APOSTLES OF DISCORD

The Author

RALPH LORD ROY, of Swanton, Vermont, is an ordained Methodist minister and, during the research for *Apostles of Discord*, a doctoral candidate in religion and society at Union Theological Seminary and Columbia University. A graduate of Mt. Hermon School and Swarthmore College, he received his master's degree from Union and Columbia. He has written articles for a number of religious periodicals, including the *Christian Century* (which carried magazine adaptations of several sections of this book while it was in press), *The Pastor, Zions Herald,* and the *Union Seminary Quarterly Review.*

Beacon Studies in Church and State

AMERICAN FREEDOM AND CATHOLIC POWER
Paul Blanshard

THE AMERICAN TRADITION IN RELIGION AND EDUCATION
R. Freeman Butts

APOSTLES OF DISCORD
Ralph Lord Roy

THE ATTACK ON THE AMERICAN SECULAR SCHOOL
V. T. Thayer

CHURCH, STATE, AND FREEDOM
Leo Pfeffer

COMMUNISM, DEMOCRACY, AND CATHOLIC POWER
Paul Blanshard

CORNERSTONES OF RELIGIOUS FREEDOM IN AMERICA
Edited by Joseph L. Blau

MY CATHOLIC CRITICS
Paul Blanshard

ONE WOMAN'S FIGHT
Vashti McCollum

THE WALL OF SEPARATION BETWEEN CHURCH AND STATE
Conrad Moehlman

Apostles
of
Discord

A study of organized bigotry and disruption on the fringes of Protestantism

RALPH LORD ROY

THE BEACON PRESS · Boston

Contents

TO MY
MOTHER AND FATHER

Preface

The program and vitality of Protestantism is threatened today by organized malcontents who zealously seek to promote hate and disruption under the banner of the Christian faith. In this book I attempt to survey, in a factual manner, many of the groups and individuals active in the current campaign of extremists to capture the Protestant mind. This study is not definitive; as the first of its kind, it has many limitations. Perhaps, however, it will serve to arouse interest that could result in the further unveiling of Protestantism's "apostles of discord."

The most important objectives of this book are:

— to warn Americans, and Protestants in particular, of the ominous threat to Christian values and to democracy which these fringe groups represent;

— to provide ministers and laymen with basic data for combatting these groups;

— to challenge the irresponsible methods and shallow principles that characterize most of their activities;

— to convince those who collaborate with "hard core" extremists, oftentimes unwittingly, that they are aiding and abetting forces antagonistic to the best American traditions and Christianity's highest ideals.

I approached the task of preparing this study — originally an academic thesis — with great reluctance. My doubts were multiplied by the prospect of its publication, and I was confronted with many baffling queries. Is it possible to prepare such a survey without committing injustices against some innocent parties? Can it be written without falling prey to the vindictiveness and unfair methods that so often typify those whom I criticize? Will readers interpret the data correctly, recognizing that all groups and individuals discussed do not promote equally dangerous ideologies or employ equally immoral methods? Is there a danger that such a book will convey to non-Protestants the impression that Protestantism is composed chiefly of crackpots, racketeers, and bigots warring with one another for control of our churches? Can such a negative study produce the positive results that merit its completion? Finally, and most important, will it promote the spirit of Christ and advance His Kingdom? These deliberations continued to hover over me as I completed the book.

With the forbearance of the reader, the preface appears to be the appropriate place to anticipate the kind of response a survey of this nature might receive from those of whom it is critical. I hope that some of them might be led to reconsider their position. Many, of course, will attempt to reply to such criticism straightforwardly, without rancor. A few will simply bathe in any publicity. From my short experience as a contributor to religious periodicals, however, I have learned that some of the most vociferous apostles of discord have only a slight regard for fair play and a minimal sense of right and wrong. No one can oppose them without becoming the butt of their merciless abuse. They seek to discredit all adversaries by echoing empty cliches and tossing hither and yon inapplicable labels.

In the first place, there are those who attempt to disqualify all critics on theological grounds. As much as possible, I have sought to avoid theological controversy so that the main issues with which I deal will not be overshadowed. In spite of this effort, however, some readers may feel that they detect certain biases. Religious liberals may be disturbed by my high regard for many leading fundamentalists. At the same time, certain self-styled "Bible believers" may seek to mislead their followers by charging that my principal target is the fundamentalist movement. They have already pressed this accusation; it is manifestly untrue.

This study does not criticize the legitimate fundamentalist movement. Where other Protestants have failed, the fundamentalists have succeeded. They have reached America's "disinherited" — the poor, the uneducated, the social outcasts. Untold millions have found life's meaning through this "old-time religion." But fundamentalists are divided. Most of them preach their interpretation of the Christian faith and refuse to become addicted to fraud, racism, or controversy. A vociferous minority, however, exert most of their efforts to promoting conflict and confusion. The difference is between genuine fundamentalists — e.g., John W. Bradbury, Charles E. Fuller, and Paul S. Rees — and those who exploit fundamentalism to preach hate and division — e.g., Gerald Winrod, Gerald L. K. Smith, and Carl McIntire.

Secondly, other extremists regularly seek to apply political labels to any who do not approve of their particular viewpoint. Those Protestants who serve the Kremlin, for example, lump all other churchmen together as conspirators or dupes of a gigantic, gangster Wall Street-Vatican axis aimed at suppressing the people and ushering in fascism. The irresponsible elements of the extreme right, now enjoying a heyday in their campaign of smear, hope to discredit all opponents by hurling about such terms as "globalist," "leftist" and "do-gooder."

So that readers will be fully aware of the political bias of this book, let me state explicitly: I am a Republican, generally a supporter of the "middle way" of the present administration, and a confirmed internationalist. Throughout this study, however, I purposely seek to avoid the legitimate controversies that rage between liberals and conservatives as attention is focused upon the enemies of both.

Thirdly, the most irresponsible critics will continue to fabricate, as they have already commenced to do, a whole series of wild arguments. They employ the usual tricks: misquoting or quoting out of context, twisting and distorting facts, leveling dishonest accusations, establishing alleged guilt by imagined associations. This is the way many apostles of discord bear their "Christian" witness.

A few other points should be noted to acquaint the reader with some of the difficult problems surrounding the preparation and use of this particular survey.

1. Perhaps the most perplexing problem involved the selection of material. Which groups and individuals should be included with the apostles of discord? The decisions were frequently very difficult. What of the Quaker humanitarian, Howard E. Kershner, now editor of *Christian Economics*, a bi-weekly paper that ignores the most elemental concepts of justice? Or, what of saintly Dryden L. Phelps, returned missionary after many devoted years in China, now under the spell of communist propaganda? These are only two of the many difficult questions of this nature that demanded answers.

2. The chance of minor errors in this kind of study, so filled with statements of facts, is always great. In some instances, different authorities — all honest men — render conflicting accounts of one episode. While more than forty specialists were invited to read all or part of the original galleys of this book, minor errors could slip through. Unfair critics, of course, will seize upon them to obscure the real issues with which the book is concerned. The Beacon Press has wisely decided to publish an addendum to correct any significant errors that may be included in the text.

3. One of the more exacting tasks during the months prior to the book's publication was the responsibility of keeping its text up-to-date. This required the constant injection of fresh material, for many of the situations discussed in the study are in a very fluid state. There may be some significant happenings between the printing of the book and its official publication — hence, not included herein. With regard to the rapid change of events, it is well to remember that both groups and individuals that are subject to legitimate criticism today are capable of experiencing a major change over the years.

4. Much information, along with some late material, is included in the notes, which the reader is urged to consult frequently. It proved impractical to include a reference for every fact, lest the notes rival the rest of the book in length. However, an effort has been made to document quotations and most controversial material of a factual nature. I shall gladly furnish additional documentation to serious inquirers.

5. My criticism of Protestantism's malcontents should not be interpreted as a defense of the *status quo* and an attack upon all who seek to alter it. In a democracy, and especially within the religious framework of American Protestantism, the malcontent has an important role to play — both as the conscience of the churches and as a symptom of their weaknesses. Thus, for example, when I am critical of those who seek to sabotage the ecumenical movement, I am critical of their methods and their arguments. Fair criticism of the ecumenical movement is healthy and often warranted.

There are many persons to whom I am indebted in the preparation of

xii   Preface

this study. All of them, of course, bear no responsibility for my presentation of facts or my expressions of opinion. Indeed, several of them have taken issue with one or more aspects of the book. Dr. John C. Bennett, professor of Christian Theology and Ethics at Union Theological Seminary in New York, was my academic adviser while I prepared my original thesis and developed it into a book. To him I am especially grateful. Among the other faculty members who assisted me in this undertaking were Dr. Robert T. Handy, Assistant Professor of Church History at Union Theological Seminary, and Dr. John Dillenberger, Associate Professor of Religion at Columbia University. I am also indebted to numerous fellow students, two of whom have given many valuable hours of their time: Miss Mary N. Levander of the East Harlem Protestant Parish and the Rev. Philip J. Ramstad, now chaplain of the Kiskiminetas Springs School of Saltsburg, Pa. Of the many organizations and organizational officials who have supplied me with valuable material, several merit special credit: Friends of Democracy, and particularly Leon M. Birkhead; the Anti-Defamation League of B'nai B'rith, and particularly Jack Baker-Bachrach and Mortimer Kass; the American Jewish Committee, and particularly Moses Jung and George Kellman; and the U.S.A. Conference of the World Council of Churches, and particularly Miss Eleanor Kent Browne. Frederick Woltman of the Scripps-Howard newspapers kindly gave me free access to his extensive files on communism. Special appreciation is expressed to Miss Jeannette Hopkins and Miss Janet Finnie of the Beacon Press, whose skill and patience carried this book through the many stages of its preparation, from my first rough drafts to the printed edition. Hundreds more across the country — ministers, secretaries, students, and others — have played a vital role by furnishing me with information from which this study has been produced. To them all, I am grateful. I hope that they will find this volume of some help in their efforts on behalf of a better America and a more vital Protestantism.

RALPH L. ROY

Swanton, Vermont
June 5, 1953

APOSTLES OF DISCORD

1
Introduction: The Ministries of Hate and Disruption

This is a survey of groups and individuals — most of them on the fringes of Protestantism — who promote hate or disruption. In America, today, the overwhelming majority of churchmen adhere to the broad principles of democracy; in fact, Protestantism has contributed many of these same principles. But a vociferous minority who solicit the support of the churches threaten to undermine Americanism and Christianity — the two systems they claim to defend. Collectively, these extremists comprise the "apostles of discord."

Protestantism's apostles of discord appear to be gaining in numbers and in strength. They have become a powerful force in the churches and the nation. All of them — the flagrant racists, the ultra-nationalists, the pro-communists, the economic extremists, and those who promote division and conflict for personal gain — threaten to secure important footholds in the center of Protestant life. Vigilance must be maintained if their influence is to be countered. This survey, originally intended for academic purposes only, is an attempt to make available significant information on many of these discordant organizations and individuals that are trying to enlist a large following among Protestants.

For purposes of clarity and in the interests of fairness, the apostles of discord are discussed under two broad headings — "The Ministry of Hate" and "The Ministry of Disruption." The first group incites hostility against Americans who are Negro and not white, Jew and not Gentile, Catholic and not Protestant.

3

The second has many branches. One faction spearheads reckless assaults upon the attempts of the major Protestant denominations to co-operate in the strengthening of mutual faith and practice. Another defames those church leaders who believe that the message of Christianity should spur Protestants to work for social improvement. A third branch of this ministry of disruption — less fiery, better financed, but perhaps more dangerous than the others — hopes to utilize religion to advance an ideology of the extreme right, promoted under the misleading label of "libertarianism." Finally, there are a handful of Protestants who twist Christianity's cardinal doctrine of love to lure people into support of the demonic doctrines of communism.

This distinction between the factions of the ministries of hate and disruption is not valid in every case — since some elements in both work closely together. The members of these groups may overlap. Many of the saboteurs of Protestant co-operation, for example, also promote flagrant calumnies against Catholics, Negroes, and Jews. Some economic extremists of the far right share the same prejudices against racial and religious minorities. Nearly all members of the ministry of hate accept the views promulgated by several groups in the ministry of disruption. Ironically, promoters of racial and religious bias, of economic injustice, of group antagonisms — all these, unwittingly but effectively, aid and abet the cause of international communism by weakening American democracy. In fact, the extremists of the left and of the right frequently work as one against the vast majority of Protestants — both liberal and conservative — who reject the inordinate tendencies of either end of the spectrum.

At a time that calls for unity, Protestantism's apostles of discord create division. At a time that demands calm judgment, they promote unreasoned hysteria. At a time that requires brotherhood, they seek to arouse group against group.

While "Apostles of Discord" has been selected as an over-all label for the Protestant malcontents discussed in this study, some groups and individuals in the ministry of hate collectively may be characterized as the "Protestant underworld." There are obvious problems arising from the use of this term. It does not intend to suggest that its members are involved in criminal activity — though often they are. The label does not seek to convey the idea that the Protestant underworld operates furtively — though it sometimes does. The phrase "Protestant underworld" is used to describe the activities of those who espouse ideologies which are immoral, undemocratic, and subversive of the Christian faith.

Many clear-cut distinctions should be made among various apostles of discord. It would be grossly unfair to equate them in every respect. They may differ greatly in their sincerity and in the nature of the methods they employ; the different ideas they advocate may not pose equal threats to democracy. An apologist for communism may be sincere — yet the cause he promotes is far more threatening to freedom than that of some other apostles of discord, who are perhaps hypocritical. Others must be condemned primarily for dishonest or reckless tactics. An obvious chasm divides "crackpots" and cultists from movements backed by affluent and well-meaning citizens of stature.

It may seem presumptuous to undertake a study of this nature. No one should claim the right to anathematize every group or individual with whom he happens to disagree. There is a great need, however, for a survey of the major danger areas — even though done in a frankly partisan manner. The principal thesis of this book may be stated simply: any group or individual seeking to exploit the Christian religion to justify racial or religious hate, discord and dissension, economic or political extremism fails fundamentally to understand the true nature of his faith.

Among the major problems encountered in the completion of this survey, two should be given special attention:

(1) *The problem of scope.* This study has made no attempt to cover the entire field. Some of the most pressing questions are not discussed — such as the extent to which prejudice exists among Protestants who have no connection with the organized ministry of hate. Many readers may feel that a major group omitted consists of the doctrinaire "reformers" who insist that only their particular interpretation of Christianity has eternal validity.

Apostles of discord flourish among adherents to other religious traditions as well. The Roman Catholic Church, for example, has been plagued with those who promote racial and religious intolerance; in fact, these discordant forces may have more prestige than their brothers-in-bigotry within the Protestant denominations. They determine the bias of several influential Catholic papers — for example, the Brooklyn *Tablet* and *Our Sunday Visitor*. But the structure of the Roman Catholic Church enables the hierarchy to still the voices of its most embarrassing agitators. Some who have been quieted have included Detroit's Father Charles E. Coughlin, former fuehrer of the Christian Front, and Alabama's Father Arthur Termini-ello, the "Father Coughlin of the South." Others have been excommunicated, such as Father Leonard Feeney of St. Benedict's Center in Cambridge, Massachusetts. Protestantism — organized along more democratic lines — often finds it difficult or considers it ill-advised to take similar disciplinary action.

(2) *The problem of presentation*. Obviously, any set of facts can be presented in many different ways. A study of such controversial material can hardly avoid partisan interpretation. Here, however, a strong effort has been made to present the material with sufficient objectivity so that it clearly establishes a legitimate case against these apostles of discord.

There are cogent arguments against bringing such information to the attention of the public at all. Some will contend that it can succeed only in opening old wounds or in inciting bitter new conflicts. Others may fear that to give publicity to professional agitators, regardless of the manner in which it is done, is merely to add strength to their efforts. A third group may believe that no person can present a totally fair picture of such controversial matters and that the inevitable result of this type of study is to commit injustice against some innocent individuals. Finally, a few may contend that the impact of this survey will be to aid the enemies of Protestantism by attributing undue influence to fringe groups that seek to corrupt the Protestant faith. These four contentions have merit. But the influence of the apostles of discord has reached such proportions that it must be challenged.

This survey is limited almost entirely to a simple presentation of facts. There is little attempt to analyze the phenomena reported. No effort is made to examine their psychological significance, weigh their total impact, suggest remedial steps, or predict their future. These must be left for other studies.

Some of the information included may disturb readers who find that criticism is directed at groups, individuals, and publications that have gained their confidence. Few, if any, will concur with all of the opinions of the author. Disapproval as expressed in this book does not imply a desire to deny anyone the right to present his own viewpoint — no matter how unsavory that viewpoint may be. The civil liberties of proponents of unpopular doctrines must be carefully protected. In a democracy, citizens are entitled to disagree.

THE MINISTRY OF HATE

2

The Protestant Underworld vs. Dwight D. Eisenhower

What a sorry, sad spectacle to see what fools Americans
are. They love to be humbugged. The Elders of Zion are
riding high and driving the nation to slavery and the suckers
love it. Instead of turning to God and first principle of right
they turned to a faked "right" — the "Republican" party
candidate nominated by Baruch and Dewey, the Jewish choir
boy — and now the fools worship Ike in place of God and
expect to be "saved" by his cabinet appointment of old New-
dealers as "Republicans": John Foster Dulles-style; to "return" to the American free enterprise system of life. They'll
lose even what little liberties they have and the shirt off their
backs by the time the Top-Jew usurers get thru with them.

With these words a typical member of the Protestant underworld comments on the 1952 election. His blast exemplifies
the all-out campaign now being waged by Protestantism's
fifth column against the Eisenhower administration.

"Few people realize who Ike is," continues *The Broom,* the
California "religious" weekly quoted above. "While the American taxpayers pay his salary, his allegiance is not to them but to
the handful of international Jewish usurers, headed by the Rothschilds and Sassoons, alias the Sanhedrin, alias Elders of Zion."

Other segments of the Protestant underworld single out
specific leaders in the Eisenhower administration for their concerted attack. John Foster Dulles, one gospel preacher writes,
is "guardian of the subversive, pro-Communist cell in the State
Department." Another has attacked the Secretary of State as
"an effective tool of extremely radical and pacifist church leaders

11

associated with the Federal Council of Churches." Still a third charges Dulles with conspiring with Alger Hiss and Dean Acheson to establish the "alien, treasonable, anti-American Jewnited Nations." Other favorite targets include Ambassador Henry Cabot Lodge, head of the U.S. mission to the U.N. (he "betrayed his grandfather"), Attorney General Herbert Brownell ("protege of Jewey Dewey"), Mutual Security Administrator Harold E. Stassen ("beggar nations will like him"), and Ambassador to Britain Winthrop Aldrich ("spokesman for Banker Bolshevik combine"). One midwestern nationalist sheet was headlined: "LODGE, DODGE, AND HODGE PODGE."

The consensus in the Protestant underworld is that Bernard Baruch has been retained by Eisenhower as the "invisible dictator." One New Jersey fortnightly said: "To anyone who has the courage to look into the facts, it becomes apparent that this man who has never been elected to office is really the president under all administrations." Baruch, it continued, "really makes the appointments for the President's cabinet and other important posts. Baruch is regarded as the most powerful man on earth. Many students of theology believe that he is the representative of the Anti-Christ here in America." The same New Jersey fortnightly summarized Eisenhower's appointments: "Eisenhower's cabinet and key positions are practically all from the Federal Reserve banking groups . . . ready to serve international bolshevism."

Other extremists on the fringe of Protestantism, uncertain over the results of the 1952 election, await patiently each new development on the political scene. They study Eisenhower in the hope that he will succumb to the "patriotic fringe" of the Republican Party. They watch Congress, anticipating new turns to the extreme right. Meanwhile, they form new political alliances, plan mass "educational campaigns," and carry out their divisive activities, ostensibly to the end that America and her leaders will be shaken from their lethargy in time to save the country from the Jews, the Negroes, the Catholics — or whatever group they consider as the root of all evil.

The 1952 election campaign effectively illustrates how Protestantism's problem children seize upon a specific situation in the hope of swelling the nationalist-racist ranks in the United

States. Nearly all extremist groups in the country appropriated General Douglas MacArthur as the symbol of their cause, and sought to spur a country-wide attempt to sabotage the national tickets of both major parties. One of their weapons was an assemblage of third parties designed to counter the "Jew-control" of the Republican and Democratic organizations.

The "professional patriots" of the churches endeavored to initiate a boom for their presidental choice long before the GOP convention. Delegates were deluged with pro-MacArthur literature — far more than flowed from all other pre-convention factions combined. In addition to their efforts to insure the nomination of General MacArthur, the nationalists directed a smear campaign against other contenders — a campaign equaled in degradation only by that staged against Alfred E. Smith in the presidential contest of 1928. Their principal target was Dwight D. Eisenhower.

The Protestant underworld inaugurated the "Stop-Ike-the-Kike" campaign in 1948, when a few leading Democrats were hoping to draft the General for their presidential ticket. The Rev. Gerald L. K. Smith and his Christian Nationalist Crusade (to be discussed in further detail in Chapter 4) reproduced and distributed an excerpt from the West Point yearbook of 1915 which referred in jest to "Senor Dwight David Eisenhower, gentleman, the terrible Swedish-Jew, as big as life and twice as natural." According to Smith, this appeared to confirm the racists' contention that the President is Jewish.

A favorite technique of racists across the world is to argue that their opponents have "impure blood." In the manner of Julius Streicher, Nazism's professional agitator against the Jews, Smith continues to distribute a chart purporting to trace "Roosevelt's Jewish Ancestry." Other bigots have developed elaborate systems for the detection of "crypto Jews" (Jews who supposedly conceal their true identity in the interest of camouflaging their anti-Christian activities). A Washington "lady patriot," Mrs. Agnes Waters, has "documentation" to prove that all but a half-dozen top American statesmen hide their Jewish origins behind assumed names; these "crypto Jews" include Dwight D. Eisenhower, Adlai E. Stevenson, Harry S. Truman, and Thomas E. Dewey. Mrs. Waters' list also includes Senators Robert A. Taft,

Joseph R. McCarthy, and John W. Bricker. Senator William E. Jenner, the nationalist favorite from Indiana, seems to be the only well-known senator who meets with Mrs. Waters' complete endorsement.

The Christian Nationalists were substantially aided in their pre-convention efforts to smear Eisenhower by a network of other members of the Protestant underworld.

From Wichita, Kansas, Gerald B. Winrod, influential fundamentalist pastor-publisher, blanketed the nation with tons of literature aimed at undermining the internationalist, middle-road elements of the GOP. A simple request for information on the Eisenhower candidacy brought one inquirer a cardboard carton, nine inches square, full of scurrilous pamphlets aimed at Thomas E. Dewey, Drew Pearson, Felix Frankfurter, and other favorite scapegoats who allegedly had conspired to force Eisenhower upon an unwilling public. The material re-echoed the customary Winrod line that "Communism is international because it emerges from the Talmudic background of the international race." The implication throughout was that Eisenhower had been selected as a front for Jewish-Marxist one-worlders bent upon scrapping the Constitution and tearing down Old Glory.

From midtown New York, Joseph P. Kamp, Madison Avenue hate-merchant, widely distributed copies of a special 16-page Eisenhower edition of his monthly publication headlined: "REDS, NEW DEALERS USE IKE IN PLOT TO HOLD POWER." Kamp contended that his careful analysis of Eisenhower's candidacy had revealed: (1) there were unmistakable signs of a "conspiracy" to prevent the American people from exercising their right to make a ballot-box decision on policies affecting the very existence of constitutional government; (2) "notorious un-American elements" were promoting Ike's campaign; and (3) the election of Eisenhower under his present sponsorship "would insure the continuance in Washington during the next four years of the same Socialist, pro-Communist and appease-Russia policies, which have brought the United States to its present precarious position, both throughout the world and at home." One Scripps-Howard journalist estimated that more than 500,000 copies of Kamp's attack on Eisenhower were distributed.

From Santa Ana, California, Robert H. Williams, editor of the *Williams Intelligence Summary,* attacked Eisenhower for his close relations with "the left wing, alien internationalists." In his Eisenhower edition, the West Coast vigilante asked: "Will the Republicans and the Southern Democrats permit themselves to be fooled by this second Franklin D. Roosevelt — this Kerensky of America's Marxist revolution?" He described Eisenhower's "middle-way policies" as "mid-way between American-ism and Communism, or half-way into Communism." Further indication of Eisenhower's sinister connections was his service as president of Columbia University, "virtually a Ghetto institution, an incubator of proselytes and international Jewish revolutionaries."

Meanwhile, Gerald L. K. Smith, eloquent minister-demagogue, was describing the capture of the GOP by "subversive elements." The whole thing was launched, Smith contended, when

. . . Franklin Roosevelt and his Jew advisers began in the late 30's to undermine the Republican Party with a "me too" fifth column. The fifth column New Dealers within the Democrat Party then began to whoop it up for Willkie, who was raised a Socialist and grew up in a Socialist home. Willkie put on a rather flabby campaign, and then came crawling to the White House with his tongue hanging out, looking for Presidential boots to lick.

According to Smith, Willkie and Roosevelt conspired to "junk" the right-wingers in both parties and form a liberal party; but "God evidently decreed otherwise because within six months of the time they cooked up this deal both Willkie and Roosevelt were dead."

Before the Republicans convened in July 1952, the Smith forces took over an office in downtown Chicago, near the center of political activities. Smith had characterized Eisenhower's buildup as a hoax engineered by "the same cheap Jew publicity machine that makes a star out of a Hollywood whore, or a hero out of a marijuana smoker."

Thomas E. Dewey, one of Eisenhower's most influential backers, was advised "to get off some place and crawl under a log. He is not a Nationalist. He doesn't deserve the respect of American patriots. He is on the wrong side of almost every issue."

All delegates received propaganda from Christian Nationalist headquarters advocating General MacArthur for president. Smith did not indulge himself in his customary gutterisms in literature aimed at the convention, and he carefully concealed his identity behind the Tulsa address of his Draft MacArthur Committee. On one deceptive propaganda folder he wrote: "This circular is printed and paid for by a committee of unnamed humble Republicans who are getting tired of living on short grass and skimpy rations."

Smith's right-hand man, the brilliant and aggressive Don Lohbeck, editor of *The Cross and the Flag* (see Chapter 4), acted as the overt director of all Christian Nationalist activities in Chicago during convention week. Among those working with him were Allen A. Zoll, director of the National Council for American Education; Ellis O. Jones, pre-war fuehrer of the National Copperheads; C. Daniel Kurts, of the New York Anti-Communist League; Forrest C. Sammons, head of the West Virginia Anti-Communist League; and many other known extremists.

On convention eve, July 6, the Christian Nationalists captured the only important pro-MacArthur rally held in the city. The audience of more than five hundred, solicited by anonymous advertisements (Smith-printed) were "taken in" by Don Lohbeck, who used an innocent Oklahoma Indian as front man. Once introduced, Lohbeck promptly organized the rally into Christian Nationalist campaign squads, equipped each group with Smith's anti-Eisenhower, pro-MacArthur literature, and sent them into Chicago's hotels and byways to carry a gospel of hate.

This tendency of Smith to "steal the show" from those who attempt to co-operate with him is the cause of great resentment in nationalist circles.

Simultaneously, two nationalist conventions were rallying 250 delegates from all parts of the country behind the MacArthur campaign. The more important caucus was organized by Mrs. Lyrl Van Hyning, long-time leader of the organization We, the Mothers Mobilize for America, and editor of *Women's Voice,* a monthly with an estimated circulation of ten thousand. Mrs. Van Hyning had announced her "Holy Crusade" in February — "to witness to our faith in God and our Republic."

"Communism, the UN, UMT, all the world schemes of planning and chaos are the anti-Christ," the "lady patriot" wrote her followers. " 'He that is not for me is against me,' and you cannot stay home and keep your mouth shut and be lukewarm and still be for Jesus Christ and this country."

The Van Hyning convention attracted extremists from all parts of the country. Following the opening invocation by the Rev. Earl MacArthur of Bensonville, Ill. — who boasts that he is a cousin of the General — the delegates were stirred by three days of harangues against "Republocrats," Wall Street international bankers, Jews, the British, and a long list of subversive alienisms. The favorite speaker of the three-day session was the Rev. Kenneth Goff, ex-communist preacher of Englewood, Colorado. Other principal speakers were George T. Foster, chairman of the convention and leader of the Constitutional Americans; Mrs. Rudolph Vincenti of Baltimore; wealthy Austin Hancock, head of the American Heritage Protective Committee in Texas; Elizabeth Knauss, author of the leaflet *Red Propaganda in the Churches;* Conde McGinley, Roman Catholic editor of the frenzied *Common Sense;* George Higgins, presidential candidate of California's miniscule Liberty Party; and many others. Among veteran nationalists who attended some of the sessions were E. N. Sanctuary of New York and Elizabeth Dilling of Chicago (both discussed in Chapter 3).

Mrs. Dilling was the only influential leader of the Protestant underworld who failed to endorse MacArthur for President. In a letter to her friends dated May 1952, entitled "The Man on a White Horse in 1952," Mrs. Dilling complained that MacArthur, like the rest of the candidates of both parties, was a servant of the Jews and their communist comrades. Her list of specific charges, ranging over twenty-two pages of mimeographed material, concluded that MacArthur's friendship with Brigadier General Julius Klein, his "pro-communist" policies in Japan, his sinister alliance with Taft, and his support of the United Nations disqualified him from serious consideration. To top it off, Mrs. Dilling contended that Franklin D. Roosevelt and Winston Churchill, both of "Jewish" ancestry, were cousins of the General.

The majority of nationalists who traveled to Chicago to put pressure on Republican delegates joined in the Van Hyning meeting. It was rivaled, however, by a handful of fervent devotees to the cult of white supremacy who met in another section of town to declaim against Negroes and to establish the NAAWP (National Association for the Advancement of White People), discussed in Chapter 6. The convention call was sent out by Joseph Beauharnais, soft-spoken boss of the White Circle League, who presided over its sessions. He had predicted that "hundreds of patriotic American organizations" would attend his meetings: "Many noted speakers will be on hand to alert us to the grave dangers that threaten our American form of government and our white Christian civilization."

The split among nationalists stemmed from a variety of factors. Beauharnais had sought the co-operation of Mrs. Van Hyning earlier in the spring, but she had firmly rebuffed him. She disliked him personally; she wanted to run her own show. Beauharnais had infuriated many nationalists when he accepted financial assistance from the American Civil Liberties Union in carrying his battle against the Illinois group-libel law to the Supreme Court. Mrs. Van Hyning also decried Beauharnais' preoccupation with the Negro — when the real enemy, she contended, was the Jew.

Disturbed by the schism, some nationalists rushed back and forth between the two meetings.

The pressure of the nationalists failed to affect measurably the proceedings of the Republican convention — though a deadlock would have given them their big chance. Some delegates sported both Taft and MacArthur buttons, but Eisenhower's quick victory rebuffed the extremists who had predicted that their candidate's keynote address would "wow 'em." Every possible device, including the cross, was employed on behalf of MacArthur. The delegates were flooded with crude anti-Eisenhower propaganda, which Taft sharply repudiated several days before the convention opened. "I cannot denounce too strongly the action of those who are making issues on anti-Semitic and other prejudices," he declared. Rallies and parades were organized by motley groups of "patriots" demanding "MacArthur for America."

The handful of supporters who had gained entrance into the convention hall to hear MacArthur hysterically shouted their adoration, and they sought in vain to start the nationalist chant, "We Back Mac." Even in the supercharged atmosphere of the convention, the General's backers were noticeable for the excessive zeal of their partisanship. Finally, at 2 A.M. on Thursday morning, June 10, when an Oklahoma delegate placed MacArthur's name in nomination, the doors of the International Amphitheatre were thrown open as Allen A. Zoll led 250 (the maximum number allowed) marching, stamping, frenzied "patriots" into the auditorium. The excited group swayed back and forth through the crowded aisles. Their candidate alone would preserve white Christian America!

Stunned by Eisenhower's first-ballot coup, Gerald L. K. Smith gave this explanation to his followers, whom he had promised victory in return for their cash:

Dear Precious Friend:

This is one of the sad, sad heartbreaking moments of my life. Three days before the Convention ended Eisenhower was stopped. A deadlock had developed. Robert Taft was convinced that he could not win the nomination. He promised Mr. Hoover and General MacArthur that he would withdraw so that the Convention would have time to stampede to MacArthur. As the delegates began to arrive New York bankers and other internationalists with great sums of money flew into Chicago. They had made a previous study of every individual delegate, including his weaknesses, whether or not he had an appetite for liquor, what his financial problems were, how much he owed on his home, etc., etc. Thereupon they began to break down his resistance with offers of money. Delegates were bought from $1,000.00 to $20,000.00 each. Even so, the majority of the delegates wanted MacArthur, and we who were leading the MacArthur campaign were assured that Mr. Taft would withdraw the moment defeat seemed certain.

What happened? The blind and egotistical advisors in the Taft organization convinced the Ohio Senator on the last night that he still had a chance to win. This was one of the most fatal mistakes in American history. Taft actually believed that he could win on the second ballot and that it would not be necessary for him to withdraw on the first ballot. You know the result. The Jew-bought candidate furnished the Republicans by Roosevelt and Truman was nominated on the first ballot. That tragic morning session of July 11 will live in the history of infamy. It seemed doubly appropriate on this occasion for treason that a Jewish Rabbi should pronounce the prayer for the session about to nominate "Ike." . . .

When the balloting started, I went into my bedroom, fell on my knees and prayed to God Almighty. I promised Him that whatever the result, I would continue to battle for the preservation of Christian America.

When the Democratic convention opened two weeks later, Smith could find no suitable candidate to back. He described Averell Harriman of New York as a "weakling if there ever was one" and "an obedient tool of an ingratiating bootlicker, a vassal of Herbert Lehman." Vice-President Barkley was "a typical old political hack whose rubber face portrays the effects of having worn too many false faces." Even Senator Richard Russell of Georgia, the choice of Dixiecrat elements among the Democrats, was characterized as "a political shyster . . . who has been used as a Judas goat to prevent the South from bolting against mongrelization and Communism within the Democratic Party."

His chief blasts, however, were reserved for Senator Estes Kefauver and Governor Adlai Stevenson. Of Kefauver, Smith wrote:

We have no genealogical report that would indicate that there was any Jewish blood in Kefauver, but he has the Jewish mouth, the Jewish nose, and the Jewish profile. He obeys Jews, he runs with Jews, he collaborates with Jews, he allows Jews to form his strategy planning, and he performs like a Broadway actor under direction of a Jewish nightclub operator. Who wants a man in the White House that looks like this? God save us from this.

Smith observed that "Jake Arvey brought Stevenson out of the stable and the New York delegation was held back by Lehman long enough to create the psychological effect that the stampede was for Stevenson." Linking him to Hiss, Smith added: "It is believed that his Republican wife divorced him because of his questionable political associations."

Both Eisenhower and Stevenson were vigorously challenged by some Protestant apostles of discord for their religious ties. The association of Eisenhower's mother with the Jehovah's Witnesses was exploited to make the GOP candidate appear as an "anti-Christian cultist" and a "foe of patriotism." The President has joined the Presbyterian Church since his inauguration. Stevenson was attacked as a Unitarian — denounced from some pulpits as "one who denies the deity of Christ Jesus." The two vice-presidential candidates, however, were more acceptable to such religious circles. Said a West Coast Methodist promoter of bigotry: "Both are teetotalers, do not use tobacco and are splendid moral and Christian men."

Encouraged by the Chicago *Tribune*'s temporary withdrawal from GOP ranks, a number of hyper-conservatives met in early August to nourish the Constitution Party, a splinter fringe born in New York City in early spring to work for the nomination of MacArthur. The new group elected as co-chairmen Percy L. Greaves, consulting economist of the Christian Freedom Foundation (publishers of the *Christian Economics* discussed in Chapter 12), and Mrs. Suzanne Silvercruys Stevenson, then head of the super-patriotic Minute Women of the U.S.A.

But both Greaves and Mrs. Stevenson resigned when the party's extremists met independently in Philadelphia and captured the movement. Their leaders included Upton Close of Washington, D. C., anti-Semitic collaborator with Gerald Winrod and former radio commentator; W. Henry MacFarland, Jr., of Philadelphia, organizer of the American Flag Committee and the Nationalist Action League (declared "fascist" by the Attorney General of the United States); George T. Foster of Chicago; and Kenneth Goff of Englewood, Colorado.

This schism within the Constitution Party dealt the group a fatal blow, although it waged an intensive postcard campaign on behalf of General MacArthur and G. Seals Aiken, little-known Georgia lawyer who was its vice-presidential candidate. When Senator Harry F. Byrd was asked to allow his name to be placed in second spot, he quickly repudiated the group. They claimed to have solicited Vivien Kellems, but she already was a candidate for Senator from Connecticut — and would not have consented in any case. The New York City segment of the party, which met regularly in Steinway Hall, was headed by a pre-war Coughlinite, Mrs. Catherine Baldwin. It was successfully infiltrated by elements originating in successor groups to the old Nazi Bund, centered in New York's east-side German area known as Yorkville. Other affiliated groups existed in Texas, California, Georgia, and Colorado.

When General MacArthur did not respond to fervent pleas

from his followers, a few nationalists reluctantly accepted the Republican national ticket and climbed on Eisenhower's wagon. Robert H. Williams — who earlier had called the GOP candidate "the man most wanted by the Zionists to head the government" — now warned that the splinter factions could split the GOP vote. "If the race is as tight as it now looks, the new parties may only succeed in electing the most dangerous man yet nominated for the presidency — Adlai Stevenson." There was little choice between Eisenhower and Stevenson, he said — a choice between a "befuddled weakling" and a "gifted revolutionary."

To defend his tardy switch, Williams rationalized: "It is the choice between Stevenson and the Communist-Zionist machine on the one hand, and Eisenhower and a tug-of-war between the same machine and a powerful group of right-wing Republicans on the other." Despite Eisenhower's internationalist friends, Williams believed the right wing would help to shape policy. One important factor in aligning some extremists with Eisenhower's candidacy was the so-called Nixon affair. A popular nationalist fortnightly, *Common Sense* of Union, N. J., headlined one story: "SENATOR NIXON VICTIM OF INVISIBLE GOVERNMENT."

Others urged that real Americans boycott all candidates. *The Broom,* a "religious" weekly published in San Diego by C. Leon de Aryan, had made that suggestion even prior to the Republican convention. Both Eisenhower and MacArthur, de Aryan warned, are "gladiators in the war-making circus. Neither is a Christian nor an American in the true sense." The solution: "That is the reason why we say to write-in Jesus Christ. . . . All the candidates for the presidency are Jew-stooges. There is not one true American in the lot."

After the convention, de Aryan dropped his write-in campaign for Jesus Christ, but kept up his barrage against the major candidates. Stevenson was "a Jew, if ever there was one: a Newdealer, a Jewdealer, a creature of Jake Arvey." De Aryan characterized Eisenhower as "Ike, the Kike, a Jew in spirit and in action who betrayed his own people and turned over half of Europe to Stalin, and now outdeweys Dewey and outwillkies Willkie in me-too-programs." Of MacArthur he wrote: "He is playing Baruch's game 100 per cent."

De Aryan produced many of the foulest libels against Eisen-hower during the course of the campaign. Referring to the West Point reprint circulated by Gerald L. K. Smith, de Aryan remarked: "There is some Spanish Jew or Jewess somewhere in his blood and his buddies sensed it and testified to it — and more — Ike's mind and mannerism as well as the history of his career prove it." Another time, the Californian cultist wrote: "Who was Eisenhower's father? Was he not one of the River Brethren? And are they not United Zion's Children? If Zion is not Jewish, what is?"

A third group stayed with the MacArthur candidacy. The Constitution Party was on the ballot in six states, including Texas, Colorado, and North Dakota; but it polled a small vote. Mrs. Van Hyning told her ten thousand subscribers to *Women's Voice* to register their dissatisfaction by a protest ballot. "In Illinois," she said, "we shall write in for president the name Douglas MacArthur, for Vice President Joseph McCarthy. This we call a protest vote. If the States in which MacArthur is on the ballot come up with some electors and if millions do not vote for either candidate, this election would be thrown into the House of Representatives, which would be a God's blessing." This was the ambitious plan of most MacArthur supporters.

The most intensive efforts to confuse the political picture were made by Gerald L. K. Smith. "With Eisenhower being groomed by Baruch and Frankfurter and with Stevenson the pick of Jake Arvey and Herbert Lehman," wrote Smith on August 10th, "we have four jews [*sic*] running both old parties for their presiden-tial ticket from behind the scenes. God save us!"

To counteract this "merger" of the traditional political fac-tions, Smith organized a "new second party" to "keep the two party system alive." Two weeks later he addressed a message to his followers: "We propose that the great White Christian vote shall be the new balance of power in American politics. . . . In many states our vote will be the determining factor in November and by 1954 we will be the most vital political entity in the United States."

Jack B. Tenney, for several years chairman of California's ill-famed "Tenney Committee" to investigate un-American activities, willingly ran for Vice-President on the Smith ticket. In his acceptance speech in Los Angeles, Tenney declared:

> In every generation God in His wisdom and compassion has set up warning signs and provided an instrumentality for salvation. In our time the warning signals are multitudinous, and He has given us — Douglas MacArthur!

Tenney predicted MacArthur's election.

Smith's chief lieutenant, Don Lohbeck, raced from state to state in a frantic effort to find a place for the Christian Nationalist Party on the ballot. Just prior to the election he claimed success in fourteen states, and it appeared as though the Smith cohorts might become a major threat to GOP prospects in several western and southern states. When they reached the polls, however, they were able to express their first choice in only seven states. MacArthur's total vote was less than twenty thousand, split between the Constitution Party and the Christian Nationalists.

With the disappointment of the election, Smith wrote a desperate appeal letter:

> I am sure you, like myself, have shed some tears in the past few hours and days. The dictator of America is now Bernard Baruch and his ruthless ilk of international manipulators. Their first step will be complete conscription of all human beings from 17 to 70. Their second gesture of tyranny will be to repeal the McCarran immigration act so that 20 million Jews and colored will be dumped on American shores. They propose to see to it that never again will the great white Christian majority population of America be able to express majority power.

By way of a consolation prize for their followers, the Christian Nationalists solicited funds for a Washington, D. C., headquarters: "Before Congress convenes we shall have established a lobby for the purposes of educating Congressmen and Senators on the true issues and the real crisis we face." Smith boasted of "confidential commitments" from United States Senators and Congressmen who "will cooperate with us fully in our Washington lobby and in the attainment of our emergency goals." First among these goals was the abolition of the United Nations. Other objectives included the immediate removal of Anna Rosenberg, then Assistant Secretary of Defense; vigorous support of the

McCarran Act against contemplated attack; and full "co-opera-tion" with the future activities of Senator McCarthy.

All other nationalists likewise refused to give Eisenhower any of the credit for his election — in spite of the fact that he had run far ahead of his ticket everywhere. *Women's Voice,* whose editor's slogan is "For Christ and the Constitution," gave a typical explanation of the result: It was not an Eisenhower vic-tory — or even the triumph of the Republican Party. "The people voted for America," she declared. "They voted for Mc-Carthyism." The Wisconsin primary was "the turning point of the campaign. McCarthyism is Americanism."

Eisenhower, in fact, had outpolled McCarthy in Wisconsin by a wide margin.

This was the role of Protestantism's ministry of hate in the 1952 presidential election. The average voter knew little or noth-ing about the shady activities of these men who cared less about electing a candidate than about creating an atmosphere of hatred. The ministry of hate is not, of course, confined to Protestant fringe groups — but the purpose of this book is primarily to cover that area.

During the dramatic process of an election, it is particularly easy to observe evidences of the pattern employed by these fringe groups: anti-Semitism and other forms of bigotry, the virulent type of false anti-communism based on smear rather than fact, the constant assault on internationalism and the United Nations.

This pattern of prejudice will be described and analyzed in subsequent chapters. It may seem alien — but it touches the lives of every Protestant, every Jew, every Catholic in the United States. Both clergy and laymen must be alert, to know the enemies of brotherhood, to answer and to counteract their in-fluence. Someday, perhaps, the principles of good-will will overcome the appeals to primitive insecurities that turn race against race, creed against creed.

It will happen only when the apostles of bigotry are rejected by everyone.

3

The Plot Against the Jews

A ll across America, a ministry of hate incites anti-Semitic bigotry. The line of these malevolent zealots is unfortunately all too familiar. It was used by medieval churchmen when they sought to exclude the Children of Israel from "Christian civilization." It was exploited by Adolf Hitler in his efforts to bolster the racial pride of his "gallant Aryans." It is used today by Stalin's followers in their drive to subordinate other nations, races, and creeds to their totalitarian methods and their imperialistic designs. All follow the same line: "Jews are international nomads who have conspired to oppress mankind through the plotting of financial intrigue and the fomenting of widespread rebellion."

Contemporary American anti-Semitism owes much of its strength and direction to a man whose central importance in the Protestant underworld is often not recognized. Gerald Winrod, 55-year-old evangelist of Wichita, Kansas, has been the most influential figure behind the hate campaign against the Jews. His activities form the background against which less important — though often more conspicuous — actors have performed the ritual of prejudice.

Winrod's admirers have frequently compared him to William Jennings Bryan. His husky voice, distinguished by a perfectly modulated tone, is almost hypnotic. Though extreme in his religious and political views, Winrod is well read and an industrious thinker.

A pained look flashes across his face at the suggestion that he has been widely accused of bigotry. But the Kansas preacher admits hatred for all "alienisms" — especially "godless, materialistic communism." This, he explains, is because he is a fundamentalist who believes in "the Whole Bible and the Whole Constitution"; the critics who charge him with prejudice are, therefore, enemies of religion, conspirators in a "communist-inspired" smear terror against the "sound" Christian ministers. But, despite his denials, Winrod has been venomously attacking other races and creeds for the past quarter-century. Through his journal, *The Defender Magazine,* he introduces into nearly 100,000 homes a monthly message of hate, under the cloak of old-fashioned Protestantism.

Most fundamentalists, of course — those Protestants who adhere to the "old-time religion" — do not share Winrod's racial and religious bigotries.

Winrod was born in Wichita in 1898, the son of a saloon-keeper turned preacher after his tavern had been smashed by axe-swinging Carrie Nation; seeing the error of his ways, he spurned the saloon for the sawdust trail of evangelism. Young Gerald left school early to become a day laborer and later a factory worker. Conversion burst upon him at a typical Kansas camp meeting. Armed with an elementary education and several years of tutoring by an itinerant evangelist, he set out during the 1920's to save America from the ravages of "godless liberalism." Later, in 1935, despite his lack of formal education, he was granted a D.D. degree from the Los Angeles Baptist Theological Seminary as "a distinguished minister of the Gospel in recognition of his valuable leadership both in the field of Christian journalism and theology."

Winrod launched *The Defender Magazine* in April 1926. His denunciations of social sins were compounded with bitter attacks against Protestants who held that the brotherhood of man is part of the Christian gospel and against those who preached that evolution is compatible with the concept of God the Creator. Advertising contracted through the Religious Press Association gave him respectable backing and put the magazine into the same class with scores of other small fundamentalist periodicals. By February 1934, the circulation was 40,000; three years later there were 100,000 subscriptions. The 32-page journal's low cost — long fifty cents a year, now one dollar — has helped spread its message among lower economic groups.

The Defender Magazine carries the customary fundamentalist attacks upon the "sins" of movie-going, dancing, and card-playing. It publishes denunciations of the "pagan" National Council of Churches, while praising those who carry the "true faith" to infidel peoples at home and abroad.

For a short time in 1934, Winrod added a newspaper, *The Revealer,* to his regular publications. Then he tried, without success, to start a Capital News and Feature Service in Washington, D.C., to send his interpretation of current events free of charge to editors of two thousand rural newspapers.

The Wichita evangelist has since 1923 sponsored the Defenders of the Christian Faith, Inc., a missionary endeavor boasting two hundred churches that spread his gospel to many parts of the globe. Five of the mission fields are in Spanish-speaking areas — Cuba; the Dominican Republic; Mexico; East Harlem, in New York City; and Puerto Rico, where Winrod finances numerous stations and a large theological seminary, established in 1946. The incorporators of the Defenders of the Christian Faith — most of them known for their racial and religious bigotry — include Edward Fehr, director of the Prophetic Bible Institute of Hoisington, Kansas; W. D. Herrstrom of Faribault, Minnesota, editor of the *Bible News Flashes;* Leland Marion, pastor of Christian Temple in Pontiac, Michigan; Harvey Springer of Englewood, Colorado, president of the World Baptist Fellowship; Sam Swain of Akron, Ohio, director of the National Spiritual Defense Crusade; and William T. Watson, president of Trinity College in Clearwater, Florida.

Winrod himself has never held a pastorate; his work has always been non-denominational. His secretary has put it this way: "Dr. Winrod has no church of his own. The entire United States and Canada are his congregation."

Originally Winrod had been concerned only with what he believed to be the papal threat; but by 1930 he was charging that Roman Catholic doctrine represented "a horrible mixture of Judaism and Paganism under the Christian name," and later charged that a "rapidly developing cooperation of Catholics and Jews is gaining control of the American government."

In the years that followed, *The Defender Magazine* all but lost sight of the threat of Catholicism in its increasing concern about the "guile" of the Jews. Winrod cited the infamous

Protocols of the Learned Elders of Zion, a collection of forged documents that are claimed to represent a plot by "international Jewry" to rule the world. *The Defender Magazine* contended that communism had been conceived by the Jews, that "foreign, apostate, renegade butcherous Jews" ruled the Soviet, that the N.R.A. was a Jewish plot, that the Jews were conspiring to inject immorality and radicalism into the movies, and that "in all parts of the world, the same cry is going up against Jewish control of finances, courts, newspapers, political machines, amusements, and industries."

He went to Germany in 1934, allegedly at the invitation of the Nazi propagandist, Otto H. Vollbehr, "to study social, political, moral, economic, and prophetic trends." There Winrod met some leading officials of the pro-Nazi church. He was profoundly affected by his trip; one of his associates has testified that, upon his return, Winrod burned the remaining copies of *Hitler's Place in Prophecy,* a Defender pamphlet that had labeled the German fuehrer an agent of international communism. Earlier Winrod had written of Nazism: "Hitler's policy against the Jews isolates Germany completely from the rest of Europe." But now he began to praise the Nazi regime and either denied that Jews were being persecuted or argued that the "Jewish-inspired" persecution of Russian Christians after the Bolshevik Revolution were much worse.

Winrod represented conditions in Germany in such glowing terms that a fellow fundamentalist, Rembert Gilman Smith — organizer of the Oklahoma League Against Communism, Nazism, and Unpatriotic Pacifism — could no longer tolerate such gross distortion. In a snappy little pamphlet, *Winrod of Wichita: A Number One Enemy of the Jews, Arch-Apologist for Hitler,* Rembert Smith complained:

It was said that Macaulay had so much pride in his style that he would "slander a dynasty in order to balance a period." Dr. Winrod slanders Jewish scholars in his efforts to exculpate and even to eulogize the blood-thirsty, "blond beasts" of Nazi-land, which are tearing and devouring Jews, Protestants, and Catholics in a fierce and fanatical rage against elemental religion in its great, historical organizations. Dr. Winrod will have a sense of chagrin at the refusal of a great multitude of people to accept his claim that the facts as to religion in Germany are to be found only in his publications.

By this time, Winrod was thoroughly involved with many leading American nationalists and pro-Nazis. Before his visit to Germany, he had become associated with Elizabeth Dilling, Robert Edward Edmondson, and E. N. Sanctuary — three Americans later put on trial for alleged sedition against the United States government. After his return from abroad, he enlarged his circle to include Harry Jung and James True. Jung headed the extremist American Vigilante Intelligence Federation and was described by Winrod as "one of the best informed men in the United States on subverters and subversive movements." James True, who had invented the "Kike Killer" — a club resembling a policeman's billy — Winrod considered to have "earned for himself a reputation of being one of the nation's most accurate business analysts." The Nazi propaganda organ *World Service* (*Welt-Dienst*) continually recommended Defender literature; and, in turn, Winrod distributed *World Service* and other official Nazi propaganda, including Goebbels' *The Trust About Spain,* and Hitler's speech "On National Socialism and World Relations."

Winrod and the American Clergy

Winrod sought allies not only among the Nazis, but also among the American clergy.

In 1936, Ralph W. Nollner, a leading Methodist pastor of Houston, Texas, issued a nation-wide call for a National Conference of Christian Ministers and Laymen, in Asheville, North Carolina; the announced purpose was to organize a "Christian American movement" to combat atheistic communism. The press gave it widespread advance publicity because of its controversial sponsorship. Nollner vehemently denied all accusations of anti-Semitism and anti-Catholicism, invited Jewish and Catholic clergy to address the meeting, and dropped the term "Christian" from the Conference's official title.

At the opening session on August 12, 1936, the delegates were sharply divided into opposing camps. Ernest P. Elmhurst, head of the Pan-Aryan Alliance, and Robert Athy, another nationalist agitator, met delegates at the door with printed announcements of a rump session to be held the following evening in Asheville's First Christian Church. The principal spokesmen for the dissi-

dent group were Winrod and Dr. Charles Vaughn, pastor of
the Christian Church of Los Angeles, both of whom strongly
denounced the original conference for "selling out" to the Jews.
In a strong protest letter to Nollner in which they implied that
he was an agent of "Judaic communism," the secessionists asked:

> Have you been paid deliberately to demoralize, weaken, and divide
> the ranks of Christian patriots who are fighting to avert the kind of
> bloody revolutions which have come upon Russia, France, Spain, and
> other countries? . . . What really is the name of your organization? Who
> are its real officers? Why does the latest issue of your publication, in a
> complete and radical change of policy, carry articles that reek of the
> subtleness that is typical of those forces which are endeavoring to poison
> and destroy the very foundations of true Christian America?

The insurgents planned another conference for Washington
on October 15 and 16; but this meeting never materialized.
Among the leading Asheville secessionists, many have continued
to align themselves with Winrod in recent years. They include
Louis R. Patmont, Disciples of Christ minister of Berkeley, California, who has traveled widely on behalf of the Defenders of
the Christian Faith; E. J. Rollings, pastor of the Metropolitan
Tabernacle in Detroit; Bruce Corbin, a former Methodist
preacher and missionary to India; Oliver E. Williams of Pittsburgh, Pennsylvania; and Andrew Johnson of Louisville, Kentucky.

Winrod's Later Career

Two dramatic episodes during these pre-war years brought
into the open Winrod's Nazi sympathies and his extreme racism.
On his return from Germany, Winrod is reported to have announced to the staff of the Defender Publishers: "I am now
absolutely sure of going to the United States Senate. When
there, I will make it my sounding board." Three years later,
in 1938, he threatened to make good his boast when he entered
his name in a four-way race, and frightened the Republican
high command into repudiating him. Said John D. M. Hamilton,
chairman of the Republican National Committee: "I certainly
would not vote for anyone who has dedicated himself to a course
of intolerance such as Mr. Winrod."
Winrod appealed to traditionally Republican Kansas with a

platform of high tariff, states rights, private enterprise, "Americanism," and isolationism. "Let's keep Christian America Christian. Let's keep America safe for Americans," he said. The New York *Times,* however, succinctly stated the case against Winrod: "If there is anybody in Kansas or out of it who speaks with more authentic voice for religious, racial, and social bigotry, he has yet to be found."

Winrod was defeated despite an elaborate campaign and despite his plea that "a vote for Mr. Winrod in the Kansas Primary will be a vote for the preservation of Constitutional Democracy." One of the most telling blows against his candidacy was made by a group of prominent Kansas ministers, anonymously led by Leon M. Birkhead, then Unitarian minister in Kansas City and after 1937 director of Friends of Democracy in New York. They published a 15-page exposé, *Drive Fascist Ideas From Kansas!* —pointing out Winrod's pro-Nazi bias, his attacks upon Jews and Masons, and his efforts to widen the gap between Protestants and Catholics.

Winrod's anti-democratic ideas were highlighted again, in 1940, by a divorce suit filed by Winrod's wife. She first asked for separate maintenance, declaring: "If there is anything un-American about his activities I hope this separation will bring these activities to a halt."

In the trial, in which Winrod contested her suit, she swore that he regularly announced that he expected to be a "nominal head of the country when the revolution came and that he wanted to take me to a secret hide-out so I could be protected when the government should close in on him." She told of his preaching the gospel with his own pro-Nazi overtones: "Every evening at home, by the radio, the children were taught that everything Hitler did was right and that everything England and France did was wrong."

Meanwhile, Winrod organized a series of "Prayer and Prophecy Conferences" with the hope that fundamentalist ministers would join him in his crusade against Jews and against the increasing number of Americans who were disturbed by Hitler's victories abroad. The leaders of the first and most important meeting, the Chicago National Prayer and Prophecy Conference (October 1940), included such well-known apostles of bigotry as: Harvey H. Springer, "cowboy evangelist"; Elizabeth Dilling; W. B. Riley of Minneapolis; and William T. Watson, president of Trinity College in Clearwater, Florida. Regional conferences were held in Denver and in Nashville; at each one, the "Jewish question" was analyzed and "modernism" was identified with a supposed Judaic plot to devitalize true, historical, evangelical Christianity. Similar meetings were scheduled for the following year, but the American entry into the war resulted in their cancellation.

Right up until the outbreak of hostilities, *The Defender Magazine* hammered out the pro-Hitler line, and Winrod became widely known as the "Jayhawk Nazi." After Pearl Harbor, however, he became a reluctant supporter of the war effort — although he attacked the administration for early American setbacks in the Far East and complained bitterly about America's wartime alliance with the Soviet Union. His assaults upon the Jews continued in slightly modified form; in March 1942, for example, he maintained that "Judaism . . . is an opposition movement to Christianity, a system of international government for the regulation of a nation within nations."

Winrod was indicted three times for sedition during World War II — in 1942, 1943, and again in 1944, when the government specifically charged that Winrod and twenty-nine other alleged Nazi sympathizers actively co-operated with one another and with leaders and members of the Nazi Party to accomplish the objectives of the Nazis in the United States. The Department of Justice accused the defendants of attempting to usher in a Nazi revolution, named Hitler as a co-conspirator, and charged that Winrod's publication was actually Hitlerite propaganda put out to undermine the American form of government.

The case went to court during the first months of 1944 and Winrod appeared in session after session — until the jury was excused in December, after the death of the judge. A higher court dismissed the indictment, censuring the Justice Department for "lack of diligence in prosecuting the defendants." Many observers of all political viewpoints believed that the case involved infringement of civil liberties, and condemned the sedition indictments.

Although *The Defender Magazine* did not miss an issue after the trial was ordered, copies were held up each month for a few days until the Post Office decided whether they were mailable under the Espionage Act. When Winrod was in Washington in 1944 for the sedition trials, his wife — whom he had remarried in 1939 — took over his publishing responsibilities.

At the end of the war, Winrod picked up almost where he had left off. He no longer championed overt fascism, but he carried on his racist and "super-patriotic" activities through his varied enterprises. In 1950 he claimed that more than a quarter of a million people were reading his monthly magazine as it entered its twenty-fifth year of publication. Immediately after the war he began to build a printing plant in Wichita, to employ fifty-five workers. When the Civilian Production Board ordered the construction suspended, Winrod howled "persecution" and united with three other extreme fundamentalists — Harvey Springer, L. L. Marion, and Lawrence Reilly, director of the Lutheran Research Society — to present a united front to the government. Consent was granted finally, and the $100,000 plant of the Defender Publishers was completed. The funds were raised through Winrod's favored technique of letters to his "Dear Christian Friends"; thousands of his followers sent in small contributions. Tons of race-baiting books, magazines, and pamphlets flow each year from Winrod's presses.

There are several theories about his basic motivation. It is, of course, possible that he is a sincere preacher of Christianity — as he interprets it. Another theory attributes to him a perverted sense of mission that leads him to seek power and position — an idea given credence by his own analogies between his plight and those of the "persecuted prophets" of the Old Testament. Perhaps he imagines himself the Jeremiah of the twentieth century, thundering denunciations against sin, vice, crime, apostasy, and corruption in high places.

Winrod's severest critics, however, contend that he is a man of avarice. One of his former allies says he has a "miser complex" and a "money-worshiping brain." If this is true, Winrod's formula has paid off handsomely. In 1950, for example, the income of the Defenders of the Christian Faith, Inc., was reported at $276,272. Winrod's comfortable residence in the best section of Wichita is valued at $30,000.

Distortions of the Talmud

Winrod is one of the cleverest of those who try to conceal their racial and religious prejudice behind the Cross. His *Defender Magazine* appears, at first glance, to be the very embodiment of piety. The front cover regularly displays a handsome church or a happy family scene. Its readers find sections devoted to sermons, book reviews, articles on home and foreign missions, Bible lessons. The impression of propriety is strengthened by advertisements of well-known fundamentalist publishing houses, including Van Kampen (Wheaton, Illinois), Higley (Butler, Indiana), Hope (Chicago), Zondervan (Grand Rapids, Michigan) and Tabernacle (Chicago). Each of these publishers therefore contributes to *The Defender Magazine*'s campaign of hate — perhaps without realizing fully the implications of Winrod's message. The magazine often includes sermons by such reputable fundamentalist leaders as Evangelist Billy Graham; William Ward Ayer, director of the "Marching Truth" broadcast; and Paul S. Rees, president of the National Association of Evangelicals.

Some leading proponents of the "old-time religion" have resented Winrod's use of their sermons. The Rev. John S. Wimbish, pastor of the famous Calvary Baptist Church in the heart of Manhattan, wrote an inquirer in 1951: "It is against my own desires and personal conviction that my messages are published in Dr. Winrod's 'The Defender' . . . What recourse we have in this flagrant violation I do not know, but we will investigate." Wimbish's sermons have not appeared in the *Defender* since.

Others do not share this concern. The Rev. R. S. Beal, for example, of Tucson, Arizona, leader in the Conservative Baptist Association, saw "no reason why my articles should not be published so long as a paper adhered to the fundamental position."

In spite of Winrod's use of material from reputable sources, throughout his magazine runs a racist sentiment that is as anti-Christian as it is anti-democratic.

Consider, by way of illustration, the monthly feature entitled "Sunday School" — which of all *Defender Magazine* features should be least suspected of disseminating racial and religious hatred into the minds of thousands of unwary "Bible-believers." The following lesson clearly demonstrates how Winrod and his colleagues of the ministry of hate use the Bible itself to propagate their bitter personal views:

Lesson Number 3
GOOD NEWS FOR ALL MEN
January 29, 1950
Acts 10:17-43

Memory Text: "To him give all the prophets witness, that through his name whosoever believeth in him shall receive remission of sins." Acts 10:43

THE KEY WORD OF THE LESSON IS "WHOSOEVER."

One of the infirmities of the early Christians, even after Pentecost, was a form of intolerance inherited from Judaism. They clung to the idea that Jews were superior, somehow, to the people around them.

Traditions, reinforced by the Talmudic priesthood which originated during the Babylonian captivity, were responsible for these prejudices. Obviously, the Church needed to be purged of this evil. Jesus fought it (see Matthew 15:1-3).

Peter had to have his thinking forcibly jolted when called to carry the Gospel to Cornelius, a Gentile. There was nothing in Old Testament Scripture which forbade him from sitting at the table with members of other races. It was the Talmudic writings, against which Jesus often inveighed, that distorted the racial ideas of the Jews.

The same false notion is responsible for much of the confusion, political and otherwise, which exists in the United States today. Jews, having isolated themselves on the assumption of superiority, have perfected powerful pressure organizations which blame others for conditions of their own creating.

The FEPC bill, and the so-called civil rights proposal, now pending before Congress, are examples. These measures, so destructive of American tranquility, instigated by Jewish organizations, stem from Talmudic doctrines. The Jews, who imagine themselves mistreated, are trying to stir up Negroes to further divide our Country into discordant racial groups.

If instead of blaming others, they would cast aside their Talmud, what seems to be persecution would vanish like a mirage.

As this excerpt suggests, Winrod uses the favorite tactic of anti-Semites throughout the centuries: tracing the roots of the "Jewish question" back to the Talmud. As early as the thirteenth century this design took form: in the year 1244, Paris witnessed the first public burning of copies of the Talmud. Charges of blasphemy, immorality, particularism, and absurdity were pressed. By 1264 Pope Clement IV appointed a commit-tee of censors, who expunged all passages that appeared deroga-tory to Christianity. Talmudic references to ancient paganism were widely misinterpreted as criticism of the Church.

The contents of the Talmud are vulnerable to the researches of anti-Semitic "scholars," who in their campaign of bigotry ransack its contents for "evidence." It is a record of opinions and discussions on all phases of law and life, by outstanding Jewish teachers in the academies of Palestine and Babylonia during the first five centuries A.D. The Talmud contains all manner of digressions: personal anecdotes, speculations upon points of theology or philosophy, fragments of history, bits of science, folklore, travelers' tales.

One serious student of the Talmud has commented:

> Modern anti-Semitism has displayed much energy in seeking in the pages of the Talmud grounds for attack upon the Jews. Those pages contain more and enough to spare of superstitions, narrowness, folly, and intolerance. But the faults are superficial, the merits fundamental; and it is because of the latter that the Talmud retains its permanent worth.

Gerald Winrod, however, maintains: "The Talmud and other writings of Jewish leaders were directly responsible for the re-jection of Christ. They produced hatred which finally resulted in the crucifixion of the Son of God." Jesus — Himself an anti-Semite to those who concur with Winrod's interpretation — allegedly objected to the Talmud in such statements as: "Why do ye also transgress the commandment of God by your tradition?"

Winrod frequently "quotes" from the Talmud. He accepts as his sources the corrupt versions that have been widely dis-tributed throughout the Protestant underworld. The father of these modern calumnies was John Andreas Eisenmenger (1654-1704) — though even more spectacular attacks have come from August Rohling (1839-1931), a Professor of Hebrew Antiquities at Prague; Aaron Briman, alias "Dr. Justus," a con-verted Jew; and Justin Pranaitis, a Russian clergyman of the Roman Catholic faith. Pranaitis based his distortions on Eisen-menger and Rohling, and his version is the one most frequently quoted by American racists.

The following passage is one of the many perverted translations from the Talmud promulgated by Winrod and like-minded hate-mongers:

> At the time of the Cholhamoed the transaction of any kind of business is forbidden. But it is permitted to cheat a goy [Gentile], because cheating a goyim at any time pleases the Lord.

The correct text, of course, states nothing of the kind. According to Ben Zion Bokser, a New York rabbi and scholar, author of the pamphlet *Talmudic Forgeries,* the passage deals with the observance of the intermediate days of a festival; it specifies, among other things, that "one may collect debts, certainly if it be from non-Jews, on these days of *hol ha-meod*" and "one may make commercial loans to non-Jews even where the would-be borrowers are new accounts." The passage, in other words, suspends certain restrictions upon commerce on a Jewish festival where the second party to the transaction is a Gentile. Thus has a forged translation used an innocuous tradition to slander Jewish ethics.

A common practice among the Winrod-variety fundamentalists is to discredit all forms of liberalism by dubbing them "Talmudic." The Talmud is viewed as the root of "Modernism, Higher Criticism, Rationalism, Evolutionism, Behaviorism, Freudianism, Communism, and Atheism [and] all other illegitimate children of so-called liberalism." In Winrod's mind, Judaism "is an opposition movement to Christianity."

The Defender Magazine's assaults upon the Revised Standard Version of the Bible show how this particular technique is utilized by Protestantism's ministry of hate. Some fundamentalists (as will be seen in Chapter 9) object to the new translation on the grounds that it is "modernistic" — i.e., that it has been corrupted by "liberal" scholars. Winrod, however, charges: "Consistency demands that portions of the new 'Bible' shall be regarded as Talmudic, rather than Christian." He adds that the most flagrant errors appear in the Old Testament, where prophetic passages attesting the deity of Christ are "slanted, twisted, deleted, mistranslated . . . and brought to conform to the prevailing Jewish attitude towards the Son of God." The Wichita evangelist suggests that these distortions may have resulted from the fact that, among the thirty-two men credited with producing the revision, one was a Jewish scholar, assigned to work on the Old Testament.

"True believers have no choice but to reject it," Winrod concludes, "and try to keep others from becoming ensnared by what Peter would call its 'damnable doctrines.'"

Talmudic "Scholars"

The discredited Pranaitis edition of the Talmud used by Winrod was introduced into the United States by one of his allies, Colonel E. N. Sanctuary, who called the document a "carefully translated and edited" work which would "stand the test of scholarship."

Sanctuary, who was also a defendant in the World War II sedition trial, is the "sage" of American anti-Semitism. He is still contributing his academic talents to the exposure of "Talmudic Jewry." Old-time baseball fans might remember him as a member of the celebrated "Green Stocking" team; but most of his career has been more unsavory. He has presented himself to church groups as "a well-known authority and lecturer on the development of communism in the United States." For many years he directed his multifarious activities from a New York office in the Presbyterian Building — from which he was later ejected.

Sanctuary won recognition as the "intellectual" of the nationalist movement for service to bigotry in a variety of ways. Perhaps his most widely circulated book was *Are These Things So?* — a collection of materials from other sources published anonymously by the World Alliance Against Jewish Aggressiveness, one of Sanctuary's numerous fronts. Another volume, *Tainted Contacts,* was a mass of disorganized attacks on the Federal Council of Churches of Christ in America (see Chapter 10). Others included *B'nai B'rith: An International, Anti-Christian, Pro-Communist, Jewish Power* as well as *The Holy See and the Jews.* In spite of his bitter anti-Catholicism, Sanctuary co-operates with certain Roman Catholics who spread hatred for Jews. Currently, his articles appear in the fortnightly *Common Sense,* edited by the Catholic extremist, Conde McGinley.

For many years, Sanctuary was allowed to bring his message of hate to influential Protestant churches; he taught a regular Sunday-school class at the Broadway Presbyterian Church, located near Columbia University in New York City. But the Colonel alienated many of his fundamentalist sympathizers when he published two pamphlets denouncing the American Board of Missions to the Jews. Both leaflets — *Making Ananias a Piker* (1939) and *Testimony of Sand* (1943) — were aimed at Leopold Cohn, founder of the Board of Missions, and at his son Joseph, its present director, whom Sanctuary charged with "hypocrisy and deceit" as well as with immorality.

Like many other anti-Semites, the nationalist leader casts suspicion upon all Jews — even those who accept the Christian faith. Though the vast majority of Jewish converts are as sensitive to racism as other democratic Americans, a few "Hebrew Christians" actually foster anti-Semitism among fundamentalists — Evangelist Jacob Rosenthal, for example, has worked closely with Winrod's Defenders of the Christian Faith, and A. U. Michelson, founder of the widely advertised Hebrew Evangelization Society and editor of *The Jewish Hope,* writes that "Dr. Winrod has given no indication of being unfair to the Jews."

The chief contemporary "expositor" of the Talmud is Elizabeth Dilling, whom Winrod describes as "a true Bible-believing child of God." This "modern Deborah" and "master of impassioned oratory" was born into a wealthy Chicago family in 1895; she gave up an earlier career as a concert harpist to become one of the most prolific writers of Protestantism's fifth column. After a trip to the Soviet Union in 1931 Mrs. Dilling embarked upon an anti-democratic and anti-minority crusade that finally led to her indictment during the war for conspiracy with the Nazis. She is best remembered for *The Red Network* (published in 1934), which attacked the Society of Friends, the Federal Council of Churches, and many other organizations as anti-Christian and unpatriotic. Winrod commented on *The Red Network:* "Will America be saved from the bloody hand of Bolshevism? It will, if several million citizens get their eyes open by reading this book."

Using an alias, "Rev. Frank Woodruff Johnson," Mrs. Dilling

also wrote *The Octopus,* considered by many the most virulent anti-Semitic tract ever published in the United States.

Between 1948 and 1952, she prepared a full-scale "study" of the Talmud, published as *The Plot Against Christianity.* Mrs. Dilling contends that she has unearthed a sinister world Jewish conspiracy to undermine Christian morality. She recounts in considerable detail — and with obvious delight — alleged Talmudic sanctions for "the raping of baby girls under three by grown men, incest with dead bodies, bestiality, burning children — all of them — to Molech as well as depraved Baal worship." Since publication of the volume, Mrs. Dilling has concluded that "in order to understand modern Talmudic Judaism, it is necessary to know enough about ancient forms of paganism to recognize that they have been preserved . . . in current Jewish ideology." Therefore she links the alleged "Jewish-Marxist" advocacy of free love and the free community of women with parallel practices in various primitive cultures. Mrs. Dilling hopes to place the results of her "study" in the hands of all Christian ministers.

Before Mrs. Dilling began her supposed "exposé" of the Talmud, she had directed the Patriotic Research Bureau in Chicago. From this office, at irregular intervals, she still circulates mimeographed letters addressed to "Dear Christian Friends." Although the Patriotic Research Bureau posed as a fact-finding agency on radicalism in the United States, over the years it concerned itself more and more with the "Jewish menace." In addition to a monthly periodical sent out over the signature of its editor, Mrs. Dilling circulated pamphlets and leaflets. In them were such poems as "Get Some Gentiles, Harry," and "Beware the Wily Jew," by Ellis O. Jones — former head of the National Copperheads, who was indicted for alleged sedition during World War II and now is a resident of Washington, D. C.

Although an Episcopalian, Mrs. Dilling has found her political views more congenial with the extreme fundamentalism of the Winrod school and with the Coughlinite element in the Roman Catholic church. She always expressed admiration for Father Coughlin's Christian Front, even while choosing to work principally with the Protestant network.

In 1950, she married 70-year-old Jeremiah Stokes, a Salt

Lake City attorney, himself well known for his role among American racists. Today, at 58, Elizabeth Dilling has lost most of her direct influence. But her discussion of the Talmud continues to circulate among anti-Semites.

The Forged "Protocols"

As harmful as the Talmud distortions is another forged document, *The Protocols of the Learned Elders of Zion,* disseminated in the United States by Winrod as early as 1933, when the Austrian paper hanger was seizing power in Germany. Indeed, Winrod admitted that one of his objectives in traveling abroad was to catch a glimpse of the original copy of the *Protocols,* supposedly on deposit in the British Museum. In 1935, when a group of Swiss nationalists were tried for distributing the forgery, sympathizers in all parts of the world made efforts to assist them in proving that it was an authentic document. Winrod dispatched a representative to Berne to co-operate with the director of the Nazi propaganda organ, *World Service,* who produced "evidence" in behalf of the accused nationalists.

A study of the *Protocols* and their use by the Winrod fringe of Protestantism would be a profitable venture in itself. But this study can only hint at the complex history and issues involved. The most widespread edition is the Nilus version, which contains twenty-four supposed *Protocols.* The first nine pretend to outline the methods by which the Jews will secure world dominion; the rest describe plans for a new world order, with the ultimate aim of making Israel supreme and choosing a world ruler from the House of David.

In the course of the *Protocols,* it is implied that the Jew is the author of filth, the father of immorality, the manipulator of depressions, the subverter of nations, the promoter of wars, the corrupter of the press, the contaminator of education, and the plotter against Christianity. In other words, he is pictured as the arch troublemaker of the world — source of all dissension, revolution, greed, hatred, malice, and intrigue.

The *Protocols* were brought to America by several persons. But they might never have reached world-wide prominence if

Henry Ford, Sr., had not publicized them in a series of articles in the Dearborn *Independent,* edited by W. J. Cameron. The translation was prepared by Boris Brasol, who was subsequently employed by the Ford Company and sent abroad in an attempt to establish the authenticity of the *Protocols.* Twenty of the newspaper articles were reprinted by Ford in 1920 in a book entitled *The International Jew: The World's Problem.* This anti-Semitic diatribe had an enormous circulation in the United States and abroad, was translated into many languages, and became a basic text for Hitler's racial theorists.

Henry Ford eventually came to realize that he had been godfather to a scurrilous fabrication; on June 10, 1927, he addressed a letter to all Jews, apologizing for the harm done and retracting the accusations he had made in *The International Jew.* "I frankly confess," he wrote, "that I have been greatly shocked as a result of my study and examination of the files of the Dearborn *Independent* and *The International Jew.* I deem it my duty as an honorable man to make amends for the wrong done to the Jews as fellowmen and brothers, by asking their forgiveness for the harm I have unintentionally committed."

Many refused to accept Ford's apology in good faith — because the book was republished in England and new editions continued to sell in the United States. As late as 1941, Friends of Democracy published a pamphlet, *Henry Ford Must Choose,* in which they demanded that he stop all further publication of *The International Jew* and sue for libel anyone who stated that he was anti-Semitic. Leaders of the Protestant underworld likewise doubted any genuine change in Ford's attitude. Gerald L. K. Smith contends that the manufacturer's confession of error had been drawn up under strong pressure from Jews and that Ford's signature had been forged to the confession by one of his employees.

When the manufacturer's grandson, Henry Ford II, gave the National Conference of Christians and Jews $1,000,000 in 1951, Smith prepared an article entitled "Shame on the Fords," in which he wrote: "The late Henry Ford must not only be turning over in his grave — but he must be revolving in his grave."

In February 1953, Smith's Christian Nationalist Crusade sponsored the "Henry Ford I, Memorial Award" — to be presented annually "to an outstanding patriot who has fearlessly and intelligently defended high American principle without concern for smear, misrepresentation, reprisal or organized abuse."

Several trustworthy studies of the *Protocols* have established beyond any doubt that they are spurious. The best volume on the subject is *An Appraisal of the Protocols of Zion* by John S. Curtiss, professor at Columbia University. In a foreword, fourteen prominent historians — including Dr. Dixon Ryan Fox, president of Union College, Dana G. Munro, director of the School of Public and International Affairs of Princeton University, and Allan Nevins, professor of history at Columbia — state that they "individually accept and endorse his findings as completely destructive of the historicity of the *Protocols* and as establishing beyond doubt the fact that they are rank and pernicious forgery."

Like the Swiss court in 1935, Curtiss concluded that much in the *Protocols* represented clumsily plagiarized excerpts from a book by a nineteenth-century Parisian lawyer, Maurice Joly — *Dialogue in Hell between Machiavelli and Montesquieu*, apparently written to discredit Napoleon III and the Second Empire. The title suggests its contents — imaginary discussions in the after-world between the authors of *The Prince* and *The Spirit of the Laws*.

Curtiss' appraisal won this comment from the New York *Herald Tribune*:

Dr. Curtiss's conclusions may be cited as the last word on the subject, the most completely crushing blow to a major tenet of Hitlerism. He brings together evidence that has appeared piecemeal in other publications — including court records — and piles up an objective indictment of the Protocols and those who spread their falsehoods which is most impressive. By writing *finis* to the Protocols, if not to their evil influence, he exposes fully the intellectual bankruptcy of Hitlerism, its satellites and its imitators.

The Protestant underworld, however, ignores all evidence it does not choose to believe; and its leaders still use the *Protocols* to "prove" the existence of an international Jewish conspiracy. In his pamphlets *The Truth About the Protocols* and *The Hidden Hand*, Gerald Winrod has outlined their alleged history and content and has poured out wrath against the Jews. "I am not an enemy of the Jews," he claims "[but] the Jews are essentially an egotistical people. . . . It is in the blood of the Jew to look with contempt upon other nationalities. No matter how he may try to overcome it, the feeling still lingers with him, that he is superior to others, that he is made of special cloth."

Winrod concludes that the conspiracy of the Jews has been amazingly successful in reaching its goals. Liberalism was started "from secret sources for the purpose of creating national unrest"; and morality, the next victim of the Jewish onslaught, has been almost destroyed through turning the schools into "hot-beds of radicalism and breeding places of atheism." Bible prophecy is fulfilled in this modern struggle between Judaic Communism and the Christian faith, and soon the world must accept a Jewish world ruler who will rule for three and a half years. This leader, in reality the Anti-Christ, will be "the world's most powerful potentate, a highbrow, a scholastic, a wizard in finance, a superman." When Christ returns, the Anti-Christ will be utterly destroyed, and a remnant of the Jews will then look to their Saviour and become His ambassadors throughout the earth.

In another pamphlet with a much heavier religious veneer, *The Jewish Assault on Christianity,* Winrod purports to show that "International Jewish Communism, which has already undermined all nations, firmly expects to exterminate all Christians." His curious argument runs like this: No sooner had the tomb of Christ whom they had crucified been sealed, than the Jews set out to destroy His church; this has been their intention through the centuries, and now it has come into the open in the form of atheistic communism. Winrod displays his total ignorance of history by his summary of alleged Jewish persecutions against Christians, concluding: "What the cause of Christ has endured at the hands of Jews through the centuries far surpasses anything the Jewish people have suffered from Christians."

The question of the *Protocols* split American fundamentalists. Winrod was joined in his espousal of the forgery by many influential churchmen, but a half-dozen fundamentalist leaders opposed him. They included H. A. Ironside of the Moody Memorial Church of Chicago, Louis T. Talbot of the Bible Institute of Los Angeles, and Keith L. Brooks, editor of *Prophecy*

Monthly of Los Angeles. In 1939 Dr. Brooks prepared a lengthy manifesto against anti-Semitism, which was signed by dozens of fundamentalist leaders. Meanwhile, a middle-of-the-road attitude toward the *Protocols* was followed by the *Moody Monthly, Revelation,* and the *Sunday School Times.*

Of those who joined Winrod in promulgating the forged *Protocols,* the most prominent was the late W. B. Riley, leading fundamentalist during the period of the so-called "modernist-fundamentalist" controversy. He was founder and director of the influential Northwestern Bible Schools, co-organizer of the Baptist Bible Union of North America, and the force behind the World's Christian Fundamentals Association. He took the primary role in the battles against the teaching of evolution in the public schools and wrote innumerable books, including *Menace of Modernism, Fundamentalism versus Liberalism,* and *The Blight of Unitarianism.* (Further data about Riley's career will be found in Chapter 14.)

This "grand old man" of fundamentalism believed in the forged *Protocols.* In his pamphlet *Protocols and Communism,* Riley complained of the Jews: "They are internationalists. They don't want a limited part of the world, but the whole world; nothing else will satisfy them." Moreover, he worked closely with Winrod in promoting racism — white supremacy as well as anti-Semitism — among Protestant clergymen. In 1936 he was a member of the advisory council of the Asheville rebels. In 1940 he sponsored the National Prayer and Prophecy Conferences with Winrod. As pastor of the First Baptist Church in Minneapolis, with a membership exceeding three thousand, he contributed frequently to *The Defender Magazine,* which he called "the most interesting, most informing, and the most patriotic magazine I receive." In Riley's three bookstores in Minneapolis, the writings of Winrod, Sanctuary, and Elizabeth Dilling were prominently on display. Of Mrs. Dilling's *Red Network,* he wrote: "Concerning Communism, the present world menace, Mrs. A. W. Dilling has given us one of the most valuable books in her volume, *The Red Network.* I have personally disposed of some hundreds of copies and expect to continue its advertisement."

Perhaps Riley's attitude toward the Jews — an attitude

deeply ingrained among many well-meaning fundamentalists—
was summarized in his autobiography *At Sunset or After 80:*

> Do you remember what the Jewish people answered and said that
> day when Pilate, washing his hands in their presence, declared himself
> innocent of the blood of Christ? "Then answered all the people, and
> said, His blood be on us, and on our Children." There is a vast deal of
> sympathy being felt in the world now with the suffering Jew, but we have
> another illustration of the truth that sin produces eternal effects and the
> rejection of God's Son involves everlasting judgment.

While this can hardly be called rabble-rousing anti-Semitism,
its implication is clear. For Riley, widespread hatred for the
Jews is determined by the will of God. This distorted logic
concludes that, because of the crucifixion of Christ, the Jews
as a people are condemned to eternal punishment.

Like Winrod and Riley, another key fundamentalist espoused
the *Protocols* — a Methodist, the late Dr. Arno C. Gaebelein.
He was an important evangelist among the Jews and editor of
Our Hope. In his book *The Conflict of the Ages,* which is still
sold among fundamentalists, he suggests that "nearly all that
these *Protocols* advocate, the destruction of Christian civilization,
has at least partially been brought about." He traces socialism
and Bolshevism to Jewish origins. Even the French Revolution
is attributed in part to the Jews. This theory — first evolved
by the English-born Mrs. Nesta H. Webster — has been accepted
by the Winrod circle.

But Gaebelein later changed his attitude toward the Jews.
In 1939, he signed Keith L. Brooks's "manifesto" condemning
anti-Semitism "in whatever form it may take, as inconsistent with
our heritage of liberty and fair play as citizens of America, and
as unworthy of those who bear the name of Christian."

By early 1953, the Winrod circle had changed. Dr. W. B.
Riley had died. Mrs. Elizabeth Dilling and Colonel E. N.
Sanctuary had outlived the period of the greatest influence. But
the most influential "master-mind" of anti-Semitism, Gerald
Winrod, still maintained a compact with allies who, like himself,
voiced crude accusations against racial and religious minorities.

The Winrod Circle, 1953

Winrod's best-known collaborator is Upton Close, one of
the nation's pioneer radio commentators, whose news broadcasts were heard by millions over the Mutual and N.B.C. networks. Today he publishes a regular newsletter, *Closer-ups,*
filled with innuendoes against minority groups. He contributes
a monthly column, "Washington Report," to *The Defender
Magazine.*

Dozens of Protestant ministers back Winrod. Many of them
have become associated with fake medical cure-alls — particularly the so-called Koch cancer treatment. The Christian Medical Research League, the "front" behind which the cancer
quacks do business, operates from Detroit, where its annual
conventions hear Winrod, Close, and other "prominent speakers"
proclaim how God has produced the new cure which the supposedly "Jewish-controlled" American Medical Association is
seeking to suppress.

All but one of the nine members of the League's board of
trustees are ministers: Sam Swain, W. T. Watson, Karl E.
Blake, W. R. Lantz, Louis R. Patmont, Dewey W. Whitwell,
J. Franklin Yount, and F. H. Harrison. In an account of a
yearly meeting, one supporter boasted: "Each of the eight sessions was opened with prayer to Almighty God to bless the
meditations and discussions and to advance this work which is
so beneficial to mankind. The spirit was one of genuine Christ-
centred Biblical faith, and it pervaded the entire three-day
meeting."

Dr. William Frederick Koch, "discoverer" of the miracle
cure, has been described by a government attorney as "probably
the smartest, brightest quack in the United States." He has been
making big business out of his alleged cancer-cure injection
ever since 1919, when he completed his studies at the Detroit
College of Medicine and Surgery; he thereupon established the
Koch Foundation as a clinic and the Koch Laboratories to secure a market for the injection. In 1942 the Food and Drug
Administration obtained a twelve-count indictment against Koch
under the Food, Drug, and Cosmetic Act. Twice he was tried —
and both times the trials resembled circuses, as Koch patients

paraded by with broad tales of impossible cures. Koch's first trial ended with a hung jury. The second was declared a mistrial when a juror became ill.

The Koch treatment has been severely attacked not only by the American Medical Association but also by popular newspapers and journals. In August 1949, the Chicago *Tribune* carried a long story headed: "QUACKS EXPOSED: STORY OF A FAKE $325 'CANCER CURE.'" Since then, *Collier's* magazine, the *Reader's Digest,* and the Scripps-Howard newspapers have all featured articles exposing Koch's fantastic claims.

After World War II, the Christian Medical Research League moved into the picture. Koch had realized that the surest way of perpetuating his fraud was to hide it behind a religious smokescreen. Dr. Lawrence Reilly, director of the Lutheran Research Society, stepped in to help the "persecuted" physician, charging that Koch's difficulties all stemmed from a sinister plot "to make the medical profession pre-eminently a Jewish profession." Reilly published an 158-page book, *The Birth of a Science,* which hailed Koch as a "man used by a kind and beneficient Providence to give new knowledge to the work for the relief of human suffering."

It is worth noting that Reilly was one of the vigorous leaders of the apostles of discord at the close of World War II. He set up the Lutheran Research Society in January 1946, for the alleged purpose of "identifying the enemies of religion, exposing the atheistic-communist plot to destroy America and the churches, and the alerting of pastors and lay people to this menace." In 1951, Reilly organized the Christian Anti-Defamation League which, with the help of Senator William Langer of North Dakota — who comes to the support of a variety of opposing groups — utilized even the pages of the *Congressional Record* to "expose" Jewish intrigue.

Reilly was born in Detroit in 1918, and received a theological diploma from Concordia Theological Seminary in St. Louis in 1945. Two years later he was granted an honorary divinity degree "by a Christian seminary in Puerto Rico" — undoubtedly Gerald Winrod's theological school. He served as assistant to the late Walter A. Maier, famous "Lutheran Hour" preacher, and simultaneously began the publication of the monthly *Eleventh Hour;* but when the St. Louis *Star-Times* exposed Reilly's association with Gerald L. K. Smith, Maier quickly repudiated the sentiments of his underling, and Reilly resigned.

One of the most pretentious documents to come from the ministry of hate during the post-war years is Reilly's elaborate booklet, *Moscow's Master Plan for Sovietizing America.* It affects to tie such anti-Communist groups as the Anti-Defamation League of B'nai B'rith, Friends of Democracy, the American Jewish Committee, the American Civil Liberties Union, and the Federal Council of Churches to a "monstrous communist plan directed from Moscow [which] seeks to destroy religion, particularly Christianity." In reviewing this book, Winrod's *Defender Magazine* claimed that it was "providentially timed . . . if sufficient number of people are quickly reached with information herein available, America will be saved from the clutches of those who are trying to pull our Country down to a Soviet state."

Needless to say, the Lutheran Research Society is in no way supported by any recognized synodical agency and, consequently, it speaks only for itself — or, more correctly, for Lawrence Reilly. The president of the powerful Missouri Synod, most conservative of the Lutheran groups, has made the following statement:

> The Lutheran Church-Missouri Synod dissociates itself from the principles of any organization operating under the name of the Lutheran Church-Missouri Synod which would tend to incite racial and class hatreds or political strife, and believes that such activities may not only be disturbing to the American people but harmful to the Lutheran Church and the cause of evangelical Christianity for which it stands.
>
> In keeping with this position, the Synod disavows any connection with the Lutheran Research Society of Detroit. Mr. Lawrence Reilly, its director, is not an ordained minister of the Missouri Synod and is not on the list of candidates for a call in that church body.

Other reputable Lutheran denominations have taken similar action.

During the past three years, Reilly has shown signs of financial trouble. His *Eleventh Hour* — once an attractive 36-page monthly — has been replaced by a single, irregularly published

mimeographed sheet. He has been sending out old documents
by Elizabeth Dilling, notably *Christians Awake!* She, in turn,
has described Reilly as "the brilliant anti-Communist Lutheran" and as "one of my valued friends."

The Christian Medical Research League was incorporated by
two extreme fundamentalist ministers who are now on its board
— Sam Swain and William T. Watson. A third sponsor was
Laurence B. Thatcher of Imlay City, Michigan, dealer in tomb-
stones.

Sam Swain, president of the League, directs the National
Spiritual Defense Crusade, with headquarters in Akron, Ohio,
whose announced aim is, in part, to unite the ministry of hate
against alleged "character assassins and smear artists." The
Bureau of Investigation of the American Medical Association
has described him as "on the fringe of quackery in religion and
an out-and-out Fascist." A spokesman for the Akron Ministerial
Association has called him "an itinerant preacher with a low
rating of respectability in the community." Swain operates a
storefront, the National Gospel Center, in Akron where he holds
services and sells books; but most of his activities he conducts
elsewhere.

William T. Watson, vice-president of the Christian Medical
Research League, is minister of the Gospel Tabernacle in St.
Petersburg, Florida. More significant, however, is his presidency
of Trinity College in near-by Clearwater, organized in 1932 as
the Florida Bible Institute. For years the Winrod circle has
used the college for its winter conference. Its executive board
and its "council of reference" include a large number of highly
controversial fundamentalists. Among them are Raymond R.
Richey, president of the Richey Evangelistic Association of
Houston, Texas; Leland Marion, pastor of the Christian Temple
in Pontiac, Michigan; Robert Parr, pastor of the Gilead Baptist
Church in Detroit; R. A. Forrest, president of Toccoa Falls Institute, Toccoa Falls, Georgia; Oswald J. Smith, pastor of the
People's Church of Toronto, Canada; Harvey S. Springer, "cowboy evangelist" from Englewood, Colorado; Henry Grube, pastor
of the Mobile Gospel Tabernacle in Mobile, Alabama; and
Oliver Williams, evangelist of Pittsburgh, Pennsylvania. And
there are more, including Winrod himself.

Some doubtless have no sympathy with the corrupt variety of fundamentalism they indirectly endorse. For example, although Billy Graham's name is included in Trinity College's "council of reference," he has given no indication of sharing the racism of some of his colleagues. Graham, like most fundamentalist leaders, appears to reject emphatically the racial and religious bigotry of the Winrod circle.

Winrod's Spiritual Cousins

Another champion of the Koch treatment, David Baxter, demands special comment because of his long-standing role in the Protestant underworld. When *Collier's* magazine carried its vigorous attack on the quack cancer cure in May 1951, Baxter retaliated with a series of articles, "The Big Lie," which were put in pamphlet form and circulated by the Lutheran Research Society. In them, Baxter contended that the *Collier's* story, in effect, blasphemed against any and all healers not approved by the "monopolists" and "so-called experts."

Baxter's involvement in the ministry of hate dates back to pre-war years, when he distributed pro-Nazi propaganda under a thin veneer of super-patriotism and the Golden Rule. In 1941 he organized the Social Republic Society in Colton, California, to work toward a corporate state modeled after European-style fascism. Five days before Pearl Harbor Baxter sent out a release entitled *Things You Ought to Know About the Social Republic Society,* in which he spoke darkly of "Jewish Conspirators and other subversive enemies of the American nation."

When a federal grand jury three times between 1942 and 1944 indicted Baxter for alleged sedition against the government, he attempted to clear himself in several letters to national periodicals, publicly expressing regret for his previous activities.

Baxter has periodically reminded his readers that "not since my conversion to Christ in 1942 have I believed in racial issues. You will not find anti-Semitism in a single issue of this newsletter over the years." His *Protestant Newsletter,* however, shifted to flagrant charges against the Catholics instead.

There is mounting evidence that Baxter is either naïve or

hypocritical in his pious disavowals of racism — for instance, such careless paragraphs as the following:

And when even hard-boiled Roman governor Pilate washed his hands of Jesus' killing, declared, "I am innocent of the blood of this just person," all the people screamed, "His blood be on us and our children." They actually asked for it. Like Cain, who killed his brother Abel, the Jews, by rejecting Christ, were doomed to be wanderers, marked men.

Baxter's anti-Semitic prejudices are revealed in an article in *The Defender Magazine.* He quotes the alleged attacks that Martin Luther and Ulysses S. Grant made upon the Jews; he condemns the "Jewish propaganda" of such highly regarded organizations as the National Conference of Christians and Jews; he finds that Christians are the real Children of Israel, the true seed of Abraham, "as distinguished from the synagogue of Satan."

Baxter's reading public was temporarily enlarged in 1951 when he became a regular columnist for the expanding Hoiles chain of newspapers in several small Western cities. Publisher R. C. Hoiles was against unions, majority rule, income taxes, public education, and foreign aid; he considered even Herbert Hoover a left-winger and said of child labor: "Give him a pick and shovel and let him get started." Baxter adhered closely to the Hoiles line, but added to it a thick religious camouflage with sporadic innuendoes against Jews and Catholics. He discarded his vocabulary of revolution, substituting pious platitudes about religious tolerance. He wrapped his abuse of the Roman Catholic Church in condescending compliments to Catholic laymen. To defend himself against the charge of anti-Semitism, he spoke of his love for "the Jew" as an individual — but then he smeared Jewish organizations and personalities.

In 1952, however, his column was discontinued. Baxter became Western editor of the *Chiropractic Home,* a long-established magazine published in Dixon, Illinois.

Another spiritual cousin of Gerald Winrod is Dr. William D. Herrstrom, of Faribault, Minnesota, editor of the *Bible News Flashes* and the *Americanism Bulletin.* An important figure in the Prayer and Prophecy Conferences of 1940-41, he has also

written numerous articles in *The Defender Magazine;* he serves
on the board of directors of Winrod's Puerto Rican theological
school. Self-described as "World Traveler, Prophetic Analyst,"
Herrstrom reaches about three thousand subscribers across the
country. He has focused his attention principally upon prophecy; and the large number of pamphlets he has circulated include
*The Atomic Bomb and the End of the World; The Five Horse-
men of the Apocalypse; Will This War End in Armageddon?;*
and *The Next Gold Rush According to Bible Prophecy.*

Herrstrom's rabid racism has led him to some startling doctrinal views. The most widely publicized is his claim that
Jesus was not a Jew — a theological notion which he advocated
in *The Defender Magazine* as early as 1940. He has more
thoroughly developed his ideas in his recent booklet, *Christ Is
Neither Jew Nor Gentile,* much of which was reprinted in Winrod's monthly. The Faribault clergyman claims that his booklet
has made "a great contribution to the spiritual life and welfare
of the people of America. . . . Since the editor's book was
published and widely circulated, most of the heresy [the traditional Christian belief that Jesus was a Jew] has been stopped."

"I am not attempting to prove that Christ was a Jew, a
Gentile, an Israelite, or a Galilean," he declares, "I am proving
that, as our God and our Saviour, Christ must, of necessity, be
entirely without 'nationality.' " To say that Christ was a Jew,
he continues, is tantamount to saying that God is a Jew; to say
that Christ is either Jew or Gentile is "as unscriptural as it is
ridiculous." Nationality, according to this view, is not one of
the attributes of God; to ascribe it to Christ is to destroy both
his deity and his perfect humanity.

Herrstrom argues that the false premise upon which all this
fallacious thought has developed is that Christ received his
human nature from Mary: "All Modernists, Atheists, and Communists will agree to that." But, he continues, no verse of the
Scripture even suggests such an idea; Mary was just an "ordinary
fallen human being like all the other sons and daughters of
Adam. . . . If Christ received His human nature from Mary,
it was A FALLEN HUMAN NATURE." Herrstrom borders on what
most Christians would consider blasphemy: "If Christ received
His Human nature from Mary, then the Holy Spirit was the first

'husband' — a husband while she was espoused to Joseph. This would make Mary an adulterer. It would make Joseph the 'second husband' of Mary." The unorthodox fundamentalist finally concludes that Mary had no role whatsoever in the birth of the infant Jesus, that "the 'HOLY THING' which was to be born of Mary, was the BODY WHICH GOD 'PREPARED' and which Mary 'COMPASSED.' " Since Mary was not His mother in any normal sense, "there were no parturition pains."

The Faribault minister keeps repeating: "We're not against the Jews — only the Kommunist kikes." The anti-Christ will be a Jew, he says, and "the spirit of Jew worship that now grips poor, deluded souls, is the spirit of the anti-christ"; the devil is preparing the world to accept a Jew, and fundamentalists who worship a "Jew-Christ" are, in fact, helping to prepare the way for the anti-Christ.

Herrstrom's bigotry has led him to disseminate calumnies against the Negroes as well. Like other members of the Protestant underworld, he contends that "you are in trouble" as soon as Negroes are granted equal opportunity. He claims Biblical sanction for his "crusade" against so-called mongrelization — the intermingling of the races. "Man, in his ignorance, his pride, his conceit, may blah-blah-blah about being against discrimination, but God is in favor of discrimination."

It has been the Jews' failure to heed God's warning against marriage with other peoples that has led to their heritage of suffering, says Herrstrom. The Gentiles must take note, for "if the races are thrown together in this country, in violation of God's commands, the glory of this nation will be drowned in a sea of blood." To Herrstrom the civil-rights program involves the "universal 'raping' of America's womanhood;" it has been promoted by "the devil and his crowd — the godless Communists and any whom they can delude." He traces communism to the Jews.

Anti-Semitism and Communism

The slogan "Communism is Jewish," espoused by Herrstrom and his anti-Semitic colleagues, has been the main stock in trade of bigots throughout the world since the Bolshevik Revolution. It was the principal weapon of Adolf Hitler and Josef Goebbels in persuading the "noble Aryans" to accept the systematic extermination of the Jews. The ministry of hate has since exploited the same argument.

The contention that "Communism is Jewish" frequently has taken on a new twist now that there is evidence to show that the Soviet Union and her satellites have been fomenting prejudice against the Jews.

According to Winrod's *Defender Magazine,* the whole affair appears to be part of a Jewish scheme to get the United States into another world war, this time with the Soviet Union fighting against the free nations — and the Jews preparing to profit from victory.

Conde McGinley's *Common Sense* offers a different interpretation. It argues the existence of a secret international plot — engineered by the Jews — to embroil the rest of the people of the world in perpetual warfare which will keep them weak and from which the Jews will supposedly gain. "Those of you who are wondering about the latest piece of propaganda concerning the execution of [Prague's] eleven Jews . . . keep in mind how the Jews bragged what they would do to incite another war." *Common Sense* attacks a number of Jews, advisors to the Eisenhower administration, and sums up: "Eisenhower, with this guidance, will lead us into war against Russia to save the Jews behind the Iron Curtain. . . . If the Russian people wish to throw off their Jewish yoke, what right have we to criticize?"

Others have begun to soft-pedal the communist-Jewish theme. *The Broom,* West Coast "religious" weekly, proposes open friendship with the Soviet Union: "This is the most serious blow that World Jewry has had and will . . . make friends for Stalin everywhere except in Jew-controlled America." At this late date, *The Broom* contends that "the expulsion of Trotsky and his assassination was largely an anti-Jewish movement."

When the communists began their anti-Semitic drive, many periodicals serving the Protestant underworld became confused. *Women's Voice,* published by Mrs. Lyrl Clark Van Hyning in Chicago, declared in its headlines: "THE ANTI-SEMITIC TRIALS; JEWS' EFFORT TO CLEAR THEMSELVES OF COMMUNIST CRIME." But her article bore no relation to the headline. Somehow, she held, the communist trials were part of the Jewish world conspiracy; Americans must not be taken in; underneath it all the Jews were contriving to start a new international conflict. But why? This crucial question she left unanswered.

Said George T. Foster, head of the Constitutional Americans, writing later in *Women's Voice:* "Obviously they [the Jews] are girding for war between the Soviet Union and the United States."

A Catholic friend of the ministry of hate, Fascist sympathizer James H. Madole, director of the National Renaissance Party, has gone further. Addressing his weekly meeting in Yorkville, the German section of Manhattan, he proposed that the United States purge its Jews, too. "Then Russia and America could come to terms and a war would be averted."

The Winrod circle — the aging Sanctuarys, the impetuous Dillings, the Koch imposters, and other vociferous Protestants from coast to coast — continue to plot attacks against the Children of Israel. In the name of Americanism they seek to undermine democracy. In the name of Christianity they assault the gospel of love. They spread their message through dozens of popular "religious" journals, hundreds of pamphlets, thousands of tracts — all carrying slurs against other races and creeds.

Among American fundamentalists, the message of the ministry of hate — though it is generally rejected — has done some damage. A few "Bible-believers" have been encouraged in open and latent prejudices that only years of careful education can dispel. The anxieties of the present period of cold war give added impetus to this unholy crusade. In their attempts to divide, Winrod and his nation-wide network of ministerial allies endorse any historical fancy, literary forgery, or medical quackery that would appear to support their case against the Jews. This pattern of lies leads them into a world of make-believe — a world as false as the distortions they promote.

The anti-Semites charge that the Jews killed Christ, that they are scheming to destroy his church, that they created communism, that they are plotting to undermine the American republic, that they are conspiring to enslave all mankind under the iron hand of despotism. In their unreasoning hatred of the Jews, some racists have stumbled into a curious "alliance" with communism; since Russia has attacked the Jews, many American hate-mongers have been tempted to welcome her as an ally.

This is the "party line" of Protestantism's fifth column. It is as ludicrous as it is subversive. But its champions unfortunately have an audience. In their fervor, they hope eventually to convince their countrymen — as Adolf Hitler convinced the Germans — that truth is falsehood, that the big lie is fact.

4

Hitler's Ghost in American Garb

Every member of Eisenhower's cabinet is for the United Nations. . . . Its flag is the same color as the Jew Palestine flag, and is the same design as the Russian military banner. Our new President has paid tribute to this internationalist organization which promises no good for the future of America. It outlaws prayer and forbids anyone to mention the name of Jesus within its halls or within its sessions without the official disapproval of the United Nations as such. It represents the most expensive denial of Christ in an attempt to please the anti-Christs in the history of the world. It is the most elite and high-toned crucifixion that our Lord has ever received. . . . [I have] brought about the formation of the Committee for the Abolition of the United Nations. Committees in this connection are being organized in every state and in every community, and at this writing a San Francisco Conference is being set up from which to launch this campaign to abolish this United Nations and to kick the United Nations out of the United States.

Thus spake Gerald L. K. Smith, self-proclaimed prophet of American patriots. His Conference to Abolish the United Nations, held in San Francisco on February 5 and 6, 1953, toed the line of all chauvinists who oppose every form of co-operation among the nations of the world. Echoing the neo-Nazis, Smith distributes large quantities of a brochure allegedly listing "Jews running the United Nations." "This should prove to the most skeptical observer," claims the pastor-publisher, "that the United Nations is in fact the 'Jew-nited' Nations. The real name for it should be the 'Jew N.' rather than the U.N."

For late June 1953, Smith scheduled another effort to dislodge the United Nations: a "Pilgrimage" to Washington, D.C. He announced that "outstanding patriots" would "assemble at the base of the Washington monument to re-commit themselves to their vows involved in the campaign to abolish the United Nations."

Although Winrod's circle of extreme fundamentalists, discussed in Chapter 3, may be the most influential of the several fanatical alliances that disgrace American Protestantism, the entourage of Winrod's former associate, the "Rev." Gerald L. K. Smith, is the most vociferous and the most widely publicized. It is important to examine some of the ramifications of his movement and the way in which it exploits the Christian gospel to the profit of racial and religious ill-will.

Gerald Lyman Kenneth Smith, now in his late fifties, was born into a pastor's family in a small Wisconsin town. He was graduated at the age of nineteen from Valparaiso University in Indiana, where he majored in literature, Biblical history, and dramatics — all of which were to prove highly useful in his later career. Smith is a tall man with huge shoulders and a striking, forceful personality. Even his most severe critics recognize his great oratorical abilities, and many who have known him intimately admit that he is dynamic, charming, magnetic, and intelligent.

For several years Smith — now a member of the respectable First Christian Church of Tulsa — served churches of the Disciples of Christ denomination in Indiana. In 1933 he left the pulpit of the fashionable King's Highway Christian Church in Shreveport, Louisiana, to join the Silver Shirt storm-troopers of William Dudley Pelley.

Pelley introduced Smith to the racist-nationalist fringe. The Silver Shirt fuehrer, who sought to become America's strong man, was a central figure in the campaign against democracy — a role to which Smith was to fall heir a few years later.

Pelley's record is an important chapter in the early development of the ministry of hate — a chapter that is worth summarizing. Before World War II, he flooded the United States with seas of anti-democratic and anti-Semitic literature. Born in New England, the son of a Methodist minister who represented "uncontaminated English stock," he came to the nation's attention when *American Magazine* published "Seven Minutes in Eternity," an account of how Pelley's spirit supposedly left his physical body and soared to other worlds to converse with the dead.

In 1932, Pelley went to Asheville, North Carolina, and announced the opening of Galahad College for the study and advancement of "Christian Economics." The following year, on January 31, 1933 — the day after Hitler became master of Germany — Pelley dramatically organized his Silver Shirts, sometimes called the Christian American Patriots, a group that at one time claimed more than two million members. They dressed in silver shirts, blue corduroy pants, and gold stockings; units were formed throughout the nation. The official voice of the movement's fuehrer was a small weekly magazine, *Liberation*.

In 1936, under the slogan "For Christ and the Constitution," Pelley established the Christian Party and nominated himself for President. His platform read, in part:

I propose to defranchise the Jew by Constitutional Amendment, to make it impossible for a Jew to own property in the United States excepting under the same licensing system successfully employed against Occidentals in Japan, and to limit Jews in the professions, trades, and sciences by license according to their quotas of representation in the population.

Pelley's activities came to an abrupt end in 1942 when he was jailed for sedition. There was a concerted drive in 1949 to rally sentiment for his release, and in February 1950 Pelley was paroled from Federal prison after serving approximately seven years of his fifteen-year term.

Today he bombards ministers with cultist propaganda published by his Soulcraft Press, Inc., in Noblesville, Indiana.

When Pelley's grab for power failed, Smith switched over to Huey Long and served as an organizer of the Kingfish's campaign for the White House. Smith delivered Long's funeral oration after an assassin had cut short the Louisiana dictator's career, and his rich voice brought the address to a stirring climax: "My head is bloody but unbowed."

In recalling his association with Long, Smith recently wrote: "The Roosevelt gang, supported by the New York Jew machine, dubbed him a fascist and screamed for his liquidation and conspired with those who effected his assassination. He was murdered because they knew that that was the only way he could be stopped and Roosevelt could be saved."

After Long's death, Smith cast his lot with the Townsend movement until Dr. Francis E. Townsend, founder of the pension-promoting scheme, sensed that Smith was not just a social reformer and invited him to leave.

Then Smith joined with Father Charles E. Coughlin of Royal Oak, Michigan, pre-war leader of the Christian Front, in his efforts to stampede the nation into fascism and to create a movement against the Jews. Though previously a Catholic-baiter, Smith could turn his prejudices off and on as it seemed to his personal advantage. Of Coughlin, Smith has written: "The secret Jew machine manipulated against this fearless cleric until he had been silenced by the authorities of his own church and by the moguls of radio control."

As early as 1937, Winrod brought the name of Smith to the attention of his *Defender Magazine* readers when he publicized the Smith Committee of One Million. Smith had ostensibly organized this group to counteract "insidious and subversive influences that are now undermining the sanctity of our churches, the integrity of our schools, the authority of our government and the sacredness of our family institutions." Actually, he wanted to frighten the middle and lower strata into the extreme rightist camp, much as Hitler had done in Germany. Prior to the war the Smith committee campaigned against democracy and in behalf of isolationism, supported by thousands of Americans who were frightened by the demagogue's radio diatribes predicting a Bolshevik revolution unless the country rushed to his aid. His slogan has always been: "For a White Christian America."

The war forced Smith into reluctant silence about the "evils" of democracy, especially after his magazine, *The Cross and the Flag*, was listed by the Justice Department as a propaganda vehicle for alleged seditionists. While he publicly gave 100-per-cent support to the war effort, he simultaneously became an obstructionist through his America First Party, which ran him for President of the United States in 1944. Its platform opposed most of the goals for which the United Nations were widely felt to be fighting — the end of racial and religious antipathies and the birth of an era of international brotherhood and good-will.

In fact, the pastor-agitator adopted a deceptive position that has led many Americans to consider him a pacifist. In 1944, for example, when the Methodist governing body appeared to endorse the war by the margin of a single vote, Smith bemoaned:

> I dread to see the Church get messed up in the bloody business of war. I like to think of Jesus hovering over all mankind. I like to think of the church ministering to the spirit of the Red Cross Nurse and the Chaplain who are duty-bound to serve the bodies of both friend and foe. I like to think of the church as the Mother of mankind — never taking sides with quarreling brothers.

Noble sentiments — with which many fellow Protestants would agree. But the enemy today is no longer Nazism, Smith has changed his tune — and the music is a military march. He calls upon the churches to lead a holy crusade — a crusade of hate "to preserve White Christian America!"

Smith has finally made clear his attitude toward World War II. "It was an unnecessary war," he has written. "Nobody wanted it but the power-mad internationalists operating under the direction of international Jewry. . . . Roosevelt, the opportunist and the hypocrite, was ready to do anything his master advisers told him to do in order to attain his ends."

When victory was at hand, Smith charted his post-war strategy and started an unprecedented barrage against democracy, the United Nations, Negroes, and Jews — his chief targets from that day until the present time.

Post-war Activity

Soon after the surrender of Japan, Gerald L. K. Smith announced his plans for a "great nationalist party" that would sweep the country. In May 1946, he called together a score of important nationalist leaders in the hope of uniting some sixty-eight extremist groups under his leadership. His associates in this enterprise included Kenneth Goff, of Christian Youth for America; the Rev. Arthur W. Terminiello, often termed the

"Father Coughlin of the South"; Frederick Kister, of the Christian Veterans of America; Larry Asman, of the Christian Veterans Intelligence Service; Jeremiah Stokes, of the Salt Lake City Pro-American Vigilantes, now husband of Elizabeth Dilling; and Kirkpatrick Dilling, who represented his ill mother.

They organized the Christian Nationalist Crusade, which is still the principal Smith organization. The movement was officially launched at St. Louis on June 19, 1947, with Smith setting a goal of three million supporters. Soon after, he announced that "the warm, strong arms of this mighty Crusade now reach from ocean to ocean and from Canada to Mexico. The enemy is so frightened over our rapid growth that at great expense he is sending out large numbers of secret agents."

Like the Communists, Smith has made use of innocent-sounding "front" groups, such as the Patriotic Tract Society, the Midwestern Political Survey Institute, the Committee of California Pastors, the Radio Petition Committee, the Post-war Recovery Commission, and the Western Hemisphere Committee Against Communism.

In 1947, Smith embarked upon a nation-wide speaking tour to stir up interest in his political activities. He addressed audiences ranging from a hundred to three thousand, and expressed optimism about support in the South. According to Smith, Dr. George Long, brother of Huey Long — and later elected to Congress — had assured him that Herman Talmadge, Governor of Georgia, would join in his "anti-communist" white-supremacy drive. Talmadge followed the advice of his political aides and backed out. Smith had more success with the late Theodore Bilbo, racist Senator from Mississippi, who invited the Christian Nationalist Crusader to dedicate his Juniper Grove Baptist Church in Poplarville, Mississippi. But, in spite of Bilbo's enthusiasm, Smith left the South without the following he had anticipated.

In the spring of 1950 he tried again, with even less success, to win Dixiecrat approval.

Smith and Winrod were allies in their common cause until a definite break occurred in November 1947. Some hint of a falling out between the two leading extremists had come during the summer when Winrod's *Defender Magazine* started to mark each of Smith's advertisements "Paid Advertisement." A few months later Winrod, joined by Lawrence Reilly and Upton Close, signed a joint statement disowning Smith's use of their names and denying any connection with his campaign. It may be significant that just before this rejection the Christian Nationalists had announced that they would expand their activities in the Wichita area. Perhaps Winrod resented this proposed invasion of his domain.

Some five hundred Smith followers who claimed to represent thirty states created the Christian Nationalist Party in St. Louis in August 1948, naming Smith as their candidate for the nation's highest office, after he had been repudiated by J. Strom Thurmond, candidate for the States' Right Party. The platform of the Christian Nationalists called for the deportation of Zionists, the dissolution of all "Jewish Gestapo Organizations," the shipping of Negroes to Africa, and the liquidation of the United Nations. The document demanded: "Shall the lovers of Jesus Christ or the enemies of Jesus Christ determine the destiny of America?"

Smith's role in the 1952 election has been discussed in Chapter 2.

Smith's Propaganda Techniques

March 1952 marked the tenth anniversary of Smith's monthly magazine. "For ten years," the Tulsa minister wrote, *"The Cross and the Flag* has been my favorite ideological child. My soul gave birth to it, my conscience nursed it, and that first little handful of readers protected it from starvation, kidnapping and death." Smith arrived at its title when "one morning in my den, as though an angel had whispered in my ear, the words came. . . ."

The Cross and the Flag usually is thirty-two pages in length. Like all Smith literature, it is loud and crude in tone, featuring two or three special articles and dozens of short editorials from the pen of the Christian Nationalist chieftain. Before a congressional committee, Smith has claimed a circulation of ninety thousand; but the Anti-Defamation League of B'nai B'rith has estimated it at only twenty-five thousand.

"This is not a church periodical," Smith acknowledges, "although we support the church. This is not a doctrinal publication, although we believe in the great fundamental doctrines of Christianity. This is a political periodical which believes that the only redemption that can save America is a statesmanship based on the dynamic of man's faith in God as revealed through Jesus Christ."

He seizes every opportunity to remind his flock of the "astounding" accomplishments of his Crusade in exposing the One World movement, communism in the churches, efforts toward racial self-respect, and many other dire threats to the Republic. The big issues, concludes Smith, are:

1. The preservation of our Christian faith against the threat of Jew Communism, a conspiracy to abolish Christian civilization and the church of Jesus Christ.

2. The preservation of our national sovereignty against the Jew-financed plot for World Government.

3. The preservation of our racial self-respect against a campaign to mongrelize our race and mix the blacks with the whites.

4. The preservation of our national independence against the threat of Jew Zionism which attempts to dictate both our domestic and foreign policies.

5. The preservation of our national tradition threatened by the immigration flood.

By means of Smith's monthly *The Cross and the Flag,* of a weekly letter to "My Dear Precious Friend and Fellow American," of his Nationalist News Service, of books sold by Christian Nationalist headquarters, and of mass rallies held across the country, the Crusade has brought its message of hate to millions of Americans. Smith claims to distribute a million pieces of literature monthly — a gross exaggeration — but even that number *per year* would constitute a significant threat to democracy.

Here is a list of some of the favorite nationalist texts sold by Smith's headquarters.

Roosevelt's Jewish Ancestry (a chart)
The Plot to Abolish the United States, by Joseph P. Kamp
Two-Party Treason, by Don Lohbeck
Trial on Trial, by Lawrence Dennis and Maximilian St. George
The Negro's Place in Call of Race, by former Governor

William ("Alfalfa Bill") Murray, of Oklahoma
The Anti-Defamation League and Its Use in the World Communist Offensive, by Robert H. Williams
The World Hoax, by Ernest Elmhurst
Third Zionist War, by George W. Armstrong
The Iron Curtain Over America, by John O. Beaty
Alien Minorities and Mongrelization, by Marilyn Allen
Collected Speeches of Congressman John E. Rankin
How Red Is the Federal Council of Churches? compiled by the American Council of Christian Laymen (Verne P. Kaub, director)
The Architects Behind the World Conspiracy, by Ron Gostick (Editor, Canadian Intelligence Service)
Atom Treason, by Frank Britton
The Tenney Committee, by Jack B. Tenney
The International Jew (reprinted from Henry Ford's Dearborn Independent)
Treason in Washington, "exposed" by Senator McCarthy
The Key to the Mystery, by Adrian Arcand
Red Treason in Hollywood, by Myron C. Fagan
The Other Plot to Destroy the Constitution, by Edgar W. Waybright, Jr.

Smith's technique is sensationalism. One of the leaflets currently distributed by the Christian Nationalists is headlined:

DANGER!
WARNING!
Pro-Stalin Politicians
and Alien-Minded Traitors
in Cooperation with
Blind Sentimentalists are
Attempting to Force
Negro Rule
Negro-White Intermarriage
Negro Invasion of White Schools
White Man, Awaken!

The race issue is fertile soil for his powers of exploitation. Smith steadily warns his followers against Negro-white "mongrelization." In one article entitled "Interbreeding the Pastime of the Betrayers," he complains:

There is a certain set of silly preachers and sentimental loose thinkers that ought to be taken by the nape of the neck and stood in a corner until someone has pounded some sense into their silly heads.

A certain type of modernist preacher, who usually denies the Lordship of Jesus Christ and the authority of the Holy Bible, specializes these days in casting about for crusades that can be used as substitutes for preaching the gospel. It is difficult to figure out what motivates these troublemakers and mischief inventors. It is puzzling to determine whether they experience a vicarious sex thrill or whether they are sadists or Communists or conspirators or downright fanatical nuts. Whatever the case may be, they have developed a mania for promoting mongrelization.

For Smith, the Negro represents a "child race." To treat him as an equal will certainly bring about intermarriage, and then the white race will fade out into "a sort of Miami tan."

"This campaign of mongrelization," writes Smith, "has been led by modernist churchmen, academic sentimentalists, Communists, and New Dealers, all operating under the leadership of Eleanor Roosevelt and her ilk. God save us!"

Under certain circumstances, Smith's methods might well incite a riot. In September 1947, as one example, his Nationalist News Service issued the following bulletin: "Reports coming out of Atlanta indicate a complete breakdown in law and order. Citizens are buying their own private guns to protect themselves from rapists and robbers . . . private citizens do not feel safe to walk on the street day or night." The only basis for this serious charge seems to have been the fact that the Columbians, a Nazi-like subversive organization, was under prosecution by Georgia authorities.

Another variation of the scare-technique is Smith's constant reference to ubiquitous enemies who are preparing to pounce upon any genuine exponent of Christian Americanism. He warns his patrons that it is impossible to trust almost anyone, in these times of "Jewish intrigue."

Smith especially enjoys portraying himself as the chief target of frantic communist plots. One letter was headlined: "KILL HIM! KILL HIM! KILL HIM!" It continued: "Christ-hating mobsters had done everything in their power to intimidate me — yes, to get me killed before the meeting came off." This time, Smith was leading up to a request, not for a bodyguard, but for contributions:

I am sorry to observe that many people receive this letter each month who seldom, if ever, respond with a contribution. Are you going to desert us? If we fail, where else can you turn? Will we stand idly by and merely wait for the savage Communist and the Christ-hating tyrant to draw a razor blade across our throat or drive a bloody dagger into our backs.

Another letter began: *"Don't read this letter* if you are weak, timid, or lack the courage to face the truth. Here it comes." It was entitled "The Forbidden Letter" and read in part:

Dumb, stupid businessmen too self-righteous and too cowardly to support people like us who have been smeared by the character assassins, will never know what hit them if the Reds have their way. They will probably die in bed or over their own executive desks with daggers in their backs.

Keep this letter. Frame it. Initial it. Lay it away, and see if it looks so crazy a year from now.

We start the year as beggars — beggars for the money to carry on the fight.

Nearly every message from Smith contains mysterious suggestions. He writes vaguely about sinister plots, strange deaths, secret meetings, imminent bloodshed. He concludes with a humble assurance that Gerald L. K. Smith will battle on, even in the face of death or imprisonment. "If my enemies could do it without unfavorable reaction, I would be murdered or imprisoned within a week."

Smith has an almost unlimited vocabulary of vilification for those whom he dislikes. One of his favorite targets is Eleanor Roosevelt, whom he describes as "the world's most evil influence, the old hatchet gal, the villainess of American history." President Eisenhower is called "a phoney who can fool only the stupid"; Thomas Dewey, the "impudent little villain" whose "duplicity and trickery has facilitated the wrecking of our Nation"; Harold E. Stassen, "a tool to be tempered, a stooge to be used, a vanity to be inflated."

The Christian Nationalist chief is especially antagonistic toward alleged "Jewish-dominated and influential bureaucrats, the captive columnists, the prostituted commentators, and the hired babblers of propaganda." Drew Pearson is called "a low-grade, highly paid renegade, hypocrite, liar, blackmailer, character assassin, working for the Jewish Anti-Defamation League."

Ralph McGill, editor of the Atlanta *Constitution,* is described as "one of the most effective, efficient and obedient bootlickers in the United States. He is a journalistic whore if ever there was one." The Christian Nationalist Crusade devotes an entire pamphlet to a discussion of *Walter Winchell: Jew Traitor?*

But Smith has his "honor roll" as well. Among the columnists, his favorites are Westbrook Pegler, John O'Donnell, and Walter Trohan. He also has congressional pets: John W. Bricker of Ohio, William E. Jenner of Indiana, Joseph R. McCarthy of Wisconsin, Martin Dies of Texas, and others — none of whom openly endorse Smith. Joseph P. Kamp of the Constitutional Educational League and Merwin K. Hart of the National Economic Council rank high on his list of "real Americans."

Smith's Religious Veneer

Gerald L. K. Smith has little time for theology in his speeches or publications. "This Crusade is in no sense denominational or sectarian," *The Cross and the Flag* assures its readers. "It is a call and a challenge to all the lovers of Jesus Christ to stand together against the onslaught of the anti-Christs." Frequently he coats his vulgar racism with a religious veneer. One of his favorite tactics is to give a pious title to an article that actually has no religious content.

On occasion, Smith pontifically lists the religious requirements for his followers:

. . . absolute love for Jesus Christ, one that knows no fear, no compromise, no turning back . . . an absolute recognition on the part of God's children of their destiny in the world . . . an absolute identification of the enemies of Jesus and the willingness to pay the price of death, if need be, in order to resist the power and force and the satanic venom of those who would take the name of Jesus Christ out of this world.

Some nationalists who oppose Smith accuse him of a Messiah complex which makes him an arrogant ally. Others contend that he is interested in one objective — making money. Smith, however, claims to labor in his crusade for a different motive: "To indict a nation of its sin and to call on a people to put Jesus Christ first." He assures his readers that he himself is "at peace with God" and that the frustration and confusion in our time can be traced to timid men who refuse to battle against Christ's enemies — those who "stand by the fire, warm their hands as did Peter, and when asked to make a public statement, as was he, they lie and profane His name. Oh, they may confess His name with their lips, but they are afraid of His enemies. They call themselves Christians, while doing the work of His crucifiers."

Unlike many of his fundamentalist friends, Smith accepts the testimony of anyone who pretends to religious piety — as long as he despises Jews and unswervingly supports white supremacy. Smith disagrees with most fundamentalists on the issue of Catholicism, for example. He warns both Protestants and Catholics that it is the strategy of the enemies of Christianity to pit one against the other "in order to divide the lovers of Christ." The Christian Nationalists welcome Catholics into their fold, and distribute *The Popes and the Jews* as part of their campaign to solicit support. This 22-page pamphlet contains alleged edicts issued by twenty Popes "designed to curb the attempt of the Jew to get control of the Catholic Church, the Catholic community, and the Catholic institutions."

Another indication of Smith's willingness to accept support from any quarter is the important role of the Anglo-Israelites in the Christian Nationalist Crusade. While professing orthodox Protestantism, the Anglo-Israelites have concocted a fantastic notion that the ten lost tribes of Israel found their way to Britain and America, and that these two nations therefore are "chosen" of God. A large portion of Smith lieutenants embrace the credo of this cult (which is examined more thoroughly in Chapter 5).

Perhaps Smith accepts these views himself. Some disgruntled former Christian Nationalists charge that he concurs with Anglo-Israelites when among them, but agrees with their critics at other times. In any case, the Crusade has widely distributed Anglo-Israelite literature, and Smith has endorsed some of their basic beliefs. Thus he maintains that Jesus was not a Jew "in the modern sense"; that the Scriptural Jew was a citizen of Judea; that these people were fair and were Galileans; that Canaanites, possessed of the devil, flooded into Galilee at the time of Christ and stole the term "Judea," and have exploited it from that day until this. "It is a matter of common knowledge," Smith contends, "that the physical Jesus was fair and blond and of open countenance and bore no resemblance whatsoever to the modern hooked nose shop keeper, money changer, brothel owner and whiskey peddler."

Like Winrod, Smith portrays Christ as the world's greatest anti-Semite. "When I am cursed by a Jew, when I am hated by a Jew, when a Jew seeks to kill me, or smear me, or brand me as an evil force, then I have fellowship with Jesus Christ."

It is absurd, of course, to attribute anti-Jewish sentiments to Jesus. Historical scholarship affirms that Jesus was a Jew — a Jew in every sense of the term, in his heritage, his culture, and his religion; a Jew who never once considered himself anything else, who never for a moment surrendered his loyalty to Jewish institutions, who hardly stepped outside of Jewish territory. Moreover, the twelve apostles were Jews, the first Christians were all Jews, and Paul, the forceful apostle to the Gentiles — viewed by many Christians as history's greatest preacher — was also a Jew. In order to "prove" that Jesus was anti-Semitic, Smith distributes the pamphlet *Jesus vs. the Jews,* listing "20 choice texts from the New Testament, which in themselves outline the conflict between our Lord Jesus Christ and those who cursed him, ridiculed him and crucified him." Sixteen of these verses are taken from the Gospel of John.

Scholars are not agreed as to whether there is anti-Semitism in the New Testament. Many contend that the passages that would appear to promote prejudice against Jews simply reflect the early ideological battle between Judaism and its offspring, Christianity.

Reputable fundamentalists are inclined to emphasize the Old Testament warning to the nations that whoever touches the Jews to do them harm will be cursed by God. "Germany now lies prostrate," one fundamentalist scholar observes, "and probably never will rise again to occupy a dominant place among the nations of Europe." In this view, Germany's defeat is traced to Hitler's refusal to acknowledge God's ancient covenant with the Children of Israel.

Many liberal scholars, however, express the concern that the New Testament, as the creation of fallible men, was influenced strongly by anti-Semitic sentiments current in the first century of the Christian era. The Gospel of John is especially full of hatred for the Jews. The worst text is John 8:44, "Ye are of your father the devil." One commentator insists, "It is simply inconceivable that Jesus of Nazareth ever said these words." Less virulent bigotry appears in Mark (where as early as the third chapter the Pharisees are represented as conspiring to destroy Jesus); in Matthew (with its inscription to the whole Jewish nation of the curse, "His blood be on us and on our children!"); and, in mild form, in Luke and Acts.

Some scholars have urged the churches to take forceful action against these corrupted passages. Dr. Frederick C. Grant, New Testament professor at Union Theological Seminary in New York City, laments:

> The shame of the church is that it has permitted anti-Semitism to survive within its own ranks. The causes, like the origins, of this disgraceful and dysgenic social attitude certainly lie outside the New Testament and are shared by Jews and non-Jews; but that the Christian sacred scriptures got infected with the virus, that the poison survives there to this day, that the church has hitherto done very little to counteract the infection — all this is inexcusable.

Grant suggests:

> What Christians can do, today, to stem the tide of anti-Semitism in the modern world may not seem of much consequence, but it certainly ought to begin with a frank acknowledgement of the seriousness of the situation within the New Testament itself. In the choice of lessons for readings at public worship, and of material for use in religious education, sermons, and confirmation instructions, the clergy and other leaders of the church should realize how far-reaching are the inferences people draw from the passages heard or read at church, and how serious are the practical consequences of our acquiescence in the inherited prejudices which the New Testament seems to support. . . .
>
> To say the very least, and to put the matter on an entirely different ground, there is no hope that Jews will ever be led to accept the gospel as long as these misrepresentations of their religion and the accusation of their responsibility as a people for Christ's death continue to be read in the New Testament.

But Gerald L. K. Smith finds co-operation between Christians and Jews definitely forbidden by the Scriptures. "There is a verse in the Bible which says, 'Be ye not yoked together with unbelievers,' but in spite of this admonition there is a degenerate tendency abroad among so-called ordained preachers to flatter and patronize the rabbi and the synagogue." Again: "Corrupted by Jewish money and flattered by Jewish-controlled newspapers, numerous flabby clergymen have become bootlickers supreme. . . . Shame on such men who call themselves Christians."

Smith is particularly upset by the efforts in behalf of the brotherhood of the National Conference of Christians and Jews. "God pity the dumb preachers and pity the sappy laymen who continue to be a part of the Jew-financed and Jew-promoted racket designed to belittle and make unnecessary in the minds of the people the name and teachings of Jesus Christ."

Needless to say, the Christian Nationalist Crusade also keeps alive the twisted versions of the Talmud and the forged *Protocols of the Learned Elders of Zion* (both discussed in Chapter 3). "The average American does not realize how serious the Babylonian Talmud is," Smith warns. "This is the textbook and the guidebook of the international Jewish machine." He finds that the spurious *Protocols,* which he sells, "constitute the most deadly revelation of the international Jew ever to be put in print."

Gerald L. K. Smith has a network of supporters stretching from one coast to the other. Many of these apostles of discord, as we have noted, are aligned with the racist cult of the Anglo-Israelites. Others, however, give lip service to traditional Protestant beliefs — while they deny the ethical principles upon which these precepts are built.

Smith's Staff

Working close to Smith at his St. Louis headquarters is a small nucleus of devoted assistants. His office manager is Opal Tanner, once aide to the late Carl H. Mote, former owner of the Northern Indiana Telephone Company and generous contributor to a number of extremist causes. When Mote died, he left her a substantial legacy, some of which she has used to purchase the present building in which the main Christian Nationalist offices are housed. Much of Smith's confidential work is performed by his private secretary, Renata Legant.

Smith has referred to these aides as "two of the most essential persons in the Christian Nationalist movement."

Don Lohbeck, until recently editor of *The Cross and the Flag,*
was perhaps the most brilliant, ruthless, ambitious, and fanatical
propagandist of the whole Smith conspiracy against democracy
in the United States — performing somewhat the same role as
Josef Goebbels in Germany. Lohbeck had originally embarked
upon a career as a concert pianist. His gradual alignment with
the Protestant underworld began by way of the America First
Committee, pre-war champion of isolationism which suffered
from pro-Nazi and anti-Semitic infiltration. In the spring of
1953, however, Lohbeck broke with Smith.

In his alarming little booklet, *Racial Aspects of the Coming
Political Struggle,* the youthful propagandist states the "intellectual" case for racism:

> Civilization, in the meaning of man's having conquered the forces of
> nature and put them to work for man's welfare — in the sense of man's
> technical knowledge being used to bring greater comfort and enjoyment,
> is the product of the white race. It is the white man — as engineer, as
> architect, as adventurer, as scientist, as mathematician, as artist — who
> has lifted mankind from barbarism to civilization. That the white race
> was able to conquer the force of nature, and the white race alone, is due
> to the inherent curiosity of the white race — the superior intelligence of
> the white race, and the quality, uniquely white, of individualism to a
> possibly exaggerated degree. Throughout the history of the white race
> the white nation, having carried its civilization to the extent of its techni-
> cal knowledge . . . became morally decadent and intermixed with the
> inferior races within its orbit. With the loss of racial integrity and the
> rise of mass politics (and the introduction of the "all men are equal"
> philosophy) political control passed into the hands of the mongrel.
> Civilization, no longer protected by the aggressiveness of the white race,
> disappeared.

Lohbeck discovers three forces at work in the world today.
The United States, he believes, represents the white race, with
its "technical civilization" and its "racial aggressiveness." The
Soviet Union, he says, represents the Asiatic and colored world,
with its "collectivistic solidarity." The two cannot both remain
powerful. If the white man wins, "Asiatic numbers must recede
back into the slumber from which they have awakened." If the
colored races are triumphant, the white race "will be absorbed
or destroyed."

The key to the struggle, according to Smith's master-mind, is the third force — the "Jewish race" — which has throughout history sought to "obliterate Christianity and destroy the individual freedom cherished by all white men." Lohbeck's incredible thesis argues that "the Jew" says in effect: Let the "dumb whites" and the "dumb colored" destroy each other while "we Jews" remain strong enough to take over when the battle is finished.

Using as an analogy Christ's parable of the sower, Lohbeck sums up his case:

> The Jew is the wayside where the seed of Christianity did not take root; and the colored races are the stony ground and the thorny places where there was only a beginning; but the white race is the good ground where the seed of Christianity took hold and multiplied and grew to strength and productiveness. And if the white race should perish — all the creative power for good in the world would perish with him.

As a candidate for various offices in Missouri, Lohbeck has had an opportunity to broadcast his racist views by radio. Two German visitors found his views so alarming that they wrote to the St. Louis *Post-Dispatch:* "Before our eyes there arose again the picture of a Germany under the bloody whip of Hitler. . . . When Hitler started in Germany nobody saw the danger that came with him. Many, many people laughed at those who tried to warn us of what was coming, but it was not long before there were tears, bloody tears." The two Germans pleaded with readers to see the danger of Christian Nationalism.

Forrest C. Sammons

If Don Lohbeck was the theoretician of the Smith faction, perhaps its most fervent disciple is Forrest C. Sammons, a retired contractor, of Huntington, West Virginia. Sammons, a large man in his late fifties, besieges ministers and laymen alike with "open letters" urging them to repudiate the historic Christian belief that the "god" of Moses was the "God" of Jesus Christ. Communist-World Jewry, he would have them believe, is exploiting Christian ignorance of Biblical history to ensnare support for their sinister goals.

Each separate Sammons letter is stamped with these words: "STOP THE JEW!"

Sammons' interpretation of history complements that of Lohbeck. The Jews are held responsible for every event that has meant unhappiness to the world. Led by their Sanhedrin, they are supposed to be carrying out a plot to control the world and oppress the Christians. Thus, in American history, for example, the Jews are held to have been responsible for the War of 1812, Jacksonian democracy, the abolition movement, the murders of Lincoln and McKinley, the sinking of the *Maine,* the First World War, the League of Nations, the depression, the New Deal, the Second World War, the United Nations, the Korean War, the dismissal of MacArthur, the nomination and election of Eisenhower, and the continual "persecution" of Christian patriots.

Sammons issues these analyses of contemporary political problems in the name of the West Virginia Anti-Communist League, Inc. — which operates from his home.

This wealthy pamphleteer has widely publicized one of the favorite hoaxes utilized in the anti-Semitic movement in the United States. In most of his writings, Sammons prominently features a "prophecy" by Benjamin Franklin, allegedly made at the Constitutional Convention and preserved in Pinckney's private diary. Franklin is quoted as saying:

I warn you, gentlemen, if you do not exclude the Jews forever, your children's children will curse you in their graves. . . . They should be excluded by the Constitution.

The fact is that this alleged statement of Franklin is a flagrant forgery. It was printed continually in the Nazi press and broadcast over the Nazi radio. It was incorporated in the Nazi bible, the *Handbuch der Judenfrage* by Theodor Fritsch. It was spread by Nazi propagandists in America. Thousands of copies, sometimes poorly typed and containing grammatical errors, are still circulated.

Many historians have exposed the fraudulent document. The late Charles A. Beard wrote: "This alleged 'Prophecy' ascribed to Franklin is a crude forgery, and his name should be cleared of the crass prejudices attributed to him. There is in our historical records no evidence whatever of any basis for the falsehood."

The director of the Franklin Institute of Philadelphia — where this Pinckney diary allegedly is lodged — has refuted this false-hood. "The truth is, we *do not* possess the notorious diary," he has written. He has pointed out that, when the Hebrew Society of Philadelphia sought to raise money for a synagogue, Franklin signed the petition of appeal for contribution to "citizens of every denomination" and himself gave five pounds to the fund — scarcely the actions of an anti-Semite.

Sammons enthusiastically supports his leader, Smith, whom he likes to compare with Martin Luther. Sammons has also had kind words for most of the other important bigots in the United States. Father Coughlin he has described as an "out-standing American radio voice that was silenced by the Jewish Gestapo in order to make the world safe for Soviet Russia"; William Dudley Pelley, as "a tireless, unselfish patriot trying to warn America of the danger in the plot between FDR and the Polit Buro"; Joseph Kamp, as "one of the oldest and best Marxist authorities"; ex-Congressman John Rankin of Mississippi, as "one of the best informed and most fearless fighters . . . in Wash-ington."

Sammons has made a special appeal to churchmen in his open letters to "Christian Churches of All Denominations." Occasionally he addresses them to newspapers across the country under the pseudonym of "M. Vespasian, Bible student." He expresses highly unorthodox interpretations of the Scriptures which should make his ardent fundamentalist friends a bit uneasy.

Most of the Old Testament "is preserved for man's enslave-ment and destruction by Zionist World Leaders," Sammons con-tends. The books of Genesis, Exodus, Leviticus, and Numbers are "allegorical." Deuteronomy explains "how Moses imposed his 'god' upon his followers in order to create a crusading army." In the Book of Deuteronomy, Sammons discovers the key to the "international Jewish plot":

When the Lord thy God shall bring thee into the land whither thou goest to possess it, and hast cast out many nations before thee . . . (by subterfuge) . . . thou shalt smite them and utterly destroy them, and shalt make no covenant with them nor shew mercy unto them. Deut. 7:1-4.

"This," continues Sammons, "proves that the 'god' of Moses was not the God of the Prince of Peace."

Multi-Millionaire Octogenarian: George W. Armstrong

The best-known financier of the Christian Nationalist Crusade is George W. Armstrong, millionaire octogenarian of Natchez, Mississippi. Armstrong operates an extensive enterprise from Fort Worth, Texas, under the innocent-sounding title of the Judge Armstrong Foundation. Ostensibly the organization exists for the "support of charitable, religious and educational undertakings." In fact, however, it underwrites a major attempt to blanket the nation with booklets from the pen of its wealthy sponsor.

In February 1953, Gerald L. K. Smith's San Francisco Conference to Abolish the United Nations voted to present Judge Armstrong with the first annual "Henry Ford I, Memorial Award." Armstrong was described in *The Cross and the Flag* as "one of few great businessmen of responsibility who have been unafraid to attack and expose the political program of international Jewry."

The Armstrong fortune, sometimes estimated in the scores of millions, came from steel, oil, and southern plantations. As the result of a temporary business failure soon after World War I, he made his first superficial study of the American scene and published it under the title *The Crime of '20*. At that time his villain was the Federal Reserve Board, which he accused of encouraging deflation "designedly for the purpose of putting down prices and wages."

In the following decade, Armstrong's concern over national finance was supplemented by his fierce hatred for the New Deal and his gradual acceptance of crude racism. During the Second World War, for example, his publication *The Corruption of America* (1943) was barred from the United States mails for contending that the conflict was provoked "to establish sovietism in America," with "Franklin D. Roosevelt as Emperor and Eleanor Roosevelt as Empress." Armstrong had demonstrated his sympathies in 1940 when he dedicated *The Rothschild Money Trust* to such self-proclaimed "patriots" as Winrod, Sanctuary, Pelley, James True, Charles B. Hudson, and Robert E. Edmundson.

Judge Armstrong, now in his late eighties, was the son of the Rev. R. C. Armstrong, a Methodist minister and a soldier in the

Confederate Army. "I was formerly a member of the Methodist Church," he testifies, "but am not now a member of any church." He claims to be "an optimistic youthful man . . . happy and unimpaired by age, except as to eyesight and hearing, whose only ambition is to be of service to our country."

The Mississippi multi-millionaire directs his venom both at Jews and at Negroes. "This is a Christian country and a white man's country," he has said in his books, "and we do not need the Ishmaelites and negroes [sic] to help us run it." Specifically, Armstrong has called for the repeal of the Fourteenth and Fifteenth Amendments to the Constitution so that "no alien or person of Asiatic or African descent shall vote, hold office, or have any interest in a newspaper, radio, or cinema, or maintain any secret organization." On one occasion, Armstrong boasted:

I am superior by blood and inheritance to any and every man of African or Asiatic ancestry. The Anglo Saxon race is superior to every other race. We are God's chosen people.

The "Jew-Zionists" are the principal targets of Armstrong's wrath. "Our Lord and Saviour, Jesus Christ, denounced these bigoted Zionists as 'liars, hypocrites, and murderers,' and they murdered Him. So they were then, and so they are today." In his 1949 book, *Zionist Wall Street*, Armstrong concludes that "Zionism is Judaism, and Judaism is communism." The only solution, he holds, is mass execution of the "Zionist Wall Street Traitors" and deportation of all rank-and-file supporters of their program. This program "has always been followed by long periods of peace and happiness in the country that applied it."

Armstrong's own estimate is that there are thirteen million Jews in America, 95 per cent of whom endorse the Zionist program. "Every synagogue Jew and every member of the B'nai B'rith should be presumed to be a Zionist communist until proven otherwise."

To bolster his anti-Semitism with religious support, Armstrong resorts to some startling re-evaluations of the Bible. In writing of the Hebrews of the Old Testament, for example, he says:

The Israelites were a cruel, predatory warlike people. They made war on the Canaanites, the Amalekites, the Edomites (descendants of Esau), the Gideonites, the Philistines, the Syrians and other peoples. Some of these wars may have been justified but some of them appear to have been only for plunder; they were all attended with great cruelty. They killed men, women and children, and made slaves of captives.

They were Nihilists — murderers. They have killed many of the Czars and other rulers. King David killed Uriah, one of his bravest and best soldiers, in order to obtain his wife. King Solomon had his half-brother, Adonijah, killed because he sought his (Solomon's) consent to marry Abishag. These were not murders of Gentiles but of Israelites, and in violation of Mosaic law and of their covenant with God. Jesus Christ and the prophet Jeremiah, whom they killed, were Jews seeking to save the Jewish race.

This interpretation is scarcely shared by many of Smith's Bible-believing followers.

The Judge subscribes fully to the Talmud distortions and to the forged *Protocols* (discussed in Chapter 3). He has praised Sanctuary, the chief distributer of the Talmudic forgeries, as "a learned American Biblical scholar." The Talmud "is worse than 'chaff'; it is malicious and vicious and is not entitled to be classed as a religious book." Of the *Protocols,* Armstrong writes:

We must accept the protocols as being authentic and as being the program of international Jewry because they are consistent with the teachings of the Talmud, the authenticity of which is not denied; the protocols are indeed a complement to the Talmud. The Talmud expresses Jewry's "limitless ambition, burning greediness, merciless vengeance, hatreds and malice." The protocols state the plan of attaining this "limitless ambition," gratifying this "burning greediness," and of satisfying this "merciless vengeance, hatred and malice." The Talmud expresses the hopes and purposes; the protocols, the means for bringing them about.

In November 1949, Judge Armstrong was dramatically brought before the public eye when he offered the small, struggling Jefferson Military College, in Mississippi, an estimated fifty million dollars on condition that it bar non-Caucasians and include in its curriculum the teaching of religious and racial bias. Front man for the negotiations with Jefferson Military College was General George Van Horn Moseley, who had retired from the Army in 1938 to become a leading contender for fuehrer of America's pre-war nationalist fringe. At one of Smith's St. Louis rallies held shortly before the military-college incident, Moseley was quoted as saying: "I have only one thing to say about the

Jews: As for me, the whole tribe should be eliminated from the human race."

As a result of widespread protest, the board of trustees of Jefferson Military College took prompt steps to dissolve the transaction. The chairman of the board firmly announced:

> There is not enough money in the world to make us adopt the philosophy of education based on religious bias or anti-Semitic feeling. *There are some things that money cannot buy*.

Some observers contend that Armstrong's primary aim was to secure publicity and that he had no intention of going through with the original offer.

While Armstrong was tempting Jefferson Military College with the fifty-million-dollar offer, he was trying also to influence the policies of Southern Methodist University. The Natchez bigot had discovered that S.M.U. was sponsoring a community lecture series in co-operation with Temple Emanu-el of Dallas — a practice that had begun in 1939. In a letter to Umphrey Lee, president of the university, Armstrong charged that the program was "obviously for the purpose of promoting internationalism and communism and the program of the communist 'Federal Council of Churches,' for the Jews are not Methodists; they are anti-Christ." He threatened to withdraw funds allegedly pledged to Texas Wesleyan College, another Methodist educational institution.

Dr. Lee naturally ignored Armstrong's protests, save for expressing his hope that "your opinion of Southern Methodist University and of me personally will not affect your relations with Texas Wesleyan College, which is quite another institution."

In other letters to Bishop H. A. Boaz in Waynesville, North Carolina, Armstrong boasted that he had never been a member of the united Methodist Church (product of the merger of three large Methodist bodies in 1939). "The Southern Methodists made a great mistake in uniting with the Northern Methodists. We are a different people from socialistic northerners, and better." Again he threatened to withhold the proposed gift from Texas Wesleyan. "I cannot support a church school that is affiliated with Bishop Oxnam's socialistic Federal Council of Churches," he explained.

Failing to influence either Jefferson Military College or Southern Methodist University, Armstrong contributed two million dollars to his own Foundation to flood the country with his own booklets. Half of this amount was allotted to the distribution of *World Empire,* an inflammatory 100-page discussion of the *Protocols,* concluding with an exhortation to "attack the Russian monster" now.

Since then, Armstrong has published a discussion of the Korean conflict, *Third Zionist War,* whose thesis is summed up concisely in its first paragraph:

> Our present war with Russia and China is obviously our Third Zionist War. All three of them were for the same purpose, viz: to establish a Zionist World Empire. All of them were initiated by a shocking disaster to arouse us to war: the first one by the sinking of the passenger ship Lusitania; the second by the destruction of our Pacific fleet at Pearl Harbor; and the third by the Korean attack. The first resulted in the League of Nations, the second in the United Nations, and the third is obviously intended to convert it into a Zionist World Empire for the *pretended* purpose of preserving peace.

Judge Armstrong has finally succeeded in his attempts to foist a fraction of his amassed fortune upon a recognized institution — the small, liberal-arts Piedmont College, in northern Georgia. In 1950, General Moseley was invited by President James E. Walter, D.D., to be the guest of honor and principal speaker at a student-faculty pre-Thanksgiving banquet. A young English instructor, Hoyt E. Bowen, remembering Moseley's racist record, objected, and others joined him in vigorous protest.

The clamor grew when it was announced that, through Moseley, Piedmont was to accept the small sum of $500 per month from Armstrong — "no strings attached." In the course of the controversy that followed, faculty members (including Bowen) were fired, trustees resigned, and students demonstrated. But President Walter, content to believe that the donor's sole intent is to aid the struggling institution, continued to accept regular allowances from the Armstrong-sponsored Texas Educational Association. The situation has continued to cause difficulties on the campus. Two more faculty members were dismissed in the spring of 1953, bringing to twenty-three the total of teachers or officials who have resigned or been discharged.

Piedmont College, which matriculates two hundred students,

maintained a tenuous connection with the Congregational Church. It was established in 1897 by the American Missionary Association, precursor of the present Board of Home Missions. By its charter Piedmont is open to all qualified students — but no Negro students have ever been admitted. The Board of Home Missions, however, is committed to a long-range policy of "a non-segregated church in a non-segregated society." It stated: "If the time comes when, in our judgment, Piedmont ceases to abide by the principles of human equality for which we stand, we shall certainly withdraw our moral and financial support and make our evaluation known to the churches." In early 1953 the showdown came — and the Congregationalists severed all affiliation with the college.

"Footnoted Hate": Professor John O. Beaty

Leaders of the Smith circle — and many other apostles of discord — welcomed a new "scholar" into their fold in late 1951. Dr. John O. Beaty, professor of English at Southern Methodist University, attempted to document the rantings of the fringe groups in an analysis of American political forces in his 268-page book, *The Iron Curtain Over America*. The volume appears to be the most extensive piece of anti-Semitic literature in the history of America's racist movement. And, early in 1953, it was continuing to sell thousands of copies in its ninth printing.

Protestants should be troubled by *The Iron Curtain Over America*. Southern Methodist University is one of Methodism's great institutions, with a faculty of over three hundred, six thousand students, and an endowment of more than $4,000,000. Beaty, who is a Baptist, corrupts his professed religious faith by using it to attack the principles of Christianity. According to the book's preface, the author "has humbly and reverently taken as his motto, or text, the promise of Christ the Saviour . . . AND YE SHALL KNOW THE TRUTH AND THE TRUTH SHALL MAKE YOU FREE."

The Beaty thesis is admirably clear. While the volume is self-described as "the first comprehensive, documented account of the origin and scope and the intentions of the 'insidious forces working from within' which are seeking to destroy America and Western Christian Civilization," it turns out to be a skillfully prepared diatribe against the so-called "Khazar Jews." These powerful "Eastern European elements" actually are not Jews in the Biblical sense, says Beaty, but "a people of mixed stock with Mongol and Turkic affinities" who accepted Judaism in the eighth or ninth century. "Various elements of this restless aggressive minority nurtured the amazing quadruple aims of international Communism, the seizure of power in Russia, Zionism, and continued migration to America."

Like Armstrong, the S.M.U. professor contends that the "Khazars" were instrumental in plunging America into the first World War against the Germans, in spite of the fact that "the friendly relationships between the United States and Germany existed not only on the governmental level but were cemented by close racial kinship." Because of these same Eastern European elements, "the defeated country was left in the precarious position which soon produced an economic collapse," enabling Jewish interests to gain control over the German economic and political structure. This development, in turn, gave rise to Hitler and the Nazis.

Meanwhile, argues Beaty, the Jews had overthrown the Czar and established international communism—through which they now agitate against the rest of the world. In America, to which large numbers of Khazars migrated between 1919 and 1924, they allegedly captured the Democratic Party by assuming the balance of power in strategic northern states; then they gradually gained positions of great prestige until, by 1933, they were able to win their "first spectacular triumph" in Franklin D. Roosevelt's recognition of the Soviet government. Since the beginnings of the New Deal, the Khazars have imposed a "black mask of censorship" upon the nation.

Beaty maintains that American policy during the New Deal era had a three-pronged purpose:

(1) As early as 1937, our government determined upon war against Germany for no formulated purpose beyond pleasing the dominant Eastern European element and allied elements in the National Democratic Party, and holding "those votes . . ."

(2) The powerful Eastern European element dominant in the inner circles of the Democratic Party regarded with complete equanimity, perhaps even with enthusiasm, the killing of as many as possible of the world-ruling and Khazar-hated race of "Aryans" . . .

(3)   Our alien-dominated government fought the war for the annihilation of Germany, the historic bulwark of Christian Europe . . .

The Iron Curtain Over America uses similar reasoning in evaluating current United States foreign policy. Beaty says of Korea, for example: "The only logical conclusion . . . is that *for some reason* certain people with influence in high places wanted heavier American casualties in Korea, the final defeat of our forces there, and elimination of General MacArthur from the American scene." Beaty sums up by saying that the Jewish Khazars, through the Democratic Party, deliberately forced upon the country "Socialistic controls" and "plenty of casualties." The solution? First, drive the "Khazars" from the government; then, "evolve some method of preventing our unassimilable mass of aliens and alien-minded people from exercising in this country a power over our culture and our lives out of all proportion to the members of this minority."

Normally one could dismiss *The Iron Curtain Over America* as simply another published example of flagrant racism — for this it is. But Beaty cannot be ignored. While he plays the same tune as full-time agitators, his work possesses a learned flavor seldom found in the standard anti-Semitic texts. It is written with a strong aura of authenticity that could easily impress the uninformed, the gullible, or the latently anti-Semitic. The S.M.U. professor relies upon sources that provide a clever "front" of reliability for his baseless arguments — such as government documents, encyclopedias, leading newspapers, popular magazines, publications of the American Legion and of the Veterans of Foreign Wars. Beaty also quotes liberally from the ultra-conservative *National Republic, The Freeman,* and *American Mercury.* He betrays himself, however, when he takes material from numerous hate sheets — including the frenzied *Common Sense,* "The Nation's Anti-Communist Newspaper."

A second unusual fact is that Beaty is far from being a "nobody" who had to turn to "footnoted hate" for financial profit or academic status. His education includes B.A. and M.A. degrees from the University of Virginia, a Ph. D. from Columbia, and graduate work at the university of Montpellier — which indicates that education alone is not a sure cure for intolerance. In 1919 Beaty joined the faculty of Southern Methodist University; he rose to be head of the department of English. He has been a visiting professor at Pennsylvania State College, the University of Virginia, and the University of Texas. In addition to his teaching posts, Beaty has written or collaborated on a dozen books. His texts have been used in more than seven hundred colleges and universities, and his historical novel, *Swords in the Dawn,* published first in New York, has had British and Australian editions and was adopted for state-wide use in the public schools of Texas. Among the dozen or more organizations to which he belongs are three honorary fraternities: Phi Beta Kappa, Delta Sigma Rho, and Tau Kappa Alpha.

The professor contends that his travel in Europe and Asia and his five years with the Military Intelligence Service in World War II "rounded out the background for the reading and research (1946-51) which resulted in *The Iron Curtain Over America.*" He advertises his volume as "neither memoirs nor apology, but an objective presentation of 'things as they are'." It differs from many other "pro-American books," he adds, in that "it not only exhibits the external and internal dangers which threaten the survival of our country, but shows how they developed and why they continue to plague us."

The book is a composite of distorted half-truths and positive falsehoods. The author's impressive — but carefully selected — array of quotations and references is deceptive. A thorough exposé of Beaty's method of documentation and of his general thesis cannot be undertaken here, but two or three examples will serve to illustrate his pseudo-scholarly technique.

In the first place, critical readers will find that the author often supplies seemingly impressive documentation for insignificant or non-controversial details that have no importance for the thesis as a whole; elsewhere, on the other hand, he offers extreme assertions without any supporting evidence whatever. For example: he gives two irrelevant references for the undisputed fact that the Kingdom of Jerusalem established during the Crusades lasted nearly a hundred years; and he quotes an encyclopedia to lend an authoritative air to the obvious assertion that Martin Luther won the sympathy of many of his countrymen.

On the other hand, Beaty furnishes no argument or authority

for his contention that drastic controls have been repugnant to the "free western mind" but quite acceptable to the Jews, "for the Babylonian Talmud under which they lived had taught them to accept authoritarian dictation on everything." The S.M.U. professor conveniently ignores the fact that it was this "free western mind" of his noble Aryan that gave rise to a variety of totalitarianisms, notably Nazism. He also fails to mention that Karl Marx — himself baptized a Protestant at the age of eight — gained most of his philosophical bearings from a Prussian Christian professor, Georg Wilhelm Friedrich Hegel.

Far more serious than his random injection of jumbled references throughout the book is Beaty's flagrant abuse of the sources that he does employ. As one of many examples, he utilizes the *Jewish Encyclopedia* in an attempt to document his charge that the Khazars were pre-Revolution espousers of Soviet communism. Thus, he quotes from the encyclopedia as follows: "reaction to those excesses was Jewish support of the Bolsheviks. . . ." This might be interpreted as a support for Beaty's contention.

If we examine the context of the quotation, however, we find that he has reversed the actual meaning. Immediately following the sentence that Beaty has repeated in part, the enclopedia author had stated: "Yet the majority of Jewish radicals adhered to democratic socialism, and among the Jewish working class the Leninist faction had a limited following. . . . The Jewish masses viewed the seizure of power by the Bolsheviks with apprehension. . . . The prohibition of free enterprises, no matter how small, meant economic disaster for them."

It is unnecessary to present here innumerable other examples of Beaty's "scholarship." Yet, because many people are awed by footnotes, *The Iron Curtain Over America* poses a dangerous threat to democracy and a new embarrassment to sensitive Christians.

Protestantism's ministry of hate hailed Beaty's hoax with enthusiasm. In a two-page spread in *The Cross and the Flag,* Gerald L. K. Smith called it

. . . the most sensational book of this generation, . . . sensational not because it contains any new truth, but because this is the first time that an instructor and military officer (retired) has dared treat the Jewish question with courage, objectivity and clearness. The leaders of the Christian Nationalist Crusade and the editors of *The Cross and the Flag* urge every reader to get this book immediately.

Most leaders of Protestantism's fifth column were similarly impressed. Gerald Winrod gave *The Iron Curtain Over America* an enthusiastic review in his *Defender Magazine,* urging that "Christians and all other patriotic Americans lose no time in ordering and circulating it among friends and neighbors." The West Coast *Williams Intelligence Summary* told its readers: "Give it every ounce of support you can. Write for copies and use them as a circulating library." *Women's Voice* called it "an absolute MUST!" Allen A. Zoll, arch-enemy of the public schools, concluded that the Beaty publication was "the most important book in the last 50 years." Smith's Los Angeles friend, Methodism's Bob Shuler, found it "conclusive" and "the most startling and sensational book of this generation."

But comment on the book has come from more surprising sources. Colonel Alvin M. Owsley, Past National Commander of the American Legion and former United States Minister to Rumania, the Irish Free State, and Denmark, characterized *The Iron Curtain Over America* as "one of the great documents of our times," which "should become the first reading of every patriot in the land." J. M. Hazlitt, Oklahoma columnist, wrote: "Nothing I ever read in my life before stirred me so deeply, caused such wonder and anger, finally called for such quick action." Hedda Hopper called it "the most revealing and frightening book that's come to my desk in ages."

The Freeman, the *American Legion Magazine,* and other widely circulated publications have carried advertisements for the book.

One of the most important episodes in the drama of the Beaty book directly involved hundreds of American clergymen. The Rev. Henry Darlington, retired rector of New York City's Church of the Heavenly Rest, where he had served as pastor for twenty-eight years, sent *The Iron Curtain Over America* to Episcopal clergymen and chaplains in all sections of the country. On the stationery of the Military Order of Foreign Wars of the United States, of which he is Chaplain, the aging minister wrote to recipients of the book:

My dear Bishop and Brethren of the Clergy:

Because I am pro-Christian and pro-American I wish you would read this great documented book, "The Iron Curtain Over America," by John O. Beaty of Southern Methodist University, Dallas. Beaty's text books are now in 700 Universities and Colleges. This book shows the anti-Christian and the anti-American *"conspiracy"* in our beloved country.

A Christian patriot has paid for these books. I hope that after you read it you will please pass it to your friends so that the facts therein will be widely known and understood by the people of America.

The "Christian patriot" who footed the bill turned out to be J. Russell Maguire of Greenwich, Connecticut, who has amassed millions from oil and manufacturing (Thompson submachine guns, electrical equipment, etc.). Maguire bought *American Mercury* in the fall of 1952, precipitating a crisis in its staff that finally resulted in the ousting of Editor William Bradford Huie. According to *Time* magazine, Maguire has been a supporter of other figures on the fringes of the Protestant underworld — men such as Merwin K. Hart, head of the National Economic Council, and Allen A. Zoll, whose American Patriots, Inc., was listed by the Attorney General as a "fascist" organization.

But later Darlington made a stout apology. On July 24, 1952, he addressed a letter to all persons to whom he had transmitted the Beaty book. It read in part:

I recently sent to you a book written by Professor John O. Beaty, entitled "Iron Curtain Over America." I was persuaded to do this, although I had not previously read the book, by someone who represented to me that it dealt with a subject in which all Americans should be interested, namely, the threat of Communism.

I now find that I was misled. The represented purpose of this book is but its ostensible purpose; actually the Beaty book attempts to engender religious hostility. As such, it is scarcely worthy of your attention. Accordingly, I apologize, for, as you know, I would have no part in promoting bigotry in any form.

Although a professor at Southern Methodist University, Beaty speaks only for himself: the university's faculty and student body completely reject his incredible thesis. The book page of the Dallas *Morning News,* edited by a Southern Methodist University professor, characterized *The Iron Curtain Over America* as "the worst book of 1952." A sharp critical review in the college newspaper, *The S.M.U. Campus,* called it "just what students of Dr. Beaty would expect . . . [but] a man should be judged on his public record, not what Dr. Beaty calls his 'racial antecedents.' " The principle of academic freedom was an important factor in keeping the university from initiating action against Beaty.

Many flamboyant racists are no longer alive and the influence of others has withered. But successors have come to replace them. The dynasty of hate is tenacious and strong. The wary citizen can spot the cold orators of bigotry without much difficulty. He must be careful also to detect the subtle hate-purveyors — men who pretend to be scholars, who pervert the American respect for education by false documentation, who hide their spiritual decadence under the mask of respectability. Street orator and scholar — all racists adopt the same unscrupulous techniques.

5

The Self-Anointed "Chosen People"

It might happen in any American town. A zealous pastor joins his colleagues in a meeting of the ministerial association to lecture to them at length on the ten lost tribes of Israel and the Great Pyramid of Egypt. "Brethren," he might testify, "I was filled with doubts and uncertainties until I discovered these great truths. I owe my renewal of faith and assurance of salvation to my discovery of Anglo-Israelism, the only valid interpretation of God's Word. I know now that the Scriptures have not remained unfulfilled."

The Anglo-Israelite creed — which also goes under the names of British-Israelism, Celto-Saxon, Destiny of America, and the Kingdom Message — has made an alarming contribution to the activity of the Protestant underworld. Its adherents have been authoritatively estimated at two million, most of them in the United Kingdom or the British Dominions. Although it would be unrealistic to single out the movement as a special menace in this country, Anglo-Israelite pastors often lend enthusiastic support to organized bigotry against Jews, Negroes, or Catholics. The cult's distinctiveness stems from the notion that the Anglo-Saxons are God's Chosen People. Its members are found in Protestant churches of nearly all denominations.

The fundamentals of Anglo-Israelism were first propounded about 1790 by a harmless madman named Richard Brothers, who preferred to be known as the "Prince of the Hebrews." Brothers was born in Newfoundland in 1757, joined the British navy while a youth, and served with some distinction until he retired with half-pay at the early age of thirty. Soon after settling down in London, he began to show signs of religious fanaticism, and by 1794 he had developed delusions of grandeur that led him to proclaim that, as a descendant of King David, he was the rightful heir to the British throne. The following year Brothers was committed to an asylum, and in 1824 he died a pauper. His ideas had caught on, however, and the mantle passed from one person to another. The British-Israel World Federation — in which some United States Anglo-Israelites play a role — dates back to 1890.

Kingdom Messengers generally scoff at the theory that they trace their creed from an eighteenth-century madman. Comments one Anglo-Israelite publication: "We could say that Abraham, Moses, David, Isaiah and Jeremiah were the earliest apostles of this truth, that the Apostle Paul was one of its keenest thinkers, and that the place of its origin was Palestine instead of England." Champions of the cult contend that from earliest times English writers, religious and secular — of all classes — have delighted in writing of England as Israel. Even the Puritans of New England called themselves "the Seed of Abraham, God's servants, and the children of Jacob, His chosen." The members of the cult regard John Wilson of Scotland, author of *Our Israelitish Origin* (1840), as "Father of the Rediscovery of Israel."

There was no concerted Anglo-Israelite movement in the United States until the late 1920's, when Howard B. Rand, a New England Bible scholar, started the propagation of the Kingdom Message. Before his ordination into the ministry, Rand had graduated from the University of Maine and passed the bar examinations in Maine and Massachusetts. He made an unsuccessful bid for the Bay State attorney generalship as the Prohibition candidate in 1914, toyed with insurance for a few years, and then became manager of a Haverhill, Massachusetts, construction company. In 1928 he started a small Anglo-Israelite group in his home city, but his early experiences were discouraging. After a trip to England to visit the head of the British-Israel Federation, he became more active, and the average attendance at his meetings jumped from a dozen to nearly two hundred.

Rand began publication of *The Bulletin,* later called *Message of the Covenant,* and now *Destiny.*

Destiny goes to about fifteen thousand subscribers and is probable the most attractive-looking of all the "hate sheets" published in the United States. It is a slick monthly with a multi-color cover, an exceptionally good printing job by the Rumford Press of Concord, New Hampshire. *Destiny* is circulated by Destiny Publishers, who also deal in vast quantities of Anglo-Israelite books and pamphlets by the most celebrated of the movement's authors.

In 1930 Rand arranged for a national convention of the Kingdom groups that had mushroomed throughout the United States. It was held in Detroit, where he met W. J. Cameron, former editor of Henry Ford's Dearborn (Michigan) *Independent* and radio publicist for Ford's "Sunday Evening Hour." It was Cameron who — together with Ford and Boris Brasol — was responsible for the infamous series of articles entitled "The International Jew." (See Chapter 3.) By 1933 Cameron was president of the newly organized Anglo-Saxon Federation of America, and Rand was serving as its secretary-general at the national headquarters in Detroit. A few years later, Clarence S. Warner, a successful advertising man for Packard Motors, joined the movement and became Rand's crack publicity expert and No. 1 disciple. Through their joint efforts many Anglo-Israelite groups were started across the country.

Today these groups have little official connection with one another, although Rand is still widely acclaimed as the patriarch of the movement. In addition to the extensive publication offices in Haverhill, his group opened a Bible Research Library in Boston — since closed down — where Rand and other teachers of the cult held forth on the deeper mysteries of their faith. Rand himself is a colorless speaker. His voice totally lacks drive or emphasis. He is a rather nondescript man of about sixty, a bit stooped, almost completely bald. His audiences are predominantly middle class, with a sprinkling of mink coats. With great confidence in the leader, the audience listens attentively to the long pseudo-scholarly lectures delivered in a dull monotone.

The theology of the Kingdom Message relies mainly upon *a priori* arguments from the Bible, and its followers believe implicitly in their own infallibility as interpreters. Each believer regards his own church or Sunday school as his divinely appointed mission field. By a slavishly literal approach to certain selected Biblical passages, and by the application of the wildest guesswork to history, they make out a case that identifies the Anglo-Saxons with the ten "lost" tribes of Israel. Without a long refutation of the cult's basic premises, it can be stated that there is not a shred of reliable evidence to support their position.

A standard, though sketchy, outline of the basic elements of Anglo-Israelite theology is Rand's booklet, *The Pattern of History,* sent to all *Destiny* patrons to "provide the essential background for reading the month after month issues of our magazine." It traces the Biblical accounts from the wanderings of Abraham to the Babylonian captivity and concludes:

After seventy years of captivity, a remnant of Judah returned to its homeland but the northern ten tribes of Israel never returned. . . . Actually, it is impossible that Israel should become extinct. Before the time of their captivity, God had promised that the Israelites would grow great in the world. . . . He had also promised that Israel would change her name and become lost to herself for a long time. Now, if you believe God, it follows that you will believe his promises. Therefore, Israel must be in existence still, though without knowledge of her true identity.

The Pattern of History then quickly "proves" that the Jews could not be Israel because the Jews are the remnants of Judah — and Judah and Israel were two separated nations. The book also discounts the notion that the Christian Church is the spiritual heir of Israel, since the Bible promises that Israel "was to become a great nation, a company of nations, and a great people." We can only discover Israel, it continues, if we find those present-day nations in which the promises of God are fulfilled. The Anglo-Israelites have sought out hundreds of such promises and find that the modern Anglo-Saxon-Celtic nations, the United States and the British Commonwealth, are fulfilling every prophecy made about present-day Israel. Among thirty-two favorite passages are:

1. A Powerful Nation (Micah 4:7, 5:8).
2. An Undefeated Race (Isa. 17:14, 41:12,15).
3. The Chief Nations (Isa. 41:8,9).
4. With Colonies in all zones, immense in size (Isa. 54:1-3, 58:12, Obad. 17).
5. Scattered everywhere among the Heathen (Ezek. 37:21).

6. Yet Mistress of the ends, sides, and uttermost parts of the earth (Deut. 33:17, Ps. 2:8, 98:3).
7. Holding a great Heathen Empire in dominion (Ps. 2:8).
8. The Chief Missionary Power on Earth, carrying the Gospel everywhere (Isa. 27:6, 49:6, Micah 5:7).

The Pattern of History hastens to assure those who do not usually consider themselves Anglo-Saxons that they, too, may be included among God's Chosen People. "The forefathers of the Anglo-Saxon-Celtic people spread slowly across Europe. . . . Many of them stopped on the way, forming 'pockets' of Israel in Europe."

How, then, does one know whether he is of select heritage? "If you have the inclinations and ideals which have made America and England great today, no matter in what country your immediate forefathers were born, it may well be that in your ancestry you are derived from one of the lost tribes of Israel."

Other favored proofs of Anglo-Israelism stem from a comparison of the Hebrew and English languages. As early as 1530, William Tyndale announced that he had found amazing likenesses between the two tongues, which made English the most suitable language into which to translate the Old Testament. The Kingdom Message expounds this general thesis in great detail. Saxon, for example, is traced to Saac's sons — Isaac's sons — thus fulfilling God's promise of Genesis 21:12: "In Isaac shall thy seed be called." British stands for *berith-ish* — *berith* being Hebrew for covenant and *ish* for man, i.e., men of the covenant. And John Bull was so named because Isaac's British sons frequently sacrificed the bullock, which in Hebrew is spelled *engle* — hence England.

The Anglo-Israelites then delve into a hodgepodge of prophecy. They find the future of Israel and the Israelites foretold in the Bible. Every indication, they claim, points to the conclusion that the time has come when the greatest prophecies will be fulfilled. The Anglo-Israelites attribute great significance to General Allenby's capture of Jerusalem on December 11, 1917; for, "according to the Bible, these prophecies are to be fulfilled within a 35-year period after the end of the war in which Israel recaptures the Holy City — Jerusalem." What are these great events that are taking place? The answer, they say, lies in the

Bible if we recognize the true identity of Israel. Some forecast Armageddon in 1953.

The case of the Anglo-Israelites becomes even more ludicrous when many branch into "pyramidology" and find corroborative evidence for Biblical prophecy in the Great Pyramid of Gizeh. They argue that the structure fulfills the remarkable prophecy of Isaiah: "In that day there shall be an altar to the Lord in the midst of the land of Egypt, and a pillar at the border thereof to the Lord. And it shall be for a sign and for a witness unto the Lord of hosts in the land of Egypt." The message of the Great Pyramid is deciphered through a study of its system of passages and chambers, which portrays the history of the "Building Race." Some students of Kingdom theology devote much of their lives to the interpretation of the allegorical significance of its internal meanderings. In fact, an entire organization, solemnly known as the Institute of Pyramidology, has been set up for "research" in this area.

The Anglo-Israelite attitude toward the Jews varies slightly from one group to the next, but most in America agree that the Jews are "a curse, a hiss, and a reproach." In a recent booklet, *Palestine: Center of World Intrigue,* Rand states that "God has declared that he will visit upon them the type of suffering they have been instrumental in bringing upon others." Therefore, as the climax of the age approaches, terrible suffering will come upon the Jews who have gathered together in Palestine. "They will be numbered for the sword and will bow down to the slaughter." Jews are hastening to Israel, Rand adds, so that they may arrive in time at the place of execution where this sentence may be carried out.

Kingdom Message believers have numerous theories about the origin of the Jews. Perhaps the most popular thesis was advanced by R. H. Sawyer, West Coast writer, in his booklet *The Jewish Question,* whose general tenor may be gathered from his first paragraph:

The Jewish question has been so long before the people of the world that many refuse to give it serious consideration. But it can not be disposed of by such indifference. While the world sleeps the Jew works, and the best interests of nations and men suffer as a result of his unceasing activities. Just now America seems to be the focal point of a combined

Jewish effort, in their persistent attacks on the Divinity of Jesus Christ and their presumptuous claims that "The Bible is a product of Jewish literary and artistic genius." A Jew controlled press is being used throughout America in an apparent effort to wreck the faith of the youth of the land.

Sawyer contends that few present-day Jews are of the House of Judah. Most of them are deemed to be the offspring of various wild tribes — notably the "Mongol Chazars," who became converts to Judaism. Moreover, even those who did descend from the House of Judah disobeyed God's "great commandment" and intermarried with the Canaanites, Hittites, and other inferior peoples. Sawyer's thesis parallels that of John O. Beaty — discussed in Chapter 4 — whose book *The Iron Curtain Over America* was received enthusiastically in Anglo-Israelite circles.

In spite of the racist tendencies of many Anglo-Israelites, anti-Semitism is not an intrinsic element of their fanciful creed. In fact, in J. H. Allen's *Judah's Sceptre and Joseph's Birthright,* the principal sourcebook of the entire movement, the Jews are recognized as "kin" of the Anglo-Saxon-Celtic peoples:

> Understand us: we do not say that the Jews are not Israelites; they belong to the posterity of Jacob, who was called Israel; hence they are all Israelites. But the great bulk of Israelites are not the Jews, just as the great bulk of Americans are not Californians, and yet all Californians are Americans.

Many Anglo-Israelites in other parts of the world — notably England — have no sympathy for their fellow-cultists in America who preach racism.

The prejudices of Kingdom leaders in the United States were brought before the public in dramatic fashion in 1941, just before the attack upon Pearl Harbor. Boake Carter, prominent radio commentator and newspaper columnist, had accepted the credo that the Anglo-Saxon-Celtic-*Judaic* peoples constitute the modern progeny of the sons of Jacob — much as J. H. Allen had taught. Rand invited him to speak at a Kingdom convention. When Carter planned to emphasize the need for unity among all of the House of Israel, Jews included, Rand balked and asked Carter to forget the whole thing. As a result of the ensuing flare-up, the commentator publicly repudiated the Anglo-

Saxon Federation as un-American, undemocratic, anti-Semitic, and "wholly in variance with the words of God in His Bible."

Rand has been especially sensitive about charges of anti-Semitism. "We are all Semites because we all stem from Israel," Rand replied to Carter. "If we were anti-Semitic we would be denouncing ourselves." More recently, the Haverhill pyramidologist traced such charges to "Communists, fellow-travelers, and all those whose purpose is to destroy our American way of life [who] are in mortal terror that the real truths will be published throughout the length and breadth of our land."

Southern Kingdom

The Southland is a spawning ground for Anglo-Israelism; their self-styled "fundamentalist" pastors and publications proclaim the myth that white Anglo-Saxons are chosen of God. In Florida, for example, there are many such groups, large and small, including the Kingdom Bible Seminary, located in St. Petersburg. The seminary is controlled by a 25-man board of directors headed by C. Lewis Fowler, A. M., Lit. D., D. D., President. Fowler once had offices in the Presbyterian Building in New York City, where he organized the Kingdom Message Association, now defunct.

Other leading Anglo-Israelite leaders in the South include A. Royal Forsythe, who operates an up-to-date printing plant in Knoxville, Tennessee; F. M. Royall, elderly director of the North Gate Mission to Israel in Greenville, South Carolina; Charles O. Benham, publisher of the *National Broadcaster* in Washington, D. C.; Otis B. Read, Jr., pastor of the Open Bible Church in Baltimore, Maryland; and many more.

Perhaps the most energetic cult leader in the United States is James A. Lovell, founder and director of the United Israel World Fellowship of Fort Worth, Texas. Lovell spends large sums weekly to carry on the "thirteen phases" of his ministry, which include the pastorate of the First Covenant Church in Dallas and the publication of an 84-page monthly, *Kingdom Digest*.

During the past few years radio broadcasting has become a major emphasis of his ministry, and he claims an air audience of fifteen million. Intermittently, Lovell's quarter-hour programs have been carried by as many as fifty different stations from coast to coast, including high-powered KRMG (Tulsa, Oklahoma) and XERB (Mexico). In 1952, for example, he boasted that more than fifty thousand persons responded annually to his programs by mail.

Lovell's propaganda campaign includes an integrated effort to circulate literally millions of books, booklets, leaflets, and tracts that sell for prices ranging from ten cents to seven dollars. He claims to distribute a million pieces of literature a year "to hungry hearts all over the world." In addition to the customary expositions of Kingdom theology, Lovell sells charts on everything from King Solomon's Temple to "vita-potent" vitamins, as well as health bulletins on tonsils, cystitis, fibroid tumors, and many other known or unknown physical ailments.

He also distributes standard racist briefs by Gerald L. K. Smith, George W. Armstrong, John O. Beaty, Kenneth Goff, and many of Lovell's cultist brethren. These or others who share their point of view regularly contribute to *Kingdom Digest*.

While Lovell modestly denies that he has any extraordinary prophetic powers, the United Israel World Fellowship does a big business in soothsaying. In 1953 its director estimated that "approximately 50,000 people, all over the nation and many parts of the world, read our predictions." His 1953 prophecies cover 125 topics, including such diverse subjects as Eleanor Roosevelt, Billy Graham, Catholics, Aliens, Tito, Breweries, Chlorophyll, Freakish Weather, Prodigality, Dope, Operations, and Intermarriage.

James A. Lovell, D. D., is a man of forty-five who boasts about his buoyant health and energy. He was born in Boyd, Texas, into a family of six boys and three girls. Lovell attended Hardin-Simmons University at Abilene and Southwestern Pre-Millenial Bible Institute in Fort Worth. He served the Baptist denomination in two Texas parishes, left to establish two Kingdom churches in California, and abruptly returned to Texas in the fall of 1946.

Lovell claims to have known Howard B. Rand for many years, but he is friendlier with other Kingdom preachers, especially the several dozen in the Texas-Oklahoma-Missouri area, who include Congregationalists, Methodists, Disciples, Baptists, as well as ministers of the Churches of Christ, "Latter Rain," and Pentecostal sects. He has shown special interest in the Christian Nationalist Crusade. He lists Gerald L. K. Smith as an Anglo-Israel clergyman and echoes the Smith line in *Kingdom Digest's* editorial columns, "Prophecy on the March." Before World War II, Lovell was quoted as saying: "God wants to destroy the Jews and He is using Hitler as His tool." In recent years he has decried, in one bundle, "One-Worlders, Zionists, pro-Communists, Liberals, and Jews." He prophesies that in the "Kingdom Age" ahead, many Jews will be converted and that their "arrogant, prideful, unregenerate, Canaanite nature" will be changed.

The most colorful of all pyramidologists is another southern pastor, and former associate of Lovell, "Dr." Joe Jeffers of Sarasota, Florida. With his wife, Helene, he directs the activities of the Kingdom of Yahweh. Jeffers claims to be the first evangelist to devote his full time to the preaching of Anglo-Israelism. "Practically all of the teachers except those in Massachusetts are students of mine," he adds, but "most of them are not progressive enough to follow with the new revelation which we have received concerning the Creator's true Name, YAHWEH (pronounced Yahway)."

Although Jeffers preaches traditional Anglo-Israelite theology, he alienated most leaders of the cult when he placed great emphasis upon the manner in which one addresses the Creator. "God is not a name, it is a title. There are over three million idols, pagan gods and deities, — all which are called 'God.' . . . What confidence can one have that we will not contact one of these false gods rather than YAHWEH, the only spirit or being that we are permitted to worship?" Since only those who use the name of Yahweh will be saved — he claims — the Creator has sent Jeffers to prepare a nucleus of believers to remain in the world after its other inhabitants have been destroyed.

The boy Joe was the sixth of fifteen children born to a poor railroad employee of Roanoke, Alabama. Joe's parents were hard-shell Baptists, and at fourteen Jeffers was state president of the Baptist Young People's Union. At eighteen he was recommended by a Baptist board of deacons as a ministerial student at Howard College in Birmingham. A few years later, after receiving a degree from Baylor University, he was ordained at Southwest Baptist Theological Seminary in Fort Worth.

Jeffers was an immediate success as a "pulpit clown," and shortly after received a promotion to evangelistic work centering in Dallas. Jeffers traveled widely; wherever he went, he attracted attention. In St. Louis he was shot at by unknown assailants. In another town he coughed his way out of a gas-filled evangelistic tent, and watched a second go up in flames. When opposition toward him became formidable within the Baptist ranks, Jeffers suddenly broke completely with the denomination and in 1935 he established Kingdom Temple, Inc., in California.

The troubles of the dynamic young cultist were just beginning when he began his ministry on the West Coast. He had allegedly added renunciation of sex to the usual Anglo-Israelite tenets, and when his first wife — the mother of his two children — objected, Jeffers secured a divorce in Reno.

A year later, in 1939, Jeffers was hauled into court on charges that he and his second wife, Joy, entertained house guests by exhibiting themselves and indulging in sexual activities. Joy stood by her husband and he was acquitted. In 1943, however, when her husband announced that he was in effect "the Christ," she sued for divorce and an equal division of all the Kingdom property. The court upheld Mrs. Jeffers; and when her husband ran off with a Cadillac that had been awarded to her, he was given a four-year term in a Federal penitentiary. In the meantime Jeffers had wed his third wife, Helene, who continued to hold Kingdom meetings and send out "prophetic messages" from the Temple of Yahweh, Cabazon, California, while he was in jail.

In 1947 Jeffers was paroled until the marshal's office came to pick him up for an alleged violation and found him in a 32-room Laurel Canyon mansion for which his followers had paid $60,000. He had five shiny chauffeur-driven cars at his disposal, as well as a houseful of servants. He headed a flock of more than five thousand who firmly believed that he was the "Son of the Creator." Jeffers headed back to the penitentiary for another two and a half years. Throughout all these difficulties, he loudly attributed his misfortunes to a series of premeditated "frame-ups."

Jeffers, who frequently moves from one city to another, currently directs the activities of the Kingdom of Yahweh in Sarasota, Florida, to which it moved last year from Houston.

The work of the Jeffers and of a number of Temple of Yahweh ministers aligned with his cause has included the publication of *Kingdom Voice,* a mimeographed bulletin issued irregularly. When in Texas, he broadcast radio messages over KTHT in Houston and XERF in Del Rio. The bulletin is filled with a weird mixture of Anglo-Israelite theology, Jeffers' prophetic utterances, and articles on "How to Increase Your Income" by the Rev. Dr. Frederick Tilney of Coral Gables, Florida. Tilney is the "World's Foremost INSPIRATIONAL TEACHER of the Science of Healthy, Happy, Natural, Successful, Vibrant, ZESTFUL LIVING." In the summer of 1951, Jeffers claimed that the annual budget for their activities was $35,000.

Before the Second World War, Jeffers had an infamous reputation on the Pacific Coast for stirring up racial and religious antagonism. One columnist reported that Jeffers had been selected by the Nazi Bund to launch a wave of attacks on the Catholics in an effort to line up Protestant support for Hitler Germany. Another charged that he showed Silver Shirt recruiting films in his Kingdom Temple in Los Angeles. Whether or not these particular accusations were justified, his slanders against Jews and Catholics are a matter of public record. At the present time, however, such bigotries have been made secondary to the promulgation of his cultist doctrines.

Western Kingdom

Perhaps Gerald L. K. Smith's most influential supporter is Anglo-Israelite Wesley Swift, who operates a hate enterprise costing over $40,000 annually in the Los Angeles area. Swift has directed the activities of the Great Pyramid Club, the Anglo-Saxon Christian Congregation, and the Anglo-Saxon Bible Study Group; collectively, they are often considered to constitute the strongest racist element on the West Coast.

At one time Swift was Smith's chauffeur, bodyguard, and research assistant. He has remained intensely loyal to his former boss, co-operating with his program and accompanying him on many of his trips. Swift is featured regularly at Christian Nationalist rallies, where he thunders his denunciations of Jews, liberalism, and the United Nations; he attempts to imitate the dramatic drive of his master's voice. Smith considers him "one of the great Bible students of the nation, and one of the three or four most eloquent preachers to whom I have ever listened."

Swift's flagrant racism — occasionally disguised for purposes of radio broadcasting — follows the general Christian Nationalist line. Introducing a typical sermon, he says: "We are living in a period of time when the enemies of the Kingdom of God are highly organized. They are falsely claiming the Kingdom for themselves. The Church, which is the Courier of the glad tidings of the Gospel, is still blinded to the reality of this Kingdom as nations on the earth and, thus, are spiritualizing away their greatest heritage." Swift charges that the "merchants of Babylon" who control the clothing industry, the drug industry, the jewelry industry, the radio and motion-picture industry — in fact, almost everything — hope to keep America from awareness of its unique destiny under God.

Around Swift and Smith is a circle of Kingdom leaders, who aid in the California activities.

One leader is Stephen Goodyear, who served as Swift's bodyguard, organized for the Dixiecrats in Los Angeles and vicinity, published the *Anglo-Israelite Guide,* and operated the Anglo-Saxon Book and Stationery Store.

Robertson Orr, a Scottish Presbyterian minister, directs the activities of the Kingdom Fellowship Church in Long Beach. A second church which he led in Los Angeles was pulled down.

Canadian-born Clem Davies spoke to a large crowd at the Shrine Auditorium before his death in early 1952. He played an active role in the Christian Nationalist Crusade.

W. B. Record, brother of an important Kingdom leader in Chicago, preaches in the Embassy Auditorium and has broadcast regularly over Los Angeles stations. Smith finds that he is one who "understands and discusses the Jewish question."

Max A. X. Clark of Oakland, an elderly friend of the Swift-Smith alliance, publishes the *National Christian Quarterly.* It carries the writings of enthusiasts for both Smith and Winrod.

And there are many more.

In the little city of Atascadero, California, one of the strangest exponents of the Anglo-Israelite creed directs the Beacon Light Ministry — a miniature theocracy with William Kullgren at its head. This 66-year-old dealer in the Kingdom Message also attempts to sell prophecy, reincarnation, spiritualism, health foods, and Hitler-like totalitarianism. Kullgren sums up his wares in his 50-page monthly, *Beacon Light Herald* (formerly *Beacon Light*), "A Magazine Devoted to the Problems of Humanity." In addition to its other amazing features, the *Beacon Light Herald* regularly brings to its favored readers a "Message from Christ Jesus Received through William Kullgren."

Kullgren was a hotel operator, a newspaper correspondent, and an employee of the New York City Board of Health before he began to publicize his unusual ideas through the *Beacon Light* in 1933. Prior to World War II he was involved in a variety of pro-fascist organizations, including service as a lieutenant in William Dudley Pelley's Silver Shirts. As a result of his seditious activities, Pelley was sentenced to fifteen years in federal prison. Kullgren's own alleged disloyalty following the outbreak of the war led the federal government to indict him twice for sedition. With the death of the judge the suit was dropped, and Kullgren has continued his verbal onslaughts against democracy and minority groups. "Seventy-five per cent of our subscribers ran for cover when the heat was turned on," he has complained, adding: "The tide is now reversed."

"Democracy," says Kullgren, "has never worked . . . and never will." He contends that the word itself, *demo-crazy*, well characterizes this form of government — the creation of a crazy demon. Unfortunately in America we have a democracy, since the Communists are in power — but "we have no use for it." World communism, Kullgren affirms, is the creation of the Jews, who are "only a fraction of the tribe of Judah; the rebel element of the tribe, who went and mixed their blood with the then scum of the earth." Through a "non-astronomical transformation process," most of Kullgren's enemies have become Jews or part-Jews, including Woodrow Wilson, Franklin D. Roosevelt, Churchill, Truman, and Eisenhower. For several years he urged that a copy of the *Protocols* be placed in every Gentile home, though God would finally settle the Jewish question "largely through annihilation and not education nor political action."

Kullgren periodically predicts an imminent revolution in the United States — followed by the end of the world. Even in the midst of World War II, he insisted that "civil war is inevitable," and in every recent issue of his periodical he has found that new signs in the "lunations" indicate that atomic warfare, wholesale destruction, famines, and pestilence will soon come upon us. Often he connects this dread fate with his health-food business, and advises his readers to make the necessary preparations by ordering a sufficient supply of his herbs, vegetable concentrates, powders, and numerous varieties of tablets. Currently, he is distributing the books of William Frederick Koch (discussed in Chapter 3) and many other medical quacks.

Kullgren's favorite among his Anglo-Israelite brethren used to be "Dr." Joe Jeffers. In 1939 when Jeffers was in court on a morals charge, Kullgren accused "a Jew District Attorney, a Jew police officer, and a Jew judge" of having framed Jeffers by recording "the intimacies of married life in the privacy of their own bedchamber." His defense of Jeffers made Kullgren unpopular in the Kingdom movement, however, since most Kingdom pastors were at the time repudiating the present director of the Kingdom of Yahweh in Sarasota, Florida.

By the end of the war, Kullgren was again attending Anglo-Israelite conventions and finding that "it would be pretty hard to beat the type of speakers who were presented and the tone that prevailed." The *Beacon Light Herald* currently carries articles by most leading apostles of the faith.

In the Northwest there are many Anglo-Israelite groups, three of which deserve brief mention.

The Anglo-Saxon Christian Association of Portland, Oregon, is directed by Colonel H. M. Greene, a pioneer Kingdom minister, and by Hugh C. Krum, co-editor of a monthly periodical, *The Reminder of Our National Heritage and Responsibilities,* which circulates to two thousand subscribers. The association adheres to the usual Anglo-Israelite line on Jews, Negroes, and other minorities, and from time to time it has distributed pamphlets of Gerald L. K. Smith's Christian Nationalist Crusade.

Illustrative of Greene's point of view are his objections to the Civil Rights program. He blames the fight for civil rights on "over-sexed people . . . white and black," who want to bathe together and "to intrude cohabitation upon God's Country." By nature, Greene continues, blacks and whites segregate, as do crows and jays, and nest alone. "Rats and skunks do not occupy the same beds." Segregation is defined as "a God-given civil right, and unalienable right."

In Tacoma, Washington, Conrad Gaard heads a Kingdom congregation, broadcasts over three Washington stations, and edits *The Broadcaster* (formerly *The Interpreter*), with the slogan, "A Voice Crying in the Wilderness; prepare ye the way of Jehovah." Gaard is an active ally of Gerald L. K. Smith, and in his publication he uses the "Biblical injunction to racial pride" as a front for a flagrant racism.

The Tacoma pastor identifies the present-day Jews as "Shelanite-Amalekite-Canaanite racial elements" united against Israel. "This Shelanite-Amalekite-Canaanite Cabal has continued its Satanically inspired Conspiracy for World Dominion ever since it was organized at Babylon and today it is nearer to achieving its goal than it has ever been since it was first organized."

Perhaps the largest and most beautiful Kingdom church structure in America is the Bethel Temple in Spokane, Washington. Its pastor, Alexander Schiffner, also edits the monthly *Prophetic News Herald,* writes pamphlets and tracts, sponsors radio broadcasts, and supports a book store in connection with his church. He shares the non-Biblical sentiments of his theological brethren. All the troubles of the world he traces to a "Fabian, Rhodes Scholar, Zionist, Pinko, Communist, New Deal, Fair Deal, Socialistic-minded gang."

Much of the inspiration for these Anglo-Israelite groups in the Northwest has come from the highly active British-Israel Association of Greater Vancouver across the border in British Columbia.

Marilyn Allen: Lady Anglo-Israelite

Probably the least refined of all the Anglo-Israelite leaders in the country is another western Kingdom teacher, Marilyn Allen of Salt Lake City, Utah. Miss Allen is a friend of the Christian Nationalist Crusade whom Smith has called a "noted author, pamphleteer and crusader," "a prolific writer . . . of no mean ability," and "one of the fightingest women in the country."

She is the author of the crudest racial treatise in current circulation, *Alien Minorities and Mongrelization,* "a CHALLENGE TO WHITE CHRISTIAN AMERICANS to protect, defend, and preserve their racial heritage." She periodically publishes booklets under such titles as *The Jewish Protocols; Judaic-Communism vs. Christian Americanism; Zionist War Mongering in the U. S. A.; Crucify Him But Hold the Jews Harmless.* Her crowning blasphemy is her pious dedication to "that High Holy One, who alone gave to America her ideals and Christian religion."

For many years Miss Allen lived in Atlanta, Georgia, where she served as secretary to a Jewish insurance agent. One account is that rumors of imminent race riots terrified her, and that she fled to Salt Lake City in hopes of finding as few Negroes as possible; her extreme fear of Negroes led her into racist circles, and soon she began to believe that the Jews were the primary agitators for equality.

Miss Allen, an unmarried and attractive woman of about fifty, is southern-born and speaks with a southern accent. In addition to making diatribes against minorities, she has been a pillar of such anti-democratic women's groups as the National Patrick Henry Organization, the Pro-American Vigilantes, and We the Mothers Mobilize for America. She has also been editor of the nationalist periodical of Walla Walla, Washington: *Northwest Defense News.*

Miss Allen's attitude toward the Negro is that "he should serve the White man, helping him till the field, and performing similar services." According to God's law, as the Salt Lake City pamphleteer interprets it, the parties to a marriage or a sexual relationship between white and black should be put to death. "The White race . . . made in His image, have time and time again been commanded and warned to keep to themselves and separate."

But "the white stock of America, and the World, is being purposefully and relentlessly destroyed, by war and every other means." At home, she warns, "mongrelization" is forcing a mixture of races. "Abroad, our white boys are mating with Japanese and other colored peoples; while the fire-breathing Chinese Reds (backed by Moscow) threaten us with a new Yellow Peril."

One of her widely circulated poems is "Ride, Clansman, Ride!" Its final stanza reads:

> Ride, Clansman, Ride: redeem the manhood of the Race!
> Ride, Clansman, Ride: and save its threatened womanhood!
> Oust the traitors, alien racial agitators!
> Grasp again firmly the reins of government,
> Righteous power that's yours alone, by Divine Fiat.
> Make supreme our *Christian* ideology,
> Hold high *our* Flag, reinvest our Constitution!

Miss Allen is even less restrained in her attacks upon the Jews, and she openly distributes the scurrilous literature of Einar Aberg — a Swede who has the dubious honor of being the world's most vulgar anti-Semite. "The anti-Semites are the true patriots in every country!" states Miss Allen. Like Aberg, she occasionally shields her sentiments behind "religious" verbiage:

> OUR Messiah has come: while the Jews yet look for theirs, to interpret their God to them. They completely rejected the sacrifice, the leadership, the authority, the philosophy of the Christ. And in rejecting Him, St. John (and other passages in the Bible) categorically said that they reject "Him that sent ME." "Ye (Jews) are of YOUR Father, the Devil." Why then do alleged Christians embrace and collaborate with the "Children of the Devil" — the enemy of Christ? I have never yet heard a reasonable explanation of this monstrosity. Christians were commanded to live *in* the world, but not to be *of* the world: Jews are definitely OF the world — they are Mammon, Babylon. "Come ye out of her and be ye separate."

Miss Allen, convinced that communism is Jewish, bitterly exclaims: "The White Cross of Christ drips RED, these days with the blood of Christian martyrs, being shed by Jew-Communists . . . abroad." We are heading toward a similar situation in this country "by permitting Jew Professors in our universities and pro-Jew ministers in our pulpits who teach and preach *against* anti-semitism. . . ." What is Miss Allen's remedy? "Only the Ideals of CHRIST-IN-ACTION can save this Republic."

Like many other "super-patriots," Miss Allen propounds a
dubious interpretation of the Bible on the question of peace and
war. Quoting from the third chapter of Ecclesiastes, she adds:
"This is not a time of peace, as our false peacemongers tell us:
it is a time of war, a time to break down a false regime, a time
to kill our enemies, before they kill us." To those who envision
Christ as a "pussyfooting pacifist," Miss Allen suggests certain
New Testament texts "where he is talking to the collaborators,
fellow-travelers, proselytes. . . ."

Anglo-Israelite theology is not very important to Miss Allen
— though occasionally she will dedicate a pamphlet to "WHITE
CHRISTIAN CONSTITUTIONAL AMERICANS, who are the backbone
of the nation; the salt of the earth; and the TRUE ISRAELITES OF
THE BIBLE." She has many friends in the Kingdom ministry,
including Wesley Swift of Los Angeles; and she particularly
recommends the writings of William Kullgren, Howard B. Rand,
Conrad Gaard, James A. Lovell, and Charles O. Benham. Although not an ordained pastor, Miss Allen is widely heralded as
one of the most useful writers in the Anglo-Israelite movement.

Dayton Theological Seminary

The principal training center for ministers of the Anglo-
Israelite creed was the Dayton Theological Seminary in Dayton,
Ohio — now temporarily closed for lack of students. It was
directed by Millard J. Flenner, deposed clergyman of the Evangelical and Reformed denomination and outspoken exponent of
racial and religious bigotry. His friend Gerald L. K. Smith
describes him as "an outstanding preacher of the gospel," while
Marilyn Allen finds that he is "doing a heroic Christian American
job at education for our young people."

In announcing the new seminary in 1947 Flenner stated that
its purpose was to acquaint students with the enemies of Christ,
identified as "Russian Yiddish speaking people," who "having
established themselves in our land . . . have sought to overturn
our way of life." The seminary's catalogue suggests that the
anti-Semitic elements of the Kingdom creed receive careful
consideration in such courses as "The Persecution of the Early
Church by the Hebrew Jews" and "The Jewish Problem in the
Light of Bible Prophecy."

Flenner also directs the activities of the Church of the Covenants, which was organized in 1940 and incorporated three years later. His labors began in a private house purchased by his congregation; but in the fall of 1951 a stone Gothic edifice was opened. The pastor regularly conducts an evangelistic program, "The New World Coming," over radio stations in the area. Although he avoids racism on the air, Flenner has launched into virulent tirades against the Jews ("Esau-Amalekite International Bankers") on many occasions.

At one of Lovell's Kingdom conventions, Flenner is reported to have said:

The Jews were murderers and liars from the beginning. . . . We should build up our barriers in America . . . this is the time for the Jews to go. . . . There will be no more Jews in Washington or to confer in Siberia or to white-wash their evil doing via Hollywood.

Dean of Dayton Theological Seminary until his death was S. A. Ackley, a former YMCA secretary and founder of the Kingdom Gospel Tabernacle in Chicago. In 1949, after fourteen years of service in the Windy City, Ackley resigned to accept his new position in Dayton. He died on December 15, 1950.

While he was active in Kingdom work in Chicago, his assistants included James McGaw, a minister of the Scotch Covenanter Church, who was widely respected among Anglo-Israelites for his presumed scholarship; and F. H. Ackley, the elder Ackley's nephew, who finally left the Kingdom Gospel Institute to go into independent evangelistic work. McGaw died in 1948, while the younger Ackley is a home missionary of the Kingdom creed and editor of *Portions in Due Season*.

The present leader of the Chicago flock is Robert B. Record, brother of W. B. Record of Los Angeles. Record claims to be a minister in good standing of the Baptist denomination. He left the West Coast in 1947 to assist Ackley, and assumed full responsibility for the church when its founder joined Flenner in Dayton. Record has tried to continue *Covenant Voice*, a small monthly with a circulation of about five thousand, which was started by Ackley in 1942 as the *Kingdom Voice*. Because of financial problems, *Covenant Voice* has not been published since 1950.

From Record's articles in other publications, however, it is possible to conclude that he shares the typical Anglo-Israelite racist attitudes. His platform advocates "keeping foreigners out of the government since America is the land of White Christians." Record recently started a series of radio broadcasts — "The Destiny of America" — over Chicago's station WGN.

Another midwestern city, Minneapolis, is also a center of Anglo-Israelite activity. Two important figures in this movement — C. O. Stadsklev and Paul Rader — minister to separate congregations, publish periodicals, and direct radio programs in the Minneapolis area. Stadsklev is founder and publisher of an attractive-looking monthly, *Truth and Liberty Magazine*, and pastor of the Truth and Liberty Temple. Radar edits the weekly *Sunshine News* and conducts services at the River-Lake Gospel Tabernacle. Until July 1952 he assisted his father, Luke Rader, who had established the Anglo-Israelite enterprise.

Stadskev has a long record of association with hate groups and personalities. One of his good friends is Gerald L. K. Smith, who finds that the Minneapolis pastor is a "courageous Christian statesman," and "thoroughly alert to the Communist menace and to the Jewish problem." Smith has several times traveled to Minnesota to visit Stadsklev; and in 1947, when Stadsklev's congregation purchased a temple of worship, Smith made the dedication address.

Elizabeth Dilling, indicted for sedition in World War II (see Chapter 3), is another long-time friend of Stadsklev. Shortly after her first indictment she defended herself from his pulpit and read aloud letters on her behalf from W. D. Herrstrom and the late W. B. Riley — two other leaders in the ministry of hate. Since then, Mrs. Dilling (now Mrs. Jeremiah Stokes) has visited Stadsklev on many occasions.

A third favorite of Stadsklev — and other Anglo-Israelites — is Kenneth Goff, who has regularly been his guest and whose articles have appeared in *Truth and Liberty Magazine*.

Stadsklev's monthly, sent to about a thousand subscribers, seldom indulges in the vulgarities that characterize many of its editor's allies. Both his radio programs and his literature are largely focused upon the theology of the Anglo-Israelite movement. From time to time, however, his prejudices come to the fore, and he concludes that the Jews are a "reproach, a proverb, and a curse," or that they are attempting to secure Palestine "in order to foster and further the aims of Communism." He publicized the racist ideas of Theodore Bilbo, the late Klan-minded Senator from Mississippi, calling them "both timely and significant." Stadsklev is particularly vexed by "Quislings of the White race" — that is, those who believe in the dignity of all men.

The Raders have generally been considered more influential in the Minneapolis area than Stadsklev, though their colorless weekly, *Sunshine News,* has had a circulation of less than half that of *Truth and Liberty Magazine.* In addition to pastoral duties at the River-Lake Gospel Tabernacle — where Luke and Paul used to preach on alternate Sundays — they ran a book-store in connection with their work. After 1949, when the elder Rader suffered a heart attack, his son shouldered most of the responsibilities of the ministry.

Luke died in July 1952. E. J. Rollings, pastor of the Detroit Metropolitan Tabernacle, delivered the funeral sermon. George Ziemer of the Wisconsin Gospel Tabernacle in Milwaukee paid a tribute "to his long-time friend."

Luke was always antagonistic toward the Jews. He contended that they were "Chaldeans . . . masquerading under the name of Jew and in conspiracy with other enemies of God . . . endeavoring to re-establish the former world tyranny of Babylon." Paul is even more vehement than his father was. Like Luke, Paul has spoken of the Jews as the "synagogue of Satan"; has distributed the discredited *Protocols* and Ford's *The International Jew;* has been vigorously anti-Catholic and has spread the traditional falsehoods about Catholic designs and institutions.

Martin Luther — Anti-Semite?

Perhaps the most important Anglo-Israelite preacher from the standpoint of rank-and-file Protestantism is Jonathan Ells-worth Perkins, builder of the Full Gospel Tabernacle of Tulsa, Oklahoma, who for several years was one of Gerald L. K. Smith's most trusted allies. In 1949, however, Perkins revealed a bitter split by publishing a book advertised as "The Plain and Naked Truth about Gerald L. K. Smith At Last!" Entitled *Gerald L. K.*

Smith Unmasked: The Biggest Hypocrite in America, Perkins'
exposé claims to be an authentic, well-documented revelation
of the real Smith and of organized anti-Semitism.

Although the book is actually nothing of the sort, it gives
valuable insight into Perkins' character and points up the fact
that individuals long active in racist circles do not easily escape
from the fundamental bias.

Perkins claims that he joined the Christian Nationalists
"largely for patriotic reasons, thinking I was doing it for my
country and the glory of God." The day that he had enough
facts to justify his conviction that Smith was an "impostor," the
Tulsa preacher contends, he quit, and felt it his duty to tell the
world his reasons why. Perhaps his most interesting observation
concerns Smith's motivation:

> Gerald L. K. Smith does not say he is God, but he has some very
> dangerous notions as to the real meaning of his destiny. I have heard a
> few folks say that they were the Almighty in human form, but in spite
> of their enthusiasm and vehemence I have always doubted their state-
> ments. . . . As for Smith, I never ceased to be shocked at his claims of
> being invulnerable. His great swelling words of pretended invincibility
> made me wonder and ponder about this man.

Perkins was an Ohio-born Methodist minister who graduated
from Southwestern College at Winfield, Kansas, and did further
study at the Moody Bible Institute in Chicago. He has been
more active as a writer than as a preacher, and before he joined
forces with Smith he claims to have been a key man in the
Gospel Publishing Company in Springfield, Missouri — a plant
serving the interests of the Assemblies of God. He has also
worked with Luke Rader; with Townsend's pension movement;
with Gerald Winrod, allegedly a distant cousin of Perkins
through common Indian ancestors; and with the late Aimee
Semple McPherson, famous California woman evangelist and
founder of the International Church of the Four Square Gospel.
According to Winrod, Perkins in almost every instance turned
on his employer — and usually offered something for sale to
the man's enemies. His *Gerald L. K. Smith Unmasked* was part
of this pattern.

While serving as a Smith lieutenant, Perkins rivaled his chieftain in scurrilous attacks upon Jews and Negroes. Because Perkins clung to the Anglo-Israelite creed, his approach to the race question was colored by a strong theological bent.

He first attracted public notice as an avowed anti-Semite in 1945 with the circulation of *The Modern Canaanites or the Enemies of Jesus Christ*. This attack upon the Jews — based largely upon Perkins' peculiar interpretation of the Kingdom Message — was widely distributed by his Anglo-Israelite brethren and by the Christian Nationalist Crusade.

In this book, Perkins develops the idea that the present-day Jews descend from Cain, "a very wicked man . . . possessed of a murderous spirit," whose nature was inherited by his progeny. The Jew "has been driven from country to country because he always seeks to rule the country he invades. He never enters a country in penitence and humility, but by arrogance and subterfuge becomes unbearable when given a place of authority and invariably proves himself unworthy of confidence." The Jews control Russia, says Perkins, and they know that they cannot control the world until they win the United States.

"Modernism," according to the Kingdom minister (and many other "reverend bigots") is a powerful weapon of the Jews. "Many people do not seem to realize that the Federal Council of Churches is largely the unclean and unsound theology of higher critics of Germany." This higher criticism, argue Perkins and other leaders in the Protestant underworld, originated among German Jews, eager to devitalize the Christian faith in the Bible.

Indeed, concludes Perkins, "the Jews are always at the bottom of every form of lawlessness in the earth if it is fully investigated."

A short while after the publication of the book, Smith and Perkins teamed up in San Francisco to oppose the United Nations Charter. In 1947 they openly joined forces and together toured the country in the interests of Smith's political aspirations. The Tulsa Anglo-Israelite pastor contributed regularly to *The Cross and the Flag* and wrote diatribes against minority groups.

In *White Man, Awaken!* Perkins warned southerners that unless they organized to combat the Negroes they would be the victims of "black rule" and "mongrelization."

In *Does Jerusalem Belong to the Jews?* he embraced the

discredited *Protocols* and the Talmudic forgeries (discussed in Chapter 3).

In *Jesus Christ Was Not a Jew,* he echoed the lie that Christ was an Anglo-Saxon and cursed the Jewish people — who collectively comprise the Anti-Christ.

In *The Jews Have Got the Atom Bomb,* he invented the fable that David Lilienthal is an agent of political Zionism in its effort to establish a world government centered in Jerusalem.

The latest Perkins booklet, his version of Martin Luther's *The Jews and Their Lies,* created something of a stir among Protestant churchmen, especially Lutherans. The public relations division of the National Lutheran Council sent a memorandum to all pastors warning them of the "dangerous anti-Semitism" implicit in Perkins' venture. It is an unfortunate truth that Luther did write a book, *Von den Juden und ihren Luegen,* which is frequently quoted by members of the Protestant underworld to justify their attack upon the Jews. It was penned by the reformer in his last days, when he was bitter and disillusioned over the unwillingness of many Jews and Catholics to leave their faith. It hardly represents the opinion of the valiant fighter against corrupted Christianity who earlier had said: "The Jews are blood relations of the Lord; therefore if it were proper to boast of flesh and blood, the Jews belong to Christ more than we. I beg, therefore, if you become tired of abusing me as a heretic, that you begin to revile me as a Jew."

Professor Theodore G. Tappert, of the Lutheran Theological Seminary in Philadelphia, sent out a pre-publication review of Perkins' book. It read, in part:

To publish this one utterance of Martin Luther, apart from his other utterances, is not only likely to do violence to Luther but is also unlikely to contribute to the "Jewish problem" today. Luther's book can be understood aright only in its historical context. If it is lifted out of this context and applied to the present "fight over Palestine" and the campaign "organized by the political Zionists," it will certainly be misread and misapplied. Luther's fundamental concern was not political, economic, or racial. His concern was theological. He was a critic not of the Jews as a race, but of Judaism and its implications as Luther understood them. To call Luther anti-Semitic, as Mr. Perkins does by implication, is therefore to give the term a connotation which it does not properly have.

It is true that in this book Luther used violent language with reference to the Jews. The fact of the matter is that most of his polemics were seasoned with earthy and sometimes (especially for modern tastes) abusive language. Princes, Luther wrote, for example, "are usually the greatest fools and the worst knaves on earth." Peasants he called "perjured, disobedient, rebellious, murderers, and blasphemers." "It is almost impossible for lawyers to be saved," he wrote. Merchants he described as "manifest thieves, robbers, and usurers." He asserted that the Pope is "anti-Christ" and monks are "tame dogs that lie on pillows and whistle with their hind-ends." But for his own countrymen Luther usually reserved his sharpest words: "I know well that we Germans are brutes and stupid beasts" and "swilling swine." "We Germans are much worse than the Jews." It would appear that, if Luther was anti-Semitic, he must also have been anti-German.

"Above all," Professor Tappert concluded, "it must be remembered that [Luther's] book was written by a very human and fallible person whose views are conditioned by the age in which he lived and by the infirmities of approaching death."

Almost unwittingly many Americans have toyed with Hitler's favorite fanaticism — the notion of racial supremacy — through the fantastic delusion of Anglo-Israelism. Some men are chosen of God, Kingdom Message believers reason. The Creator is a God who sets apart one race.

These self-appointed heirs of the Biblical covenant view themselves as the world's elite. They may be motivated by an innate desire of man for special grace. Based on spurious interpretations of the Bible, superstitions, and false logic, Anglo-Israelite "philosophy" lends credence to the familiar adage: "A little knowledge is a dangerous thing." They add a beaker of learning to a vat of error; the mixture is a concoction that threatens to poison its addicts on the fringes of Protestantism.

6

Fiery Crosses, the Shame of America

On July 4, 1952 — anniversary of the Declaration which affirms "that all men are created equal" — elaborate red-white-and-blue posters adorned a meeting hall above a small Italian inn in Chicago. One poster read: "Serve White America, Join the White Circle League, We Fight to Uphold the White Man's Rights." Another, aimed at the United Nations, proclaimed: "Our Battlecry: No Mongrel UN Flag. Tear It Down!"

Joseph Beauharnais, Chicago dealer in leathergoods, led a small group of "White Christian Patriots" in invoking divine guidance upon the meeting to save the United States from "mongrelization" — a fabricated word to describe intermingling between Negroes and whites. His advance bulletin to "fellow-Americans" early that spring had summoned them to the three-day meeting "to maintain white racial integrity against the long train of evils under which our nation is sinking to destruction."

"Noted orators" were on hand to alert their listeners to the "grave dangers" threatening white civilization. The convention's boyish co-chairman, Peter L. Xavier, gave a "gripping" address to frenzied applause from the small but enthusiastic audience. "We are met for the purpose of helping build a national pro-American atmosphere in advance of the Republican convention," he shouted.

Other leading race agitators were on the roster of "interesting and colorful" speakers. John W. Hamilton, executive director of the Citizens Protective Association of St. Louis, attended with a small delegation of elderly women, whose stern, desiccated faces showed horror and disgust as they spoke of the gradual "corruption" of white civilization. To the handful of assembled "delegates," the United Nations, with its program to encourage

118

good-will among men of different races everywhere, represented a communist-inspired plot to force "mongrelization" upon "decent white Americans." Particular targets were the Genocide Pact and the Universal Declaration of Human Rights — two historic documents symbolizing the hopes of mankind for a world free from caste based on artificial barriers of color and creed.

Present also were C. Daniel Kurts, director of the letterhead New York Anti-Communist League, active in the pre-war Coughlinite movement; Mrs. Ed C. Alumbaugh, editor of the bizarre Georgia publication *The Spider;* Mr. and Mrs. Austin Hancock, an elderly and wealthy San Antonio couple, whose Negro chauffeur waited quietly outside in a Cadillac. The convention's visitors numbered among them some whose chief concerns were other "causes" — anti-Semitism, anti-Wall Street, and anti-British fanaticism — people like George Sudbeck, self-described "learned authority on the money question"; George D. Higgins, Los Angeles Liberty Party candidate for President, who traces the world's dilemmas to the Rothschild family; and Mrs. Catherine Baldwin, an Anglophobe, later chairman of the 1952 Constitution Party, a splinter group designed to sabotage the GOP ticket by posting a MacArthur-headed rival slate on the ballot.

This feast of hate — one of the periodic anti-Negro gatherings planned to hold together the deteriorating pattern of racism — proclaimed the founding of the National Association for the Advancement of White People.

The story of anti-Negro prejudice, unfortunately, can be traced far back in American Protestantism—although, of course, the notion of white supremacy has not been the monopoly of adherents to any one religious faith. Protestant entrepreneurs from New England were among those responsible for selling African slaves to Protestant plantation owners in the South. Many Protestant ministers, working industriously to find scriptural arguments to justify the evils of the slave trade, ripped from context portions of the Bible that implied sanction of barter in human lives. In the Old Testament, the account of God's curse upon Ham in the story of Noah, the condemnation of Abraham's handmaid Hagar to bondage, the laws of Moses regulating the relationship between slaves and their masters — these and other passages were exploited to bolster the institution. From the New Testament, proponents of slavery claimed support from verses in Matthew 8 and Luke 7, describing how Jesus befriended a slave-holder; and from St. Paul's exhortation to slaves to "obey" their masters.

The Ku Klux Klan

The most flagrant organized hostility against the Negro can be traced to the Reconstruction era and the formation of the Ku Klux Klan. The Klan, founded ostensibly to protect "white civilization" from a coalition of liberated Negroes and northern "carpet-baggers," accepted sympathizers from all faiths — Catholics and Jews included. The Klan succeeded temporarily in nullifying the Fourteenth and Fifteenth Amendments by placing on Dixie statute books laws depriving the former slaves of social and political equality. Intimidation and actual violence — including lynchings — scarred the history of the period. Hooded "Knights," hiding behind the anonymity of white sheets that symbolized the "supremacy of the white race," rode under cover of darkness in a conspiracy to "keep the Negro in his place." Only after the rigid patterns of segregation and enforced inequality were firmly established did the activities of the Klan subside.

Following the First World War, they were revived — this time to foster antipathy toward Catholics and Jews as well as Negroes. The militant Protestantism of the Klan was symbolized in its leader, William Joseph Simmons of Atlanta, who boasted: "I am a churchman and proud of it. . . . I'm a member of two churches — the Congregational church and a full-fledged associate member of the Missionary Baptist Church, given me as an honor." On many occasions, he recounted with an unseemly show of reverence the experience that led him to revitalize the terrorism of the Klan. Winfield Jones, Klan historian, tells the story of Simmons, the confederate veteran, in *Knights of The Ku Klux Klan*. (This apology for Klan activities was issued in 1941 by the Tocsin Publishers of E. N. Sanctuary, whose connection with various branches of the Protestant underworld is described elsewhere in this volume.) Jones writes:

The young veteran, back on the farm, was converted at a Methodist camp meeting — "got the old-time religion," as he expresses it. The conversion was thorough, for young Simmons determined to become a minister. . . . The "Imperial Wizard" says he does not believe in visions, and yet he relates a mysterious and interesting occurrence which he says he does not understand to this day. He was then a poor minister in Alabama, and one summer night . . . he thought he caught sight of something mysterious and strange in the sky, and as he looked at the clouds a row of horses seemed to be galloping across the horizon. White-robed figures were on the steeds. The clouds seemed to disperse, and a rough outline of the United States appeared as a background. The horses remained, and then one big problem after another of American life moved across the map.

He fell to his knees and offered a prayer to God, so he said, to help solve the mystery of the apparitions he had seen in the sky. He then registered a vow that a great patriotic fraternal order should be builded as a memorial to the heroes of our nation. That was the real beginning of the Knights of the Ku Klux Klan.

The new clandestine movement reached into all parts of the nation, until some authorities estimated its membership at five million. Underlying this fresh outbreak of Klan activity was widespread ignorance, successfully harnessed by unscrupulous leaders seeking political prestige. The lynching of Negroes was the best-known activity of the Klansmen, but in many states, especially of the South, flogging of both whites and Negroes — men and women — was a regular occurrence. The Klan committed many of these atrocities in the name of "Protestant morality"; it took upon itself the responsibility for enforcing individuals' adherence to its own hide-bound conceptions of good and evil. Resolute clergymen who battled against such terrorism were themselves often threatened or accosted. But at the same time, some churches across the country welcomed Klan members when they visited services en masse — frequently in the regalia of their cult.

The Klan's use of religious symbols is most conspicuous in the *Kloran,* secret ritual book of the organization. It is filled with a pseudo-religion that makes a mockery of genuine Protestant faith. For example, in the "naturalization" services in which "aliens" are inducted into the "klavern," initiates must answer many questions on their religious beliefs. They are asked if they are "native-born white, Gentile American" citizens and if they accept the tenets of the Christian religion. As a façade for the unethical practices of the Klan — the most sacrilegious of which has been the burning of the cross — its literature abounds in pious platitudes and lengthy prayers. When the new Klansman is admitted to the "holy order," he is anointed with oil from a vessel on the "sacred altar" with the words: "With this transparent, lifegiving, powerful God-given fluid, more precious and far more significant than all the sacred oils of the ancients, I set you apart from the men of your daily association to the great and honorable task you have voluntarily allotted yourselves as citizens of the Invisible Empire. . . ." Then, before departing on a midnight expedition of terror, the initiate and his new "friends" invoke divine blessing upon their nefarious mission.

The Post-war "Knights"

Between the late 1920's and the end of World War II, the Klan declined sharply. Then a new surge of fiery-cross activity threatened to engulf the South. The Ku Klux Klan was legally dissolved in 1946, when the federal government levied a $685,355 assessment against it for tax evasion. To avoid payment, the hooded order surrendered its corporate charter, but, under the leadership of mild, bespectacled Dr. Samuel Green, an Atlanta obstetrician, a new movement was incorporated — the Association of Georgia Klans. Green utilized the outdated application blanks of the old movement, stamping on them the insignia of the new organization. He proclaimed himself Grand Dragon at a $10,000 annual salary, later changing his title to Imperial Wizard. He took control of "klaverns" in South Carolina, Tennessee, Florida, and Alabama.

When Green died on August 18, 1949, the situation became confused as several contenders jockeyed for power. Samuel W. Roper finally succeeded Green as the head of the Association of Georgia Klans, but complicated internal problems have led to continuous conflict. In late 1949, Roper's appointee as Grand Dragon for South Carolina, ex-grocer Thomas Hamilton — by 1953 in jail for terrorist activities — suddenly withdrew to set up his own organization. Meanwhile, an Alabama roofing contractor, William Hugh Morris, and a Florida plumber, Bill

Hendrix, conspired with Hamilton to ignore Roper and act as the "governing council" of a national Klan.

Post-war Klan groups mushroomed beyond the Mason-Dixon Line — especially through Ohio, Indiana, Michigan, California, and Pennsylvania. In Chambersburg, Pennsylvania, for example, "Exalted Cyclops" H. F. Shaffer — a disciple of Gerald L. K. Smith — bombarded the area with evangelistic gospel tracts and "open letters" soliciting "white, Gentile Protestants" for membership in his Franklin County Klavern. One of his pamphlets, *America for Americans,* added: "It is and always will be the earnest endeavor of the Knights of the Ku Klux Klan to preserve this great Nation for its native born through Christ Jesus our Criterion of Character."

Religion and the Klan

Several ministers have been active in Klan circles. Editor of the *Southern Gospel* and the *American Klansman* (suspended publication of the Roper faction) was the Rev. A. C. Shuler, Klan Imperial Kludd (chaplain) and pastor "emeritus" of the Central Baptist Church of Jacksonville, Fla. On August 12, 1950, Shuler was the main speaker at the annual "naturalization ceremony" at Stone Mountain, Georgia — traditional site for mustering of the robed "Knights." Said Shuler in the *American Klansman:* "No sordid, selfish, grasping horde of men or devils, steeped in ideologies foreign to our Christian religion and our concepts of liberty, shall ever be allowed to exploit us." Of the purpose of the Klan, the Jacksonville minister has declared: "Today the Invisible Empire, with the help of God, . . . is engaged in the most momentous struggle in the history of the Invisible Empire. . . . The Klan sounds the clarion call. The day for heroic action, my citizens of the Invisible Empire, is now."

Although Shuler is a Baptist, he has no respect for the Southern Baptist Convention, largest denomination in Dixie. When the World Baptist Congress passed a resolution against segregation in July 1950, he complained bitterly: "Thus it was [that] the Southern Baptists in this hybrid assembly of all faiths and creeds — even though they're labeled 'Baptist' — sold the birthright of Bible Baptists for a mess of pottage and became parties to a brazen, open repudiation of traditional Baptist doctrine and practices."

In January 1951, Shuler announced that he would leave the Klan to devote more time to preaching and to the publication of a "religious patriotic monthly magazine." Since then he has been sending out a small, mimeographed paper, *The Crusader* — "Devoted to Religion and the Constitutional Rights of the People."

Another leading minister-Klansman has been the Rev. Alvin Horn, who played an important role in the Federated Ku Klux Klan of Alabama. A Baptist minister from Talladega, he joined William Hugh Morris, the organization's Grand Dragon, in 1948 after reading a Klan advertisement in a local newspaper. Horn accepted the assignment of building "klaverns" in Talladega and in other parts of the state. Later the same year, he rose to be fourth man on the Klan's board of governors, where he continued his highly successful work until early 1950. Then suddenly he switched allegiance to the faction backing Samuel W. Roper. Morris promptly dubbed him a "traitor" and claimed that less than a hundred Klansmen followed Horn's lead. In February 1950 Horn was indicted in the slaying of a storekeeper in Pell City, Alabama, but he was later exonerated.

Perhaps the most influential of the clergymen who champion the Klan in the Southland has been the Rev. Evall G. Johnston — better known as "Parson Jack." Johnston has been publisher of several anti-labor and anti-Negro weeklies, notably *The Trumpet* and the *Georgia Tribune,* both distributed from Columbus, Georgia. He came to Columbus in 1929 and soon had established the influential Baptist Tabernacle — which left the Southern Baptist Convention in 1938 and proclaimed itself an "Independent Missionary Baptist Church." Johnston's involvement in Klan activity began many years ago; and in the years following World War II he began to rival Dr. Samuel Green — the Imperial Wizard himself. A year before Green's death, Johnston broke with him, and "klaverns" in several towns of the Columbus area established themselves as the Original Southern Klans, Inc. "Parson Jack" remained behind the scenes throughout the controversy, ostensibly abdicating control in favor of A. E. Pate, editor of *The Klansman,* the new faction's publication.

In August 1947, Johnston tried to organize the White Protestant Christian Party. This was the new party's old line:

WE DECLARE THAT THE WHITE RACE IS STILL SUPERIOR TO THE NEGRO RACE. . . . THE NEGRO IS BLACK BECAUSE OF GOD'S CURSE. . . . The Negro is black because he was cursed by the Almighty God, and that curse will never be lifted in this world. We believe that a Negro has a soul, and that in heaven, his color will not be recognized, for there will be no physical distinguishing characteristics there, but let it be understood that WE ARE NOT IN HEAVEN YET.

Application blanks for membership in Johnston's short-lived political party urged prospective members to help keep America from becoming "a mixed and mingled mass of isms."

During recent years Johnston's Klan activities have become secondary to his attacks upon Protestantism's church-unity movement. In January 1953, he announced he had sold the *Georgia Tribune* so that he might devote his full time to the ministry. In fact, he has expressed fear that the Ku Klux Klan can no longer perform the functions for which it had been organized. In a *Georgia Tribune* editorial of March 13, 1952 — entitled "Do We Need the Ku Klux Klan?" — Johnston wrote:

We would say yes if there was very much principle left among the rank and file of the people; but we make the charge that principle is almost totally gone. . . . The thing America needs is for the Almighty God to handle our case for us. . . . This country is bound to wallow in her own blood; and there is very little that can be done about it.

His principal suggestion was that the Negro be encouraged to migrate to the North: "In the early days of this country, we heard a lot about 'Go West young man, go West' but we advise the Negro generation to go North, go North!"

"Parson Jack" played host to an "anti-U.N." convention held in his Columbus Baptist Tabernacle, which — like the Chicago meeting four months later — brought together leading agitators against the Negro. Arrangements for this "Save America" meeting were handled by other second-string leaders of the Protestant underworld — Mrs. Jessie W. Jenkins, 1950 Liberty Party candidate for Governor of Georgia, and Frank B. Ohlquist, secretary of the so-called Constitutional Alliance of Los Angeles. One hundred and thirty-two "patriotic" organizations were allegedly represented.

Among the featured speakers were Thomas Hamilton, Grand Dragon of the Carolina Klans; Bill Hendrix, Florida Grand Dragon who recently ran for governor of Florida; Joseph Beauharnais of the White Circle League; C. Daniel Kurts of the New York Anti-Communist League; Mrs. Ed C. Alumbaugh of Macon, Georgia, editor of *The Spider,* representing the Temple Cleansing Crusaders; D. L. Churchwell, Macon lawyer for the same group; Peter L. Xavier, author of *Rise America!* and head of the National Security League; and G. Seals Aiken, Atlanta attorney and later vice-presidential candidate of the Constitution Party.

When Georgians, led by many ministers, protested against the meeting because of Klan participation, "Parson Jack" explained after the event: "We were not aware that the Klan would be represented. . . . However, it matters little with us . . . because we are in accord with the principles of the Klan, and we have no apology to offer for their appearance in Columbus." In the same issue of the *Georgia Tribune,* Thomas Hamilton sought to answer the Anti-Defamation League of B'nai B'rith, which had condemned the convention:

The KKK had received, through the press, much abuse, but let's pause for just a moment and go back to the Holy Bible, God's inspired Word. . . . Who were the people who objected to Jesus Christ? It was the JEW. . . . Behind Communism in America and the World stands the JEW. The KKK is fighting Communism.

The high point of the convention was the reading of two congratulatory telegrams. One came from Congressman John T. Wood of Idaho, author of the House resolution to withdraw the U. S. from the United Nations and favorite legislator of the Protestant underworld until his narrow defeat in November 1952. The other was from General Douglas MacArthur, who expressed his regret that many commitments prevented him from accepting their invitation to speak before the "Save America" gathering. MacArthur probably did not know the character of this meeting.

The Dayton (Ohio) *Independent,* mouthpiece for leaders in the National Association for the Advancement of White People, boasted that "ex-soldiers, Klansmen, preachers, lawyers, farmers, publicists assembled to do honor to Old Glory and the Stars and Stripes as [a] symbol of endangered States Rights." The *Independent* was particularly impressed by the co-operation of traditionally antagonistic elements: "The eyes of America was [*sic*] focused upon this gathering where Klansmen and Catholics gripped the hand of fellowship in a vow to stand together against the enemies of Christ and America." Said C. Daniel Kurts, nominal Roman Catholic: "You Klansmen have a great organization. You have a right to be proud of it."

Such co-operation between Roman Catholics and the Klan has been urged by other cultists of white supremacy as well. In the newsletter of the Imperial Council of the Ku Klux Klan, edited by Bill Hendrix, pro-Catholic sentiments are regularly expressed. Said one such communication:

> The Washington Bureau warns that there is a well-organized and vicious campaign by books, magazines and radio against the Roman Catholic Church today from a leftist or pro-Communist viewpoint. This is because the Roman Catholic Church is a tower of strength against Communism. . . .
>
> There are just two organizations which the Communists fear, namely, the Roman Catholic Church and the militant Protestants organized as the Ku Klux Klan. They are spending millions against both of them, but money cannot defeat a vigorous fight for American liberty and Christianity and Christian morals, because God fights on our side.

And in Hendrix's pamphlet *The Ku Klux Klan and Its Story,* the Catholic Church is again assured of the amity of the Klan:

> Every well informed person knows that the Roman Catholic Church does not constitute any present or imminent danger to the freedom and liberty of the individual citizen in the United States, but upon the contrary is waging a vigorous fight against Communism. We have, in fact, no fight against the Roman Catholic Church today.

The anti-Catholic bias demonstrated by the Klan shortly after World War II has now been replaced by a bitterness toward Jews and broadminded Protestants similar to that which characterizes most of the Protestant underworld. In the pamphlet quoted above, Hendrix sharply condemns "Judeized [*sic*] Christianity." Like other Protestant malcontents, he traces an alleged subversion of "old-time religion" to the influences of Khazar Jews. He attacks the National Council of Churches for supposedly favoring "a Judeized economic theory of Government dictatorship abolishing free enterprise." Hendrix charges that there are more than twelve thousand ministers in the United States "who can definitely be termed Red." In another newsletter, he characterizes the Protestant church-unity movement as "one of the most dangerous Communist front organizations in this nation. . . . The ministers under its influence preach the Modern or Social Gospel. They talk against free enterprise, where it dares; it also advocates the 'New Morality' which is a form of free love." He recommends that Klansmen write for information concerning the "anti-Christian, pro-Communist" National Council to such organizations as the Conservative Baptist Fellowship, the *Southern Presbyterian Journal,* and the Church League of America. Hendrix advised his readers to "purge" their churches of any "subversive" influence.

Despite the tolerance that Hendrix and other KKK leaders show toward the Church of Rome, most "klaverns" still exclude Catholics. One post-war guidebook, *Principles and Purposes of the Knights of the Ku Klux Klan,* warns its followers:

> We often boast that this is a Protestant nation. If this boast is to mean anything, the Protestant Christians of the United States must assert themselves. They must unite in one concerted effort to save America or the time is rapidly approaching when we can no longer claim the United States as a Protestant Christian nation. The Protestants must co-operate and co-ordinate their efforts, not only along social and religious lines, but in politics and business as well. . . . We cannot preserve this nation as a Protestant Christian democracy by placing the enemies of Protestantism and those who deny Jesus Christ, in control. This Protestant nation must be preserved and it can be done only by seeing that none but Protestant Americans are placed on guard.

The guidebook's reference to Protestant Americans, of course, does not include 10,000,000 Negro churchmen — who comprise one-fifth of all Protestants in the United States.

Lay Leaders in the Anti-Negro "Crusade"

Despite the Klan's professed devotion to Christianity, its chief preoccupation is with inciting anti-Negro prejudice. In this campaign, it has many allies — chief of whom is Joseph Beauharnais, a good friend of Bill Hendrix. There is an ironical contrast between this man's mild manners, his habit of reading poetry with tearful sentimentality, his calm discussion of "racial history," on the one hand — and his unreasoned hatred of the Negro, on the other. His White Circle League claims eleven thousand members — a gross exaggeration. His aim is to enlist "50 million white people to uphold the white man's rights in America." The *White Circle News,* his irregularly published mouthpiece, often states: "North and South Unite to Preserve And Protect The White Race, Christianity and America." Below this slogan are the flags of the United States and the Confederacy, crossed in a symbolic union against attempts to "mongrelize" America. Beauharnais blatantly and defiantly boasts:

> *The white man's rights shall never die!*
> *And federal bureaucrats, federal guns*
> *Shall not deter the white man's sons*
> *From fighting for God's racial plan*
> *Of segregating beast and man.*

The 54-year-old Chicago propagandist, who runs a struggling leathergoods enterprise, has made race agitation his principal concern. He distributes hate literature in white neighborhoods, urging readers to sign pledges that they will not employ Negro domestic help — or that they will refuse even to admit a Negro to read gas or electric meters in their homes. His chief aim, however, has been to preserve segregated neighborhoods. One inflammatory appeal to wild prejudice which gained mass circulation in parts of Chicago carried this banner head: "THE ARROGANT NEGRO HAS STRUCK AGAIN IN HIS CONQUEST FOR ANOTHER WHITE NEIGHBORHOOD." Beauharnais continued:

> I welcome you to join with me in a program that will stand up against any force that is anti-white, be it the negro, the religionists, the politicians, the pro-negro white groups or the so called CHRISTIAN DEMOCRATS and misguided liberals. Let us stand up and be counted in our mutual efforts to preserve the WHITE HERITAGE that we have always enjoyed until the arrogant and scheming negro came along, with his political WHITE COHORTS, to desecrate and destroy our standards.

Hate of the Negro, Beauharnais maintains, is "normal, natural and exactly the way the Creator intended it."

Beauharnais received nationwide publicity in April 1952, when the United States Supreme Court, by a 5-4 decision, upheld an Illinois "group libel law," under which he had been convicted for his calumnies against the Negro. The case was taken to the

Supreme Court by the American Civil Liberties Union, which contended that the state law violated the right of free speech and that Beauharnais was convicted without a finding that a "clear and present danger" existed. Justice Frankfurter, speaking for the Court, gave the majority opinion; four separate dissents were submitted. The *White Circle News* charged that Frankfurter "deliberately engineered what he considered a clever piece of judicial trickery . . . in performing a service for certain minority groups."

Beauharnais was born a Roman Catholic and, when dealing with Catholics, he still professes to accept their faith. But at one time he attended Episcopal and Presbyterian churches. Now, Beauharnais openly disavows all organized religion, charging that the major denominations have been hoodwinked into teaching false notions of "brotherhood." Nevertheless, his cohorts are largely churchmen — some of them "pillars" in churches of the Chicago area and in the South.

In recent issues of the *White Circle News,* increased emphasis has been placed upon the "threat" of the Jews — chiefly the "conspiracy" of the Jews to force "mongrelization" upon "white Gentile America":

> Squarely behind this plot to mutilate Nature's perfect laws and destroy God's Holy Creative wisdom is the Communist Plan to control the world and enslave all peoples. The Zionist Jew is the power behind communism and uses communism as a weapon to rule the peoples of earth and to foment and cause wars among the white Gentile race so that through fratricide, white brothers will weaken and destroy one another, to the end that the JEW POWER will triumph and rule the world as they have plotted for three thousand years.

This argument is not original with Beauharnais. In fact, in Atlanta, Georgia, there exists a Christian Anti-Jewish Party whose sole concern is to promote the idea that Jews are responsible for attempts to "mix the races." The group is the brainchild of Jesse B. Stoner, a Ku Klux Klan figure still in his twenties. In 1942, when he was only seventeen, he began his career of bigotry as "Kleagle" — Klan organizer — for a "klavern" in Chattanooga, Tennessee. Later, he published a book called *The Gospel of Jesus Christ Versus the Jews,* in which he tried to prove from the Bible that the Jews are "the children of the devil, vipers, poisonous snakes, serpents, world's chief liars and the leading murderers."

One of Stoner's targets is alleged "Jew control" of the National Association for the Advancement of Colored People, which has led in the movement for equal opportunities for the Negro. Stoner writes: "It has surprised some people to find out that the president of the National Association for the Advancement of Colored People (NAACP) is NOT a Negro BUT the JEW ARTHUR SPINGARN. It is the Jews who are leading the fight to destroy segregation in Atlanta schools."

In contrast to Stoner's evolution from an anti-Negro emphasis to anti-Semitism, others have moved in the opposite direction — from anti-Semitism toward "white supremacy." Such was the case with John W. Hamilton, now head of the Citizens Protective Association of St. Louis, a constituent group of the National Association for the Advancement of White People. Hamilton claims to have been a communist and atheist; at the age of thirty he became a key lieutenant in the Christian Nationalist Crusade of Gerald L. K. Smith. His own version of his life appears in the Christian Nationalist pamphlet *I Was Branded With The Number 666,* marked by an unctuous pseudo-religious tone. After describing a clash with Jewish "Anti-Christs" in his native Boston, Hamilton adds:

I moved to St. Louis, determined to join a church where I could make full surrender to my Lord. I was led to attend where it was easy to see that the preacher and his people were completely devoted to our Lord Jesus Christ. I fully surrendered my life and was baptized in the Name of Jesus Christ, and for the first time I realized to the fullest extent the power of our Lord to save all who will call upon His name.

His "conversion" only led him deeper into the Protestant underworld. After Hamilton broke with Smith because of the domineering manner of the director of the Christian Nationalist Crusade, he established his own anti-Negro organization to "preserve racial purity by maintaining the time-honored custom of separation of the races which is the law of God." In his promotional literature, Hamilton asks his readers:

HOW DO YOU LIKE:
1. Negroes in White Swimming Pools?
2. Negroes Buying Homes Next Door to You?

3. Negroes Playing with Your White Children in School?
4. Negroes Attempting to Force Themselves into White Restaurants, Theaters, Parks?
5. Communism and Mongrelization being Taught Your Children in School?

If YOU like these things, then YOU should be happy. But, if YOU don't like them, there's something YOU can do about it.

Help the CITIZENS PROTECTIVE ASSOCIATION to help YOU.

He publishes a monthly propaganda sheet, the *White Sentinel*, dedicated to "racial integrity — not amalgamation." It features crude accounts of alleged crimes committed by Negro citizens. Hamilton's general thesis is that every great civilization known to history was built and developed by the white race and then weakened and finally destroyed by the "curse of race-mixing." He contends that "the Bible very clearly shows this as does secular history. Separation of the races is the law of God. Any people who have violated this law have been cursed." He shows particular impatience with "the modernist clergy," whom he charges with encouraging "mongrelization" of the United States. One interesting twist of the Hamilton line urges a "Soviet-American alliance against the colored races" everywhere:

> Preserve the white stock and you preserve the Christian way of life.
> . . . Invite the Russians to help preserve the white blood which is a minority stock. If we would do this, we would recover our sanity and lose our fear, and Russia would respect us as she does not wish to be classed as colored any more than we do.

This curious attitude demonstrates again how professional bigots are willing to accept any ally in their unholy crusades.

Hamilton idolizes the 79-year-old Prime Minister of South Africa, Daniel Malan, head of the extremist Nationalist Party. When Malan's racist faction won a national election in April 1953, Hamilton's *White Sentinel* was jubilant. "Dr. Malan's splendid victory is a victory for the White Race the world over," said the publication.

Hamilton's Citizens Protective Association has tried to establish affiliated groups in other states. Greatest success has been in Tennessee, where a chapter has been set up to agitate for white supremacy in the eastern section of the state. According to the *White Sentinel*, this is the first of numerous affiliates to be organized. In Memphis the racist cause is bolstered by the *Political Report,* a 20-page mimeographed monthly edited by Harry William Pyle, which carries the harangues of Protestant underworld spokesmen. Because Missouri twice refused to grant the Hamilton group a charter, it has been incorporated in Tennessee.

Among the several women who occupy important positions in the loose anti-Negro coalition is Mrs. Ed C. Alumbaugh, editor of *The Spider* of Macon, Georgia, and an ardent Protestant. She has been in the hate profession for more than a quarter-century — a modern-day "Know Nothing" who has slandered many races and creeds. In 1927, for example, she widely circulated her attack upon Roman Catholicism, *The Struggle of The Ages.* Mrs. Alumbaugh, who was national secretary of the ultra-patriotic American Rangers, contended that the Catholic Church should be outlawed, that no subject of the Pope should be allowed to vote, and that every convent should be abolished and every confessional box locked. She charged that Negroes were being duped or bribed into joining the Catholic Church — which was promoting "hate-breeding" between Negroes and whites — in a calculated effort to incite a race war. Mrs. Alumbaugh's cheerful grandmotherly demeanor is contradicted by her fiery speeches against a wide variety of targets. *The Spider* voices a weird concoction of prejudices from hatred of Wall Street's "Bankers Kingdom" to endorsement of the Ku Klux Klan ideology.

Another "lady patriot," Mrs. Jessie W. Jenkins, heads the National Patrick Henry Organization in Columbus, Georgia, where she co-operates closely with the followers of "Parson Jack" Johnston. Although she is strongly anti-Semitic, Mrs. Jenkins' principal attacks are directed against the Negro. She undergirds her defense of white supremacy with Biblical "proof" of God's condemnation of Negroes — the story of Ham, son of Noah:

> The negro [sic] is NOT a part of the CREATION, and did not appear until long after the destruction of the "Creation Civilization" by the flood. . . . Cush, the son of Ham, became father to the blacks, as punishment pronounced upon Ham for his great sin in ridiculing his old father. . . . Therefore, the negro does serve a very definite purpose, in that he is a perpetual reminder *to all people,* of the wages of sin. He is of the unholy

seed of corruption, and whoever takes him into the Holy family of God's own *created* in His own image, must certainly incur the wrath of God.

"God Himself practiced segregation," according to Mrs. Jenkins. She attributes the flood in the time of Noah to the fact that "the holy seed, bearing the image of the Creator, began to be enticed by the overflowing Cainites, and to mix with them, becoming incurably immoral."

Like other members of the Protestant underworld, Mrs. Jenkins also claims to find Jewish intrigue in the history of Negro-white relations in America. Concerning the Civil War, she inquires: "Wasn't it the agents of the Rothschild-gang of revolutionists who plotted and promoted the war? Old Thad Stevens admitted the purpose was to amalgamate the races to crush the South in order to confiscate the property of the Southerners — in boasting of his own rascality."

In the preceding chapter appeared a discussion of the activities of Marilyn Allen, Salt Lake City pamphleteer who left the South for fear of a Negro uprising, only to become convinced that "mongrelization" was a plot of the Jews. Her 475-page volume, *Alien Minorities and Mongrelization,* charges that the "MONGRELIZING (mixing of the races) of America is THE No. 1 plank of the Communist Party. . . . It has as its purpose the lowering and degrading of the white race, and making of our people a hybrid nondescript mixture, who can then the more readily be taken over by Communism." Miss Allen condemns this attempt to repeal what she calls "GOD'S DIVINE LAW AGAINST THE MIXING OF THE RACES."

The Anglo-Israelites and "Race Superiority"

Marilyn Allen is only one of the many advocates of Anglo-Israelism (see Chapter 5) who engage in anti-Negro activities. In Salt Lake City she has been allied with another Anglo-Israelite "messenger," Keen Polk, in efforts to propagandize against "mongrelization."

Polk is considered by this faction of the ministry of hate as a leading "scholar." Two of his pamphlets, *The Negro and the Constitution* and *Everything After Its Kind,* are distributed by many extremist groups. His general conclusion in the first of these is that God gave Adam, a "white man," dominion over all the men of the earth, that He strictly forbade intermingling, that He destroyed the world when the "sons of God (white)" married the "daughters of men (colored)," and that Christ was sent to remind mankind of the subordinate role of the non-white races — as when He referred to the Canaanites as "dogs." Polk warns "those ministers who are advocates of racial and social equality . . . that the Lord will have a controversy with them."

In Polk's second pamphlet, *Everything After Its Kind,* the author pretends to give "a new and critical study of the origin of the Negro according to the Holy Scriptures." One of his absurd theories is that the Negro represents "the beast of the field." This conclusion he derives from a variety of disconnected Biblical references to "beasts" — "a beast that can talk," Genesis 3:4; "a beast that has a hand," Exodus 19:13; "a beast that has a foot," Ezekiel 29:11; "a beast that can cry unto God," Jonah 3:8.

Polk's ideas have gained currency in other Anglo-Israelite circles. In Denver, for example, William L. Blessing, 53-year-old director of the House of Prayer for All People[!] and editor of the monthly *Showers of Blessing,* circulates a "treatise," *White Supremacy,* whose thesis (similar to Polk's) is frankly stated: "White Supremacy is taught in the Bible, verified by history, justified by civilization and instinctively believed in by all races."

Blessing, who was born into a poor West Virginia farm family, boasts of past membership in the Ku Klux Klan and persistently calls for "a 100 per cent American Protestant organization like the Ku Klux Klan to rise in order to protect Americans and our Christian way of life." The Denver pastor-evangelist becomes greatly disturbed at the prospect of the "wholesale mongrelization" of America. "The wrath of God will come," he warns in his *Showers of Blessing.* His slogan is "Every race in its place and a place for every race." But the Negro, according to Blessing, is not alone guilty of violations of God's command to segregate the race: "The modernistic preachers, the One World 'do-gooders,' the influence of Eleanor Roosevelt . . . [are] indirectly responsible for the tendency toward race suicide in America."

For ten years, Blessing has been active in this three-fold crusade "for the establishment of Christ's Church according to the perfect New Testament pattern, for the Restoration of the

Israel laws of God in Government, and for the defense and maintenance of the Constitution and the Republic of the United States of America." At the age of twenty-one, he began his studies for the ministry, and he claims to have been affiliated with the Disciples of Christ for twelve years. By 1936, however, he had started to preach open racism; when criticized, he resigned from the denomination. "I could not be contented to draw my breath and my salary," he complained.

Blessing boasts that long before Gerald L. K. Smith launched the Christian Nationalist Crusade, his own House of Prayer was exposing "Jewish influence and power over the Protestant churches." In addition to his distaste for Negroes, Jews, and the major Protestant denominations, Blessing is vigorously anti-Catholic and advocates the legal abolition of "immoral priestcraft." He complains in his sporadic "Blessing Letter" that other Protestant underworld figures do not boldly oppose Roman Catholicism. Referring to Smith and Winrod, he asks, "Have you ever heard them say a word against the Pope or the Roman Catholic system?"

But his major attacks are reserved for the Negro. He even contends that "God is white; Christ is white; the angels are white. The Bible is a white man's book and every colored person who is saved and accepted and adopted into the family of God will be 'made white.' "

Occasionally an Anglo-Israelite minister launches a "crusade" against the Negro. In the fall of 1949, for example, the Rev. M. W. Howard, pastor of the Tulsa Gospel Tabernacle, founded a new group whose stated purpose was to "Keep the White Schools White." It was innocuously called the Oklahoma Public School Defense League, and behind this façade it attempted to enlist 100,000 citizens in support of its racist program. The enrollment card circulated by the League read:

> As one who believes that white and black children of the State of Oklahoma should continue to be separated in their schools and as one who realizes that a highly financed campaign is being carried on to break down our traditional system and mix the black and white, I desire to enroll and give my moral support to the preservation of the segregation system.

Howard is another of the many Anglo-Israelites who have

been aligned with the Christian Nationalist Crusade of Gerald
L. K. Smith. In 1948, for example, the Tulsa minister joined
with other Smith associates to organize the Oklahoma Anti-
Communist League. Working with Howard were three other
Tulsa "clergymen": W. T. McMullan, John Hanover, and Jonathan Perkins. Perkins was a key Smith aide until their alliance
was dramatically severed in 1949 (see Chapter 4). In one of
Perkins' many inflammatory pamphlets, *White Man Awaken!*,
he wrote: "God save America against the filthy plots of Christ-
hating Communism, one of which is to destroy the dignity, leadership, and purity of the white race."

Despite such protestations against Communism, of course,
the fact is that the racists serve as Russia's most powerful fifth
column within the United States. For among the colored peoples
of the world the Soviet Union has been exploiting American
racial discrimination to great propaganda advantage in the cold
war.

The "Repatriation" Cult

One reaction to Bible-quoting racists, such as the Anglo-Israelites, has been the development of several very small cults proclaiming that the Negroes are themselves the "chosen people."
These groups usually also claim Biblical proof that the principal
personalities of both the Old Testament and the New Testament
were black — including Jesus Christ.

Some of these Negro cults are more political than theological
in orientation. The United African Nationalist Movement, for
example, suggests to its members a program of action:

1. Establish a world-wide confraternity among the Black Race.
2. Promote the economic and industrial development of Independent
   Black Nations.
3. Promote economic self-determination in all Black Communities in-
   stilling the slogan: "Buy Black."
4. Conduct a militant and consistent campaign against colonialism by
   European nations in Africa. AFRICA MUST BE FREE.
5. Insist that the curricula in schools attended by children of African
   stock contain African history.

A better-known organization, the Universal African Nationalist Movement, Inc., promotes a program identical with that of

the earlier "Garvey movement," which had been established in 1917 by Marcus Garvey, a native of the West Indies. He had a sizeable following in the early twenties, and soapbox apostles of his ideology continue to interest passing crowds. Garvey started the Black Star steamship line, raised large sums of money, and planned to transport millions of Negroes "back home" to Africa. Troubles developed and the movement sharply declined; but it left behind in many Negroes a legacy of pride in blackness and a strong feeling of group identity.

Endorsement of the proposal to "repatriate" American Negroes to Africa has come from many white members and friends of the Protestant underworld. In Indianapolis, for example, Frank Ellison Best, a successful manufacturer, seeks to stir up widespread support for his resettlement plan: to transport all Negroes to Africa, establish a forty-ninth state, and limit the elective franchise there to Negroes. Best actually succeeded in winning the approval of one Negro pastor, the Rev. Warren A. Rogers of the First Colored Nazarene Church of Indianapolis. "I believe that slavery was one of the blessings of God," Rogers declared. "For God 'works in mysterious ways His wonders to perform,' so that my people might come here to the United States to become prepared along all lines and return to their native country with the 'know-how' to better enjoy God-given blessings."

The "repatriation" plan was brought before Congress on several occasions by the late Mississippi Senator, Theodore Bilbo, whose name became a world-wide synonym for race hate. He introduced a Greater Liberia bill proposing the settlement of American Negroes in the Republic of Liberia and such neighboring territory as could be acquired by the United States from France and Great Britain. Bilbo inserted generous doses of white-supremacy "ideology" in the *Congressional Record,* particularly in the section carrying the "extension of remarks," designed for free mailing to constituents. He announced in the spring of 1944 that he wished to send all Negroes to Africa with Eleanor Roosevelt as "queen" of the Negro nation.

A bill introduced by Senator William E. Langer of North Dakota in 1953 would provide "aid to persons in the United States desirous of migrating to the Republic of Liberia." John

W. Hamilton urged his followers to write their senators to support the bill. Meanwhile Joseph Beauharnais of the White Circle League attempted to organize a "Back to the Fatherland" group, whose program approximates that of the Garvey movement — but motivated by hate rather than genuine concern for the Negro.

Bilbo, who was an ardent Baptist, carefully exploited the Bible for the advancement of bigotry. In his book *Take Your Choice: Separation or Mongrelization,* published in 1947, he devoted an entire chapter to a discussion of "False Concepts of the Christian Religion." After badly distorting several scriptural texts he concluded:

> Whenever and wherever you hear a Negro preacher or a white negro-philistic minister or layman advocating social equality of the races under the high and ecclesiastical sounding terms of "all one blood," "brotherhood of mankind," "the golden rule," or "the fatherhood of God," you will instantly know that he is either a fraud and hypocrite or an unthinking and ignorant man. . . . To make secure the purity and integrity of both the white man's blood and the Negro's blood, every congregation whether white or colored in this broad land should promptly and unhesitantly unfrock the pastors in the pulpits who desecrate their sacred calling by preachments which through direction or indirection seek to destroy and mongrelize both races by advocating or even tolerating social equality in the name of the Christian religion.

Across the South other influential politicians have written in the same vein. Particularly offensive in recent years has been William H. ("Alfalfa Bill") Murray — colorful ex-Governor of Oklahoma, who in 1932 had offered himself as a Democratic presidential candidate. His incoherent 100-page book *The Negro's Place in Call of Race,* published in 1948, was hailed and sold by the Protestant underworld. "Only the Christian, blue or gray-eyed races can govern themselves," Murray declared. He cited the "curse of Ham" as the Biblical basis for his contentions of white supremacy. The book utilized "information" supplied by a long list of professional bigots, including Harvey Springer, Robert H. Williams, Keen Polk, Jessie W. Jenkins, and Gerald L. K. Smith.

Hate Sheets Across the Nation

Stretching across the nation is a network of small publications — all with a strong religious veneer — that headline the notions of the Bilbos and Murrays, the Howards and Hamiltons, the Shulers and "Parson Jacks." In Danville, Virginia, for example, Guy C. Stephens rushes to the defense of the Klan in his 4-page monthly *The Individualist*. The Dayton *Independent* — which in 1952 enthusiastically hailed "Parson Jack" Johnston's "Save America" meeting — is edited by Mrs. A. Grace Silvey of Dayton, Ohio. It has served as a sounding board for such Bible-quoting bigots as Hubert H. Heath of Anthony, New Mexico, such self-admitted fascists as J. H. Madole of Beacon, New York, and such religious racketeers as Edward James Smythe of Washington, D. C. The small National Farmers Guild has adopted the *Independent* as its official organ.

Georgia is a nest for racist publications. Through the Augusta *Courier*, the political machine of Governor Herman Talmadge strives to preserve anachronistic patterns of discrimination. The weekly publication of the state's Department of Agriculture, the *Georgia Farmers' Market Bulletin*, edited by Commissioner Tom Linder, carries virulent anti-Negro diatribes to 250,000 readers. And in Clayton, Georgia, a close personal friend of Talmadge, the Rev. Blake Craft — who will be discussed at greater length in Chapter 13 — abuses the name of Protestantism's largest denomination by circulating *One Methodist Voice*, a bitter exponent of white supremacy.

Illustrative of the numerous papers that bring together not only those that promote hatred for the Negro but nearly all "branches" of the Protestant underworld is *Militant Truth*, of Atlanta, Georgia. Published by the Christian Citizens Crusade, Inc., it is edited by Sherman A. Patterson, anti-labor spokesman, who ostensibly dedicates his 8-page monthly to "Interpreting Current Events From A Fundamental Christian and Constitutional American Viewpoint." At one side of the masthead of *Militant Truth* is the picture of an open Bible superimposed upon a cross, and the legend "Word of God"; at the other is an American flag with the phrase "Constitutional Americanism."

Patterson fans the flames of racial bigotry in a deliberate effort to associate labor unions with "mongrelization." Typical of his language aimed at inciting Southern workers is this "warning" to textile millhands:

Yes, from the "so-called melting pots" of northern cities, where people of strange races and imbued with alien ideologies are blended together to produce all manner of men, including numerous arrogant mongrels, come emissaries of misinformation and hate to tell the textile workers in this section of America what they should think, believe, and do.

According to *Militant Truth,* tolerance "is the plea of the political 'anarchist' and the person 'morally bankrupt.' "

The writings of many hyper-conservatives contribute to the extremist tenor of Patterson's paper — George Washington Robnett of the Church League of America; Merwin K. Hart of the National Economic Council; Joseph Kamp of the Constitutional Educational League; George S. Benson, president of Harding College in Searcy, Arkansas; Thurman Sensing of the Southern States Industrial Council; Economist Alfred Haake; Columnist George Peck; and others. Extreme cartoons by Bill Paulson and Tom Kay are included for good measure. Robert P. Shuler, Sr., editor of the *Methodist Challenge,* W. D. Herrstrom, editor of *Bible News Flashes,* Carl McIntire, editor of the *Christian Beacon,* and other clergymen-bigots have articles in Patterson's paper. McIntire's American Council of Christian Churches has enthusiastically listed *Militant Truth* as one of the papers "serving" its constituents.

The Cross and the Flag, The Defender Magazine, Destiny, Kingdom Digest, and many others — the hate sheets which specialize in bitterness toward Jews — without exception also promote unreasoned prejudice against Negroes.

As long as there are Americans who reject the basic premises of democracy and deny the concept of brotherhood inherent in the Judeo-Christian tradition, anti-Negro sentiment will persist in the United States. Some forms of expression involve actual violence — the lynchings and floggings and bombings perpetrated by the Ku Klux Klan. Fortunately, such outbursts have diminished sharply; 1952 was the first year on record during which no reported lynchings occurred in America. Another form of "white supremacy" depends upon twisted and distorted interpretations of religious belief — usually the product of sick minds. The unholy crusade of this "lunatic fringe" continues to influence many thousands; the ranting Negrophobe of the Protestant underworld still pounds his pulpit, slanders his fellow-citizens, and above a roar of "Amens!" warns his flock against the "menace of mongrelization."

The greatest obstacle to genuine democracy in the United States, however, is the vast reservoir of prejudice still lurking in the minds of citizens who accept without protest injustices against minority groups. Sometimes this attitude is expressed through open antagonism toward persons of another race. More often it remains latent, until efforts to eliminate the inequalities rooted in discriminatory customs bring it to the surface in open hostility.

Protestantism has an obvious responsibility for the improvement of Negro-white relations. Church membership and participation, with only few exceptions, reflect the segregated pattern of American society. It is an ironic truth that each Sunday morning at eleven o'clock more people are divided by a rigid color line than at any other time during the week. But every major Protestant denomination has taken definite steps within the last decade to break down these color barriers. The National Council of Churches, on behalf of its thirty constituent denominations, has been in the forefront in urging Protestants to purge themselves of all attitudes and practices that deny the fatherhood of God and the brotherhood of man. Ultimate success in the elimination of racial injustice depends upon the commitment of the churches to Christian ideals and the readiness of the members to put their professions into practice.

7

"No Popery!" — Bigotry's Battlecry

ew prejudices have affected Americans more deeply than anti-
Catholicism. All regions, nationalities, political parties, and
economic groups have suffered from hatred or distrust of
Roman Catholics.

It is not within the scope of this study to discuss the complex
problem of how to achieve better relations between Catholics
and non-Catholics. Instead, the purpose of this chapter is to
determine which organizations are being used by today's anti-
Catholic bigots to promote their brand of unreasoned prejudice.

As early as the colonial period, most American settlers hated
and feared Roman Catholicism. In England, stronghold of
European Protestantism, many of them had been reared in
homes where the Pope symbolized the devil, where Jesuits
were considered subversive aliens, and where tales of convent
and monastery life portrayed gross licentiousness and immorality. These settlers brought across the sea their ingrained
prejudices, strong enough to influence the governments of the
colonies for many years to come.

In Virginia, as in England, the Anglican Church was established by the state; other Protestants were taxed to support
the rector and fined when they failed to attend Sunday services.
Roman Catholics were totally excluded. The Puritans of New
England, even though they now enjoyed the religious freedom
of which they had been deprived in the Old World, in turn displayed intolerance of other minorities. They frowned upon all
who worshiped according to the Anglican Book of Common
Prayer. In 1635 Massachusetts banished Roger Williams be-

cause of his unpopular beliefs. Several Quakers were hanged. From the beginning, the laws of the Puritans reflected bitter hatred of the Catholics, reinforced by the belief that Indian raids upon Massachusetts settlers had been plotted by Jesuit missionaries.

Conditions were no better in many other colonies. In 1700, for example, New York decided to imprison every Roman Catholic priest who entered the domain. South Carolina law denied liberty of conscience to any "papist." New Jersey placed severe restrictions on any of "the Romish religion." In Maryland, originally founded as a haven for persecuted Catholics, goodwill later surrendered to intolerance; in 1654, Puritan settlers repealed Maryland's Act of Toleration. Pennsylvania, established by William Penn and the Quakers, and Rhode Island, founded by Roger Williams, succeeded in preserving religious freedom; but even in these colonies there were signs of anti-Catholicism. In Pennsylvania, by the charter of privileges granted in 1701, Catholics were excluded from public office; in Rhode Island, a law denied Catholics the rights of citizenship.

The American Revolution led to a temporary decline in anti-Catholic feeling, partly because of Catholic enthusiasm for the colonial cause and the aid that came from Catholic French and Polish military leaders. Article VI of the Constitution of the United States incorporated the new spirit of tolerance by declaring that "no religious test shall ever be required as qualification for any office or public trust under the United States." Later, in 1791, the First Amendment stated that "Congress shall make no law respecting the establishment of religion or prohibiting the free exercise thereof." State governments, however, were free to enforce discriminatory statutes, and anti-Catholic legislation remained on many books for generations.

The influx of Europeans after the Napoleonic wars caused a new outburst of religious antagonism. The large number of immigrants who came to America from Ireland were Roman Catholics. As early as 1829, homes of these immigrants were besieged by a Boston mob. Three years later, a frenzied group in New York invaded St. Mary's Catholic Church and burned it to the ground. In 1834, the Ursuline Convent in Charlestown, Massachusetts, was ransacked and gutted. Such anti-Catholic violence was fanned by pulpit diatribes and scurrilous literature; the attack on the Ursuline Convent has been blamed on the inflammatory sermons of the Rev. Lyman Beecher, Congregational minister and father of Henry Ward Beecher and Harriet Beecher Stowe. In the same year, inventor Samuel F. B. Morse, using a pen name, published in the New York *Observer* a series of anti-Catholic diatribes later brought together in a book, *Foreign Conspiracy Against the Liberties of the United States.*

Probably the most conspicuous anti-Catholic agitation in United States history came in the 1850's with the organization of the Know-Nothing party — so named because its members answered all questions about the organization with the words "I don't know." Each member was required to prove that he was "a native-born citizen, a Protestant, either of Protestant parents or reared under Protestant influence, and not united in marriage with a Roman Catholic." At first the Know-Nothing faction confined itself to endorsing candidates chosen by the older political parties. But in 1854 it had nominated candidates of its own and succeeded in electing governors in nine states. Of the 62 members of the Senate, 8 were Know-Nothings; so were 104 of the 234 members of the House.

The problems of the Civil War turned the attention of the public from the Catholic "menace" to grave questions of tariff, states' rights, and slavery. But in 1887 the American Protective Association took up where the Know-Nothings had left off. Catholic progress in industry and commerce, scandals among Irish-American politicians in New York, widespread political and social unrest — these and other factors allowed the American Protective Association to gain a foothold in at least twenty-four states, while numerous weekly newspapers devoted to anti-Catholic propaganda helped spread its message to millions of readers.

Organized anti-Catholicism increased even more after the turn of the century. The most significant evidences were the publication of *The Menace,* which boasted in 1914 of a circulation exceeding 1,400,000; the capture of numerous state, county, and local offices by the Pope-baiting Ku Klux Klan; and the campaign of bigotry waged against Roman Catholic Alfred E. Smith during the 1928 presidential race. Smith's overwhelming defeat even in areas of the "Solid South" — largely on the grounds of his religious faith — proved once more that few prejudices have struck more deeply into American life.

How is "anti-Catholicism" to be measured? Before discussing several organizations that blatantly appeal to bigotry, we shall consider the two major groups accused by American Catholics today of anti-Catholicism. The more influential of these is Protestants and Other Americans United for Separation of Church and State (POAU), characterized in some Roman Catholic circles as "a revival of the Know-Nothing movement, the APA, and the Ku Klux Klan." POAU represents objections to the political and social policies of Roman Catholicism.

The second is Christ's Mission, Inc., of New York City, classed in the Catholic press as a haven for ex-priests who have broken their celibacy vows. Christ's Mission, which has strong fundamentalist backing, places major emphasis upon doctrinal "errors" embraced by Roman Catholics, and in its zeal occasionally oversteps the boundary between fair play and untamed bigotry.

Let it be stated emphatically: Neither POAU nor Christ's Mission can fairly be classified as part of the ministry of hate. They are considered here because they are the most popular targets of Roman Catholic attacks — and because *some* adherents of both groups, especially Christ's Mission, carry their "anti" emphasis beyond the point of legitimate vigilance.

Protestants and Other Americans United

On January 12, 1948, in Washington, D. C., Protestants and Other Americans United for Separation of Church and State was launched "to assure the maintenance of the American principle of separation of church and state upon which the Federal Constitution guarantees religious liberty to all people and all churches of this republic." The founding of this movement was marked by the issuance of a manifesto signed by five eminently reputable church leaders — men who certainly are not allied with the ministry of hate. They were John A. Mackay, president of Princeton Theological Seminary; G. Bromley Oxnam, then bishop of the New York area of the Methodist Church; Louie D. Newton, then president of the Southern Baptist Convention; Edwin McNeill Poteat, then president of Colgate-Rochester

Divinity School; and Charles Clayton Morrison, former editor of the *Christian Century*. The thesis of the manifesto was clearly stated:

(1) Its all-inclusive premise was that the Roman Catholic Church "holds and maintains a theory of relation between church and state that is incompatible with the American ideal."

(2) This theory determines Catholic policy — a policy "plainly subversive of religious liberties as guaranteed by the constitution."

(3) Catholics pursue this policy by the camel's nose strategy of seeking limited objectives. The design is to "fracture the constitutional principle at one point after another where the action can be minimized as trivial or disguised as falling within some other category than that of its ultimate intent."

(4) Rome's principal objective is to nullify the First Amendment to the United States Constitution by securing for the Catholic Church "a position of special privilege" from which it will be able "to deny or curtail the religious liberty of all other churches" and "to vitiate democracy."

(5) Two dangerous steps toward this end have been: (a) the appointment of a personal envoy from the President to the Vatican; (b) the practice in some states of providing free textbooks and bus transportation for Catholic school children.

The manifesto made meticulous disavowals of any anti-Catholic animus; its objection to the Roman Catholic Church was not on the basis of "No Popery!" but under the banner of "Separation of Church and State." Declared the manifesto:

Protestants and Other Americans United does not concern itself with the religious teaching, the forms of worship, or the ecclesiastical organization of the many churches in our country. It is no part of our purpose to propagandize the Protestant faith or any other, nor to criticize or oppose the teaching or internal practices of the Roman Catholic Church or any sect. We have no connection or sympathy with any movement that is tinged with religious fanaticism. Our motivation arises solely from our patriotic and religious concern for the maintenance of the separation of church and state under the American form of government.

POAU invited all citizens who "believe in the American system of separation of church and state" to "join with a united Protestantism which is sinking its own differences in a common front to make sure that legislatures and executives and courts shall defend the constitutional guarantee of religious liberty against all attempts to subvert it." Those who professed the "faith of Judaism" were particularly singled out, and the hope was expressed that many "sound, intelligent and sincere" Catholics would also join.

Protestant attitudes toward the church's function in society have varied through the centuries and conflict at the present time. There are three chief positions.

First, there is the "secularist" or humanist position, with effective spokesmen among the theological "left-wing" of all major denominations. While less numerous than others, those who hold this position include many professional educators who have more influence than their numbers might suggest. They claim to find in the First Amendment a "wall" between church and state — and they are very vociferous in espousing this interpretation of the Constitution.

Second, the pietistic or "free-church" position is often found in curious alliance with the "secularists." It is numerically more significant and exerts great influence, especially in the South. Its position can best be explained in historical terms: Because its adherents have often been the victims of persecution by an established state church, they are wary of any interference by the state in the affairs of any church. The "free-church" position exists in most large denominations, but with special strength among Baptists and Disciples. From time to time the pietists flatly contradict their basic church-state tenets by lobbying vigorously for various kinds of "morality legislation." They were a major force, for example, behind the introduction of prohibition in the United States.

The third Protestant position is based on the principle that friendly and co-operative "separation" has a role under the American constitution and in American society. Its adherents contend that public education today is promoting a "religion" that rivals the churches — "secularism." As a reaction to increased "secularist" and "free church" agitation, this third force has become more articulate in recent years.

In POAU, the first and second of these positions are strongest — though occasionally a few members of the third force have allied themselves as well. POAU claims the endorsement of the Council of Bishops of the Methodist Church. Other Protestant individuals and groups that figure prominently among POAU supporters include the Seventh-Day Adventists, many Unitarians and Universalists, the National Association of Evangelicals, and numerous regional associations of denominational churches (e.g., Episcopal, Lutheran, Baptist), and councils of churches.

Who are the "Other Americans" in POAU? The managing editor of the monthly review is Stanley Lichtenstein, of the Jewish faith. Among the members of the national executive committee have been two Christian Scientists, James Watt and his successor, Harold C. Fitz. A third, Arthur Todd — active until his death in 1948 — was a pioneer in organizing similar but less potent groups that preceded POAU, and he served as one of the original members of POAU's executive committee when it was founded. Important backing of the group stems from some of the leaders of the American Humanist Association, the American Jewish Congress, and the American Ethical Union. Certain vehement critics of POAU contend that the "other Americans" have more influence than the Protestants in the policies of the organization.

POAU boasts of strong support from various educational groups. Dr. Charl Williams, past president of the National Education Association, is a member of its executive committee and one of its most ardent supporters; Willard E. Givens, the Association's past executive secretary, also demonstrated sympathy for its program. POAU claims that its principles have been endorsed by such groups as the American Association of School Administrators, the American Association of University Women, the National Congress of Parents and Teachers, the National Council of Chief State School Officers, and the American Federation of Teachers.

In recent years POAU has utilized two interesting personalities: Vashti McCollum, plaintiff in the famous Champaign "released-time" case, and the late Thomas Sugrue, author of the book

A Catholic Speaks His Mind. Mrs. McCollum is a professed freethinker. Sugrue was a reporter for the New York *Herald Tribune,* foreign correspondent for *American Magazine,* book reviewer for the New York *Times,* and author of a number of books. He became an occasional feature of POAU rallies and propaganda. A great deal of libel was published against him by some extreme elements of the Catholic press. Among other charges, he was accused of being mentally incompetent, "kept" by anti-Catholics, and a social climber — "always running around with Jews and Protestants."

POAU's advisory council of more than a hundred has a diverse membership, including James Luther Adams, Mary McLeod Bethune, John W. Bradbury, Rutherford L. Decker, Charles Fama, Clark Foreman, Frederick C. Fowler, Donald Harrington, Alvin W. Johnson, Thomas E. Little, Clyde R. Miller, Lewis Mumford, James DeForest Murch, Harry A. Overstreet, Charles E. Schofield, Guy E. Shipler, Rex Stout, Stanley I. Stuber, and J. Elwin Wright — an unusual combination of the right and the left, both theologically and politically.

The only thing that could possibly hold together such divergent forces is the issue of "Catholic power" — which they are all *against.* POAU rallies have been given greatest support by fundamentalists — who shout "Amen!" after the denunciations of Catholic policy uttered by such religious liberals as Paul Blanshard.

Blanshard is among those who have suggested that the name of POAU be changed to "Americans United for Separation of Church and State," for several reasons: (a) "Protestants and Other Americans United for Separation of Church and State" is too long and too clumsy a name; it can create a titter in an audience; (b) non-Protestants feel that they don't really belong; people do not like to be classified with "others"; (c) the term "Protestant" in the title conveys the impression that religious issues are involved, and leads to misinterpretation. Many POAU leaders now speak of their group as "Americans United."

On the national level, POAU is a simple organization. It has begun to build up its Washington headquarters into four departments: publications division, research and legislative division, promotional and organizational division, and legal division. Increasingly, however, the emphasis of POAU is upon local and regional units. On November 1, 1950, the first regional office was established in Chicago; six more are planned for the future. Some cities have affiliated committees.

POAU has attempted to promulgate its message in various ways. In keeping with its increased scope, it has developed a monthly bulletin — originally *Church and State Newsletter,* now *Church and State* — which has doubled in size and appears as an 8-page paper. The group makes determined efforts to obtain broader publicity and charges that "in this crusade . . . the secular press is throttled by fear of boycotts and reprisals," and that "it is next to impossible to enlist the support of the public press in any way to criticize even in a constructive manner the political activities of the Roman church." The *Christian Century* has been the most influential supporter of the POAU position among the religious journals, while wide publicity has also come from such publications as *The Churchman, Zions Herald, United Evangelical Action, Liberty* (of the Religious Liberty Association), *The Watchman-Examiner, The Michigan Christian Advocate,* and the monthly newsletter of the Baptist Joint Conference Committee on Public Relations.

POAU distributes a large number of pamphlets and urges the sale of many books. Among the "best sellers" are:

Separate Church and State Now! by Joseph Dawson
American Freedom and Catholic Power, by Paul Blanshard
Communism, Democracy, and Catholic Power, by Paul Blanshard
The Vatican in World Politics, by Avro Manhattan
The Wall of Separation between Church and State, by C. H. Moehlman
The Attack Upon the American Secular School, by V. T. Thayer
The American Tradition in Religion and Education, by R. Freeman Butts

Mass rallies have been successfully utilized to reach potential supporters. POAU's speakers' bureau supplies many leading churchmen to audiences across the nation. Paul Blanshard has toured from coast to coast on its behalf; in his 1951 tour, he reached more than thirty cities, where average attendances were over 1,500. Bitter Catholic opposition has met Blanshard in some cities, usually spearheaded by the Knights of Columbus and the Catholic War Veterans. Members of POAU are themselves sharply divided in their attitude toward Blanshard.

POAU, always politically alert, exerts influence upon national policy in many ways. It is caught in the dilemma, however, of deciding how to insure separation of church and state without itself using methods that would contradict this basic principle. On the subject of party platforms, for example, POAU claims that it is not political: "POAU abstains from approaching the platform committee of any party with an argument for including separation of church and state, because we believe that the adoption of any plank in support of the principle should be voluntary, apart from all pressure from groups."

One of the main concerns of POAU has been aiding plaintiffs in suits alleging church-state violation.

POAU claims to have a number of friends in Congress, some of whom are willing to be identified. The names of Senator Olin D. Johnston and the late Representative Joseph R. Bryson, both of South Carolina, have appeared on the list of members of its national advisory council. Several of the first informal meetings preceding the formation of POAU were held in Senator Johnston's office. Representative Brooks Hays of Arkansas was an early supporter of the movement. Senators Walter George of Georgia, Robert Kerr of Oklahoma, Willis Robertson of Virginia, among others, have been regarded as friendly to POAU, "not because of pressure but because of their culture."

Criticism of POAU

Protestants and Other Americans United has been attacked from many quarters — and on various grounds. The loudest denunciations naturally have come from spokesmen for the Roman Catholic Church. As soon as the POAU manifesto was released, numerous members of the hierarchy hit back.

Speaking for the National Catholic Welfare Conference, the Most Rev. John T. McNicholas denied the assertion that the Catholic hierarchy pursues a policy subversive of separation of church and state. "To say that the hierarchy of the United States is not wholly devoted to the maintenance of the Constitution in all its provisions, and that it is seeking for its own church advantages and privileges is, in plain language, an untruth," said the Archbishop. He charged that POAU was bound "to arouse intolerance, suspicion, hatred, and conflict between religious groups." He associated it with "Know-nothing-ism," "APA-ism," and "Ku-Klux-ism."

At Manchester, New Hampshire, on February 2, 1948, Archbishop Richard J. Cushing said that, while Catholics usually remain silent when their church is attacked, "silence would be craven and unworthy of decent men" at a time when Catholic loyalty to the United States is questioned. In answer to this implicit accusation, Cushing asked: "Who, then, are the Catholics who are conspiring against the American Constitution? What Catholic group, past or present, strikes at the American way of life or at civil liberties? Let their names be named so that we, the Catholics, can repudiate them." He called attention to the fact that anti-Catholic organizations in the past usually paraded behind a screen of "Patriotism." "If there is danger to the American way of life," declared Cushing, "it is to be found in the conduct of men who will fight their fellow Christians here at home and defend the real assailants of Christianity abroad."

An interesting analysis of the POAU manifesto came from the pen of the Rev. John Courtney Murray, S. J., editor of *Theological Studies*. Murray did not pretend to refute the charges; he blandly assumed they would fall of their own weight. Finding encouragement in the fact that POAU does not echo the references to the Hôtel Dieu, Maria Monk, the Scarlet Whore, and the Great Babylon, characteristic of vulgar anti-Catholicism, Murray said:

The ancient spectral threat is now made to walk in the night in much more civilized garb. To change the metaphor, the cry through the palace windows is not a hoarse shout, edged with frenzy, the articulation of something elemental in the mob. The voice indeed still carries to the Governor, but its tone is quiet, its accents cultured, its rhetoric restrained.

After proposing that another organization be founded — with

a "still lengthier but still more meaningful title, Catholics and Protestants and Jews and Other Americans United for Cooperative Relations between Church and State in View of the Peril of Secularism, Especially in Education" — Murray made the unfair suggestion that "the Manifesto of 1848 [Communist Manifesto] should set the Manifesto of 1948 in its ultimate perspective, certainly to Catholics — and perhaps even to the men who signed it."

The most severe and irresponsible critics of POAU have been the editors of America's most widely-circulated diocesan newspaper, *Our Sunday Visitor,* published at Huntington, Indiana. During recent years this weekly has printed two bitter pamphlet attacks upon POAU: *Whose Friends Are They — America's or Russia's?* and *Who's Who in the POAU?* The first, as its title suggests, attempts to prove that the enemies of Catholicism are friends of the Soviet Union. The second is equally glib, though much more complete and up-to-date. It introduces the reader to the leaders of Protestants and Other Americans United in the following words:

> Not only have they been obsessed with anti-Catholicism all their lives, but for the most part, they have had un-American connections. If that had not been true, they certainly would not have chosen the time they did for the formation of the POAU — a time when national unity was so badly needed, when any effort to divide our citizenry delighted the heart of God's and our nation's arch-enemy, Stalin.

The cry of "Red!" directed at the chief figures in POAU is wholly unjustified and Roman Catholics who succumb to such unethical tactics have slowed progress toward interfaith goodwill.

It is not only Roman Catholics who reject the position of POAU. Extreme atheist groups, such as the militant National Liberal League, tend to look upon it as "a bit too pious." Certain rabid fundamentalists, represented by the American Council of Christian Churches, accuse POAU of serving as a haven for "modernists" and "pro-communists." Other fundamentalist groups, such as Christ's Mission, publishers of the *Converted Catholic Magazine,* while certainly not opposed to POAU, feel that the best way to defeat Catholicism is "to combat its false doctrines and superstitions." Some Jews and humanists shy away from the church-state organization because they are convinced that it takes a primarily Protestant view of the problem.

A large number of Protestants — including some who are themselves strongly anti-Catholic — feel that POAU divides America at a time when it should unite against the communists. Fundamentalist Luther C. Peak, Dallas editor of the *Evangelist and Bible Teacher*, for example, has charged that the organization "is dragging the red herring across the trail. It is an effort to raise a pseudo issue of the union of Church and State, in order to throw the American people off the track, in their thinking, as to the menace of Russia and of Communism, to the peace of the world." Another Protestant "leader," the late Howard Kiroack, founder of the Laymen's National Committee, Inc. — which, as mentioned in Chapter 12, sponsors Sunday School Week — charged that "these spokesmen for the Protestant Church are playing right into the hands of those who would replace our American way of life with godless communism."

Influential Protestant thinkers have challenged the aims of Protestants and Other Americans United as well as its techniques. Writing immediately after POAU was founded, John C. Bennett of Union Theological Seminary in New York City expressed concern that "the only winners in this kind of struggle are likely to be the aggressive secularists." He wrote:

It is too early to estimate the significance of the new organization that calls itself "Protestants and Other Americans United for the Separation of Church and State," but serious questions can be raised concerning the wisdom of its approach to the problem of Catholic-Protestant relations. The reference to "other Americans" suggests that this may become an alliance between Protestants and secularists who also strongly oppose any connection between church and public education, but who themselves have developed in many cases a humanistic religion of democracy which they seek to incorporate in public education.

Bennett's colleague, Dean Reinhold Niebuhr, had expressed a similar opinion when he stated that "there is a greater danger that the separation of church and state be interpreted too rigorously in our country than that Catholics achieve some undue advantage."

Americans, regardless of creed, must decide for themselves

whether POAU expresses its legitimate views through legitimate means. Protestantism historically, of course, has been concerned with both the political and doctrinal aspects of the Roman Catholic Church; impetus for the Reformation itself came from sharp conflict in these two realms. Such concern is a natural interest of Protestants. But they must be vigilant in maintaining methods which do not foster intolerance.

Most of POAU's leaders have attempted to avoid any concession to unreasoned hate. A few, however, stand upon the edge of the chasm of bigotry. The future will show whether POAU's reputable leadership — which includes some of Protestantism's key spokesmen — can keep in check the less responsible elements which would like to involve POAU in the activities of the ministry of hate. If they can, POAU may serve a useful purpose in alerting Americans against attempts by any church to gain special government favors.

Christ's Mission, Inc.

While POAU has sought to prevent bigotry in its ranks, an important fundamentalist group, Christ's Mission, Inc., has often lost control of the reins of prejudice. Christ's Mission is best known through its slick monthly, the *Converted Catholic Magazine,* a 32-page journal that claims 100,000 readers, including 8,000 ministers, from all denominations. Recently it reports gains of more than 500 new subscribers each month. Editorial offices are at 160 Fifth Avenue in the "church-office" district of downtown New York, where operations are directed chiefly by former Catholic priests and monks.

Christ's Mission was incorporated in 1887 by "Father" James A. O'Connor, Irish-born ex-priest — compared by his admirers to Martin Luther. Incorporation papers stated that it was "for benevolent, charitable and missionary purposes, and also for the purpose of mutual improvement in religious knowledge and *for the furtherance of religious opinion.*" O'Connor published the *Converted Catholic Magazine* from its first issue in 1883 until his death in 1911.

The leading spirit of Christ's Mission in recent years was Leo H. Lehmann, who died in 1950. Another Irish convert, he claimed to have been ordained in 1921 in the Pope's own church,

St. John Lateran in Rome, after four years of study at the international seminary for the Propagation of the Faith. After transfer to a parish in Florida, Lehmann left the priesthood in 1929. The theological reasons leading to his decision were, he declared, the same as those which have motivated other priests who turn to conservative Protestantism:

The Catholic Church rejects the all-sufficiency of the sacrifice of Christ upon the cross. In its doctrine additional sacrifice must be made daily by priests, that is, the ritual of the mass. This reenacting of the sacrifice is even said to add to and improve upon Calvary.

The doctrine of purgatory is just another name for the pagan doctrine of reincarnation, which means that the sinner must go on suffering and expiating for his sins after death. This purgatorial suffering may be shortened by indulgences which are dispensed for cash or certain observances and thus priests hold their people through fear.

We now believe that sacrificial priests do not belong in Christianity. We believe that the sacrifice of Christ was perfect and therefore complete, that he suffered once and for all, that through him and him alone is salvation assured, and that there is no need for further suffering in purgatory.

As director of Christ's Mission, Lehmann did not content himself with theological discussion. He wrote several booklets of a political nature, charging Rome with intrigue to undermine American democracy. In *Behind the Dictators,* for example, Lehmann claimed to present "a factual analysis of the relationship of Nazi-Fascism and Roman Catholicism." His expressions were hardly in accord with judicious study of the facts and could only give rise to irrational prejudice against Catholics. He traced the whole Nazi-Fascist movement to sinister plots of the Jesuits. "The real motivating force behind Nazism-Fascism has been the thrust of the Jesuit counter-reformation . . . aimed to crush out of existence the hated principles of the Protestant democracies." Lehmann asserted blandly: "Hitler is a product of the Catholic church." Even the forged *Protocols of the Elders of Zion* — accredited, of course, to Jews in anti-Semitic circles — Lehmann traced to Jesuits, who fabricated them for use against Protestants and Masons.

Since Lehmann's death Christ's Mission has continued to peddle such blanket condemnations of Roman Catholicism. In 1952 the same line was promoted in a booklet, *Vatican Policy in World Affairs,* actually a revision of Lehmann's earlier *Vatican Policy in the Second World War.* The new version was edited by Walter M. Montano, new executive director of Christ's Mission and editor of the *Converted Catholic Magazine.* Montano, grand-nephew of a former president of Bolivia, also directs the Western Hemisphere Evangelical Union, Inc., with headquarters in Hollywood, California.

Ex-priests, at some time affiliated with Christ's Mission, evangelize across the country. Joseph Zacchello, a young Italian immigrant, now edits his own magazine, *The Convert,* in Clairton, Pennsylvania. Two of his books, *Secrets of Romanism* and *Ins and Outs of Romanism,* were widely heralded in fundamentalist periodicals, in which most anti-Catholic literature wins enthusiastic publicity. Co-editor of *The Convert* is William E. Burke, ex-priest of the Diocese of Scranton and former field representative for Christ's Mission, with his center of operation in Covington, Kentucky.

Sometimes priests who find a haven with the Mission later turn against their fellow-converts. Peter J. Doeswyk, for example, ordained in 1933 in the Diocese of Omaha, travels widely in midwestern Lutheran and Reformed circles, declaiming equally against Catholics and against the *Converted Catholic Magazine.* Such schisms — often the result of power struggles, personality conflicts, or monetary problems — frequently have led to bitter rivalry among the anti-Catholics.

Converts from Catholicism complain that their adoption of the Protestant faith is surrounded by a deliberate fog of silence, while converts to Catholicism are bathed in the sunlight of publicity. Some charge that at the time Clare Booth Luce was embracing the Catholic Church — to the accompaniment of day-by-day press accounts of her progress — the Rev. Noel Patrick Conlon, member of the Order of Franciscans and of the faculty of St. Bonaventura College, Allegheny, New York, was received as a minister into the Protestant Episcopal Church. But his conversion was not news around New York.

Many respected ex-Catholics have been associated with Christ's Mission. In 1946 the Rev. Frank Payas, former colleague of Lehmann, was elected moderator of the Presbyterian Church by the Presbytery of Santa Fe, New Mexico. Dr. George

Barrois, former priest and professor in the national Catholic University in Washington, is now a professor at Princeton Theological Seminary. Among the many who have joined the Lutherans are Andrew Sommese, ex-priest of the Augustinian order to which Martin Luther belonged, and Father John Zerhusen, formerly a secular priest of the archdiocese of Baltimore. The Rev. Chris DiPietro, formerly a priest in Brooklyn, now preaches Protestantism among the Italians in Pennsylvania. The late Rev. Aristide Malinverni worked among a similar group in the Bronx. Jose Vega, once director of the seminary of a Catholic order, received aid from Christ's Mission and today is assistant dean of an Episcopal cathedral in Mexico City.

These are a few of the dozens of priests who have been associated in some way with Christ's Mission. Obviously, not all of them display the same degree of bitterness toward the Roman Catholic Church.

Christ's Mission has successfully solicited the support of a large number of Protestant leaders, chiefly fundamentalists. It gets little support from leaders of the National Council of Churches, some of whom are aligned with POAU. But, in general, members of the National Association of Evangelicals (discussed in Chapter 8) are far more responsive. The names of the members of the board of trustees of Christ's Mission (formerly twelve in number, now more) are a carefully guarded secret in order to protect them from public abuse.

In November 1947, when the *Converted Catholic Magazine* sponsored a prayer crusade for the conversion of Monsignor Fulton J. Sheen (now a bishop), endorsements came from such eminent conservative leaders as the late Harry A. Ironside of the Moody Memorial Church in Chicago; President Dean G. McKee of the Biblical Seminary in New York City; Donald Grey Barnhouse of Philadelphia, editor of *Eternity;* T. Christie Innes, former general secretary of the American Tract Society; William Ward Ayer of the International Marching Truth broadcast; and many more. Ayer, who formerly filled the pulpit of the Calvary Baptist Church in New York City, has himself written a pamphlet attacking Sheen, entitled *Romanism's Pied Piper*.

The *Converted Catholic Magazine* boasts that it keeps its

discussion of Catholic-Protestant relations on a high level. "Christ's Mission's staff of converted priests does not indulge in mud-slinging against Catholic nuns and priests," says one pamphlet. "They are primarily concerned with bringing their Catholic people into the knowledge of the saving power of the Lord Jesus Christ."

But too frequently the *Converted Catholic Magazine* incites irrational hatred against Catholics based upon false premises. Consider, for example, its views of Roman Catholic politics. In the issue for March 1952, Montano announced boldly and without qualification: "One cannot be a true Catholic and loyal American at the same time. Allegiance to the Vatican is betrayal of the American Constitution." This attitude closely reflects the Ku Klux Klan mentality of the 1920's.

The *Converted Catholic Magazine* also tries to impugn the moral standards of the Roman Catholic Church. An article entitled "Catholic Invasion of Rural America" expressed these sentiments:

Now, why all this cry "to bring Christ to the country" and save America for God, by settling Roman Catholics in rural America where Protestant culture has kept life clean and wholesome for more than 100 years? How will it help to bring to those country districts, Roman Catholics with their liquor, gambling, bazaars and raffles, their parochial schools, and priests and nuns? So far, these . . . small places have done very well without the Catholic Church and those appurtenances that make up "Catholic culture."

In the same issue appeared this generalization:

[An] atmosphere of "joy and merriment" in the material and fleshly sense, is the hall-mark of Roman Catholic communities where the three great (and profitable) vices of drinking, gambling, and prostitution abound.

Conservative Protestants may feel justified in attacking the moral code of Roman Catholicism in areas where it is less rigid than their own. But such sweeping, irrational condemnations do not contribute to interfaith goodwill.

Contrary to its boast, Christ's Mission does not keep itself completely free from the "nun-priest" theme that marks so much of anti-Catholicism in American history, though it refrains from dealing in most scandalous "best sellers." One of its favorites, however, is *The Priest, The Woman and the Confessional* — a standard "work" among professional haters that is currently in its forty-fifth edition.

It was written by "Father" Charles Chiniquy, a French Canadian ordained in Canada in 1843 and suspended from the priesthood eight years later for "irregularities." Coming to the United States, Chiniquy began to capitalize on his former connections, and traveled under the auspices of the American Protective Association and other such bigoted groups. Lehmann has called him "one of the most eloquent and successful preachers of the Gospel among both Roman Catholics and Protestants that the world has ever seen." Chiniquy had phenomenal success in converting Catholics, especially among the French-speaking. His book *Fifty Years in the Church of Rome* still commands a wide sale in fundamentalist circles.

Chiniquy's book *The Priest, The Woman and the Confessional* is a sensational "exposé" of the Catholic confession. Wrote Chiniquy: "The confessor is the worm which is biting, polluting, and destroying the very roots of civil and religious society, by contaminating, debasing, and enslaving woman." Of the confessional he said:

> The confessional is like the spider's web. How many too unsuspecting flies find death, when seeking rest on the beautiful framework of their deceitful enemy! How few escape! and this only after a most desperate struggle. See how the perfidious spider looks harmless in his retired, dark corner; how motionless he is; how patiently he waits for his opportunity! But look how quickly he surrounds his victim with his silky, delicate and imperceptible links! How mercilessly he sucks its blood and destroys its life!
>
> What remains of the imprudent fly, after she has been entrapped into the nets of her foe? Nothing but a skeleton. So it is with your fair wife, your precious daughter; nine times out of ten, nothing but a moral skeleton returns to you, after the Pope's black spider has been allowed to suck the very blood of her heart and soul.

Christ's Mission has been sharply criticized from many quarters. Some, for example, have accused it of financial racketeering. A recent blast appeared in the April 1953 issue of *Exposé*, a sensational New York tabloid. *Exposé* charged that Christ's

Mission only gives help to ex-priests when it can exploit them. The article quoted several ex-priests, one of whom reportedly stated: "The claim that Christ's Mission is interested in helping former priests is absolutely false and absolutely despicable. Christ's Mission isn't interested in working for Christ. It is interested in working for money." Of the alleged $45,000 annual revenue from the *Converted Catholic Magazine* and the estimated $125,000 additional obtained from contributions, the article charged that never in its history has Christ's Mission spent as much as $10,000 a year to aid ex-priests.

Christ's Mission denied the charges, tracing most of them to a "professional critic," John J. Arrien, an ex-priest who, they claimed, had been rebuffed in his attempts to exploit the organization for his own personal gain.

Members of Christ's Mission are harshly censured by the Roman Catholic press. In the little pamphlet, *Did They Leave or Were They Put Out?* (angrily subtitled "Brief Character Sketches of Wilful Deceivers"), the inflammatory diocesan paper *Our Sunday Visitor* states: "We can say irrefutably that no priest ever left the Catholic Church in order to become better." One by one the pamphlet takes up leading converts to Protestantism, many of whom have been connected with Christ's Mission. L. H. Lehmann, for example, is charged with entering into civil marriage and fleeing with the parish automobile. W. M. Montano is described as a "fake" priest. The assumption appears to be that no normal, intelligent priest can leave Rome to embrace Protestantism.

Significantly, certain anti-Semitic elements of the Protestant underworld hailed the Roman Catholic attack upon Christ's Mission. Mrs. Elizabeth Dilling recommended the *Our Sunday Visitor* pamphlet, adding: "I, myself, have proof that the very Leo Lehmann ENDORSED by the leading Fundamentalist ministers is a speaker for atheist societies like the Freethinkers, and his books are part of the catalogue of the American Association for the Advancement of Atheism." She charged that "every anti-Catholic movement in this country is Communistic and Pharisaic."

Kenneth Goff, ex-communist youth leader, now a Colorado race agitator, has charged that Lehmann was an ace ally of the

Communist Party. Describing his own activities as a Party member, Goff has testified:

> Our main project was to get the *Converted Catholic Magazine* circulated among Protestants. The editor . . . was well known to us. He attended our meetings, gave lectures and made "helpful" suggestions. . . . While Lehmann's magazine displayed itself as a publication for Bible-believing Christians, it always followed the Communist Party line.

Under Lehmann's leadership the *Converted Catholic Magazine* carried articles that easily could be interpreted as mild doses of Soviet propaganda. On one occasion, it ran an item entitled "Russian View of the Pope," which quoted the Soviet *New Times* as saying that the Vatican was plotting a move to Washington. Lehmann expressed his hope that this communist report would "serve to sharpen the focus in the sleepy eyes of over-intolerant, indifferent American Protestants." Furthermore, Christ's Mission advertised in *The Protestant,* the pro-Kremlin, anti-Catholic "religious" journal, long after *The Protestant*'s sympathy for communism became obvious (see Chapter 11). In conspicuous contrast to its own fundamentalist position, the Mission has promoted the anti-Catholic writings of such vehement critics of all organized religion as Joseph McCabe and H. G. Wells. (Until 1950, most of this literature was distributed under the aegis of the Agora Publishing Company, now dissolved.) The truth is that Christ's Mission, though obviously not pro-communist, sometimes has found itself in strange and mixed ideological company.

No one can object to the efforts of Christ's Mission to promote its own version of theological truth in opposition to the doctrines of the Church of Rome — but criticism of any religious system should always be fair.

The American Protestant Defense League

Christ's Mission has a loose fraternal relationship with a more extreme anti-Catholic group in New York, the American Protestant Defense League. Founded in 1932, it has been described by the *Converted Catholic Magazine* as "a Protestant patriotic society [which] aims to help with legal assistance and advise Protestants who suffer discrimination because of their faith." For several years the circulation and shipping departments of Christ's Mission were housed in the basement of the Manor Community Church at 350 West 26th Street, where the League has its office.

Founders of the organization were the Rev. Thomas E. Little, present director-general, and Dr. Charles Fama, prominent New York physician, who serves as chairman of its national advisory board. There are few well-known names on its letter-head; but over the years testimonials have been secured from William Ward Ayer, Donald Grey Barnhouse, H. A. Ironside, Louis T. Talbot, John W. Bradbury, and other reputable funda-mentalist leaders. The American Protestant Defense League holds irregular meetings, distributes books and pamphlets, and publishes the *American Protest,* a 16-page periodical issued monthly. The League's principal claim to fame rests on a single case in which Little secured the release of a Protestant woman committed for disciplinary reasons to a House of the Good Shepherd, a Roman Catholic institution in New York.

The American Protestant Defense League habitually has re-sorted to unethical attacks upon the Roman Catholic Church. One of its favorite themes is that the Vatican is plotting a war against the Soviet Union in which American Protestantism will serve Rome's ambitious designs. "We say, here and now," begins one League leaflet, "that if the Vatican wishes a war against Russia, let the Vatican call for volunteers among the Catholic men. . . . As a Protestant, I do not like to think of my sons and grandsons engaged in a fight to pull Roman Catholic chestnuts out of the fire."

The same line is followed in an Australian pamphlet circulated by the League, *Will the Vatican Plunge Us Into a Third World War*:

> The Roman power is an exclusive power — scheming, intransigent, domineering. . . . This ideology is far more dangerous to democracy than ever communism was, because Romanists are all over the world, in all democratic governments, trade unions, councils, to bring the Papal ideology to reality. . . . [The Catholic] clerical-fascist International [is] actively at work projecting the organizational plans for the rebirth of a Fascist Axis and another attempt at a Third World War.

Little's one-man organization recently boasted that it had circulated 100,000 copies of a special Latin American issue of the *American Protest*. Typical of the inflammatory articles in this edition and other League literature are these: "The Vatican Declares War On Our Constitution." "Jesuits Overplaying Their Hand," " 'Card Carrying' Romanists Vs. 'Card Carrying' Communists."

"Deny it as they will," stated a recent issue, "the aim and purpose of the Roman Catholic Church is not primarily the worship of God. It is the conquest of the world and specifically, the conquest of the United States of America, admittedly the greatest prize in the world."

For the past several years, the American Protestant Defense League has been featuring, as guest speaker for its anniversary events, James McGinlay, radio preacher of "The Baptist Hour" (broadcasting station WABC) and pastor of the Baptist Temple in Brooklyn. The League demonstrated its distaste for fellow Protestants as well as Roman Catholics in 1953 when McGinlay gave four bitter diatribes against the new Revised Standard Version of the Bible. "As far as I'm concerned, I wouldn't wipe my feet on it," shouted McGinlay. It was translated, he said, by "ignoramuses" and "enemies of Jesus Christ." McGinlay warned that this "apostasy" is leading Christendom to a huge "one-church" headed by the Anti-Christ. This Anti-Christ would be the Pope.

The climax of the anti-Catholic crusade of the American Protestant Defense League was reached many years ago, and it appears that Little now maintains a lonely vigil, fortified with the memories of a more fruitful past.

American Council Bigotry

Perhaps the most vociferous attacks upon "Romanism" stem from the American Council of Christian Churches, the uneasy coalition of fundamentalist sects ostensibly organized to combat "soul-destroying modernism." As will be shown in the next chapter, the most powerful cannon of this schismatic element have been aimed at fellow Protestants; but another favored target is the Roman Catholic Church.

The principal figure in the American Council, Carl McIntire of Collingswood, New Jersey, set the tone for post-war anti-Catholicism in his *Christian Beacon,* saying in September 1945:

As we enter the post-war world, without any doubt the greatest enemy of freedom and liberty that the world has to face today is the Roman Catholic system. Yes, we have Communism in Russia and all that is involved there, but if one had to choose between the two . . . one would be much better off in a communistic society than in a Roman Catholic Fascist set-up. One wonders sometimes if all the antagonism of the Roman Catholic Church to Communism . . . is not being played up especially in the United States at the present time for the purpose of gaining advantage for the Roman Catholics. . . . America has to face the Roman Catholic terror. The sooner the Christian people of America wake up to this danger the safer will be our land.

McIntire's most vociferous ally in this campaign against Catholicism is Harvey H. Springer, "cowboy evangelist" of Englewood, Colorado, president of the splinter World Baptist Fellowship, and executive officer of McIntire's global arm, the International Council of Christian Churches. For many years, Springer has criticized "baptized paganism," as he calls the Catholic creed. (When he was allied briefly with Gerald L. K. Smith, however, he attacked those "who are trying to divide Protestants and Catholics in their fight against heathen Communism." In 1946, he asked: "Is *Converted Catholic Magazine* Just Another Red Front Publication?")

Springer has established the Protestant Defense League to combat "the inroads of Romanism," and the Protestant Information Bureau to flood the fundamentalist camp with scurrilous material directed against the Church of Rome. (It is reported that anti-Catholic printed sermons and pamphlets constitute a profitable line for the stores that carry them.) Springer fills the pages of his *Western Voice* with such insulting verse as "The Pope's New Theme Song":

> O, give me a Rome
> 'Tween Buffalo and Nome
> Where the priests and cardinals prey,
> Where seldom is heard
> An heretical word,
> And Protestants burn everyday.

Or "Ring Around the Rosary":

> Eenie, meenie, minie, moe,
> Round my rosary now I go,

Counting my beads and mechanical prayers.
If I say them quite often, I may get Upstairs.

One of Springer's main activities has been the distribution of
the bogus "Knights of Columbus Oath." POAU's *Church and
State Newsletter* — itself no friend of the Catholic hierarchy —
has exposed this aspect of Springer's Ku Klux Klan variety of
hate:

As an organization which has repeatedly expressed its admiration for
"Christian Spain," the Knights of Columbus can be justly criticized on
various counts — but all persons of good will should beware of a forged
document which is being distributed in some communities as the "Knights
of Columbus Oath." According to the spurious "Oath," members of the
Knights of Columbus must "hang, burn, waste, boil, flay, strangle, and
bury alive . . . infamous heretics, Protestants, and Masons." Although
a Congressional committee called the document "fake and libelous and
spurious" back in 1913, a cowboy evangelist named Harvey Springer
has reprinted it for widespread distribution, and already an Oklahoma
minister has had to plead guilty in a libel action brought against him by
the Knights for having read the Springer reprint from his pulpit.

Though Springer is the most outspoken anti-Catholic of the
group, he is one of many leaders in the American Council who
promote irrational hostility toward the Roman Catholic church.
Another example, Dr. T. T. Shields, heads the Conservative
Baptist Association of Canada, serves the large Jarvis Street
Church in Toronto, directs the Canadian Protestant League,
and edits the *Gospel Witness and Protestant Advocate* — which
has circulated to as many as 30,000 subscribers. Shields has
always been on the warpath against his brother Baptists, Methodists, Anglicans, and anyone else who dares differ from him,
on such diverse issues as bobbed hair ("the Lord never intended
women to go to the barber"), and athletics ("the Lord hath no
pleasure in the legs of a man").
Shields is the most vociferous anti-Catholic in Canada. He
has carried his message of hate to pulpits around the world, and
his lusty blasts against "Romanism" over the conscription issue
during the war brought him into the limelight in his own country
and in the United States. He charged that "it was the aim of the
Roman Catholic hierarchy to keep their men at home to breed

their kind, while they were willing to have non-Catholics killed off in any number."

On another occasion:

> The Papacy is the world's greatest enemy, the destroyer of the individual, the corrupter of society, of governments, and nations, the greatest of war-mongers, and the earthly source of the intensest hatred of every kind of human liberty. . . . [The Roman Catholic Church] represents the most criminal institution in the world. I say "criminal": by that I mean that it is utterly lawless; a clerical humbug with a Roman collar.

In a recent address to a regional conference affiliated with the American Council, Shields well summed up the doctrine that some of his fundamentalist colleagues promote but are too timid to state: "The principal enemy of the Christian Church today is not Communism, but Roman Catholicism."

"Free the Nuns!"

Perhaps the favorite thesis of professional anti-Catholic organizations has been that the vow of celibacy required of priests fosters gross immorality in convents and monasteries.

Literature emphasizing this theme still floods fundamentalist circles and serves in place of "thrillers" for otherwise pious readers. Some fundamentalists, forbidden common sources of "worldly pleasure" — smoking, dancing, card-playing, movie-going—may find vicarious enjoyment in such lurid paper-bound books as *Convent Horror, Forgotten Woman, Secret Confession of a Roman Catholic Priest,* and *Why Priests Should Wed.*

Perhaps the leading center in the United States for scurrilous literature of this kind is the Book and Bible House in Decatur, Georgia. The organization — formerly located in Toledo, Ohio, and in St. Petersburg, Florida — was founded by "Evangelist" L. J. King, active Klansman, self-proclaimed defender of Protestantism, and a man with a police record. Before his death King circulated numerous "best sellers." "God has specially sent me after the nunneries and the confessional box," he wrote. "Destroy these two institutions and Romanism is ended."

Among King's "basic works" was *Abolish the Nunneries and Save the Girls.* "We demand it in Jesus name," he began. "The thousands of white slaves confined in them are groaning and crying, and praying for deliverance." Of the confessional, King wrote:

This devil-invented clap-trap, laid across the path of virtue to catch girls, to railroad them into the Convent, to fill up the place of poisoned, deluded, outraged, starved, raped, and murdered victims of priestcraft in the nunnery, to feed the lust of the adulterous bachelor, overfed, drunken, priesthood of the Romish fake, the Mother of Harlots and abominations of the earth must be stopped.

King's most extensive volume is *House of Death and Gate of Hell,* "exposing Rome's heathen, pagan, unnatural, unamerican convent system." The promotion flyer, which reads like a side-show barker, cries:

See nun who dug hole under wall and made her escape from Detroit nunnery. . . . See nun bound hand and foot, gagged, lying in dungeon because she refused to obey a priest. . . . See the iron virgin with steel teeth, a murder device. . . . Get ready for convent abolition — the world needs this message. Stir up the people. Agitate, educate, organize and legislate this pagan, heathen, monastic system out of America.

Such books as these are advertised in many fundamentalist publications, including the *Christian Beacon, United Evangelical Action,* and *Western Voice.* One typical Book and Bible House advertisement recently appearing in such periodicals reads:

CONVENT HORROR

Court record. Most horrible Revelation of Convent cruelty on record. Beautiful, Innocent Barbara Ubrick locked in a Nunnery Basement Dungeon 6 x 8 feet for 21 years. Total darkness. Fed on potato peelings, crusts of dry bread and cold water once per day. Weighed 40 lbs. when taken by government. See photo of Iron Virgin, an instrument of death torture.

At the present time, the Book and Bible House is directed by the Rev. Fred J. Junior. Junior represents himself as a former Catholic altar boy, who became a Protestant fourteen years ago. He describes his lurid selection of anti-Catholic literature as "the greatest books ever printed, eye-openers for sleepy Protestants and blinded Catholics. America faces a grave crisis. Years ago Rome said, 'We will take America.' "

The most widely distributed "exposé" of convent life, *Awful Disclosures of Maria Monk or The Secrets of the Black Nunnery*

Revealed, is circulated by another outlet — the Gospel Art Shoppe of Rowan, Iowa, also known as The Old Authors Shoppe. First published more than a century ago, the book produced a powerful reaction in America as well as abroad. Its current distributor, specializing in out-of-print anti-Catholic books, finds customers through the columns of many fundamentalist periodicals, including Winrod's *Defender Magazine* and the *Converted Catholic Magazine.*

The Gospel Art Shoppe advertises *Maria Monk* as "the most extensively read book ever printed on the papal curse. . . . Rome fought bitterly, but in vain, to suppress this book. Read this frightful, heart-breaking story and see how Roman priests perpetrate every crime from seduction to murder." It is estimated, the flyer continues, that 10,000,000 copies have been read throughout the world — a gross exaggeration. "Little did Maria Monk dream, when she gave her book to the world, that from her saddened mind and broken heart she was sending forth a masterpiece that would carry its wringing message and vital warning through the ages. No book like this in print! *Maria Monk* contains 106 burning pages."

These "awful disclosures" are known to be absolutely false. The events allegedly took place in the Hôtel Dieu nunnery in Montreal. The "heroine" describes in detail sadistic practices that finally caused her to flee and volunteer her own experiences to arouse the outside world.

Fair-minded Protestants early repudiated this book. In 1836, William L. Stone, a Protestant layman, personally investigated the truth of these stories and concluded from Maria Monk's unreliable description of the convent that she could not have lived within its walls. His article, which originally appeared in the New York *Commercial Advertiser* for October 8, 1836, is currently distributed by the Paulist Press, Roman Catholic convent-seeking publishing house. Stone concluded:

I will, therefore, now close this protracted narrative, by expressing my deliberate and solemn opinion, founded not only on my own careful examination, but upon the firmest convictions of nearly the entire population of Montreal — embracing the great body of the most intelligent Evangelical Christians — *that Maria Monk is an errant impostor and her book, in all its essential features, a tissue of calumnies.*

The woman Maria Monk, it was discovered, had a police record and at one time had been confined in a Magdalene Asylum for rehabilitation of prostitutes. She died in prison in 1845. In the meantime two editions of her book — numbering 40,000 each — were quickly exhausted and her royalties were estimated at $30,000. Since her death, more than 300,000 copies have found customers — though current editions have been somewhat edited to comply with Post Office obscenity regulations.

"Protestant" Racketeers

Several unscrupulous organizations have exploited the good name of Protestantism to promote bigotry against Catholics, as well as against Jews and Negroes.

One of these is the Protestant War Veterans, "Sentinels of Liberty." Edward James Smythe, "executive chairman," operates his letterhead organization from Connecticut Avenue in Washington, D. C. His involvement in extremist activities began in the 1920's. By the beginning of World War II, he had become a central figure in the nation's racist element. His Protestant War Veterans, set up in 1937, was placed on the Justice Department's list of subversive organizations in 1943 — and again in 1947. It was charged with "a policy of advocating or approving the commission of acts of force and violence to deny others their rights under the Constitution of the United States."

During World War II, Smythe was indicted three times on sedition charges. Among his many affiliations were the German-American Bund and the Ku Klux Klan. Before the war, he organized and spoke before a joint meeting of the two groups at Camp Nordland, New Jersey, popular center for Bundist activities. Attacking Roman Catholicism in the same breath with Judaism and communism, Smythe once told his Protestant War Veterans:

NAZISM AND HITLERISM is PROTESTANTISM IN ACTION, the highest form of Christianity. . . . We Christian Americans will swing into ACTION, we will STRIKE LIKE LIGHTNING against these MONGOLIAN JEWS who have seized control of our country, now comes the question. . . . Will we ask support of HITLER? Yes we may do so, if we need help. . . . We will destroy JUDAISM and COMMUNISM in America, we will likewise DESTROY ROMANISM here as HITLER has in the NEW GERMANY. . . . Every PROT-

ESTANT throughout the world (except those in the employ of the JEWS) look upon HITLER [as] the greatest LIVING CHRISTIAN SINCE JESUS CHRIST. . . . This Nation belongs to the Protestants to them we will return it this year, or as soon as HITLER HAS DEFEATED THE JEWISH EMPIRE OF GREAT BRITAIN.

Smythe has regularly exploited Protestantism not only for the Protestant War Veterans, his principal front, but for numerous other letterhead organizations as well. They have included Protestant Servicemen's Club, Protestant War Veterans Memorial Fund, Protestant Gold Star Mothers, Sons and Daughters of Protestant Veterans, Protestant Loyal Legion of the U.S., Protestant Fife and Drum Corps of the U. S., and the Protestant Church Boys Brigade of the U. S. He prints impressive-appearing letterheads and envelopes — which have convinced some contributors of his integrity. His current interest is the Protestant News Service and Trans-Radio Agency, Inc., which he calls "the only Protestant news and radio-television agency in America serving your best interests." There are no known clients.

Smythe has never been drawn into theological controversy. He belongs to the Protestant underworld not because of any denominational affiliation but because of his flagrant exploitation of the name "Protestant." His "philosophy" is straightforward: he hates almost everyone. This is one of his slogans:

> God Bless America
> The Jews own it
> The Catholics run it
> The Negroes enjoy it
> The Protestants founded it
>   But
> The Communists will destroy it.

Before assuming the role of "champion of the faith," Smythe devoted several years to a salesmanship racket. He had booklets printed containing tenets of the U. S. Constitution, the Declaration of Independence, and benefits of the G.I. Bill of Rights; then he sold them — at $35 per 100. This venture collapsed when it was discovered that these documents were free on request from the Government Printing Office. Next Smythe turned to the sale of "Victory Stamps," another short-lived racket.

Attacks on Roman Catholicism are a constant feature of

Smythe's irregularly published bulletin, *Protestant War Veterans,* "representing the religious, political and economic rights of over twelve million Protestant war veterans." He has warned:

> You must not forget, that the Roman Catholic Political Hierarchy is a dead duck over in HATE RIDDEN Europe, and this conspiracy, is working night and day to make Protestant America their seat of Empire, when that day arrives, you Mr. and Mrs. Protestant American will be on the same status as an African Black man, for as it is in all Roman Catholic controlled countries you will have no rights, your Churches will be closed, as they are in Spain under Roman-Catholic Franco, where Protestants can only worship their GOD in their own homes, and where they are denied their civic and political rights, remember there is no such animal as minority rights in Roman Catholic countries, in those countries. the Roman Catholics only have rights, history will tell you that. . . . SO WAKE UP — WAKE UP — WAKE UP — The hour is later than you think.

On another occasion, Smythe wrote: "Thousands of Priests and NUNS are coming into this country every week from Europe in preparation of taking this country over." He traces this "plot" to the House of Rothschild, which "owns the Roman Catholic Political State BODY AND SOUL."

In spite of his contempt for racial and religious minorities, Smythe has not been on good terms with some extremists of the Protestant underworld. Although he calls Gerald Winrod "one of our greatest Americans," he characterizes Gerald L. K. Smith as an "18 CARAT PHONY." For a time Smythe labeled Elizabeth Dilling "that most outstanding Christian American Patriot"; he urged all Protestant veterans to obtain from 1 to 12 copies of her book *The Octopus.* Mrs. Dilling, however — not impressed by "his illiterate correspondence"—broke off relations with Smythe.

As a result of such disputes, he once bitterly complained:

> No Preacher, No Clergyman, No Religionist, has any place in this Nationalist Political Movement, Religion has no place in this STRUGGLE, and when they bring it in here, it is nothing more than to use two baits in order to catch more SUCKERS — We will keep striking at these RELIGIONISTS and PARASITES until they run back in their holes, or PULPITS or whatever you want to call them.

Smythe, labeling the Federal Council of Churches of Christ in America a "Jew Communistic Church Organization", concludes with a vulgar flourish: "So I say to HELL with such LOUSY PROT-

ESTANTS — they do not represent PROTESTANTISM." He considers the American Council of Christian Churches as "the ONLY (Protestant) Church Council in the United States."

Another "religious" racket exploiting Protestantism has been the Puritan Church — "the Church of America" — with headquarters in Washington, D. C. It is a "church" only because its "chancellor," Harrison Parker, calls it that. It has no formal membership, no edifice for worship, no ritual. It holds no meetings. In the past, the Puritan Church has maintained a small office to handle mail at 1612 I Street, N. W.

On a small but valuable piece of property in another section of the city, the Puritan Church has planned a "Protestant Embassy" to "pressure the United States out of the Pope's European Wars." A statement soliciting funds anounced:

This Embassy is sponsored by the Puritan Church — the Church of America, in which Methodists, Baptists, Presbyterians, Congregationalists, Lutherans, Episcopalians, Quakers, Mormons, Unitarians, Christian Scientists, Americanized Roman Catholics, Reformed Jews and Converted Freethinkers are united for the first time.

One immediate objective of the new "Embassy" was to secure the abandonment of the "Vatican Embassy" at 1312 Massachusetts Avenue, N. W. — actually the offices of the National Catholic Welfare Conference — in order "to preserve the national integrity of the United States from utter destruction and encroachments upon it by the 189,000 'paid agents' of the Pope of Rome, now collecting money and circulating Roman Catholic propaganda."

Chancellor Parker, a benign-appearing gentleman of seventy-four, prides himself in his direct descent from Deacon Thomas Parker who led the first boatload of Puritans to come to America. The chancellor's story discloses a gradual involvement with anti-Catholicism. At one time he held the well-paid position of advertising manager of the Chicago *Tribune*. Later he became the $45,000-a-year publisher of William Randolph Hearst's Chicago *American*. Parker resigned in 1917, according to his testimony, because he felt that Hearst was not trying to keep America out of the war. He moved from one job to another until he decided to embark upon "church work." In 1943 he

was "ordained" by the College of Divines of the Puritan Church
— a sect that he and a few friends had organized — and two
years later assumed his present role as "chancellor" of the "denomination."

From then on Parker became more deeply entrenched in what
developed into a religious fraud. Several wealthy patrons contributed to his various projects, notably his Puritan Church Building Fund for the construction of the "Protestant Embassy."
Meanwhile, Parker sought smaller donations through a mail
puzzle contest which proved to be a hoax. Sensing irregularities,
the Post Office authorities stepped in and filed a fraud order,
while the Treasury Department simultaneously began action
against Parker on tax-evasion charges.

Catholics were responsible for this "persecution" — or so the
chancellor contended. He charged that certain "Roman-Catholic payrollers entrenched in the Department of Internal Revenue
of the United States" were responsible for the Treasury Department's income-tax suit against him; that the "100-per-cent
Roman Catholic censorship maintained by the Roman Catholics
in the U. S. Post Office" was behind the mail-fraud indictment;
that the "religious bigots of the foreign Church of Rome were
either influenced, intimidated or bribed" to destroy his puzzle
contest.

Parker published other blistering attacks upon Catholicism
in *Liberty Bell*, his irregular but well-printed periodical —
"maintained at Washington, D. C., by the free-will donations
of Americans to defend the American way of life (Christianity)
from the destruction by either the Roman-Catholic way of life
(Paganism) or the Russian way of life (Communism)." *Liberty
Bell* has sought to interpret most political events in terms of
a world-wide papal conspiracy. One of its favorite themes —
echoing that of other anti-Catholics — is that the Pope is deliberately pushing the United States into war. On the outside
cover of many issues of *Liberty Bell* appears the startling announcement:

JAIL, OR NO JAIL

WE WILL NOT

FIGHT IN EUROPE

IN WORLD

WAR III

Inside the editor continues:

> If the present European struggle between Roman Catholicism and Soviet Communism — a struggle in which the Pope of Rome is taking a personal hand — leads to World War III, the Puritan Church WILL DO EVERYTHING IN ITS POWER TO PREVENT THE UNITED STATES FROM ENTER- ING THAT WAR.
>
> Neither the Puritans nor their children nor their grandchildren will fight in Europe in World War III to uphold there the tottering "throne" of the Pope of Rome.

In another issue Parker advises Protestants and Jews "to keep arms" in their homes "to protect the Constitution of the United States from its destruction by Roman Catholic scoundrelism." The Smith Act, according to *Liberty Bell,* outlaws the Church of Rome. "The Roman Catholics are a 'clear and present dan- ger' to the United States and to World Peace; the Smith Act should be upheld; Roman Catholics as well as Communists should be outlawed in the United States." One "Fellow Pil- grim," in a letter to Parker published in the same issue, stated: "McCarthy attacks about anybody that isn't Catholic."

Parker has hammered away at another favorite theme of anti- Catholics — that the Pope caused World War II. His particular version of the theory is unique: "Documentary evidence . . . now available to the United States military authorities shows that an Italian, Eugenio Pacelli, as Secretary of State of the Vatican Government of Europe, promoted World War II in an attempt to compel a 'merger' of Stalin's Greek Catholic Church and his personally owned Roman Catholic Church." One issue of *Liberty Bell* ran the headline: "TRY EUGENIO PACELLI, ALIAS POPE OF ROME, BEFORE THE INTERNATIONAL COURT OF JUSTICE IN GENEVA."

Parker charged that Europe had collaborated with two "Roman Catholics" — Hitler and Mussolini — in promoting World War II, and maintained fifty-five ambassadors "to and from the Vatican to agitate war." He warned that the "Vatican Government of Europe" seeks to recast the "whole social and political structure of the United States after the Spanish model of police-state dictatorship." Once the Catholics gain control of America, Parker continued, the Constitution will be scrapped so that the hierachy can "wipe out" all Protestants and Jews.

In the field of anti-Catholicism, the harangues of the rabid bigots — the Harvey Springers and Edward James Smythes and Harrison Parkers — are of course shocking. But they may not be as dangerous as the more subtle anti-Catholicism lurking on the edges of responsible Protestant circles.

Protestants have, with some justification, voiced many complaints against the policies of the Church of Rome. They have been aroused by efforts of the Catholic Church to obtain government support — in whatever form — for her parochial schools. They have been disturbed by the attempts of the hierarchy to censor public entertainment, as in the famous *Miracle* case. They have reacted with alarm to reports of religious persecution in Spain, Italy, Colombia, and other countries where Catholicism is the dominant faith.

But "Pope-baiting" and the circulation of scandalous literature are not a worthy Protestant answer to the challenge of Roman Catholicism. If Protestantism is to merit the confidence of its adherents — and the respect of other Americans as well — the negative emphasis of anti-Catholicism must never be allowed to replace a firm dedication to the tenets of democracy and to the principle of brotherhood that is rooted in the message of Christianity.

THE MINISTRY OF DISRUPTION

8

Saboteurs of Protestant Co-operation

> The Federal Council is a Goliath of power, a wild Absalom
> of rebellion, a loathsome Judas of treachery, a deceiving
> Sapphira of falsehood, a cruel Ahab of covetousness, a bold
> Belshazzar of Irreverence, a merciless Nero of evil, a haughty
> Nebuchadnezzar of pride, and a painted Jezebel of murder.
> . . . I ask you again, will we tolerate such? I say a thousand
> times, NO, and again I say BY THE GRACE OF GOD, THEY SHALL
> BE EXTERMINATED!

So spoke an influential southern evangelist in condemning
the church-unity movement among Protestants. His blast
echoes in violent form the sentiments of a vociferous minority intent upon sabotaging attempts to unite churchmen in their
common faith.

Protestants are separated by wide chasms of doctrine. They
embrace many divergent forms of church government. They
adhere to different historical traditions. But the majority feel
that Protestantism's effectiveness is imperiled by division —
that the churches can exert greater force for good if they act
co-operatively.

Regardless of their religious preferences, Americans have a
casual familiarity with the "church-unity movement," often referred to as the ecumenical movement. In the United States it
arose in the nineteenth century, when Protestants of most of
the major denominations sensed the urgent need for closer co-
operation in attaining common goals. In 1832, the National
Sunday School Convention marked an early instance of wide-
scale co-operation among various churches. This was the fore-
runner of the International Council of Religious Education,

181

founded in 1922 and responsible for a many-sided program that
has reached millions of children and adults.

December 1908 witnessed the establishment of the Federal
Council of the Churches of Christ in America, an association
of twenty-seven denominations, organized "for the prosecution of
work that can be better done in union than in separation." The
Federal Council proved to be a highly successful vehicle for
united Protestant endeavor, in spite of bitter attacks on the enlightened social program of its leadership.

By the middle of the twentieth century, the main stream of
Protestantism again demonstrated its willingness to work together. Eleven large interdenominational organizations joined
with the Federal Council to form a new co-operative agency. November 29, 1950, was a great day in the history of religion:
representatives of twenty-five major Protestant and four Eastern
Orthodox churches officially launched the National Council of
the Churches of Christ in the U. S. A. In a memorable ceremony
in Cleveland, against the backdrop of the banners of the constituent denominations, the twelve agencies pledged their support to
an interchurch enterprise linking 35,000,000 Protestants in
150,000 churches across the country.

Simultaneously, the principal Protestant and Eastern Orthodox
denominations were striving toward closer co-operation on the
international level as well. Beginning with the famous Edinburgh
Conference in 1910, a series of productive meetings led to the
formation of the World Council of Churches in August 1948.
The official representatives of 147 denominations from most of
the great communions of non-Roman Christendom gathered in
the Nieuwe Kerk at Amsterdam, Holland, to establish an official, permanent, universal free fellowship of churches united
by a common acceptance of Jesus Christ as "God and Saviour."
Divisions of nation, class, and race, as well as those of faith and
order, were transcended in the delegates' dedication to a common
religious purpose.

While constructive criticism has been necessary and indeed
welcome, the ecumenical movement has had more than its share
of unfair critics. A few of these represent anti-religious elements
which, while possessing little prestige in this country, persistently
propagandize against all traditional religious faith. Certain in-

flammatory elements of the Roman Catholic press have also deliberately attempted to detract from the gradual emergence of co-operative Protestantism.

Here, however, special consideration will be given to those among Protestant fundamentalists who strongly attack the ecumenical movement. Most adherents of the "old-time religion" dedicate themselves to the constructive aspects of their faith; they are sincere and earnest heirs of an honorable religious tradition. Other fundamentalists — a minority — have been sidetracked into devoting their chief energies to attacking their fellow Protestants.

National Association of Evangelicals — Fair or Unfair?

Since the early 1940's, top fundamentalist leaders have sought to form a single co-operative group. The National Association of Evangelicals, a cluster of thirty denominations with a total membership of more than a million, through its affiliates claims to serve 10,000,000 Protestants. Its theological viewpoint is presented by men like the influential evangelist, Billy Graham, and by groups like the well-known Youth for Christ. While many fundamentalists support the ecumenical movement, as represented in the National Council of Churches and the World Council of Churches, others are critical. They fear that the church-unity movement will completely abandon "old-time religion." A few dread the emergence of a "super-church."

The National Association of Evangelicals was established in 1942 by a coalition of ministers and laymen "to represent all evangelical believers in all denominations and groups." Several important Pentecostal groups are in the Association, among them the Assemblies of God and the International Church of the Four Square Gospel. The latter, founded by the late Aimee Semple McPherson, is now directed by her son in Los Angeles. Other affiliated denominations include the National Association of Free Will Baptists, the Free Will Methodist Church of North America, and the Wesleyan Methodist Church of America. In 1951, however, the 150,000-member Christian Reformed Church withdrew.

In addition to member denominations, the Association includes more than six hundred individual congregations, eight conferences of other churches, and nearly one hundred colleges. It reaches many millions of individuals at home and abroad through its loosely associated, single-purpose commissions on evangelism, social action, missions, and world relief. The Association's religious point of view is carried to the public through frequent radio programs.

To counteract secularism in the public schools and alleged "modernism" in the National Council of Churches, these fundamentalists have set up the National Association of Christian Schools. Comparable to the parochial-school philosophy of the Roman Catholic Church, the Association of Christian Schools disapproves of all teaching "which may speak *about* God but which does not *make Him central in and through Christ.*" Therefore it promotes separate Christian schools "in opposition to secular instruction."

United Evangelical Action, the biweekly organ of the National Association of Evangelicals with a circulation of sixty thousand, is harshly critical of other Protestants. Its editor, James DeForest Murch, has been particularly immoderate in his treatment of the ecumenical movement. On one occasion, for example, he carried a series entitled "Ecclesiastical Octopus," a virulent attack taken from a book of the same name written by Ernest Gordon, contributing editor to the *Sunday School Times.* Murch himself wrote a pamphlet now being promoted by *United Evangelical Action* — "The Growing Super-Church." One of its principal theses is that ecumenical leadership has abandoned religion in order to promote "social revolution."

Leaders of the National Association of Evangelicals generally tend to support ultra-conservative political, economic, and social views — although there are some exceptions. Their lack of the idealism that has characterized the mainstream of Protestantism has been typified in the Association's outlook on world affairs. Its Washington office, for example, has vigorously battled against UNESCO and the Universal Declaration of Human Rights. The editorials of *United Evangelical Action* express similar views in opposition to international co-operation. Recently, for example, in an editorial entitled "International Rot," Murch adopted an extreme viewpoint on philanthropic foundations. "One of the gravest situations ever to confront the

American people," Murch complained, "is the growing human-istic-socialistic internationalism backed by some sixty foundations financed by men like Carnegie, Rockefeller, and Ford. These subversive elements are likely to destroy all we hold dear in Christian America."

The isolationist sentiments of *United Evangelical Action*—akin in many respects to those of the Chicago *Tribune* — do not keep the Evangelicals from making contact with colleagues overseas. Largely through the efforts of J. Elwin Wright, one of the Association's most energetic leaders, a World Evangelical Fellowship was established in 1951. The work of the Fellowship is being administered through the offices of the British Evangelical Alliance in London and the Association's Commission on International Relations in Boston. Dr. Paul S. Rees, president of the Association and pastor of the First Covenant Church in Minneapolis, joined Wright in 1951 on a global journal in the interest of securing evangelical co-operation.

Because of the divisive activity of some of its key figures, the National Association of Evangelicals unfortunately must be mentioned in a study of the apostles of discord. At the same time, it must be made clear that there are among its leaders many outstanding conservatives who do not stoop to the depths of their extremist colleagues. Some of the more moderate leaders include President Paul S. Rees; Rutherford L. Decker of Kansas City, executive secretary of the Association; John W. Bradbury, editor of *The Watchman-Examiner;* Donald Grey Barnhouse, editor of *Eternity;* President Stephen W. Paine of Houghton College; and Harold J. Ockenga of Boston's Park Street Congregational Church.

On September 7, 1941, just prior to the founding of the National Association of Evangelicals, the representatives of two splinter denominations, the Bible Presbyterians and the Bible Protestants, met in New York City to establish the American Council of Christian Churches, dedicated to the battling of alleged "soul-destroying modernism."

From that day until the present this dissident group has fought to gain recognition as the rival of what they picture as giant ecclesiastical machines hiding behind "a breastwork of halos" —

the ecumenical councils. But the American Council's claims to success have been consistently illusory. At the very outset its leaders announced "that most if not all of the denominations not in the Federal Council will in due course become members." They also made "guarded predictions" that the swing of other bodies within the Federal Council to their camp would result in "a revolutionary realignment in American Protestantism."

The creedal basis of the American Council immediately set it apart from the bulk of American Protestantism. Instead of the broad basis of doctrinal unity existing in the National Council — a belief "in Jesus Christ as their divine Lord and Savior" — the new group required an exhaustive testimony "to the glory of God and the historical faith of the Church universal." Among the beliefs deemed necessary to its fellowship were:

> The full truthfulness, inerrancy, and authority of the Bible, which is the Word of God; the holiness and love of the one sovereign God, Father, Son, and Holy Spirit; the true deity and sinless humanity of our Lord Jesus Christ, His virgin birth, His atoning death, "the just for the unjust," His bodily resurrection, His glorious coming again; salvation by grace through faith alone; the oneness in Christ of those He has redeemed with His own precious blood; and the maintenance in the visible church of purity of life and doctrine.

In addition to accepting these dogmas, constituent denominations are not permitted to have any connection with the larger ecumenical movement.

Carl McIntire — Twentieth-Century Reformer?

The principal figure in this insurgent movement is Carl McIntire, president of the International Council of Christian Churches, editor of the weekly *Christian Beacon,* and pastor of the 1,600-member Bible Presbyterian Church in Collingswood, New Jersey. McIntire, Bible in hand, towers above his congregation — when he takes time off from his "missionary" activities to serve his home parish. He has a vivid personality, unusual preaching ability, crusading zeal, and a feeling of a mission to free Protestantism from the shackles of the "modernist" bogey.

In addition to numerous pamphlets on theology and politics, McIntire has written several books, including *Twentieth Century*

Reformation, Modern Tower of Babel, The Rise of the Tyrant, and *Author of Liberty.* He is president of the board of directors of Faith Theological Seminary; a member of the Independent Board of Presbyterian Foreign Missions; a director of Shelton College (New York City), of Highland College (Pasadena, California), and of Harvey Cedars (New Jersey) Bible Presbyterian Conference.

Many of his critics — including some who observe him closely in Collingswood — think that McIntire is a man who enjoys the opportunities for personal power. Some believe that, through the American Council of Christian Churches, he may be trying to avenge himself on the Presbyterian Church in the U. S. A. for having deposed him from its ministry. Others conclude that he envisions himself as another Luther or Calvin, leading the forces of righteousness in his "Twentieth-Century Reformation."

The McIntire family of five lives in a comfortable house in residential Collingswood, five miles across the Delaware River from the City of Brotherly Love. In fairness to McIntire, it should be noted that most of his congregation have stood behind him when he has blasted the ecumenical movement. As one pillar of his parish phrased it: "You're either a Christian or you ain't. You either agree with Rev. McIntire or the Devil. Take your choice."

Carl McIntire was born in Ypsilanti, Michigan, on May 17, 1906. At an early age, he moved to Oklahoma with his rigid Presbyterian parents. After earning a B. A. degree at Park College, Parkville, Missouri, in 1927, McIntire traveled east to enter Princeton Theological Seminary. When Professor J. Gresham Machen, an eminent fundamentalist scholar, withdrew from Princeton in 1929 to found Westminster Seminary at Chestnut Hill, Pennsylvania, McIntire followed; he received his divinity degree there in 1931, the same year he married his southern-born college sweetheart. In the spring of 1950, the Toronto Baptist Seminary, a small ultra-fundamentalist institution connected with the American Council, gave McIntire an honorary degree of Doctor of Divinity — a title he has regularly employed since that time.

After his ordination, he became active in the Machen struggle against the increasingly enlightened views of the Presbyterian

Church in the U. S. A. The position of these extreme fundamentalists gained strength within the denomination. They became more and more punitive in language, finally repudiating
the regular mission board of the church and establishing their
own — the Independent Board of Presbyterian Foreign Missions.

By 1934 the schism had become so threatening to the integrity
of the denomination that the General Assembly felt obliged to
take a firm stand. It overwhelmingly voted to order "that the
Independent Board of Presbyterian Foreign Missions . . . desist
forthwith from exercising any ecclesiastical or administrative
functions" and "that all ministers and laymen affiliated with the
Presbyterian Church in the U. S. A. who are officers, trustees, or
other members of the Independent Board of Presbyterian Foreign Missions . . . sever their connection with this Board." The
refusal to comply would be just cause for deposing the dissidents.

But the Machen group became more defiant than ever. Therefore, in 1936, the denomination brought them to trial before
the Synod. McIntire was charged on six counts:

1. Disapproval, defiance, and acts in contravention of the government
and discipline of the Presbyterian Church in the U. S. A.
2. Not being zealous and faithful in maintaining the peace of the
Church.
3. Contempt and rebellion against his brethren in the Church.
4. Conduct unbecoming a minister of the Gospel.
5. Advocating rebellion against the constituted authorities of the
Church.
6. Violation of his ordination vows.

The tribunal dismissed the third, fourth, and fifth charges, but
found McIntire guilty of the other three.

From the Synod, McIntire brought his case to the General
Assembly. His appeal was one among the many that marked
that particular session as decisive in American Presbyterianism.
The denomination as a whole had grown tired of the assaults
by a handful of the dissidents upon its respected leaders. With
full realization of the seriousness of their action, with doctrinal
lines nearly obliterated, the decision made clear the position of
the overwhelming majority: To preserve the unity of the church,
the rebels would have to go.

Machen thereupon established the Presbyterian Church in America, a sect whose eight thousand members now refer to themselves as Orthodox Presbyterians. McIntire, however, split with his former professor over several petty doctrinal matters, and the Orthodox Presbyterians have been strong critics of McIntire's methods. He subsequently established his own denomination — the Bible Presbyterian Church — and the Faith Theological Seminary (in Elkins Park, Pennsylvania).

The Collingswood preacher has alleged that the issue at stake in the 1936 trial was doctrinal, and that he was disciplined on mere technicalities. But an official church statement commented as follows:

In its final decision, the General Assembly, as the supreme court of the Presbyterian Church in the U.S.A., made it perfectly plain that those persons being disciplined had defamed the character of their fellow Christians, had broken certain of the Ten Commandments, and were instrumental in "causing dissension and strife" in the Church, were engendering "suspicion and illwill" and "seriously injuring the peace of the Church."

Nothing could be further from the truth than to intimate that these persons who were disciplined were guilty of mere technical breaches of ecclesiastical law. These offenses as enumerated in the cases against these men were specifically against the moral law. The Presbyterian Church determined that it must defend its loyal ministers and members who were defamed and its agencies who were being opposed. In bringing the offenders to trial and in inflicting upon them definite censures for their offenses, the Presbyterian Church took the only recourse that it was possible for it to take to exonerate the innocent ministers and lawful agencies upon whom the offenders were heaping unmerited abuse and malicious slander.

Editorializing on the "unfrocking," the *Christian Century* said:

It will be a mistake for the public to assume from the outcome of this long-standing controversy that the Presbyterian Church has become "modernist" in its doctrine. It is true that the origin of the dispute was doctrinal, but it has long passed that stage. The real issue in the minds of the rank and file of the church has been the question of respect for the official decision of the church courts. If these were not respected then obviously there would be no longer a constitutional court. Men of the most conservative doctrinal view joined with those who were liberal in insisting that no group within the church be permitted to defy its official mandates.

Commented the *Presbyterian Banner,* an important denominational periodical:

> In rendering judgment against them, the Assembly was not passing upon their devotion to the word of God, or their loyalty to the faith of the Church. It was not a question of modernism judging fundamentalism. Such a charge is untrue and groundless. If doctrine was involved, it belonged in the ethical sphere of brotherly love and honesty to ordination vows. . . . We have no unkind feelings toward these brethren but hope they will treat one another better than they have treated us. It is to be regretted when such divisions occur, but the church has passed through many of them that have had their little day.

A series of legal battles followed the General Assembly decision, as the ousted pastors sought to take their parish properties with them. At the Collingswood church — which had been firmly fundamentalist for many years before the advent of McIntire — guards took their places in the front pews during the services, a 24-hour watch was maintained, and the West Jersey Presbytery was refused permission to declare the pulpit vacant.

Of the fight McIntire led to secure the property for his followers, he has written in terms that illustrate his sense of the dramatic:

> Thank God, my congregation in Collingswood, the largest missionary church in the Presbytery at that time, with 1275 members, renounced the jurisdiction of the denomination. We fought for our church property and every penny we had in the bank. The congregation — 1200 — walked out of the beautiful Gothic structure which they had themselves built; sang "Saviour, Like A Shepherd, Lead Us," went down to an empty lot, put up a large chautauqua tent . . . took communion in paper cups, built a wooden tabernacle in which we still worship.

Promoting Discord at Home and Abroad

Upon the establishment of the American Council of Christian Churches in 1941, Carl McIntire became its first president, with Harold S. Laird (his predecessor in the Collingswood church, now pastor of the First Independent Church of Wilmington, Delaware) as vice-president. Among the sponsoring committee members were the Rev. Fred Meldau, editor of *Christian Victory;* Ernest Gordon, religious-survey editor of the *Sunday School Times;* Dr. William H. Houghton, president of the Moody Bible Institute in Chicago; J. David Adams, president of the Philadel-

phia School of the Bible; Allan A. McRae, president of Faith
Theological Seminary; and J. Oliver Buswell, Jr., former president of Wheaton College (Illinois), now president of Shelton
College of New York. Some of the original reputable backers of
the American Council have since broken with it.

For several years, a comparative calm hung over the American
Council. Up to 1948, it was primarily concerned with informing
"tens of thousands of Christians all over America of the dark
record and paganizing influence of the Federal Council." By
exaggerating its membership the American Council gained
free radio time over major networks, to proclaim that it would
protect all Christians from "unconstitutional government regi-
mentation."

The Council's most blatant attempts to harass the movement
toward Protestant unity have been made since 1948, when it
adopted a policy of holding its own meetings at the same time
and in the same place as the larger ecumenical gatherings — a
deliberate attempt to create confusion.

Not long before the World Council of Churches held its first
great meeting in Amsterdam in 1948, the McIntire faction announced that it would organize a huge international gathering
in the same city just before the World Council met. McIntire
called it "the most important meeting of any church group in our
lifetime." The American Council framed an "International
Call," mailed to Protestant leaders all over the world. It painted
a lurid picture of the harm the ecumenical movement would do
"in misleading the nations, in opposing the pure gospel, in
closing doors to faithful missions, and in advancing socialism,
and political intrigue with the state."

The *Christian Century* was quick to warn the press to avoid
the trap of confusing the two conferences. This warning in
itself was hailed as a tremendous victory by the American Council. McIntire's *Christian Beacon* boasted:

At last the *Christian Century* has come to life, and for some reason or
other, they have taken the movement not only seriously, but they have
had to come out in vigorous opposition to it. Did it ever dawn upon
the editors of the *Christian Century* that there is perhaps a God in the
heavens to undertake for the splinter bodies which are standing true to
the infallible Bible?

As for what actually happened at the Amsterdam conference of this ministry of schism, Dr. Donald Grey Barnhouse, editor of *Eternity* and a leading fundamentalist, wrote:

In Amsterdam, the main event was the great meeting of the representatives of a vast proportion of organized Christendom. Before this main event there was a side show that finished in fiasco. The American Council of Churches, whose general history has been one of bitterness and negation in the United States, sought to extend its divisive work in Europe. A little group, less than fifty, of whom half were Americans, plus a small group of "observers," met for a few days before the World Council of Churches in order to form the International Council of Churches. So that there might be as large a number as possible, the American Council took several men from various parts of Europe who should not have been at any Christian meetings, men who had been fired from work, one at least on moral grounds. The Americans of course, were ignorant of this; it is so easy for a man to raise a flag of fundamentalism in order to hide deficiencies in other phases of life. . . .

The Council's position was sold out at Amsterdam. There was such a lack of enthusiasm by competent European leaders that the American leaders were forced to announce, grandiloquently in order to cover the defeat, that the actual organization would take place in 1950. One of the wisest comments which the Editor heard of this movement was from an outstanding French Christian. He said, "You in America suffer from the scores of divisions in the Church of Europe which were carried across the Atlantic to be perpetuated there. Now we are getting a reverse lend-lease that we could well do without. The American Council is seeking to sow the divisions of Americans among the Christians of Europe."

Obviously McIntire could not boast of success at Amsterdam. Instead, he devoted most of his efforts to minimizing the success of the founding assembly of the World Council of Churches. In an editorial entitled "When God Rebukes," he declared:

It was to represent 300,000,000 Christians. The Rev. Frederick Reissig was so obsessed with the bigness of the world assembly that there was no room for the *Christian Beacon* press to be represented or to have accreditation. Numbers — bigness — greatness! The leaders seemed intoxicated with it! But in the providence of God, when they came down to the closing days of the assembly, on one vote they had only 107 present, and on another only 155. It was a terrific letdown.

McIntire's greatest targets, however, were what he termed "the carefully watched, coached, and protected" press, as well as the

World Council's resolution condemning extreme laissez-faireism along with communism.

In 1949 occurred what has probably been the most extreme action of the American Council — its attack on the broadcast "One Great Hour of Sharing," a concerted appeal by many Protestant denominations to raise funds for the hungry, sick, and homeless overseas. The American Council made a last-minute attempt to disrupt this widely praised relief appeal in the Lenten season of that year. This ministry of schism charged that the appeal was for "cash to purchase . . . socialistic propaganda."

"Christians in this land," it said, "opposed to socialism and believing in our private enterprise society and the blessings of liberty attendant upon our capitalistic system, are the tools who are unwittingly to finance this one greatest drive ever put on to advance the socialistic world."

The American Council asked radio stations not to broadcast the program; if they did, the McIntire faction demanded equal time to "refute" the appeal. Although the major networks rejected this reckless demand, the *Christian Century* reported that some damage was done. It added:

> The religious, moral and humanitarian callousness of the effort to disrupt co-operation in Christian charity cannot be too strongly condemned. But some good will come of it. The ACCC has shown itself to be a group which will stop at nothing, even at snatching food from the mouths of the hungry, if it thinks it sees a chance to gain time for itself on the radio.

The next aim of the American Council was to sow discord among Christians in the mission fields. For many decades the Protestant churches of America have contributed heavily to the support of evangelism in other lands; strong Protestant movements now exist on every continent. McIntire and his colleagues, eying these mission fields, decided to solicit abroad the support that they had failed to obtain at home. First target of this effort was Latin America.

In 1949, the Inter-American Evangelical Conference — associated with the World Council of Churches — called a meeting in Buenos Aires. The June issue of the *Christian Beacon* thereupon headlined: "GARMAN, SHARP, MCINTIRE TO ATTEND BUENOS AIRES MEETING: WCC LEADERS, MACKAY, NEILL, BOEGNER TO PARTICIPATE." But the American Council, of course, had not been invited to send delegates. Dr. Jorgo Federico Wenzel, executive secretary of the Conference, informed them that only accredited delegates would be admitted. American Council representatives, ignoring the warning, went to Buenos Aires anyway; they saw in the meeting an opportunity for their favorite technique of stirring up incidents in the hope of obtaining free publicity. The conference agreed to ignore the American Council group on the grounds that they had not been invited. The McIntire faction then set up a rival meeting in a public hall, under the auspices of the International Council of Christian Churches, where — to the seventy-four persons present — they repeated their charges against the ecumenical movement.

In the summer of 1951, McIntire's International Council sponsored a Pan-American Evangelical Conference in São Paulo, Brazil. The conference established the Latin American Alliance of Christian Churches to promote further discord in the mission field.

Regardless of the effect his crusade may have upon the success of Protestantism in this section of the world, McIntire is determined to block the efforts of the ecumenical mission activities. Protestant leaders in Latin America, by and large, have carefully avoided the "Twentieth-Century Reformation." One native churchman has queried: "Why should we team up with an outsider who is more interested in promoting division than in furthering the cause of Christ?" Nevertheless, the intrusion of McIntire's International Council opened old wounds between the fundamentalists and other missionary groups in South America. McIntire's visit particularly stirred up the conservative Presbyterians and Baptists, leading to fresh attacks on "modernism" and ecumenicalism.

The "Bangkok affair" of December 1949 provides further evidence of the purposes of the American Council. McIntire and a small group of supporters headed for the Far East with the expressed purpose of opposing "efforts of the World Council of Churches to dominate the Christian churches of southeast Asia." Their particular target was a conference of Asian churches in Bangkok, sponsored by the World Council and by the International Missionary Council — which is affiliated with the World Council. Again McIntire and his friends were refused admittance on the ground that they had come to disrupt the gathering. Again they set up a rival meeting, at which they accused the missionary and ecumenical movements of communism. Of the score who attended this rump conference, several later repudiated it.

Dr. John A. Mackay, president of Princeton Theological Seminary and chairman of the International Missionary Council, issued an acid rejoinder to attacks by the McIntire faction:

This group, while paying lip tribute to the Bible and Jesus Christ, represents an unbiblical Christianity. While being concerned about Communism it carries on work with Communist technique. Wherever they go and in all they say about those whom they love to malign and to traduce, they act without the slightest interest in truth and with terms of a Jesuitical ethic.

At McIntire's "Conference of Christian Churches in Asia," held in Manila in November 1951, the Far Eastern Council was established. Its purpose: to promote discord in that part of the mission field.

Meanwhile, at home, the McIntire movement sought to distract attention from the ceremonies marking the formation of the National Council of Churches in November 1950. As early as 1948, McIntire had stated the American Council line on the proposed organization. "There is little doubt," he wrote, "that the name of the Federal Council has become so unpopular, and it has become such a target in Christian circles across the country that these Federal Council leaders have decided that the time has come to get another name." This he compared to the manner in which communist fronts, once they are exposed, change their names. In McIntire's view, the new National Council would be simply a larger organization which would give its leaders even greater scope to propagate modernism and socialism. "The present liberal leaders," he concluded, "are imbued with the idea that the bigger their organization the more power they are going to have. For some reason or other, they are simply intoxicated with the passion for power which they themselves will exercise."

Shortly after Cleveland was selected as the birthplace for the National Council, it came as no surprise to hear that the American Council would hold its annual conference in Cleveland, too — just a week before the National Council. At its sessions, the American Council attacked the merger of the ecumenical agencies as "another mile-post on the road to a super-church" and "a whistle-stop on the train back to Rome." The event, predicted McIntire, would be a "sad and dark occasion" for American Protestantism.

Evidence of the "validity" of McIntire's prediction was "miraculously" provided. He wrote: "As if displeased with the whole affair, the Almighty God visited Cleveland with the most frightful snowstorm in all the city's history, utterly paralyzing the community for several days."

For McIntire and the American Council, the high point of the National Council convention came when Charles Taft publicly mentioned Carl McIntire "by name." To the dissidents, this represented the beginning of the end for the "apostate" ecumenical movement. "The new council," announced the *Christian Beacon*, "has been placed on the defensive; there has been a public unmasking; and telling blows have been struck, the extent of which we were not aware."

More recent incidents developing out of attempts by Carl McIntire and the American Council of Christian Churches to promote discord and gain publicity are discussed in Chapter 9.

Allies in the Ministry of Schism

Chief objective of the American Council of Christian Churches has been to make itself appear important to its members, dangerous to its foes. After more than ten years, the American Council makes confusing claims as to its size. In May 1948, for example, one newspaper reported that the American Council estimated its membership at 2,000,000. A few months later, it claimed "a total membership of 1,213,000." Still later during the same year, claims were publicized ranging from 1,000,000 through 1,800,000. Recently, the McIntire faction settled for 1,500,000 — a highly exaggerated figure.

The National Association of Evangelicals was the first to accuse the American Council of deliberate distortion. In a letter dated June 5, 1948, Dr. J. Elwin Wright challenged McIntire to prove his figures. He wrote, in part:

It is widely believed, and I share the belief, that your membership figures are highly inflated. You can understand, under these circumstances, that your rigid insistence on a "pure" church falls on deaf ears so far as we are concerned because we feel that the sin of misrepresentation of membership is just as bad as the sin of modernism. If you will submit your records to any disinterested statistical organization on which we may mutually agree, I will pay to any missionary cause you would like the sum of $1000 if you can prove that you have even 20% of the number of members claimed in the *Beacon* of February 19, 1948 — "of approximately 1,213,000 in fifteen national bodies."

McIntire did not take up Wright's offer.

To this day it has been difficult to secure an accurate tabulation of the total membership of the American Council. It has doggedly refused to publish any detailed breakdown of its statistics and nearly all denominations affiliated with the American Council withhold membership data from the *Yearbook of the Churches,* published annually by the National Council of Churches.

Only one American Council affiliate, the General Association of Regular Baptist Churches, has existed long enough to have been included in the most recent governmental census of religious bodies — issued in 1936. Within this denomination, nearly one-third of the individual congregations have kept apart from the American Council — though McIntire literature inaccurately states: "Individual churches approving, nearly 100% members."

Only this one sect — the Regular Baptists — claims any substantial following (130,000), over three-fourths of the total membership of all American Council sects combined (approximately 170,000).

The Old (Evangelical) Catholic Church — described by McIntire as the first "denomination" to join the American Council — appears to be defunct.

The "American Episcopal Church (Evangelical)" was dropped from American Council rolls only after its "Primate Bishop" — "Dr." Denver Scott Swain — was revealed as an ex-convict and a religious racketeer.

The "United Christian Church" is directed by Herbert J. El-liott, "Bishop of the Eastern Territory," from a hardware store in Brooklyn. Its late "Presiding Bishop," Alexander A. Lowande, was involved in a number of suspect activities. (See the Notes for a discussion of these and other activities by affiliates of the American Council.) This "denomination" is not to be con-fused with a reputable sect of the same name in Pennsylvania.

Among former affiliates of the American Council that have withdrawn are the Independent Fundamental Churches of Amer-ica, the Evangelical Methodist Church, and the Iowa Eldership of the Churches of God in North America.

Two affiliates are insignificant regional bodies — the Tioga River Christian Conference and the Union of Regular Baptist Churches of Ontario and Quebec. Some observers think that this latter group may desert the American Council — leaving behind a tiny splinter segment, the Conservative Baptist Associa-tion of Canada (1,500 members).

Four affiliated denominations are ones that refused to join the Methodist merger of 1939. These are the Associated Gospel Churches, the Bible Protestant Church, the Southern Methodist Church, and the Methodist Protestant Church (which has a doubtful legal status). The largest of these splinter groups has less than 10,000 constituents.

Two more, the Conference of Fundamental Churches and the Fundamental Conference of America, are denominations in name only.

The Bible Presbyterian Church, McIntire's own sect, has a membership of less than 8,000.

Recent statements by various American Council leaders place the number of constituent denominations between fourteen and eighteen. A careful examination reveals that the unsteady coali-tion at present includes twelve sects — perhaps fewer — none of which can be considered important in the total picture of Protestantism. But these denominations come and go with such fluidity that an exact listing is impossible.

Key Figures in the American Council

Carl McIntire has secured the co-operation of malcontents from various parts of the country for his "Twentieth-Century

Reformation." A key figure in the movement is Harvey Springer — the "cowboy evangelist" whose anti-Catholic activities were described in the preceding chapter. Springer is not only executive officer of the International Council of Christian Churches, but also president of the World Baptist Fellowship, a splinter coalition organized around the late J. Frank Norris, Texan supporter of the McIntire faction (see Chapter 14). Springer is noted for his previous alliance with Gerald L. K. Smith, and for his present alliance with Gerald Winrod. Springer, for instance, is a director of Winrod's Puerto Rican seminary, which McIntire visited in 1949.

The "cowboy evangelist" claims to preside over the largest Baptist church in Colorado, and publishes a weekly newspaper, *Western Voice,* "From Out of the Rockies." He is one of the most popular of extreme fundamentalists, and annually brings together leading evangelists and pastors for his summer Bible-school sessions.

After early years of herding cattle, Springer drifted west to Denver from his home in Oklahoma. He became a book salesman and insurance agent. But, according to Winrod, "a change took place in this cowboy's life. He embraced Jesus Christ as his Saviour, climbed down from his saddle and went East to school." He graduated from an anonymous "practical Bible-training school," and his success as a pulpit buffoon was immediate. Today his large tabernacle congregation consists for the most part of families from the cattle country around Englewood. Every Sunday morning they gather in their simple wooden church to enjoy their minister's energetic condemnation of the Pope, "modernists," and government bureaucrats — Satan's trinity.

Springer exploits the stereotype of a lanky, easy-going, drawling cow-puncher, complete with a ten-gallon Stetson and a fringed vest. Once he finds his way into the heart of his sermon, he works himself into a frenzy. The tall, handsome minister knows how to dramatize his role as a champion of the "old-time religion." He has even cleared the distance between the pulpit and the front row of seats in one leap.

Springer's chief target for many years was "Jewish intrigue." As early as 1940, he stepped into the center of Winrod's ministry of hate — a position he still holds. In that year, 2,400 people crowded into his church to attend one of Winrod's Prayer and Prophecy Conferences, to hear Springer's "analysis of the Jewish question." According to *The Defender Magazine:* "Springer warned against allowing Judaism to infiltrate church circles. He showed that Modernism is nothing in the world but a restatement of Judaism."

In 1940 also, he published his booklet *Termites* — an assault upon the Federal Council of Churches which concluded that the church-unity organization was "infested with . . . vicious termites which are robbing it of spiritual power, reducing it, figuratively speaking, to ashes." Both Judaism and the Federal Council, in his opinion, had the same central belief, that the mother of Jesus "was a woman with a questionable character. . . . Modernism and Judaism, they are the one and the same!"

The cowboy evangelist rode the Christian Nationalist bandwagon of racist Gerald L. K. Smith from the spring of 1943 until soon after the war. "Dr. Smith," he wrote, "is one of the most brilliant minds in America, a sincere Christian, and a loyal patriot."

At the same time that Springer was co-operating with Smith, he teamed up with McIntire to come to the defense of J. Harold Smith, influential southern evangelist who glories in sensationalism. When the latter was banned from Station KNOX in Knoxville, Tennessee, for broadcasts against the public interest, the two extremists rushed to his aid. McIntire saw in the situation a chance to vent his scorn for the ecumenical movement. He expressed the belief that the action against J. Harold Smith was "mainly the result of Federal Council influence, and its program to get Gospel preachers thrown off the air."

In early 1948, Springer began holding his annual "revivals" in McIntire's church, where he distributed his booklet *Termites.* At the founding convention of the International Council of Christian Churches in August 1948, he was elected to the executive committee and appointed head of the Commission on Information and Publicity. Since then he has made "missionary" jaunts to Latin America and elsewhere in the interests of the divisive movement.

The presidents of the American Council have had careers

involving sensational episodes similar to those in the lives of Springer and McIntire. Robert T. Ketcham of Waterloo, Iowa, who held the office from 1944 to 1947, took twenty-two churches out of the Northern Baptist Convention in 1932, to form the nucleus of the General Association of Regular Baptist Churches. W. O. H. Garman of Wilkinsburg, Pennsylvania, president from 1947 to 1950, was deposed as a minister of the United Presbyterian Church in 1939. It was charged that he "slanderously defamed those responsible for the doctrinal training of the ministry," "contemptuously repudiated for himself the ecclesiastical authority, and control of the United Presbyterian Church," and "violated his ordination vows." In 1945 Garman was characterized by a high government official as the only religious representative in America who consistently obstructed the wartime efforts of the Office of Defense Transportation.

The current president of the American Council of Christian Churches, W. W. Breckbill of Altoona, Pennsylvania, was repudiated by the Evangelical Methodist Church — a sect he had helped to found in 1946 — when it voted in 1952 to secede from the separatist group and join the National Association of Evangelicals. Breckbill dramatically led a fraction of the denomination out of the meeting and promised to organize an "Evangelical Congregational Methodist Bible-Believing Church." Soon after this incident, the American Council re-elected him to its highest office.

The vice-president of the International Council of Churches, T. T. Shields, underwent a similar experience in 1949. He was, in effect, renounced by the Union of Regular Baptists of Ontario and Quebec, over which he had earlier presided. This was only one of a long series of battles he had waged against those who learned to resent his domination (see also Chapters 7 and 14). His record speaks for itself:

1921: Shields' congregation splits; dissenters start new church.
1927: Baptist Convention splits; Union of Regular Baptists organized by Shields' insurgents.
1929: University students run Board President Shields off the campus; university forced to close.
1930: Shields' congregation splits again; another rival church is started.

202 Apostles of Discord

1931: Union of Regular Baptists splits; rebels expelled by Shields; they establish a new group.

1948: Shields' seminary splits when dean is fired; ousted dean leaves with most of students and staff to launch a new school.

1949: Union of Regular Baptists splits again; Shields is ousted as president while he is in Asia with McIntire; upon his return he forms another splinter group.

This entire "Twentieth Century Reformation" is, therefore, only a tiny splinter movement, bringing together a curious assortment of "leaders" and a handful of "denominations" — some legitimate, others fraudulent. It can do harm only in so far as the press and individual church members accept its pretensions at face value.

The first step in combatting the divisive influence of the McIntire faction is to make public the facts concerning its personnel, aims, and methods. This chapter has presented the basic data on the American Council; the next chapter will deal with several other aspects of its activities and those of its brothers-in-disruption.

In these times of confusion, this ministry of schism is exploiting every opportunity to call attention to itself. Controversy, smear, divisiveness, sensationalism — these characterize the American Council in its drive to turn Protestant against Protestant in order to build up its own power.

To ecumenically-minded churchmen, the American Council of Christian Churches presents a challenge to exhibit more enthusiasm for bringing Christians together than these saboteurs demonstrate for driving them apart.

9

"Modernism" — and the "Battle of the Bible"

On a day in December 1952, the Rev. Martin Luther Hux, pastor of the Temple Baptist Church of Rocky Mount, North Carolina, gathered his congregation together to witness a twentieth-century book-burning. He tore a page from the "new" Bible, set it afire, and hurled the rest into an ashcan. He denounced the handsome maroon-and-gold-bound Bible that had sold 1,600,000 copies in the eight weeks after publication. "A deliberate attack on our historic faith," he cried. "A scheme of the modernists to make the Lord Jesus Christ the son of a bad woman!"

One North Carolina newspaper ranked the burning with gold-fish-swallowing and flagpole-sitting. Another observed wryly that Hux seemed interested in being photographed. A third commented: "Brother Hux, to put it mildly, is in the religious furore business." When the president of the North Carolina Baptist Convention said that it was "inconceivable" that anyone should burn part of the Bible, Hux protested bitterly that he had mutilated not the "Word of God," but "a fraud that has been palmed off on the people of God." Letters had come to him from as far away as Canada and California, he claimed, "telling me to go to it and Godspeed."

"It shouldn't be necessary in these times to recall the ignoble heritage of book-burning in Germany," the Greensboro *Daily News* commented, "or the inquisitorial tortures of the Middle Ages or the parade of bloodpaths across the world which preceded establishment of free speech and the right to differ."

Many fundamentalist journals that disapproved of the "new" Bible expressed concern. A warning came from *The Christian Standard*, organ of ultra-conservative members of the Disciples of Christ: "Book burning is for the middle ages; and if widely indulged in will lead back to the middle ages. . . . For, if I burn your book today, what is to prevent your burning my book tomorrow? . . . The logic of burning books leads to burning churches, and then to burning preachers."

The North Carolina book-burning was only one of several in various parts of the country. In some communities, ordinances were passed to prohibit the burning of the Bible. The city council of Crestview, Florida, for example, prescribed a $500 fine or ninety days in jail for offenders.

Shortly after the Rocky Mount incident, Carl McIntire, president of the International Council of Churches (see Chapter 8), directed a "Back to the Bible Rally" in Denver, timed to coincide with the opening of the National Council of Churches' four-day biennial congress in the same city. To the chagrin of some members of his audience, the American Council chieftain announced that he wouldn't burn a Bible, but added: "I'm kind of glad that old boy down in North Carolina did." Draping the front wall of the hall was a huge banner which read: "Crusading for an Uncorrupted Bible." Other signs proclaimed: "King James Did It Better," "Modernism's Bible," "No Official Protestant Bible," "Shall We Deny Prophecy?" and "Words Added to the Bible Not God's."

McIntire branded the sale of the "new" Bible as the "biggest, slickest promotion ever put over on the American people." The enthusiastic crowd chorused "Amen" thirty-four times during his speech, but varied the pattern with a sharp "No" to the question whether it would accept the "new" Bible. "An unholy book," McIntire shouted, "the work of Satan and his agents!" He found "communism in church circles . . . at the bottom of this."

The publication of the Revised Standard Version of the Bible ushered in the best-organized attempt in recent years to discredit the church-unity movement. A committee of distinguished scholars, who had labored over the ancient text for many years, finally produced the most accurate and the most lucid version of Christian scripture to date. Its publication was sponsored by the National Council of Churches; Protestants across the country marked its appearance with enthusiastic celebrations.

But zealous fundamentalists — many of whom eagerly seek opportunities for combat with less belligerent churchmen — delighted in condemning the "new" Bible. Well typified by Carl McIntire and his American Council, these self-styled champions of "inerrant Scripture" seized in particular upon the substitution of the term *young woman* for *virgin* in Isaiah 7: 14, a verse familiar in fundamentalist circles as an alleged prophecy of the virgin birth of Jesus. "To break the force of the predictive nature of this passage in Isaiah . . . in such a way is inexcusable," McIntire charged, "and we do not believe the true church will accept such handling of God's infallible Word."

An unofficial reply was issued by Dr. Luther A. Weigle, dean emeritus of the Yale Divinity School and chairman of the revision committee. *"Young woman* was used simply because that's what the Hebrew means. You can take it for granted that whatever is printed there is what the original language said. We can't be influenced by what people like or don't like in the way the words affect their theology." A footnote for *young woman* — "Or, *virgin"* — was included, Dean Weigle continued, "to show that this had been the traditional translation of the Hebrew. In contrast to the correction in Isaiah, *virgin* was retained in the New Testament prophecy (Matthew 1: 23) because the original Greek could be translated accurately only in that manner."

McIntire, however, was not satisfied with Weigle's explanation. The Collingswood preacher was concerned primarily with gaining publicity for his own position and with discrediting the ecumenical movement. He immediately voiced other objections to the new version, its translators, and its National Council sponsorship.

In the first place, McIntire described the new version as part of a careful plot designed to break the "widespread" influence of his own "separatist" cause — i.e., the American Council's plea that fundamentalists avoid all association with "modernists." "It is the separatist emphasis that is the greatest possible threat to the rising ecumenical movement and blocks the fulfillment of its one-world church dream," McIntire boasted. He contended that II Corinthians 6: 14, "which has been at the very heart of the separationist movement of the Twentieth Century Reformation movement, has also been seriously tampered with." The King James Version, which most Protestants have used since its appearance in 1611, reads: "Be ye not unequally yoked together with unbelievers"; this text has been misinterpreted by McIntire as a basis for his own action. The Revised Version correctly applies the verse to the marriage relationship — "Do not be mismated with unbelievers" — instead of to religious separatism. Other key "separatist" passages include II Timothy 3:15, Ephesians 5: 6-11, II John 9-11, and Jude 3.

McIntire also condemned the committee for including among its members one Jewish scholar, Harry M. Orlinsky of the Jewish Institute of Religion in New York City: "There can be little doubt that in the inclusion of this man of unitarian belief there is definitely reflected the toning down of the Old Testament in regard to Messianic passages and the teaching of the deity of Jesus Christ."

The other members of the committee McIntire described as "modernist liberal scholars." "There is not a man on the list," he said, "who would be considered a fundamentalist or evangelical in the historic sense of the word." He expressed displeasure over the alleged "red" affiliations of two members of the committee, Dean Weigle and Professor Walter Russell Bowie of Virginia Theological Seminary. He also complained that seven of the translators were from Union Theological Seminary in New York or Yale Divinity School — pictured in the *Christian Beacon* as "hotbeds" of modernism and socialism.

Another criticism constitutes a direct attack upon the National Council of Churches — undoubtedly the real target of McIntire's campaign. The National Council he accused of "making merchandise of the Scriptures for their own pecuniary profit." McIntire warned his followers: "Anyone who desires to assist and aid the National Council of Churches financially may do so by purchasing their Bible. Those who do not approve of the National Council, its modernism, its inclusivism, and socialism, and do not desire to contribute to it financially should not purchase a copy of their Bible or encourage the sale or promotion of it." Ecumenical leaders were maligned as having "an ax to grind and a financial profit and religious prestige in the promotion of the book."

McIntire saw the publication of the revised translation as a great opportunity to rally support around his own banner. He made a strong effort to gather fundamentalist support from all parts of the nation to combat this "planned, deliberate effort on the part of the modernist leadership in the churches of this country to remove the Bible from the hands of the Lord's people and give them another Bible." Implying a groundswell revolt, banner headlines in the *Christian Beacon* for weeks read like this:

OPPOSITION TO NEW BIBLE ARISES; ADVERTISEMENTS PLACED IN PAPERS; REMOVAL OF VIRGIN BIRTH FROM OLD TESTAMENT BY DROPPING "VIRGIN" IN ISAIAH 7:14 CENTER OF PROTESTS; BIBLES RETURNED; CHURCHES STIRRED

The editor suggested nine specific steps against the new translation — steps which show how the American Council seeks publicity by exploiting a variety of issues:

1. By word of mouth tell neighbors and friends of what has happened, particularly with Isaiah 7: 14, the virgin birth.
2. Circulate leaflets and pamphlets giving evidence.
3. Ask Sunday school teachers to call it to the attention of their classes.
4. Ask pastors to speak against it to their people.
5. Write letters in the "Voice of the People" columns in the newspapers such as are reported in this issue of the *Beacon*. Any attempts to answer will reveal the weakness of the other side.
6. Whenever favorable mention is made of the new Bible in the press or elsewhere, immediately offer additional information.
7. Place information in the hands of Bible-believing radio broadcasters and request them to call it to the attention of their listeners.
8. God's people who have bought the Bible and found out that they have secured something that they did not want should take back the Bible. Return the Bible and request the money back. The claim on the flap of the Bible justifies this. The publishers claim that no doctrine or fundamental concept has been altered. The changing of the text proves this not to be true.
9. Use this occasion to explain further the nature of the National Council of the Churches of Christ in the U. S. A., its modernistic leadership, its socialistic program of the "kingdom of God," its radical influence

in our national political life, and the maintenance of the NCC's lobby in Washington, D. C.

Other newspapers serving the constituency of the American Council took up the cry against the Revised Standard Version and pursued McIntire's basic arguments. The *Baptist Bible Tribune* of Springfield, Missouri, organ of the Baptist Bible Fellowship — a splinter of a splinter — called the revised New Testament "a very subtle attack upon the deity of Christ." *Militant Truth,* an anti-Negro, anti-labor newspaper of Atlanta, Georgia, featured a McIntire diatribe under the heading: "Christians Should NOT Accept the New Bible!" The *Evangelist and Bible Teacher* of Dallas, Texas, characterized the new translation as "such a 'monster' that the Bible believers are against it, and the modernists, the liberals, the pinkos, the 'one-worlders,' the National Council and the World Council are for it." Harvey Springer's *Western Voice,* an American Council favorite, carried many stories, one entitled: "Anti-Christian Jews Hail National Council-Revised Version."

Vigorous support for McIntire's position came from other leaders in the ministry of hate. Their sentiments were well represented in the remarks of Gerald Winrod, Wichita's bigot-evangelist (discussed in Chapter 3), who warned his quarter-million readers:

A false and treacherous "Bible" is being palmed off on the religious people of the United States by a shrewd advertising campaign, as part of a master plan to denature and devitalize our historical and evangelical Christian Faith. The old Federal Council of Churches, operating under a new name, is responsible for this unprecedented deception. Behold the glove of Esau covering the hand of Jacob!

Winrod concluded by saying that the Jews were linked to this gigantic plot. "Consistency demands that portions of the new 'Bible' shall be regarded as Talmudic, rather than Christian," he claimed. Like McIntire, Winrod suggested that the alleged attack upon the deity of Christ resulted partly from the fact that a Jew had been assigned to work on the Old Testament.

Winrod has been a firm friend of the McIntire movement. His *Defender Magazine* finds that the American Council "loyally represents the real Protestant viewpoint and attitude" and "is causing an awakening among loyal Americans who are devoted to truth and basic fundamentals." McIntire, in turn, has aided Winrod's missionary endeavors. A leading American Council spokesman of the South, Henry Grube of Mobile, Alabama, used the columns of *The Defender Magazine* to rant bitterly against "a left-wing oligarchy" which "printed a private interpretation of the Scriptures, which denies cardinal truths of the Christian Faith."

Other boosters of the American Council enthusiastically took up the arguments. Gerald L. K. Smith, who has said that McIntire "is to be congratulated on his crusading activities," helped to distribute his widely circulated, 24-page pamphlet, *The New Bible: Why Christians Should Not Accept It*. In a letter to his followers on February 7, 1953, Smith promised to send contributors "a copy of Dr. McIntire's sensational exposure of the new apostate Bible, a scheme to change the meaning of the Scriptures, supervised by modernists, Communists and Jews."

To many, of course, the American Council attack upon the new translation was completely unjustified. Typical of much comment was this paragraph from a letter sent to McIntire by a Methodist clergyman in Pennsylvania:

For years the *"Christian" Beacon* has been pouring out untrue and slanderous accusations upon all kinds of Christian leaders from Stanley Jones to Billy Graham. I have shuddered to think that men should even think, let alone print, such vile untruths in the name of Jesus Christ. This latest attack on the Revised Standard Version of the Bible, however, tops all. . . . I realize that the attack on the RSV of the Bible is really an attack on the National Council of Churches, which you hate (I John 4: 20,21). If the King James Version of the Bible were sponsored by the National Council of Churches, you would oppose it. Of that I have not the slightest doubt.

The McIntire faction was not alone in objecting to the new translation and great pressure has been applied upon those who have supported the Revised Standard Version.

The National Association of Evangelicals, for example, issued a statement on December 16, 1952 — pending a later detailed evaluation — that protested the manner in which the new version was promoted, and certain minor changes which the translators had adopted. *United Evangelical Action,* the Association's official organ, carried the case much further. Editor James DeForest Murch singled out the publication of the Revised Standard Version to prove his favorite thesis that the National Council is a monstrous "super-church." He envisioned a conspiracy of gigantic proportions in which the new translation was being exploited (1) to establish the ecumenical movement as the supreme authority over and above scripture, (2) to propagate liberal theological viewpoints, (3) to finance operations of the ecumenical movement, (4) to coerce non-members into joining its ranks, and (5) to increase the prestige of the National Council. But Murch predicted: "The ecclesiastical endorsement of a Super-Church will never make, nor can it break, the Word of God."

Meanwhile, *United Evangelical Action* and other fundamentalist periodicals carried extensive critiques of the new translation. While most disapproved, a few hearty fundamentalist scholars withstood the pressure from their more dogmatic colleagues and spoke their minds on the matter. Several such as Professor J. Harold Greenlee of Asbury Theological Seminary, found the new translation acceptable. Said Greenlee:

The careful student of the Scriptures will not rely completely upon one version of the Bible, and he will seek to recognize the strength and weaknesses of the versions he uses. . . . In this writer's opinion, the Revised Standard New Testament is a good version, translating well, on the whole, the Greek text of the New Testament. It will certainly be easier for the uninstructed to understand than the King James. The RSV may safely be read "for teaching, for reproof, for correction and for training in righteousness, that the man of God may be complete, equipped for every good work." (II Tim. 3:16-17, RSV)

While tending to favor the King James Version, John W. Bradbury, fundamentalist editor of the national Baptist weekly, *The Watchman-Examiner,* stated:

Whatever the critics have to say about the RSV, it is still the Bible. There is not one Christian doctrine corrupted or even affected by the translation. With all its divergences in expression from that of the Authorized [King James] Version, it has not changed any of that great body of Christian truth which theologians and expositors have derived from the Bible. It remains the Bible.

Bradbury expressed the hope that the "heat which some have

engendered" regarding the Revised Standard Version would soon be forgotten. "It certainly does not encourage unbelievers and sinners to turn to the Bible for light and salvation," Bradbury concluded, "when they see Christians fighting each other over matters involving the sincerity of translators and the value of a translation."

Other fundamentalists, too, voiced concern over the general tenor of the controversy. "From where we sit, at least, it appears that more heat than light has been generated," said *The Fundamentalist,* a weekly founded by the late J. Frank Norris, explosive Texas preacher.

Other observers complained that the onslaughts on the new translation usually appeared simply to be vehicles for divisive attacks on the ecumenical movement.

"Old-Time Religion" vs. "Modernism"

This "Battle of the Bible" demonstrates that the full-time job of fringe fundamentalists, especially those in the American Council, is to undermine the broad Protestant movement which is advancing toward interdenominational co-operation. "The dream of the apostates is that the little schisms and finally the 'great schism' will be healed," McIntire has charged. "The great ecumenical mission is to heal these schisms, but God calls it 'Mystery, Babylon the Great, the Mother of Harlots and Abominations of the Earth.'"

This reference to the last book of the New Testament (Revelation 17: 5) traditionally has been reserved by fundamentalists for denunciations of the Roman Catholic Church; but these "separatists" apply it to the World Council of Churches instead.

Startling examples of this name-calling technique appear from time to time in McIntire's weekly *Christian Beacon.* A front-page article carried the following diatribe by J. Harold Smith, colorful, influential southern preacher and close ally of the American Council:

You cannot destroy the pollution of leprosy by clothing its victims in purple and fine linen. It is impossible to drown the stench of the Federal Council under the flood-tides of philosophical perfume sprayed on by certain preachers. The Federal Council is not a pen-knife, it is a guillotine to behead every "faithful preacher." It is a demoniac vulture sitting upon the pinnacles of our churches waiting to devour their carcasses. The Federal Council is an internal cancer, gnawing at Divinity's vitals.

There is an even more frantic tone to other charges by the southern evangelist:

The Federal Council of Churches of the Anti-Christ would make prostitutes out of your daughters and libertines of your sons. This is the dirty, hellish, gang of sex-mad devils that some of the Knoxville preachers are falling over themselves to defend. Leave this atheistic, communistic, Bible-ridiculing, blood-despising, name-calling, sex-manacled gang of green-eyed monsters and hell-bound devils before God's judgment is poured out on them.

Aside from these harangues, the most important accusation against the ecumenical movement is that it is "modernist." By systematically picking apart the thought of certain important figures in the church, often misinterpreting or quoting them out of context, the American Council tries to prove that they deny the historic faith. It accuses them of theological liberalism, of rejecting basic doctrines, such as the deity of Christ, the Trinity, and the authority of the Bible.

Favorite targets of American fundamentalists include Methodism's Bishop G. Bromley Oxnam; President John A. Mackay of Princeton Theological Seminary; E. Stanley Jones, missionary evangelist; Henry Smith Leiper, former American secretary of the World Council of Churches; Professor Reinhold Niebuhr of Union Theological Seminary; Dr. Ralph W. Sockman of Christ Church (Methodist) in New York City; and many more. The pastor emeritus of famous Riverside Church in New York, Dr. Harry Emerson Fosdick, has been perhaps the target of the most bitter attacks; he has even been dubbed "modernism's Moses."

To most Protestants the orthodox nature of the ecumenical movement has been demonstrated time and again. The Affirmation of Unity of the famous Edinburgh conference of 1910 has served as a basis for subsequent theological pronouncements. It read:

We are one in faith in our Lord Jesus Christ, the incarnate Word of God. We are one in allegiance to Him as Head of the Church, and as

King of kings and Lord of lords. We are one in acknowledging that this allegiance takes precedence of any other allegiance that may make claims upon us.

This unity does not consist in the agreement of our minds or the consent of our wills. It is founded in Jesus Christ Himself, Who lived, died and rose again to bring us to the Father, and Who through the Holy Spirit dwells in His Church. We are one because we are all the objects of the love and grace of God, and called by Him to witness in all the world to His glorious gospel.

Every member denomination of the World Council must "accept our Lord Jesus Christ as God and Saviour." The Preamble to the Constitution of the National Council of Churches reads in part: "In the providence of God, the time has come when it seems fitting more fully to manifest the essential oneness of the Christian churches of the United States of America in Jesus Christ as their Divine Lord and Saviour." Only communions which accept this basis for church co-operation are admitted to membership. The Council itself imposes no other requirements because it believes that each denomination should have the sole authority over its members. To assume such authority would be inconsistent with its nature as a "co-operative agency."

In fact, with the formation of the National Council, doctrinal lines appear to have been, not loosened, but tightened. To the disappointment of those Protestants who believe that the ecumenical movement should serve as a genuinely free fellowship of all Protestant churches, the ban against Unitarians and Universalists has been enforced with great rigidity. Thus, the United Church Women — one of the twelve agencies that had merged to establish the National Council — in 1951 took steps to oust all Unitarians and Universalists from its national boards, noting that "these persons are from denominations which are not thought to be in agreement with the preamble of the constitution."

Theology and the "Social Gospel"

In spite of all this, it is no secret that there are important theological divisions among Protestants in the ecumenical movement. During the first twenty-five years of the twentieth century many leading Protestant thinkers — theological conservatives and liberals alike — waged a dramatic battle to extend the horizons of Protestant thought. A broader Protestantism emerged, and fundamentalists have since been seeking ways to regain ground against "modernist" ascendancy. These conflicts, basic and bitter though they may be, often have not affected the vast majority of Protestant churchmen, who are more interested in the practical value of religious faith and in the local churches than in the learned debates that engage the theologians.

Two opposing schools of thought have battled for supremacy within the major denominations. Doctrinaire theological liberals (articulate and influential, though never numerous) contended that the "old-time religion" was intellectually unbelievable, psychologically catastrophic, and ethically reprehensible because it deflected the moral energies of many away from the concrete problems of the world. They sought to give science a more important role in determining religious truth. Fundamentalists, on the other hand, rested their case upon a literal interpretation of the Bible — in the belief that the Bible is the infallible Word of God, the only absolute rule for faith and morals. In between liberals and fundamentalists stood the majority of Protestants — moderates who rejected the tendencies of both extremes.

Many fundamentalists voiced particular disapproval of the "social gospel," often identified with economic as well as theological liberalism. One fundamentalist summed up his attitude toward modern church interest in social action in these terms:

> We are sent to preach Salvation, not Society; Evangelism, not Economics; Redemption, not Reform; Conversion, not Culture; Pardon, not Progress; a New Birth, not a New Social Order; Regeneration, not Revolution; Revival, not Renovation; Resurrection, not Resuscitation; a New Creation, not a New Organization; the Gospel, not Democracy; Christ, not Civilization; to be Ambassadors, not Diplomats.

The tragic world-wide depression of the 1930's, the later international conflict, and the post-war "age of anxiety" brought disillusionment to many liberals. Some of them sought a more "realistic," and less optimistic, view of the nature of man and of the universe — one that might explain the strength of disaster and evil in the world without reverting to the Biblical literalism from whose bonds they felt emancipated. There arose the new conservatism popularly known as "neo-orthodoxy" — more properly called "neo-Reformation theology" or the "theology of crisis" — with its roots in the Christian existentialist philosophy of Europe. It has placed marked emphasis upon the Lordship of Christ, the authority of Holy Scripture, the fallen state of man, justification by faith, and other traditional Protestant doctrines.

The dispute over the "social gospel" also divides the leading European exponent of neo-orthodoxy, Swiss Theologian Karl Barth, from the American leader, Reinhold Niebuhr, professor of Christian ethics at Union Theological Seminary in New York City. According to Niebuhr, who retains much of the spirit of the "social gospel," Barth preaches a dangerous doctrine. The American charges that Barth offers "a too simple and premature escape from the trials . . . duties and tragic choices which are the condition of our common humanity." The European leader places greater emphasis on the Bible and contends that Anglo-Saxon theologians in Britain and America "theologize on their own account . . . without asking on what Biblical grounds one put forward this or that professedly 'Christian' view."

Although liberalism, fundamentalism, and neo-orthodoxy are all represented in the church-unity movement, neo-orthodoxy seems to be emerging in the dominant position. This school of thought has become so influential, in fact, that the major conflict in the World Council today is between the "Anglo-Saxon" and the "continental" interpretations of the Christian faith. The latter — led by the Barthians — has shown signs of greater power in recent international conferences, and in both liberal and neo-orthodox circles in America there are considerable misgivings over the Barthian neglect of the Church's social mission.

While fundamentalists vigorously reject neo-orthodoxy as a "new modernism," they are divided as to their expectations for the future. *United Evangelical Action* finds recent ecumenical pronouncements evidence of a "swing to the Biblical eschatology and the Biblical hope." As a result, the National Association of Evangelicals took a sympathetic attitude toward the 1952 World Council conference on "Faith and Order" at Lund, Sweden. McIntire, on the other hand, snapped: "It was a conference from beginning to end which was in the hands of the liberals to promote the cause of an apostate Christianity. . . . It is the spirit and power of Babylon, and we want none of it."

McIntire shows little understanding of the intricacies of thought in neo-orthodoxy, but he is certain that this "new modernism" is bad — very bad. American Council scholars — of whom there are very few — attempt to buttress this point of view. Francis A. Schaeffer, described by McIntire as a "brilliant and consecrated young man" trained at Faith Theological Seminary, declares that the neo-orthodox "have evolved the cleverest of counterfeits of true Christianity, yet actually they are farther from us than the Roman Catholic Church, and they are even farther from us than the Old Modernists." Schaeffer — who has been director of Children for Christ, Inc., secretary of the International Council of Christian Churches and of the Foreign Relations Department of the American Council — charges the neo-orthodox with "mental gymnastics" and "black magic in logic." "Contradictions and change," he says, "are accepted with complacency, and paradoxes with joy."

With the charge of "modernism," the American Council attempts to discredit the social views of ecumenical leaders. Three related accusations are (a) that the ecumenical movement is pacifistic; (b) that it works for interracial harmony; and (c) that it is pro-Catholic. We shall discuss these three charges in detail.

The Charge of Pacifism

McIntire contends that the ecumenical movement is pacifist, that "radical pacifism stems logically and naturally from the denials of faith and the departure . . . from the teachings of the Bible." Two member denominations of the National Council — the Society of Friends and the Church of the Brethren — historically have taken the pacifist position, but the Council as a whole, while respecting their position, has neither endorsed pacifism on the one hand, nor condemned pacifists on the other. In 1948, the World Council of Churches recognized that the Christian tradition had produced several conflicting views on the question of participation in warfare. All agreed, however, that war is contrary to the will of God, and the churches were asked to avoid the theory that war is inevitable: "War, being a consequence of the disregard of God, is not inevitable if man will turn to Him in repentance and obey His law. There is, then, no irresistible tide that is carrying man to destruction. Nothing is impossible with God."

McIntire and the American Council reject this view. They appear to believe that any attempt to rid the world of war is both futile and contrary to the Christian faith. McIntire has written: "We live in a world of power. Force rules. It always has, since the day that sin entered it, and it will continue to do so until the day when the Lord Jesus Christ himself returns. . . . We should frankly concede that the vision of universal world peace is impossible of fulfillment with man's heart so wicked and sinful."

The American Council, in its views on international co-operation and good-will, displays a strong nationalistic bent. It has shown little concern for understanding among nations. In 1948, for example, the annual convention of the Council appeared to call upon the United States government to initiate warfare through the immediate use of the atomic bomb. In 1951, the American Council resolved that should the American people believe that Russia is preparing to wage war, America has "a moral responsibility . . . to strike first."

When pressed, McIntire concedes that the ecumenical movement has really left churches and individuals free to decide their own attitude toward war. But this very silence he argues "is sufficient to condemn the Council before every true American. It has not endeavored to persuade the young people of the country that they should defend their country, and that they should beware of the spurious teaching of the pacifists."

W. O. H. Garman, president of the American Council from 1947 to 1950 (see Chapter 8), has charged that the leaders of the Federal Council were to be held "co-responsible for the unnecessary slaughter of thousands of our men and the unnecessary prolongation of World War II, caused by the nation's lack of preparedness."

In contrast, the McIntire faction boasts that it has been a staunch supporter of the "armed camp" point of view. It has called a universal military training program "absolutely in-

218 Apostles of Discord

dispensable." The American Council's only fear is that U.M.T. might be used "to influence the American people to change their social concept or even their racial relations." In 1948, the McIntire faction called upon the House Committee on Un-American Activities to investigate a hundred clergymen who had protested the passage of the draft act.

The Charge of Interracial Activity

McIntire and the American Council charge the ecumenical movement, in effect, with accepting the brotherhood of man. Fortunately, this accusation is true. The major Protestant denominations have often been in the forefront of the battle for racial and religious equality. But McIntire flatly rejects their basic premises, dismissing them as "utterly in conflict . . . with all the teachings of the Lord Jesus Christ." The American Council has publicly denounced Brotherhood Week, sponsored annually by the National Conference of Christians and Jews, as a "gross perversion of the Scriptural teachings." Whenever church literature pleads for understanding between different racial groups, McIntire charges that such "propaganda" logically "will destroy the races."

McIntire and his small but noisy faction have pressed the accusation that anyone who makes an effort through legislation to secure equality for all Americans is pro-communist. Of the civil-rights program, McIntire charges that it is "serving the ends of radical powers that are working for a socialistic order in this free land." More recently, he stated that "the racial brotherhood emphasis produces the class and racial strife in which the Communists delight."

It is, of course, possible for Protestants to differ on the ways in which they seek to obtain equal justice for all citizens of the United States. Many believe that legislation is not the best solution to the problem. But the American Council's suggestion that the civil-rights program is a communist-inspired plot reveals an inability to accept the responsibility of Christians toward all peoples, regardless of race, color, or national origin.

The American Council has been particularly antagonistic toward the establishment of a Fair Employment Practices Commission (FEPC), whereby an attempt would be made to dis-

courage racial discrimination in industry. It has had representatives testify before legislative committees against the passage
of such legislation. One of these representatives was John W.
Hamilton, now head of an anti-Negro group in St. Louis (see
Chapter 6). McIntire himself has promised to write a book
opposing FEPC — under the extreme title of *Making Black
White*.

Regardless of the fact that millions of Americans, including
leaders of all minority groups in the United States, support the
civil-rights program, the American Council has officially, by
resolution, attempted to smear it. On one occasion the Council
resolved that "The F.E.P.C. . . . is a vital part of the Communist
program at the present state of their developing blueprint."
In 1950 the American Council passed another resolution, again
raising the false issue of communism and calling upon President
Truman "to abandon the so-called Civil Rights legislation."

It is not clear whether the American Council opposes civil
rights merely because some figures in the ecumenical movement
favor them — or whether it is fundamentally antagonistic to the
idea of the equality of all men.

The American Council has also been associated in the minds
of many Americans with some of the country's most notorious
peddlers of anti-Semitism; there have occurred incidents troubling to those who feel that Christians must be sensitive to discrimination against Jews. It would not be fair to say that the
American Council is anti-Semitic; but the William Denton incident of 1949 furnishes a lucid illustration of the dubious
position of many leaders of the Council in the matter of Chris-
tian-Jewish relations.

English-born Evangelist William Denton, director of the
Furnace Street Mission in Akron, Ohio, in 1948 used his December 5 broadcast time for what was one of the most flagrant
attacks upon the Jews ever heard over the American radio. In
preparing his remarks, Denton employed materials circulated
by fanatical opponents of racial equality, notably Robert H.
Williams of Santa Ana, California. Marxism, Denton said,
was brought to America "from the ghettos of Europe and Russia,
where it long had flourished in the form of hatred of Christianity
and the successful white races of Christendom."

In spite of a clear case against Denton, the American Council rushed to his defense. The Washington bureau of the American Council, under W. O. H. Garman, issued a news release that distorted the incident by omitting any reference to the content of Denton's "Bible" address and by attempting to raise the false issue of communism. The release brutally attacked an Akron rabbi, and contained innuendoes against Negroes.

Subsequently, in the "Battle of the Bible," Denton — unlike Brother Hux in North Carolina — burned an *entire* copy of the Revised Standard Version. When it had smoldered for a few minutes, Denton joked: "It's like the devil, it's hard to burn." A retired Baptist minister, Benjamin H. Jeffreys, chimed in: "I wish we had all of the copies here today to burn." In a service preceding the "ceremony," Denton had solemnly read from Carl McIntire's pamphlet, *The New Bible: Why Christians Should Not Accept It.*

The Denton affair of 1948 served to indicate that the American Council often does not abide by Christian principles in its approach to race problems. The McIntire faction, of course, vehemently denies such conclusions. They cite a few resolutions; they refer to a sermon or two; they mention a handful of Negroes and one or two Jews who have supported their disruptive designs. Some members of the American Council undoubtedly feel a genuine concern for the improvement of race relations in the United States. But the Council itself has clearly sought to slow down the national trend toward the equality of all citizens.

It is not surprising, therefore, to note that the McIntire faction has been a favorite of nearly all the other extremists of the ministry of hate. Elizabeth Dilling, "student" of the Talmud, has considered the American Council necessary and sound. J. A. Lovell, Anglo-Israelite leader, has been favorably impressed by the McIntire schism. The *Georgia Tribune,* racist publication of "Parson Jack" Johnston, has given support to the American Council in its fight against the ecumenical movement. Charles B. Hudson, indicted for alleged sedition during World War II, has listed McIntire as a sympathetic commentator. Robert H. Williams, anti-Semitic editor of the *Williams Intelligence Summary,* states that McIntire is "doing a great work." Even the

Ku Klux Klan has recommended American Council literature to its members who wish to learn the "truth" about the National Council.

The Charge of Pro-Catholicism

McIntire contends that the ecumenical movement has sold out historic Protestantism — particularly by its "union with the Greek Orthodox Churches with their idolatrous mass, superstitious intercession to the Virgin and the Saints." Every step toward church unity is a "whistle-stop on the train back to Rome." When Dr. John A. Mackay, president of Princeton Theological Seminary, referred to Catholicism as a "sister Christian communion," McIntire burst forth in indignation. "The historic Christian faith will never admit for a moment," he declared, "that the Roman Catholic testimony is Christian. Surely any thinking man can realize the unlimited implication of such a surrender." When Bishop G. Bromley Oxnam — surely no friend of the Pope — noted that Protestants and Catholics worship the same God, McIntire objected: "The truth is that we do not have the same faith. The difference between Romanism and Protestantism is life and death."

Many Protestants contend that divisive groups like the American Council actually strengthen the position of Catholicism in competition with Protestantism. In the first place, they argue, such groups stand in the way of a vibrant, co-operative Protestant movement. In fact, they furnish certain inflammatory Catholic newspapers with propaganda against the entire Protestant movement. *Our Sunday Visitor,* for example, widely circulated diocesan paper, regularly has quoted with obvious enjoyment McIntire's extreme charges against the ecumenical movement.

There are many specific illustrations of this. In 1951 *Our Sunday Visitor* published a booklet assailing the leadership of Protestants and Other Americans United for the Separation of Church and State (discussed in Chapter 7). Throughout the booklet, supporters of the American Council were quoted in such a way as to aid the Roman Catholic position. Among many other references, it contained a long letter from William Harllee Bordeaux, executive secretary of the American Council, which repeats in great detail the familiar charges against the Federal Council. The letter is used by *Our Sunday Visitor* to assure readers that "all Protestants do not see alike."

In light of McIntire's extreme anti-Catholicism, it is of interest to note his participation in the so-called "Frank Fay Rally" of 1946. The late British political scientist Harold Laski, in a message to a New York gathering, had attacked the Franco regime in Spain and the role of the Catholic Church in creating and sustaining it. Frank Fay, star of the Broadway hit *Harvey*, criticized several of his colleagues of the Actors Equity Association for participating in the program during which the comments were made; he, in turn, was censured by the Equity council. The outcome of the incident was the "Friends of Frank Fay," organized specifically to protest against religious intolerance. On January 10, 1946, they staged a mass rally in Madison Square Garden.

Long before the rally was held, its pro-Catholic character became evident. It was hailed by Catholic newspapers everywhere, as well as by the Catholic Institute of the Press. The Ancient Order of Hibernians and sixty thousand members of the Knights of Columbus in the State of New York threw their support behind Fay and the Catholic War Veterans were instrumental in planning the rally. It was generally agreed that the primary purpose of the rally was to protest against anti-Catholicism.

Carl McIntire was on the speaker's platform. He later claimed that it was simply a protest against communism, and nothing more. What had happened — as McIntire himself admitted — was that the American Council chieftain attended a small luncheon that initiated plans for the rally; the host had been Merwin K. Hart, a friend of McIntire and of the American Council. (Hart will be discussed at greater length in Chapter 10.)

McIntire thinks that Hart is waging a commendable fight against communism; Hart, in turn, is highly pleased with the activities of the American Council. For a time the Council's first executive secretary served as assistant in the New York office of Hart, president of the National Economic Council and a favorite of all the anti-democratic forces in the United States — a man probably best known for his strong affection for fascist

Spain. The American Union for Nationalist Spain, a pro-Franco lobby, was organized and directed from Hart's office, and he has called Franco "one of the strongest characters in the world today."

Yet Hart's friend McIntire accuses the ecumenical movement of being "pro-Catholic!"

It is interesting that Carl McIntire does not scruple to co-operate with certain anti-Semites, "white supremacists," pro-fascists, and militant Roman Catholics — while he insists that his followers keep entirely apart from all Protestants who do not see eye to eye with him on every issue.

In line with McIntire's charge of "pro-Catholicism," he depicts the ecumenical movement as "a Protestant Vatican" or "a super-Church."

The truth, of course, is that the World Council and the National Council are not "churches." They baptize no members, ordain no ministers, consecrate no bishops, govern no parishes, command no proscribed forms of worship, issue no orders, claim no authority, and have no right to levy apportionments or to command any of their member churches. They are co-operative fellowships.

There is, in fact, a sharp contrast between this free fellowship, with its diverse leadership, and the American Council, considered by many to be a one-man organization. Carl McIntire appears to have initiated it, held its important offices, used his periodical as its principal mouthpiece, coined its catch-phrases, elaborated its attacks upon the ecumenical movement, and written the books that proclaim the American Council's cardinal dogma of "separation."

Indeed, the charge of "super-Church" tendencies appears misdirected.

Rival Factions in Fundamentalism: A.C.C.C. vs. N.A.E.

Although other fundamentalists also sometimes accuse the ecumenical movement of modernism, Carl McIntire and his "Twentieth-Century Reformation" certainly do not speak for all "Bible-believing Christians," as he would have the public believe. The fact is that most of the important fundamentalist leaders in the United States have repudiated this "separation movement."

The National Association of Evangelicals resents the effort of the American Council to pin the label of apostasy wherever it pleases. "For any inter-church group to dictate in this area," argues one top Evangelical spokesman, "is assuming that type of supervision which is usually left within the province of a denomination. Indeed, if we may so in kindness, we would feel that this is quite un-Protestant — it is in the direction of popery."

Because of the Evangelicals' reluctance to follow his lead, McIntire has been especially bitter in his attacks upon the Association. "It has not, does not, and cannot call for separation," McIntire contends. "If it did, it would destroy itself. It will not affirm belief in the purity of the church, but in its creed talks about an infallible Word, not an inerrant Bible, thus leaving room for Barthians and the neo-orthodox to fellowship with it." In fact, McIntire accuses the Association of "aiding the enemy by making flank attacks on the forces which are engaged in open battle with the enemy of the cross. This position is one of unquestioned compromise of the Gospel and the commands of Christ."

Nearly all of the leading religious personalities who accept the position of the National Association of Evangelicals — including the popular young evangelist Billy Graham — have been the target of sharp criticism from the American Council camp. The Council has refused to co-operate with the Graham revival campaigns; McIntire has declared that Graham and his Association colleagues "are occupying the middle road. They are driving on the center of the road, instead of keeping to the right. They are typical of pragmatic evangelicalism, aiming at success by means of toleration and compromise."

He has been particularly brutal in his comments about the Pentecostal groups that have flocked to the Evangelicals' banner. "The Tongues groups never had historically been counted among the Protestant churches, and to recognize them would promote and advance their error of tongues which depreciates so much their testimony . . . they are a most disruptive force and always have been, and their presence in any council of churches would well-nigh stultify it."

The American Council has even officially expressed regret at the continued success of respected fundamentalist movements. In Denver, Colorado, in April 1949, the Council resolved:

That the American Council of Christian Churches deplores the fact that such movements as the National Association of Evangelicals, Youth for Christ, and Youth for Christ International, International Child Evangelism Fellowship, and similar groups, along with a certain section of the Bible institutes, evangelical Christian colleges and seminaries, etc., which have refused to take a clear-cut stand on scriptural separation from modernism and all other forms of religious liberalism, on the one hand, and socialism and near-communism, on the other hand, continue to enjoy both the confidence and support of a segment of Bible-believing Christians and churches.

The Inter-Varsity Christian Fellowship was likewise condemned in an official resolution adopted at the next Council convention in Washington, D. C.

One of the leaders of the American Council and the International Council, Dr. T. T. Shields, has expressed a similar conviction: "After a long experience, we can say, without fear of successful contradiction, that these extra church movements have done but little good." He lists the Christian Businessmen's Association and the Gideons as detrimental, reserving particular venom for the Youth for Christ. "It has been, in most cases, a kind of religious debauch," he charges.

Several reputable fundamentalist leaders have expressed themselves freely on the subject of McIntire's movement. Dr. J. Elwin Wright, the "father" of the National Association of Evangelicals and chairman of its Commission on International Relations, recently wrote regarding the International Council of Christian Churches:

We regard the International Council of Christian Churches as divisive and destructive of fellowship among believers. They are all right doctrinally but they need to purge their hearts of bitterness, backbiting, and evil reports, which hurt the work of God. . . . They follow leaders who misinform them of the true situation among evangelicals.

Dr. Harold John Ockenga, popular fundamentalist minister of the Park Street Congregational Church on Boston's Brimstone Corner, has characterized the American Council leaders as "barking dogs" and "gadflies."

Billy Graham has regularly repudiated what he calls "ultra-fundamentalists" — meaning the divisive factions. "These dissensions in the ranks of evangelical Christians are a stench in the nostrils of God," he has added.

William Ward Ayer, another popular radio evangelist, has given this warning to his fundamentalist brethren:

I am a fundamentalist in Christian doctrine, but I realize that the movement now more than a quarter of a century old is in danger of being blighted by religious froth, acrimonious debate and a stern and unlovely religious objectivism which demands strictest adherence to creed, while failing to create the inner content of brotherliness, tolerance and deep Christian character. Doctrines are necessary but they are not an end in religion. The doctrines must be incarnated in practical everyday living if the multitudes are to see and appreciate the great truths of our faith.

John W. Bradbury, editor of *The Watchman-Examiner,* has also bemoaned the activities of "religious vigilantes" who, according to Bradbury, "cannot be classified in any sense whatever with the original Fundamentalists. They may appropriate the name, but these know not the spirit of the movement. They have brought no intellectual, moral, or spiritual contribution to the exposition of eternal truth, their chief work being in the area of religious competition." In the same vein, Bradbury concludes:

Intolerant religionists of the vigilante spirit menace all possibility of a revival because of incapacity to cooperate with their coevangelicals; they ignore or repress New Testament ideals and prostitute what should be fellowship into warring camps or into suspicious, subdued, and unfaithed satellites. . . . Christ has no part with the intolerant.

At the eleventh annual convention of the National Association of Evangelicals, held in April 1953, President Paul S. Rees joined the growing chorus against the McIntire faction. "We here and now protest the severe, misleading and irresponsible attacks by evangelicals upon evangelicals," he asserted. "These assaults dot the land with emotional situations full of half-truths, innuendoes and acrimony." Although Rees did not refer to the American Council by name, his references were quite clear to his audience.

For thousands of Protestants these problems of doctrine are of major concern. Fundamentalists speak of a "Christian" as someone well defined — as a person who accepts a specific set of dogmas. Fortunately, those who would divide are divided; extreme fundamentalists spend much of their energy battling one another. Meanwhile, the main stream of Protestantism is free to move toward closer harmony and deeper understanding.

The "Battle of the Bible" was one episode demonstrating how Protestants can be aroused by reckless name-calling. Many of the critics are sincere. Others, however, are "religious racketeers," bent upon exploiting every available issue for their own profit. As a result the work of the churches is injured by fringe Protestantism's assault upon respected religious leaders on the ground that all who disagree with air-tight theological thinking are "modernists."

Indeed this epithet has become an instrument of smear in other areas as well. When a churchman expresses a desire for peace, some will condemn him as a "modernist." When a churchman professes a belief in racial equality, some will seek to discredit his position on the same grounds. When a churchman adheres to a code of religious good-will, some will misquote the Bible and charge heresy.

In ultra-fundamentalist circles "modernism" has become a favored label to pin upon any opponent. It is comparable, in Protestantism, with the indiscriminate exploitation, in politics, of the epithet "Red!"

10

Seeing "Red"

Self-appointed "guardians of the Republic" — who have provoked flagrant injustices in government, in education, and other spheres of American society — also threaten to reach into the churches and cast suspicion upon the leadership of Protestantism. Vigilante groups, large and small, have sprung up across the nation, endeavoring to replace apostles of prophetic Christianity with those faithful to the *status quo*. Some of these factions are denominational in scope, such as Methodism's Circuit Riders, Inc. (see Chapter 13), and the Committee Opposing Congregational Political Action (see Chapter 14). Others thrust in many directions, indiscriminately indicting the ecumenical movement, church-related agencies and commissions, leading centers of ministerial training, and such non-denominational groups as the YMCA and YWCA.

At the outset, it is important to note that those who launch harmful attacks upon Protestant leaders apparently seldom *intend* to subvert traditional American civil liberties. In fact, they earnestly believe that they are exposing the actual enemies of freedom who, unwittingly perhaps, have become tools of the Kremlin in its drive to undermine America by destroying its capitalistic system. With incredible political naïveté, these "patriots" link certain liberal Protestant leaders to the worldwide communist conspiracy, often by means of inapplicable and deceptive clichés. Thus, for example, anyone who believes in social legislation is likely to be called a socialist — and a communist is simply a "socialist in a hurry."

Many of these vigilantes have been subjected to similar unfair labels themselves, especially during the war when those who did not concur with every phase of government activity were too frequently dubbed "fascist" or "un-American." These critics, in particular, share an intense desire to justify their bitter estimates of liberalism during the New Deal era. Therefore, they devote themselves unsparingly to the task of exposing "ecclesiastical reds."

It is a well-established fact that, in the past, pro-communist elements were able to infest a few areas of church life — as was also true in some agencies of government, education, and other fields. In a few instances, they succeeded in gaining the support of idealistic churchmen — among them some of stature — for their skillfully disguised efforts to undermine American democracy. A small number of these apologists for the Kremlin remain active today, though isolated from their fellow-churchmen and closely watched by the government. These are discussed in Chapter 11.

Hate Publications

The use of the Red bogey in opposing progressive church leadership is not a new phenomenon, though it has gained alarming impetus in recent years. Much of the basic ammunition utilized by today's sentinels has been culled from abusive books and pamphlets circulated many years ago.

Among the earliest volumes of importance was *Tainted Contacts,* an unwieldy conglomeration of materials published in 1931, claiming to demonstrate the "socialism, communism, internationalism and pacifism" of the former Federal Council of Churches. *Tainted Contacts* was compiled by E. N. Sanctuary, "scholar" and "elder statesman" of America's racist, nationalist fringe. It may be recalled from Chapter 3 that among his other "works" were such flagrantly anti-Semitic diatribes as *The Talmud Unmasked* and *Are These Things So?* From his offices in the Presbyterian Building in New York City, he shipped large quantities of literature and promoted his one-man organizations; these included the American Christian Defenders, the World Alliance Against Jewish Aggressiveness, and Tocsin Publishers.

Three years later, in 1934, Elizabeth Dilling published *The Red Network* — described as "A 'Who's Who' and Handbook of Radicals for Patriots." This book examines 460 organizations allegedly supporting "the Communist-Socialist world conspiracy with its four horsemen, Atheism, Immorality, Class Hatred, and Pacifism-for-the-Sake-of-Red-Revolution." Among her choice targets were the Federal Council of Churches, numerous church-related groups, and "those present-day Moscow-loving intellectual ministers who rewrite the Bible and teach it in modernist style so as to leave faith in little besides its covers."

In recent years, Mrs. Dilling has renewed her attacks upon the social policies of the ecumenical movement. In a typical newsletter addressed to fellow "Christian Americans," the self-described "lady patriot" charged that "the Federal Council has been following the Red line since its formation. While about 75% of its income has remained anonymous, its listed contributions from anti-Christian Jewish organizations is supporting evidence that the Federal Council is not Christian in its policies but Judaistic-Communistic." Mrs. Dilling has been particularly critical of the race-relations policies of the church-unity movement, which, she complains, "follows the Communist line" in sponsoring Race Relations Sunday and urging pulpit exchange between white and Negro ministers.

In *The Red Network*, Elizabeth Dilling lifts lengthy quotations from countless dubious sources to prove her case against her exhaustive catalogue of "suspect" organizations and individuals. She relies heavily upon E. N. Sanctuary's *Tainted Contacts,* and incorporates the inflammatory charges of Harry Jung, head of the American Vigilant Intelligence Federation; of Nesta Webster, author of numerous anti-Jewish diatribes; of Walter S. Steele, editor of *National Republic;* of Smith-Jones' volume on *Pastors, Politicians, and Pacifists;* of General Amos Fries, head of the misnamed Friends of the Public Schools; and of the notorious Lusk committee of New York State (1920).

Attacks upon the churches stemmed from other sources as well. The late Henry B. Joy of Detroit published and circulated free of charge a thick *Green Book* — "documents referring to the Federal Council of Churches of America" — as well as a supplement entitled *Our Pro-Socialist Churches.* In the first he cited Mrs. Dilling twenty-four times; in the second he named the same "authority" twenty-three times and recommended *The Red Network* as "a work of infinite labor and invaluable education." Joy also distributed copies of a pamphlet, *The*

Federal Council's "Tainted Contacts," which contained a long editorial from the *Sunday School Times* in support of Sanctuary's accusations.

Among other pamphlets worth mention are *Is the Federal Council a Dead Issue?* by Genna Robbins Post of Grove City, Pennsylvania; *The Federal Council of Churches* ("an infidelist, modernistic and unpatriotic organization"), by the Rev. W. Lee Rector, of Ardmore, Oklahoma; and the *Federal Council of the Churches of Christ in America Speaks,* anonymously circulated by the American Women Against Communism. Mrs. Post and Mr. Rector relied heavily upon the sources noted above. The American Women Against Communism, a one-woman project directed by Mrs. A. Cressy Morrison of New York City, used a chart "Termites Within the Temple Gates" — prepared by the late A. Cloyd Gill, director of research for Joseph Kamp's Constitutional Educational League.

Kamp continues to operate one of the more extensive "smear-bunds" from elaborate headquarters in midtown New York. From behind a façade of anti-communism, he battles social progress of any kind through the circulation of *Headlines,* his monthly bulletin, and a score of slick pamphlets financed by wealthy businessmen. In 1950, he spent four months in jail for refusal to reveal the officers and contributors to his League. Kamp always has worked closely with other native extremists, including such Protestant-underworld leaders as Gerald L. K. Smith and Gerald Winrod. Among the groups on his blacklist of communist "fronts" or "transmission belts for Red propaganda" are the Congregationalist Council for Social Action, the Fellowship of Reconciliation, the National Council for Prevention of War, the National Conference of Methodist Youth, the Student Christian Movement, and many more. His most sensational propaganda piece sought to discredit the work of the YWCA; he charged: "There is plenty to be found in YWCA publications . . . to gladden the hearts of Joe Stalin, William Z. Foster, Gerhardt Eisler, and all the other disciples of Karl Marx the world over."

Robert H. Williams, editor of the *Williams Intelligence Summary,* of Santa Ana, California, has attempted to revive the nation-wide reaction to Kamp's 1949 "exposé" of alleged YWCA intrigue. Williams has described the YWCA as "a propaganda center for Marxism," which "goes on using good people, many of them ardent Christians, to advance the Marxist world revolution against Christianity and the white race." Like Kamp, he accuses the YWCA of distributing literature "all on the side of the Marxist social-racial-economic anti-Christian revolution, all in support of the Truman-Acheson-Frankfurter subversion."

The most resounding attack against Protestant leadership in recent years was delivered by John T. Flynn in *The Road Ahead,* published in 1949. A nation-wide controversy raged over Flynn's Chapter X, "The Kingdom of God," in which the author charged that "a clique of Christian ministers and laymen" is engaged in "using" the Federal Council "to promote a socialist revolution." Flynn's chief targets included John C. Bennett, E. Stanley Jones, Reinhold Niebuhr, and G. Bromley Oxnam.

Protestants generally resented such an attack from the pen of a Roman Catholic layman. Flynn failed to demonstrate any understanding of the nature of Protestantism; moreover, at no point did he mention that the powerful National Catholic Welfare Conference had endorsed the same "socialistic" policies approved by the Federal Council.

The Road Ahead had by early 1953 sold almost a million copies, of which over 725,000 were distributed through the Committee for Constitutional Government of New York, an ultra-conservative pressure group that considered this economic treatise the "greatest book of our time." The Committee was formed under a slightly different name in 1937 to oppose President Roosevelt's court-packing scheme; it drew support from such conservative clergymen as Bishop William T. Manning, and such liberal ones as John Haynes Holmes. In 1941, the Committee was reorganized and chartered as "an educational, non-profit, eleemosynary corporation" to "uphold constitutional government and the system of free enterprise." It prides itself on maintaining one of the most extensive lists of Protestant ministers in the country. The Committee's executive secretary has been energetic Edward A. Rumely, and its chairmen have included Frank Gannett of Rochester, New York, publisher of the Gannett newspaper chain; former Congressman Samuel B. Pettengill; Willford I. King, professor emeritus of New York

University; and Norman Vincent Peale, pastor of Fifth Avenue's Marble Collegiate Church, whose weekly radio program, "The Art of Living," is sponsored by the National Council of Churches.

During Peale's term as chairman of the Committee, he exploited his ministerial position to disperse extreme political and economic theories. In 1944, for instance, he boosted — through mailings to Catholics and Protestants — a book which tried to establish parallels between Franklin Roosevelt and Adolf Hitler.

Called *For Americans Only*, this book accused Roosevelt of "dictatorship" and charged that he followed Hitler-like practices when he instituted Lend-Lease and internal-security measures. Ignoring the influence of the war on taxes, the book stated that the New Deal had harmed the churches because high taxes cut church revenue. Roosevelt's references to "freedom from want" and "freedom from fear" were compared with excerpts from some of Hitler's speeches.

On his own stationery, Peale urged the nation's Catholic priests to read *For Americans Only*, stating that, "as religious leaders, it is our duty to be wise and informed . . . in current movements, many of them swordlike, which may seriously effect the perpetuity of freedom. . . . This book, written jointly by a former member of Congress [Samuel B. Pettengill] and a distinguished Catholic economist [Paul C. Bartholomew] will give you a deeper insight into contemporary trends."

A few days later, letters went out from Peale's study to friends of the Committee, pointing out that "it would be helpful to the cause of constitutional government to place in the hands of all Protestant ministers, Pettengill's book 'For Americans Only' which is a stirring, factual and enlightening discussion of the dangerous trends toward collectivism in the United States." The amount solicited to send this book to the Committee's list of 62,000 Protestant ministers was $15,000.

While no longer connected officially, Peale continues to work closely with the Committee for Constitutional Government — and other similar groups of the extreme right.

Hart, Robnett, and Steele

Among others who use religion in the propagation of their extreme economic and political views are Merwin K. Hart, in

New York; George Washington Robnett, in Chicago; and Walter S. Steele, in Washington.

Merwin K. Hart — an usher at the fashionable Calvary Episcopal Church in New York — is founder and head of the National Economic Council, with offices in the Empire State Building, and editor of the semi-monthly *Economic Council Letter*. He freely employs conventional Christian symbols to lend religious authority to his immoderate point of view. He has a strong affection for fascist Spain, together with an equally vehement distaste for the United Nations ("fathered by Communism, mothered by Socialism and wet-nursed by power-hungry bureaucracy") and for Zionists ("this aggressive Jewish group can wreck the United States"). The Buchanan committee of the Eighty-first Congress, set up to investigate lobbying activities, charged the National Economic Council with "an ill-concealed anti-Semitism."

George Washington Robnett, Chicago advertising agent, tours the country as a "nationally known lecturer on Communism" to declaim against "Stalinism, Welfarism, and Minorityism." He directs the Church League of America, founded in 1937 to carry on "an educational program designed to bring the influence of the clergy and educators more solidly behind the laymen in . . . their common ideal of preserving Constitutional rights and the basic traditions of the American Way of Life." The Church League claims to have a sponsoring committee of more than nine hundred ministers, an equal number of laymen. In his monthly *News and Views,* Robnett attacks specific "religionists . . . of the intellectual-Left helping the Socialist-Communist cause by following their own prejudices against 'the profit system.' "

"Minorityism" Robnett has characterized as "a new national disease which has grown out of New Deal Marxism where class is pitted against class and race against race to serve political expediency." He asserts that "nothing could be more menacing to the American way of life than the minority consciousness that has been encouraged during the past twenty years."

In Washington, Walter S. Steele, a convert to the Roman Catholic Church, publishes the well-edited monthly *National Republic,* "A Magazine of Fundamental Americanism," which has considerable prestige among ultra-conservative members of Congress. *National Republic* has made a few contributions to the exposure of communism in the United States, but more frequently it discovers the disease where it does not exist. One flagrant example was a recent article by Presbyterian Herbert G. Moore, managing editor, in which he bluntly charged that "you can visit any divinity school in America and find the pro-Kremlin friends planted in the faculty." In documenting this rash statement, he examined Union Theological Seminary in New York, "for purposes of illustration." He denounced three of Protestantism's most articulate spokesmen against communism: President Henry P. Van Dusen, Dean Reinhold Niebuhr, and Professor John C. Bennett. Moore concluded that similarly dangerous radicals also haunt the faculties of "Yale Divinity School, Crozer, Oberlin, Auburn, Colgate-Rochester, and scores of other theological seminaries."

National Republic's weakness, therefore, stems from its tendency toward blind "super-patriotism" and its inability to distinguish among different political viewpoints. While posing as a reliable research enterprise which unearths communist activities, Steele's organization seeks to discredit competing groups or ideologies by dubbing them "Red" — whether they are liberal, middle-road, or even conservative. It condemns all international co-operation as "globalism." Its fanaticism on some issues has led it to cater to the writings of such totalitarian-minded allies of the ministry of hate as W. Henry MacFarland, Jr., of Philadelphia, head of the American Flag Committee. MacFarland's earlier organization, the Nationalist Action League, is listed as "fascist" on the official list of subversive activities prepared and distributed by the United States Attorney General.

Ultra-fundamentalist Criticism

Today, the most persistent criticism of alleged "fellow-traveling" among the clergy stems from ultra-fundamentalist sources, who sometimes cry "Red!" to buttress their accusations of widespread theological apostasy. As pointed out in Chapter 8, both the National Association of Evangelicals and the American Council of Christian Churches have been critical of the social policies of the ecumenical movement — although the two rival fundamentalist coalitions frequently disagree as to the specific policies that warrant disapproval.

The National Association of Evangelicals has won a reputation for fair-mindedness — which, however, it may soon sacrifice by growing carelessness in its treatment of certain controversial questions. During the past few years, *United Evangelical Action,* the Association's official organ, has become vituperative in its attacks on the "political power" of the ecumenical movement. This attitude may be partly due to the pressure from extremists, both within and without the Association.

Perhaps another important factor is the personal prejudices of its editor, James DeForest Murch, who echoes the sentiments of Robert McCormick's Chicago *Tribune.* Murch recently wrote a series of articles called "The Growing Super-Church," in which he charged that the ecumenical leadership spends "more time on idealistic and visionary plans to ameliorate the material conditions of man than it spends on the fundamental doctrines of the Christian faith and the dissemination of the Gospel Message."

"World revolution is now the goal of these dreamers," exclaims Murch. He conjures up a sinister alliance between the political "liberals" of the National Council and "a very 'hush-hush' group of bankers and lawyers." In the manner of Carl McIntire, Murch caustically complains that John Foster Dulles is an "internationalist" who was responsible for "getting Protestant support for the United Nations." The politics of the U.N., Murch adds, are "foreign to our American way of life."

Murch likes to denounce other ecumenical leaders in equally bitter language. As an example: he has represented Dr. John C. Bennett of Union Theological Seminary in New York as one of "the half-dozen most radical theologians of the day." Murch adds: "He long has been an apologist for Communism; his most recent books, including *Christianity and Communism,* attempt to correlate the ethics of the Christian faith with Marxism Communism." Obviously, Murch had never read *Christianity and Communism* — not even its opening sentence which sums up Bennett's actual position:

This book is written by one who believes that Communism as a faith and as a system of thought is a compound of half-truth and positive error, that Communism as a movement of power is a threat to essential forms of personal and political freedom, and that it is the responsibility of Christians to resist its extension in the world.

Under Murch, *United Evangelical Action* has carried other attacks upon the church-unity movement and its leaders. One series, entitled "Ecclesiastical Octopus," was based upon a disjointed "study" of the same name written by Ernest Gordon, a contributing editor of the *Sunday School Times*. Gordon's thesis parallels Murch's: subversive pro-communist elements and radical pacifists have joined international money-changers — notably the Rockefeller interests and certain munition-makers — to rob Americans of their freedom and evangelical Christians of their faith. Gordon singles out several targets, particularly New York's Riverside Church, Colby College in Maine, the Northfield Schools in Massachusetts, the YMCA, and the YWCA. Gordon reserves a special blast for the "quack-liberal" National Conference of Christians and Jews, which he claims is financed by the "Semitic whisky interests" and controlled by "Catholic clericalism." Ironically enough, he quotes as his "authority" for the latter contention Kenneth Leslie, editor of *The Protestant*, the pro-communist periodical, now published in Canada, which utilizes religion to serve the ends of Moscow (see Chapter 11).

Shortly after the Gordon series, *United Evangelical Action* carried new attacks upon the political loyalty of ecumenical leaders. It ran three articles by George Washington Robnett entitled "The Hammer and Sickle Over the Churches." Without distinguishing between pro-communists and liberals, Robnett sought to create suspicion of such reputable Protestant figures as Dean Liston Pope of the Yale University divinity school; Henry Smith Leiper, former American secretary of the World Council of Churches; John Haynes Holmes, pastor emeritus of Manhattan's Community Church; Henry Sloane Coffin, president emeritus of New York City's Union Theological Seminary — and many more. He lumped together non-communist groups such as the Congregationalist Council for Social Action and the National Religion and Labor Foundation, with organizations steered by "party-liners" — for example, the Peoples' Institute of Applied Religion (see Chapter 11) and the Methodist Federation for Social Action (see Chapter 13).

The American Council Cries "Communist"

As might be anticipated, the American Council of Christian Churches has been the sharpest critic of the social policies of the ecumenical movement. "America must not listen to the voice of the modern church," Carl McIntire warns, "or she shall go on to communism with its tyranny." He describes the National Council as "the strongest ally of Russia and the radical labor movement within the U. S." According to the American Council's unique appraisal, the principal Protestant leaders are members of communist fronts, their resolutions approximate the party line, and their interest in bettering society reveals their intent to collectivize the world.

This charge that the church-unity movement is pro-communist is so patently false that one wonders how it is possible for the enemies of the movement to continue promulgating it. The National Council of the Churches of Christ in the U.S.A. has stated its firm anti-communist conviction, in the following terms:

It [Communism] is atheistic in its conception of ultimate reality and materialistic in its view of man and his destiny. Its utopian philosophy of history lacks the essential Christian notes of divine judgment, divine governance, and eternal victory. Its revolutionary strategy involves the disregard of the sacredness of personality which is fundamental in Christianity. Such differences can never be resolved by the compromise or surrender of faith by Christians.

American communists and fellow-travelers, in fact, regularly attack the National Council as "a war-mongering foe of the people" and "tool of Wall Street imperialism."

The case of John Foster Dulles, upon whom the American Council heaps considerable abuse, demonstrates the extreme position of those who fling the Red gantlet at Protestant leadership. The *Christian Beacon,* McIntire's weekly, strongly opposed the appointment of Dulles to any government position because he has been "long associated with extremely radical and pacifist leaders in the Federal and World Councils."

On the other hand, Dulles has been a prime target of organized communism, both in the United States and throughout the world. In the spring of 1950, for example, the pro-communist periodical *The Protestant* complained: "The Federal Council Bulletin takes us to task for reckless language in criticising John Foster Dulles. We do not criticize Dulles. He is what he is, legal servant of big money, by profession cold and ruthless as a rattle-snake."

The *Daily Worker,* like *The Protestant* and the *Christian Beacon,* sharply disapproved of the appointment of Dulles as Secretary of State. In its issue of April 28, 1953, for example, William Z. Foster, top man of the Communist Party in the United States, demanded that President Eisenhower fire Dulles — whom Foster characterized as "a confirmed warmonger, an agent of Wall Street, and a close cooperator with the most malignant pro-fascist elements here and abroad."

It is interesting to find that McIntire's views are in agreement with other specific planks in the platform of the Communist Party. This is typical of many persons who hold the views of the far right. In the area of foreign policy, for example, communists and ultra-nationalists have united in the past to battle against such proposals as the Marshall Plan, the North Atlantic Treaty, the Point Four program, and United States co-operation with UNESCO.

While claiming never to dabble in politics, the American Council has pushed itself into several purely political battles. In January 1952, for example, the *Christian Beacon's* lead head-line read: "CHARLES P. TAFT, FORMER FC HEAD AND WCC EXECU-TIVE COMMITTEE MEMBER, SEEKS GOVERNORSHIP OF STATE OF OHIO." At great length, the articles "exposed" the "radical record" of Taft, including his association with the ecumenical movement. William E. Ashbrook, president of the Ohio affiliate of American Council of Christian Churches and author of the article, charged that Senator Robert Taft's brother "is probably the most affable, the most subtle, and the most dangerous threat to our American system of free government." Mr. Taft was further described as "an exponent of a socialized America and a church-sponsored internationalism" and "a New Deal co-worker and state department wheel horse."

The World Council of Churches, according to McIntire, has become "an ally with Russia in the struggle to undermine the capitalistic West. They are united in that purpose." The supposed basis for this charge is the widely discussed resolution passed by the World Council in 1948, condemning both communism and unrestrained laissez-faireism.

In July 1950, the Central Committee of the World Council of Churches, meeting in Toronto, Canada, took a bold stand with the West when it condemned the communists as the aggressors in Korea and warned Christians everywhere against the Kremlin-inspired Stockholm "Peace Appeal." The communists had already shown their distaste for the ecumenical movement in their flat refusal to let Christians behind the Iron Curtain attend the Amsterdam meeting in 1948. Moreover, missionaries connected with the International Missionary Council — an affiliate of the World Council — have been maltreated in communist countries and forced to leave their stations.

In spite of these facts, the American Council and other elements of the ministry of disruption continue to call the ecumenical movement "communist-controlled." "Do we actually have in the WCC [World Council of Churches] an effective powerful instrument for pro-Soviet propaganda for the destruction of the West?" McIntire asks.

McIntire and other extremists have now opened fire on the only two World Council leaders behind the Iron Curtain, Professor Joseph Hromadka of Czechoslovakia and Bishop Albert Bereczky of Hungary, hoping to prevent their entry into the United States for the second plenary assembly of the World Council at Evanston, Illinois, in 1954. In November 1952, in anticipation of this World Council meeting, the American Council called upon the State Department to make "a full and complete investigation" of this "communist leadership." It also asked that "representatives of Communist or pro-Communist churches and views be not admitted to the United States to carry on their propaganda and further strengthen the pro-communist elements already active within certain churches in our country."

Many church leaders view the American Council's attempt to promote schism in certain crucial areas of the world as aid and comfort to the Soviet Union in its attempts to split the West.

An American Council public-relations man, Edgar C. Bundy, is an influential leader of the ultra-fundamentalist wing of the ministry of disruption. Bundy travels around the country as a self-advertised "lecturer, soldier, traveler, journalist, evangelist," with fanciful accounts of intrigue between communists and top Protestant leaders. A Baptist who received his religious education at Wheaton College, Illinois, Bundy gives "lectures" that impress uninformed hearers with their academic façade — usually sponsored by fundamentalist churches and conferences. Occasionally, however, Bundy is able to present his unfair accusations before reputable civic and fraternal organizations. Sensational announcements of his appearances fill local newspapers before his arrival. On January 12, 1953, for example, the Wichita Falls (Texas) *Record* carried a quarter-page advertisement of a series of three addresses to be given by Bundy under the auspices of twelve fundamentalist Baptist churches in the area. Said this announcement:

How are the Communists Invading the Churches? Congress says they are! Mr. J. Edgar Hoover says they are! Captain Bundy will tell how they are, with explosive documentation which will make some people sore and others shocked! *Russia's Religious Fifth Column Within the U.S.A.* Moscow's dearest friends discovered in pulpits and seminaries in the USA. Captain Bundy exposes a man honored by the largest Protestant group in the USA and identifies him with numerous communistic organizations. *The Master Stroke of the Communists — the Perversion of the Bible.* Who was behind the new Standard Version of the Bible? Captain Bundy reveals the subversive activities of so-called "scholars" who worked on the unauthorized changes made in the RSV and explains why no American Christian should own one.

Captain Bundy — who likes to be called "Cap" — exploits his association with Air Force Intelligence in Alaska. He considers himself an authority on a host of political questions, especially regarding the Near and Far East. He boasts that he is known "internationally" for his prediction in June of 1949 that war would break out in Korea. Bundy is a master at taking material out of context. He assumes the air of an unbiased student, ready to accept the material in the essential documents. In fact, however, he throws together a hodgepodge of isolated facts so as to create a false picture. Using such techniques he describes the famous missionary-evangelist E. Stanley Jones as a "silver-tongued . . . dangerous man"; John A. Mackay, president of Princeton Theological Seminary "a Presbyterian Red"; and

Methodism's Bishop G. Bromley Oxnam as "the Red Dean of North America."

"We are witnessing the sad spectacle today of religious forces joining hands with Communist leaders in promising the people economic freedom," declared Bundy. He sees "modernism" as "the most potent and subtle means of bringing in Communism in its full form." He adds: "Having done away with the infallible Word of God and the authority contained therein, they [the "modernists"] have substituted the teachings of Marx and Gandhi for the teachings of Holy Writ. They have set aside the primary business of the church, evangelism, and are calling for a Protestant Vatican which will attack the economic and political problems of the world in general."

Investigating the Churches?

When Representative Harold H. Velde suggested on March 9, 1953, that the House Committee on Un-American Activities (of which he is chairman) might investigate the churches, the American Council was jubilant. Its general secretary, William Harllee Bordeaux, commented: "The searchlight on religious leaders has long been urgently needed." On March 13 the executive committee of the American Council voted to circulate a petition among clergy requesting such an investigation for "the preservation of both civil and religious liberty."

Later, the McIntire faction announced a "mass meeting" in Washington for May 8 to "strengthen the hand of all defenders of freedom against communism and center attention upon the glories of the historic Christian religion." One of the purposes of the rally was to petition Congress "to investigate communist clergymen in the churches."

Other Protestants were divided on the issue. Some contended that clergymen should not be exempt from investigation, that Congress has as much of a right and a responsibility to unearth communist influence in the churches as in the colleges, in labor unions, or in the film industry. Others objected. A few argued that any such inquiry into the realm of religion would constitute a clear violation of the principle of the separation of church and state. Most were fearful that the House Committee was incompetent to undertake such an investigation. G. Bromley Oxnam, Bishop of the Washington area of the Methodist Church, voiced this opinion when he stated: "I believe the Communist party is a conspiracy and that conspirators should be discovered, tried, and, if guilty, punished. I believe that the Federal Bureau of Investigation is far better qualified for that duty than Mr. Velde's committee."

Because of his straightforward retort to the Velde suggestion, Oxnam was subjected to an avalanche of criticism. A member of the House Committee, Representative Donald L. Jackson of California — enjoying congressional immunity — delivered one of the most violent attacks on a clergyman ever made on the floor of the House. He charged: "Bishop Oxnam has been to the Communist front what Man O'War was to thoroughbred horse racing." Jackson added:

If reprinting Bishop Oxnam's record of aid and comfort to the Communist front would serve any useful purpose, I would ask permission to insert it here, but suffice it to say that the record is available to any member who cares to request it from the Committee [on Un-American Activities].

Two days later, Representative Jackson declined to make public this information that he said was available. The Washington *Post* finally secured Oxnam's "record" from the House Committee, asked the Bishop for his comment, and printed the entire report, together with Oxnam's reply. There were 305 typewritten lines in the House report; Oxnam divided them into the following categories:

Two are introduction;

Sixteen are a summary of the organizations mentioned in the report;

One hundred twenty-eight concern organizations never listed as subversive, or quotations from journals that are not related to subversive organizations or activities;

Seventy-two are from an obscure newspaper in Princeton, Ill., the utter falsity of which might have been disclosed in half an hour's conversation had a committee investigator bothered to walk the 300 yards from the Capitol to my office;

Sixty-four are devoted to organizations to which I never belonged;

Twenty-three refer to organizations listed as Communist fronts to which I once belonged but from which I had resigned prior to the publication of the Attorney General's list of subversive organizations and concerning which I have made full explanation above [in the same issue of the Washington *Post*].

244 Apostles of Discord

At his own request, Bishop Oxnam appeared before the House
Committee on July 21, 1953, to answer its charges against him.
He accused the Committee of playing "into Communist hands
. . . by bearing false witness against fellow Americans," and of
using methods that give rise to a "new . . . Ku Kluxism."

After a grueling, sometimes short-tempered, hearing, the
House Committee voted Oxnam a clean bill of health as regards
Communist Party affiliation. While some argued that the Bishop's
zeal for social reform occasionally had led him into suspicious
company, his testimony succeeded in bringing before the public,
in dramatic fashion, the fallacious methods that have marked the
operation of the House Committee for many years.

McIntire, of course, quickly joined the fray. He began
circulation of a pamphlet, *Bishop Oxnam, Prophet of Marx,* in
which he charged that "as perhaps no other man, Oxnam represents the popular, radical, pro-communistic element in religious
circles in America." McIntire's case was marred by his usual
distortion of the facts. He sought to get his pamphlet to all
government officials. In an obvious attempt to rally Roman
Catholic support, McIntire completely omitted his customary
references to Oxnam's "pro-Catholicism." (As noted in Chapter
9, McIntire has bitterly criticized Oxnam for taking a courteous
attitude toward the Church of Rome.)

Kaub and His Christian Laymen

In 1949 the apostles of discord hailed a new ally. A retired
70-year-old utilities agent of Madison, Wisconsin, Verne P.
Kaub, organized the American Council of Christian Laymen
"to meet the need for united action in opposition to the teachings
of communism and socialism in churches and church connected
organizations." According to Kaub, the top leadership of every
major Protestant body ("except the more conservative Lutheran
bodies") is controlled by clerics who cast aside "the American
system" to accept "basic Marxist doctrines." Since the clergy
have been so successfully duped, Kaub contends that "only
an organized movement of laymen can reverse this tragic trend."

The American Council of Christian Laymen claims that it
has a small mailing list of three thousand persons — who apparently share Verne Kaub's peculiar notions on politics and

religion. Kaub has had amazing success, however, in propagandizing his accusations against Protestant leadership, and his literature appears wherever divisive groups seek to promote their case against the ecumenical movement. His success in distributing large quantities of literature from his one-man headquarters in Madison is explained by his untiring devotion to his self-styled role as a champion of "Christian Americanism." He toils day in and day out to call attention to the charges he seeks to spread.

Until recently Kaub was a publicity agent for the Wisconsin Power and Light Company, a unit of the old Insull empire. His own mind reflects the sentiments exemplified by the Insull forces in the pale sunlight of Coolidge prosperity. Currently, for example, Kaub's organization is distributing a leaflet entitled *Jesus: A Capitalist,* which describes how "Jesus worked with his father in the construction business" in that glorious age when "there was no labor union to meddle with prices and wages."

In 1947 Kaub published a book, *Collectivism Challenges Christianity,* in which he placed his archaic political philosophy under a religious halo. His thesis was briefly thus: America was founded on Christian principles — especially that the individual is the basis of society. Out of this belief developed the system of private enterprise. Collectivism is opposed to free enterprise; hence collectivism is opposed to Christianity. While the study began with some commendable basic propositions, Kaub's distaste for democracy and his fear of social progress robbed it of any vital ideas which it might have contributed.

Kaub has been somewhat of a gadfly around his native city, snooping into labor and liberal meetings to heckle speakers. For several years he has been crusading against William T. Evjue, editor of the Madison *Capital Times;* and against Alfred W. Swan, long-time leader in the Congregationalist Council for Social Action and pastor of Madison's First Congregational Church, to which Kaub belongs. But Kaub's influence in the city is negligible.

Verne P. Kaub has been closely associated with the efforts of the American Council of Christian Churches to sabotage the church-unity movement. Although the Madison pamphleteer himself remains affiliated with a denomination that is in the National Council, he lauds McIntire's books, contributes to the *Christian Beacon*, circulates American Council literature, and in other ways aids and abets the so-called "Twentieth Century Reformation."

Kaub, who has also befriended the National Association of Evangelicals, carefully sidesteps the controversy between the two fundamentalist coalitions. Perhaps Kaub's main point of conflict with fundamentalists stems from his attitude toward the Roman Catholic Church. On one occasion he wrote to the virulent Catholic weekly *Our Sunday Visitor*: "Not all Protestants are as narrow-minded and viciously biased toward another Christian communion as people of the [Paul] Blanshard stripe." This is unusual talk for a man who gives full support to forces inciting widespread hatred of Catholicism. McIntire, for example, refuses to recognize that the Roman Catholic faith is Christian.

Kaub has distributed thousands of copies of *How Red Is the Federal (National) Council of Churches,* a six-page brochure coated with a hammer and sickle superimposed upon a cross. The leaflet claims to list "just a few of the hundreds of present and past officers, leaders, and prominent members of the Federal Council who have aided and abetted God-hating, un-American organizations." Among these so-called "subversive" churchmen are Harry Emerson Fosdick, pastor emeritus of the famous Riverside Church in New York; Ralph W. Sockman, pastor of Park Avenue's Christ Church (Methodist); E. Stanley Jones, famous missionary and author of many popular inspirational books; Bishop G. Bromley Oxnam, a president of the World Council of Churches; Henry P. Van Dusen, president of Union Theological Seminary in New York; Samuel McCrea Cavert, executive secretary of the National Council of Churches; and many others.

Kaub's brochure was immediately acclaimed by the hate press across the nation. Gerald L. K. Smith, for example, boosted Kaub as "a Christian Patriot" whose "magnificent bulletin . . . summarizes the personnel among church leaders who have been instrumental in promoting Marxism in the United States." Smith suggested that "every leading churchman and active Sunday School teacher and churchworker should have a copy of this brochure." It is significant that the Christian Nationalist Crusade has distributed large quantities of the leaflet from its St. Louis offices under its own imprint.

Brochures like *How Red Is the Federal (National) Council of Churches?* are a threat to intelligent efforts to battle communism at home and abroad. In the first place, Kaub includes among alleged "communist organizations" several that are obviously not communist. The Fellowship of Reconciliation is an excellent example. Although the Fellowship is acknowledged widely as one of the most reputable pacifist organizations in the country, Kaub describes it as a "radical-pacifist group using Christian terms to spread communist propaganda." The original source for this characterization seems to have been *Thc Red Network,* although the identical description has been used by numerous other critics of the Fellowship of Reconciliation since 1934, when the *Red Network* first appeared. Other non-communist or anti-communist groups labeled "subversive" by Kaub include the American Civil Liberties Union, the Committee on Militarism in Education, the League for Industrial Democracy, the National Religion and Labor Foundation, and the War Resisters League.

A second error of Kaub's brochure is its misrepresentation of the records of church leaders whom it mentions. Let us note, by way of a single illustration, the alleged associations of President Van Dusen of Union Theological Seminary. According to *How Red Is the Federal (National) Council of Churches?* Van Dusen has been "affiliated" with five "subversive" groups: the American Committee for the Protection of the Foreign Born, the Committee on Militarism in Education, the War Resisters League, the National Religion and Labor Foundation, and the Socialist Party.

Of these, only the first, the American Committee for the Protection of the Foreign Born, *eventually* became a communist front. Van Dusen has said he has no recollection of any contact with this organization. Upon further investigation it appeared that on April 17, 1943 — when the Soviet Union and this country were allies against Nazi aggression — Van Dusen joined with William Allen White and Dorothy Thompson as one of more than a hundred sponsors of a United Nations dinner, allegedly sponsored by the American Committee for the Protection of the

Foreign Born. Miss Thompson and Mr. White, the two principal speakers, were well-known foes of communism and close friends of Union Seminary's president.

Van Dusen was connected briefly in the 1920's with the Committee on Militarism in Education, an "affiliate" of the Fellowship of Reconciliation designed to attract non-pacifists who opposed military units in American colleges. He was never affiliated in any way with the War Resisters League, a legitimate pacifist group with a secular bent. On the contrary, those familiar with Van Dusen's background will recall that he was a leader among the clergy who favored the interventionist cause before World War II.

Union Seminary's president has had no connection with the fourth organization, the National Religion and Labor Foundation, since the early 1930's. Incidentally, the Foundation has taken vigorous steps during the past few years to oust its small, pro-communist minority so that it might retain the democratic viewpoint that characterized it when Van Dusen was a member.

Finally, like many other leading ministers, Van Dusen had a nominal connection for a period of about two years in the late 1920's with the political movement led by his friend Norman Thomas. The American Socialist Party under Thomas' leadership has always, of course, vigorously opposed communism; and even George E. Sokolsky, conservative columnist for the Hearst newspapers, has included Norman Thomas in his list of "most patriotic Americans."

Similar facts, in contrast to Kaub's misrepresentations, could be recounted for most of the other leading churchmen attacked in *How Red Is the Federal (National) Council of Churches?*

In its efforts to discredit the ecumenical movement, the Kaub brochure exhibits a third fallacy that demonstrates its unreliability. In listing "present and past officers, leaders and prominent members of the Federal Council," the booklet includes persons who have had no connection whatsoever with the ecumenical movement except as members of affiliated denominations.

Highly influential personalities, however, are omitted. There is no reference, for example, to the two most recent presidents of the National Council, the Rt. Rev. Henry Knox Sherrill and Bishop William C. Martin; no reference to any of its vice-presidents, including such hyper-conservatives as Jasper Crane, Mrs. Norman Vincent Peale, and Mrs. Olive Ann Beech (see Chapter 12); no reference to such presidents of the Federal Council as Bishop John Stamm, Rt. Rev. Henry St. George Tucker, and Charles P. Taft; no reference to dozens of those who have held important positions with the ecumenical movement, including such lay leaders as Secretary of State John Foster Dulles, Harold E. Stassen, Mutual Security Director under President Eisenhower, and Charles E. Wilson, former president of the General Electric Corporation. A fair sampling of National Council officers would have shown that they do not represent political opinions at variance with the American people as a whole.

In addition to the customary attacks upon the ecumenical movement, *How Red Is the Federal (National) Council of Churches?* makes a bid for the support of anti-Semites with the assertion that "the Federal Council receives large sums from various Jewish and other non-Christian or anti-Christian groups, so . . . the withdrawal of your church's support won't put them out of business." Variations of this falsehood have been made many times before by the ministers of hate. It may be significant that Gerald Winrod — who preached that the Federal Council leadership was "fundamentally Judaistic" — voiced this charge just before Kaub did, in strikingly similar language. The principal contributors to the Federal Council, Winrod said, "are Jews and Jewish organizations . . . The Federal Council could sever all connections with the Protestant bodies it professes to represent and continue functioning just the same."

Many of Kaub's errors, in fact as well as in judgment, may be traced to the sources from which they came. We have already seen that he appears to have made use of *The Red Network*. Other important aids were the reports of various governmental agencies and legislative committees. Some of these reports, such as the widely used Attorney General's list, are accurate as a whole; others, however, are of doubtful reliability, such as the reports of the defunct Tenney Committee of California and those of the Congressional Committee to Investigate Communism, headed by former Congressman Hamilton Fish.

A third source of Kaub's material was the files of the American Intelligence Agency, organized by Allen Alderson Zoll. Zoll also directs the National Council for American Education, of which Kaub is vice-president in charge of research. The Council has been attacked by the National Education Association as an irresponsible foe of the public schools which attempts "to undermine education and educational institutions under the guise of patriotism."

Before his current venture, Zoll had a lengthy record of boldly anti-democratic activities. His enterprises included the founding in 1936 of the American Patriots, a group that has been officially labeled "fascist" by the Attorney General of the United States. With full knowledge of Zoll's background, Kaub says he is "a personal friend of mine and a fine Christian gentleman. I will go all out for him." Some observers find this attitude consistent with Kaub's own disapproval of democracy; on one occasion, the Madison pamphleteer wrote: "Democracy is not a Christian word and has no meaning for Christians."

Those who make such accusations seldom appear capable of discriminating between communism and decent citizenship; glibly they insist upon equating these two opposing viewpoints by means of misleading clichés. Some of them cease pressing unfair charges when the facts are revealed. A few of them, however, persist in the technique of the unsubstantiated charge. They harm innocent people and, in addition, confuse American's effort to root out actual pro-Kremlin enemies of democracy.

By the false smear and the big lie — creating division among Americans and ill-will abroad — these men actually aid communism, the foe they intend to combat.

11

The Hammer and Sickle Behind the Cross

Lights dim. Loudspeakers blare out the message that all good people want peace. The crowd is asked to sing "The Star Spangled Banner," as a spotlight turns on the American flag to the left of the stage and a fan sets it floating in the breeze. A narrator — a sonorous-voiced Protestant minister — stands behind a pulpit-like lectern, reading dramatically from his script. In the background hangs a huge drawing of terrified Korean women clutching their babies in their arms as flaming napalm bombs burst around them. On the side of the hall are draped two demanding banners: "BRING THE BOYS HOME." "SALUTE THE WORLD PEACE COUNCIL."

This is a communist rally in the United States — 1953 style.

Folk singers appeal for peace through song. An African trio presents a rendition of native "peace" rhythm. Ukrainian dancers perform "peace" dances. A People's Chorus translates "peace" songs into French, German, Spanish, Russian, Chinese, English. A church choir sings of "peace" in gospel hymns and triumphant anthems.

At this rally — typical of many — the oration of the evening is delivered in stern ministerial tone by a Congregational pastor from a small New England town. With him on the platform are a score of his brethren, all in the garb of their profession. They speak grimly of the sin of war and remind their audience of God's command for peace.

In such fashion, the Communist Party is using a small but active group of Protestant ministers to further its cause in this country and throughout the world.

From time to time the communists and willful fellow-travelers

have sought to exploit traditional religious symbols and sentiments in an attempt to influence church members. They fail
to point out that communism is, in fact, a rival "faith," with an
opposing set of symbols and sentiments. Its central credo is
dialectical materialism; its saints, Marx and Lenin; its scriptures,
the *Communist Manifesto* and *Das Kapital;* its hierarchy, the
Politburo; its priests, the commissars; its chosen people, the
proletariat; its redemption, the revolution; and its heaven, the
New World Order.

A startling example of the way in which the communists dis-
tort religion to advance their plot against democracy was the
so-called Peace Prayer Vigil, held Sunday, October 7, 1951, in
New York City. Manipulating widespread pacifist sentiment,
an Interfaith Committee for Peace Action, including more than
thirty ministers and rabbis, sponsored three meetings in different parts of the city.

The largest meeting, at Manhattan Center, was led by the
Rev. Edward D. McGowan of the Epworth Methodist Church,
Bronx chairman of the American Labor Party. A second meet-
ing, at Rockland Palace, was directed jointly by churchman Wil-
lard Uphaus, co-chairman of the Kremlin-inspired American
Peace Crusade, and the Rev. Thomas Kilgore, Jr., pastor of
Friendship Baptist Church in New York City. A final meeting,
held in St. Nicholas Arena, was chaired by the Rev. J. Spencer
Kennard, Jr., lecturer, former missionary in China, and author of
Render to God.

Many other clergymen, most of them old-timers in extremist
circles, gave their blessing to the Peace Vigil. Their roster in-
cluded Dudley Burr of the South Congregational Church, East
Hartford, Connecticut; Professor Joseph F. Fletcher of the
Episcopal Theological Seminary, Cambridge, Massachusetts;
Charles A. Hill of the Hartford Avenue Baptist Church, Detroit;
Donald G. Lothrop of the Community Church, Boston; Wil-
liam B. Spofford, Sr., editor of *The Witness* (Episcopal); and
Kenneth Ripley Forbes, executive chairman of the Episcopal
League for Social Action.

"Close to the people of our congregations, we know that their
most fervent desire is peace now," began an advance release

from the Interfaith Committee for Peace Action. Newspaper
advertisements called upon churches of "all communions and
faiths" to help fill the meeting halls. It was part and parcel of
the world-wide "peace offensive" characterized by Dean Acheson, then Secretary of State, as "the most concentrated and
far-flung propaganda effort of the International Communist
movement in the post-war world."

In typical party lingo, the *Daily Worker* summarized the proceedings:

> Workers, housewives, students, professionals, merchants, Negro and
> white, of all political opinions and denominations joined in united prayer
> for immediate cessation of war in Korea. They cheered clergymen, labor
> leaders and Negro spokesmen who challenged the bipartisan warmakers
> and pleaded for a great people's peace coalition.

The Communist Party organ boasted that there had been nine
thousand participants. Other observers estimated the audience
at a fraction of the number.

Disturbed by the publicity given such events, churchmen are
asking: Are there Protestant communists? Who are they?
Where do they do their work? Have they actually been successful in insinuating their views into denominational publications? How much of a threat do they pose at the present time?
What have the churches done about them? What *should* the
churches do about them?

There are no simple answers to these and similar inquiries.
The genuine subversive keeps well hidden. In these days of
confused issues, he may seek to exploit conservative causes as
well as liberal, isolationist as well as internationalist. Added to
such complications is the necessity for broad insight and careful
discretion. Civil liberties must be maintained. The reputations
of honest men must be protected; the innocent must be spared
from wild accusations. It is of the greatest importance that the
churches refrain from excessive emotional indulgence, and study
all charges of subversive influence with objectivity, thorough-
ness, and justice.

Contrary to those who want to discredit forward-looking
Protestant leaders, there has been very little infiltration into the
churches in recent years. In fact, the situation today is consider-

ably better than in the 1920's and 1930's — and especially in the period during World War II — when many of Protestantism's top leaders, for various reasons, loaned their prestige to Soviet Russia. Today, in 1953, only a handful of apologists for the Kremlin remain active in the churches.

Nevertheless, the churches are a key target for communist infiltration. The Communist Party has stepped up its program to enlist religion in the service of Moscow.

By and large, it is as individuals that pro-communists have sought influence among churchmen. They have established few church *groups* specifically to serve as smokescreens for subversive activity. But special attention must be given to one publication, *The Protestant,* and one organization, the People's Institute of Applied Religion, both of which once claimed widespread support among reputable clergymen — because they have become the personal property of those who devote themselves to playing the Moscow game. Then several case histories will be examined — to show how a few pro-communists still carry on in major Protestant denominations.

Kenneth Leslie and The Protestant

The Protestant (formerly the *Protestant Digest*) was published in New York City until 1951, when it was moved to Nova Scotia, by its Canadian Baptist editor, Kenneth Leslie. In its first issue — December 1938 — it carried a strong hint as to its future policy. Leslie asked: "Is it not possible for both Christians and Communists, instead of condemning each other in their mutual weakness, to contribute the best they each have and work together for the common good?" By the height of World War II, *The Protestant* claimed a hundred thousand readers and boasted that it represented more than six thousand Protestant clergymen.

Within a few months after its debut, *The Protestant* adopted a bitter anti-Catholic attitude, rooted in part in its abhorrence of fascist Spain. Even during the war, however, when American Catholics and Protestants were united in fighting the common fascist foe, Leslie spoke jeeringly of "the Hitler-Vatican shenanigans," denounced Fulton J. Sheen as a "dangerous . . .

subtle Fascist," and held that the Papacy was interested in "a Fascist world hegemony." The National Conference of Christians and Jews was controlled by "Catholic clericalism," Leslie complained. "Behind the Inter-Faith cloak flashes the stiletto aimed at the heart of our free democracy."

In contrast to Leslie's unreasoning anti-Catholicism, *The Protestant* posed as a special friend of the Jews. Frequently Protestant Associates, Inc. — the official publishers of the magazine — inserted large advertisements in metropolitan newspapers to protest against anti-Semitism. Leslie organized two committees for this purpose: the Textbook Commission to Eliminate Anti-Semitic Statements in American Textbooks, and the National Committee to Combat Anti-Semitism. Both attracted large numbers of supporters.

These groups were immediately repudiated by the leading Jewish agencies in the United States. The American Jewish Committee quickly advised its followers

. . . to give no financial support to these affiliated organizations. Backed by no official Protestant organization, *The Protestant* further belies its name by circulating largely among Jews and by seeking a major part of its financial support from Jewish organizations and individuals. This, we believe, is inherently wrong, the more so when a careful study of the files of *The Protestant* reveals that the periodical tends to arouse animosity and distrust among people of different creeds.

The Anti-Defamation League of B'nai B'rith expressed a similar opinion:

We look with disfavor on any controversy between Protestant, Catholic, and other religious publications or groups. Indeed, we are interested in any move to counteract prejudice or defamation of Protestant, Catholic or Jew, Negro or White. Therefore, we do not favor *The Protestant* or its Textbook Commission or approve any sectarian publication which does create such controversy.

When Jewish groups showed reluctance to recognize Leslie's concern, he vigorously denounced them as "deceivers of the public," "betrayers of Jewish interests," "promoters of fascism." Outbursts of anti-Zionism during recent months in the Soviet Union have led to parallel anti-Zionism in *The Protestant*. In early 1953 Leslie wrote:

US Zionism, involving world Zionism, is offering itself and its cause as a sacrifice to the appetites of anti-Soviet money imperialism. . . . The sad truth is that it is American Zionist leadership (along with its hired Christian attendants) which has sold itself to the service of the Napalm Knights of the new world aggression.

He accused pro-Western Jews of failing to understand "that an anti-Semite is always a red baiter and a red baiter is always an anti-Semite."

Originally, *The Protestant* had been able to gain widespread backing from reputable clergymen. Among the "advisors" of its editorial board who came to realize that they had been co-operating unwittingly with a tool of the Kremlin policy were such active non-communist Protestant figures as Dwight J. Bradley, Charles S. Braden, L. M. Birkhead, Frederick May Eliot, John A. Mackay, James Moffatt, Louie D. Newton, G. Bromley Oxnam, Wilhelm Pauck, Edwin McNeill Poteat, W. Stanley Rycroft, Douglas V. Steere, Paul Tillich, Channing H. Tobias, and many more. Of those who remained on *The Protestant's* advisory board, the majority still involve themselves in innumerable front activities. These include the Rev. Reginald H. Bass of Central Community Church, Brooklyn, co-chairman of New York Peace Institute; the Rev. Joseph F. Fletcher, professor at the Episcopal Theological Seminary in Cambridge, Massachusetts; the Rev. J. Spencer Kennard, Jr., author and former faculty member of West China Union University; the Rev. Donald Lothrop, minister of Community Church, Boston; the Rev. E. D. McGowan of the Epworth Methodist Church of the Bronx; the Rev. Dryden L. Phelps, former Baptist missionary to West China; and the Rev. Claude C. Williams, director of People's Institute of Applied Religion. Phelps and Williams will be discussed later in this chapter.

The Protestant also receives the moral support of Hewlett Johnson, Britain's "Red Dean," and of Bishop Albert Bereczky of Hungary.

Leslie himself has had a novel and varied career. One source reports that he has taught, lectured, farmed an apple orchard, bought and sold stock, led a dance orchestra, studied acting, written poetry, operated a buttermilk restaurant in Los Angeles, sung Hebredian songs over the radio, written and published popular songs under the firm name of Leslie and Fitzgerald. For a short period he was on the staff of the First Baptist Church of Montclair, New Jersey. Former associates say that at one time he was strongly interested in Catholicism, studying its ritual and teachings and even carrying a St. Theresa religious medal.

Many of the original sponsors of *The Protestant* withdrew their support soon after the magazine began. Later, in 1946, the entire executive force of the magazine resigned, led by Pierre Van Paassen, contributing editor. The issue was not ideological; the rebels charged: "Mr. Leslie's adamant stand that *The Protestant* is not an organizational movement but his privately owned enterprise under his control" had resulted in the "tragic collapse" of the magazine. Joseph Brainin, associate editor and spokesman for the group, said the withdrawal was not related to Leslie's political views.

Immediately after Henry Wallace announced his availability for the presidency in January 1948, *The Protestant* came to his support. In a telegram to Wallace signed by the six ministers of the board of publishers, and by the chairmen of the most important Ministerial Action Committees in Chicago, Hartford, Philadelphia, and New York, its sponsors declared: "*The Protestant* urges the people of America to support the peoples' party of Wallace not merely as a political party but as a profound spiritual revolt against the business and church cartels which led us to war and want. *The Protestant* recognizes in your Third Party the renewed spirit of our revolutionary forefathers and the true promise of world peace."

Chairmen of the Ministerial Action Committees sponsoring the telegram were Wilfred Wakefield and William T. Baird of Chicago, Chester E. Hodgson of New York, George F. Conner of Philadelphia and Edward L. Peet of Hartford. Only the first two of these five clergymen today remain among *The Protestant's* advisors.

The final split came in 1950 when Leslie devoted an entire issue to Korea, referring to America as the "aggressor" and Korea as the "oppressed." "No braver and decenter people exist than the Americans," he wrote. "But they are being involved by their Bankers, Bishops, and Brass in a COWARDLY AND IN-

DECENT ADVENTURE." The whole conflict, Leslie claimed, was a "Dulles baby," the work "of the Wall Street evangelist John Foster Dulles." Leslie charged that the American government had forced the United Nations Security Council "to make an honest woman out of the U. S. and to 'legalize' her illegal intervention."

A direct result of the special Korean issue of *The Protestant* was the resignation of several more editorial advisors. Adam Clayton Powell, Jr., Harlem clergyman and member of Congress, and John Hammond, wealthy patron of swing music, demanded that the publisher immediately remove their names from the masthead. Others followed, including Lee H. Ball, Methodist minister of New Paltz, New York, and treasurer of the Methodist Federation for Social Action. Congressman Powell telegraphed Leslie: "I THOUGHT THE PROTESTANT HAD STOPPED PUBLICATION. JUST SAW ARTICLE ON KOREA. EMPHATICALLY DISAGREE. REMOVE MY NAME IMMEDIATELY." He told the New York *World Telegram and Sun* that he started to "clear out of all left-wing organizations" in 1949 — in protest against Paul Robeson's assertion in Paris that Negroes would not support the United States in a war with the Soviet Union.

When the central committee of the World Council of Churches, meeting in Toronto in July 1950, approved United Nations action in Korea, Leslie sharply dissented: "Western leaders of the new ecumenical Christianity . . . accept with realistic fortitude the fact that innocent must die that the Kingdom of Profit must stay." He carried his case further against the World Council: "The whole artillery of the World Council is thrown against the peace movements of the hundreds of millions of ordinary people everywhere encircling the entire world and threatening the profits of the merchants of death."

The Protestant continues to follow the same rigid line. Its editor recently praised party-line religious figures in contrast with conservative World Council leaders. "We can see no common ground," he said, "between a Hromadka [Czech] and a Leiper, a Bereczky [Hungarian] and a Van Dusen, an Endicott [Canadian pro-communist] and a Visser t'Hooft." Leslie wrote: "We do not believe in the good faith of the World Council of Churches." He charged it with deliberately cultivating "animosity" against the Soviet Union and the other Socialist countries. "How can the Hungarians (and we shall let them symbolize all Eastern churches) sit down and hold communion with a group of men who serve not the God of peace but the God of war?!"

Fifteen years after its birth *The Protestant* had shrunk from a 64-page monthly journal to a thin, irregular multigraphed bulletin. Its influence has deteriorated rapidly as its party line has become more and more evident.

The People's Institute of Applied Religion

The People's Institute of Applied Religion, one of America's most incredible "religious" organizations, has from the outset been geared to the service of communist aspirations in the United States. The institute was founded in Arkansas in June 1936, "to give positive Leadership Training — in the principles and practice of brotherhood — to the natural and accepted leaders of the peoples of the rural South."

The power behind the People's Institute has been the Rev. Claude Clossey Williams, a Presbyterian minister whose services were refused recently by the fellowship committee of the American Unitarian Association when he attempted to join that denomination. Williams was born in the Tennessee hill country, the son of very poor parents who were devoted fundamentalists. His childhood and personal growth has been dramatically chronicled by a sympathetic editor, Cedric Belfrage of the Progressive Party's official weekly, the *National Guardian*.

Young Claude had a difficult inner struggle before he finally succumbed to the call of the ministry. Slowly he swung away from the faith of his parents until he had rejected the basic concept of organized religion and substituted for it a belief in Karl Marx. "Neither Protestant nor Catholic church religion can accept the implications of a people's world," he complained. "Together and of one accord they will lead the counterattack against the democratic peoples of the world."

In 1938, Williams was made director of Commonwealth College in Mena, Arkansas. On one occasion, when visiting the president of the Southern Tenant Farmers' Union, of which he was a member, Williams left behind a secret report to communist headquarters. The Union's president acted promptly. "The enclosed report shows conclusively," he wrote, "that you have connived and that you are still attempting to connive with the Communist party to 'capture' the Southern Tenant Farmers' Union." At an ensuing trial, Williams denied the authenticity of the document, claimed that it was written by someone else, and insisted that he had left the Communist Party when he was called to head Commonwealth College.

Later, Williams was quoted as saying: "Denominationally I am a Presbyterian, religiously a Unitarian, and politically I'm a Communist. I'm not preaching to make people good or anything of the sort. I'm in the church because I can reach people easier that way and get them organized for Communism."

Early in the Second World War, Claude Williams was named by the War Emergency Committee of the Presbyterian Board of National Missions to be their industrial chaplain in Detroit. Hordes of people from the South were moving into Detroit at that time, and they were being drawn in two directions. On the one hand, certain industrialists in the city encouraged a group of disruptive ultra-fundamentalists, led by Gerald L. K. Smith, J. Frank Norris, E. J. Rollings, and others. Simultaneously, Detroit was studded with hundreds of tiny store-front churches which attempted to meet the needs of the mass migrations from Dixie. The Presbyterian Board of National Misssions sent Claude Williams to counteract the detrimental effects of both movements.

The Tennessee-born preacher, however, was never free from trouble, largely because of his lack of discretion and his basic antipathy toward the creed he professed. For example, he visited churches in the area to tell the congregations that their ministers were more interested in Shakespeare than the gospel of Christ. Because of Williams' poor public relations, the Presbytery unanimously decided that his work must be discontinued. In fact, Williams' failure to achieve the co-operation of Detroit's churches has seriously delayed the work of Protestantism among trade unions in that area.

Undaunted by his Detroit failure, Claude Williams returned to the South in 1946 to continue his efforts on behalf of his

unique interpretation of Christianity. For a number of years
the People's Institute had been reasonably successful. In fact,
its national board at one time included more than fifty important
churchmen. Among those who have showed a consistent tendency to remain complacent in the face of Soviet aggression
even after World War II are Jack McMichael, executive secretary of the Methodist Federation for Social Action; William B.
Spofford, Sr., editor of *The Witness* (Episcopal); and Willard E.
Uphaus, co-chairman of the communist-sponsored American
Peace Crusade.

Also involved, however, was a scattering of non-communist
clergymen who no longer supported Williams when the real ob-
jectives of his group became evident. These included Dr. James
Luther Adams, professor at Meadville Theological School of the
University of Chicago; L. M. Birkhead, national director of
Friends of Democracy; Liston Pope, dean of Yale Divinity
School; Edwin McNeil Poteat, former president of Colgate-
Rochester Divinity School; Charles C. Webber, Methodist mini-
ster, president of the CIO in Virginia.

Williams' main thesis has been that organized "church" religion is the enemy of the people. "Catholic church religion,"
he argues, "came into being to buttress the decaying Roman
Empire. . . . Today this church religion is controlled by a
closely-knit politico-economic leadership." But Protestantism
he condemns in even sharper terms:

> Protestant church religion came into being to enhance the rise of
> capitalism. It proclaimed the divine right of property. It deified the
> kings of finance, the lords of commerce and the captains of industry.
> Today, this church religion is directed by remote control from the
> Chamber of Commerce, the National Association of Manufacturers, and
> the offices of cartel imperialists.

Two of his favorite targets have been the ecumenical movement
and Youth for Christ, which he has characterized as "another
Hitler youth movement."

Williams traces the failure of Protestantism to the "Christ-
centered theology of Paul." In his "handbook for progressive
leaders" entitled *Religion: Barrier or Bridge to a People's World*,
he writes:

The Christology of Saul became the theology of the Protestant church, the ideology of "Christian" capitalism; and has been the basis of religious anti-Semitism, Catholic and Protestant, from Paul to Hitler. Today every anti-Semitic, anti-Negro, anti-Labor, Nationalist sermon of the Norrises, Springers, Loves, MacAllisters, Rollins is studded with quotations from "St. Paul."

The only exception to Williams' blanket condemnation of Protestantism is "a sprinkling of Unitarian liberalism and ethical culture" which "are not essentially Protestant."

In fact, the People's Institute has been loud in its denunciations of individuals and organizations whom ultra-conservative Protestants sometimes consider part of their "pink fringe," including John Haynes Holmes and Henry Hitt Crane, two eminent liberal pacifists, and such organizations as the National Religion and Labor Foundation and the Conference of Southern Churchmen.

"Instead of using religion to unite labor and the progressive forces," contends Williams, "these groups have fallen into the fascist-inspired, Vatican-directed 'anti-Communist' trap. Together with their smart boy Reuther, with the Social Democrats, Ethical Socialists, Thomasites and Trotskyites, they can be expected to support the biggest union-busting program the Master Capitalists of America have ever inaugurated."

Williams has been adept in claiming support from the Bible for his Marxist views. In fact, his chief effort has been to attract fundamentalists in the Bible Belt on the grounds that he bases his credo completely on Biblical texts — that he is a "fellow-traveling fundamentalist." Thus, for example, he summarizes the role of Jesus Christ as follows:

The Nazarene Carpenter was "kangarooed" and lynched because he stirred up the people, the common people; and in such numbers that the agents of Rome said, Behold the whole world is gone after him (Luke 23: 5; Mark 12: 37; John 12: 19). The Nazarene was a class-conscious leader of the people, the common people (Matt. 26: 5).

At another point, Williams gives the reader this version of Christ's life and death:

Rome had organized the oppressive forces of the whole world against the people (Luke 2: 1-3). The Galilean began to organize the oppressed of the whole world against Rome (Matt. 11: 28-30). He was shadowed and framed by the stooges of the Roman Empire (Luke 20: 20).

On the night before he was lynched, he called his disciples together in an underground meeting (Luke 22: 1-12). Here he expounded the nature of the people's movement (Luke 22: 25-27), the danger of traitors (John 12: 38), the nature of the opposition (John 15: 18-20). He pointed out the need of the closest possible organization — that of a vine and its branches. He warned against individualism or shooting forth as a branch lest they be plucked off. He stressed the power of unity (John 15: 4-7). Early the next morning he was condemned by religious Quislings and crucified by a Gentile Gestapo (Matt. 20: 18,19).

Williams' "theology" runs true to Marxist form. Common sense, he contends, "will expose the fallacy that religion implies belief in the 'supernatural' — an un-scriptural invention of theology." True religion, he says, uses the class struggle as the most effective weapon of constructive social change in a class society. The end in sight is "to put down the mighty from their seats, to exalt them of low degree, to fill the hungry with good things, and to send the rich empty away (Luke 1:52-3)."

The People's Institute of Applied Religion increasingly has become the sole instrument of its director, until its support is limited to "party-liners" and a smattering of deluded idealists. Williams' organization struggles to keep alive at its headquarters in Helena, Alabama.

"ELSA" and the Party Line

As will be seen in Chapter 13, the Methodist Church, the nation's largest Protestant group, has a "party-line" faction that has been the cause of severe denominational conflict. But equaling Methodism's Soviet apologists in effectiveness is an influential faction within the Protestant Episcopal Church, collectively organized as the Episcopal League for Social Action.

In spite of the conservative views of many Episcopal laymen, League supporters have important positions within the denominational framework. Some, of course, are alert liberals without a tinge of communism; but a minority of League members, strategically located, faithfully meet the Kremlin line at most points.

Local branches of the Episcopal League for Social Action have been active in several of the larger cities, but it is directed from

Philadelphia, Pennsylvania, where the 74-year-old Rev. Kenneth Ripley Forbes, retired clergyman, serves as executive chairman. The League has a governing committee of nine, a membership of two hundred, and a mailing list of a thousand. Information bulletins go out regularly, with recommendations for "appropriate action" in the fields of world peace, civil rights, and social change.

Typical of the League's national meetings was their 1952 discussion of peace, as recorded in the columns of *The Witness*. The Rev. William Howard Melish, controversial acting rector of Holy Trinity parish in Brooklyn, delivered an address, giving his support to the communist-inspired "peace" movement, criticizing United States policy, without a word directed against the activities of the Soviet Union. In the discussion that followed, similar views were expressed by most of the speakers. Professor Joseph F. Fletcher, for example, characterized the communist-inspired World Peace Council (of which he was vice-president) as "the only genuinely international, interideological, unofficial peace-making activity that goes on in the world today." Most of the discussion was carried on under the banner of "Christian reconciliation."

Perhaps the most influential member of the League is William B. Spofford, Sr., managing editor of *The Witness*, a church journal which claims to have the largest circulation of Episcopal weeklies. The 61-year-old clergyman has been with *The Witness* since 1919 and served for many years as executive secretary of the Church League for Industrial Democracy (predecessor to the Episcopal League for Social Action). The magazine's editor is Roscoe T. Foust, rector of the Church of the Ascension in New York City. In the study of his church, articles and editorials for *The Witness* are discussed at editors' meetings held for a half-day twice each month.

Many of those affiliated with the magazine — such as Foust — do not agree with Spofford's extremist views. They support *The Witness,* in spite of its slant, because they believe in Spofford's right to be heard, and because they consider the publication a careful reporter of Episcopal news.

The Witness is an important cog in the extremist, pro-communist faction in the Protestant churches. Most of the magazine's space is devoted to the usual church news, because in some American communities the journal is the only Episcopalian publication read. Politics receives only secondary emphasis. Nevertheless, news stories and editorials dealing with controversial international issues almost invariably follow the current Communist Party line. *The Witness,* for example, displayed great enthusiasm for the communist-inspired Peace Prayer Vigil (described above), in spite of the fact that the religious world at large ignored it — or heard nothing of it. A few months previously, Kenneth Ripley Forbes had written the lead article in lengthy praise of the Crusade for Peace — another communist-inspired program that won no space whatever in most of the religious press. Echoing a familiar line, Forbes said in part:

> The immediate, crucial need for action on the peace front is the withdrawal of American soldiers and sailors from Korea, where they never should have intervened in a Korean civil war, unsanctioned by Congress and regretted now by probably a large majority of Americans, and simultaneous negotiation with the Peoples' Republic of China for permanent peace on that tortured peninsula.

The balance of this article — like many others in the magazine — read much like the columns of the *Daily Worker,* employing the same traditional vocabulary with its emphasis upon the "rank and file" pitted against the "warmakers" and marching en masse to Washington to demand peace. Like the communist and pro-communist press, *The Witness* frequently pictures the American "people" on the brink of revolt against "Big Business taskmasters," who are rushing the nation into an international slaughter to avert the inevitable crash of an economic system based upon savage exploitation.

Perhaps an even more significant demonstration of how *The Witness* twists and turns with the serpentine movements of the party line has been its attitude toward the so-called germ warfare. In the issue for August 21, 1952, for example, the lead editorial, "Our Ostrich Government," repeated, with implicit approval, most of the communist misrepresentations of United States policy. Although the magazine did not give full endorsement to the germ-warfare hoax, it rushed to defend those who pressed the charges, including certain "distinguished" persons from the West. Who were these individuals? "The best known of these are Dean Hewlett Johnson of Canterbury, and the Rev. James G. Endicott, a former missionary of the United Church of Canada, who was born in China and worked there as a missionary for 22 years." The first, of course, is better known as the "Red Dean." Endicott, as *The Witness* editor must have known, is an important figure in the communist world "peace" movement, which he has characterized as "the greatest, most universal, most effective movement of the people of the world that has so far appeared in all history." In 1952, Endicott was one of six recipients of the "International Stalin Prizes," presented "for outstanding services in the struggle to preserve and consolidate peace." He is a leader in the small group of former American and Canadian missionaries to China who now follow each twist of the Moscow line.

Nevertheless, *The Witness* gives credence to the charges of these men and concludes: "Suspicion is mounting throughout the world that the American authorities have no better defense than to abuse the opponent's attorney."

Among the many pro-communist articles carried in *The Witness* in early 1953 was "Korea Is on My Conscience," by Willard Uphaus, Methodist co-chairman of the American Peace Crusade. The author introduced his subject with the question: "Must our boys go on dying and killing to keep up a war prosperity?" He continued in a similar vein:

"Stalemate hostility" is a neat phrase for what is going on in Korea. While it lasts we can extract more precious tungsten from the hills of Korea. We will go on with the British and French imperialists, expending blood and treasure, in a futile effort to stop the onward march of the colored peoples to freedom and independence.

Spofford himself is very frank about his admiration for American communists. "The evidence seems abundant that we are fast approaching fascism of the German variety," he writes, "and as I look around, the only organized group that is consistently fighting it is the Communists — certainly not organized Christianity." He shrugs off critics with this statement: "If that makes me a Fellow Traveler, then I will merely have to take it and grin."

Guy Emery Shipler and The Churchman

In addition to the problems raised by the Episcopal League for Social Action and its leaders, the denomination has been troubled by at least two other cases involving left-wing bias — one centering around another Episcopalian clergyman and his magazine, the other around a complicated legal case involving a minister's right to his pulpit.

The first of these is the Rev. Guy Emery Shipler, 71-year-old editor of the independent Episcopal-oriented semi-monthly, *The Churchman,* founded as an organ for theological liberalism. Shipler has been the target of even sharper criticism than his colleague Spofford, although the circulation and influence of his journal is considerably less than that conceded to *The Witness.* Shipler became managing editor of *The Churchman* in 1917; Edna Ruth Johnson, a dominant figure on the staff and frequent champion of communist causes, now holds that strategic position. The Churchman Associates include more than a thousand dues-paying members, the majority of whom are Episcopalians. Among the associate trustees are dozens of distinguished non-communist Protestant leaders, including Dr. Henry A. Atkinson, general secretary of the World Alliance for International Friendship Through Religion; Dr. Georgia Harkness, professor at the Pacific School of Religion, Berkeley, California; Dr. Harry A. Overstreet, author of *The Mature Mind* and other well-known books; Dr. Ralph W. Sockman, pastor of Park Avenue's Christ Church (Methodist); and Dr. Carl Hermann Voss, chairman of the executive council of the American Christian Palestine Committee. More than a half-dozen Episcopal bishops are on the list. Professor W. Russell Bowie of Virginia Theological Seminary is president of the Churchman Associates.

The *New Leader,* anti-communist social-democratic weekly, has gone so far as to suggest that Shipler is "the closest thing America has to the Red Dean. His attachment to the Communists dates back a decade, and what started as a coy flirtation is now a full-fledged affair." Frederick Woltman, Scripps-Howard's professional exposé artist, has often attacked Shipler as "a constant backer of Communist fronts [who] usually brought in the name of *The Churchman* to give them added prestige." L. M. Birkhead, of Friends of Democracy, has charged that *The Churchman* is among those magazines serving as "very helpful agencies by which the Communist party does its work in America."

Shipler's harshest critics have contended: (1) that he has a long record of extensive involvement with communist-front organizations; (2) that his editorials have run parallel to many points on the Communist Party line; and (3) that he has defended the freedom of expression of some who have been accused, tried, or convicted of communist intrigue. The editor of *The Churchman* has also pursued what many feel to be an unjustly harsh policy toward Roman Catholicism. The *Living Church,* for example, one of the foremost Episcopal magazines in the country, has gone on record with a statement that *The Churchman* "is more and more becoming the leading anti-Catholic magazine in America."

It seems fair to say that the magazine is slanted toward the far "left." Fellow-travelers, including many leaders in the Episcopal League for Social Action, contribute frequently. The activities of Protestant Stalinists are faithfully reported in the large section of the magazine called "People — Opinions — Events." On the other hand, *The Churchman* has carried an effective exposé of communism by Professor John C. Bennett of Union Theological Seminary in New York, and has featured the ideas of such critics of communism as G. Bromley Oxnam, Edwin McNeill Poteat, Ellis H. Dana, Theodore Cuyler Speers, Frederick C. Grant, Robert J. McCracken, Carl Hermann Voss, and others.

Shipler has many champions among reputable clergymen. Some contend that he seeks only to give unorthodox ideas a fair hearing. Others trace his point of view to a sincere pacifism. Still more believe that any echoing of communist propaganda stems from naïve idealism rather than from any deliberate co-operation with the cause of the Kremlin. A few attach significance to his open admiration for Yugoslavia, which has continued since the abrogation of the Tito-Stalin pact.

Readers of *The Churchman* are in the best position to determine whether its editor's views are reflected in the anti-communist articles or in those that appear to advance the Kremlin cause.

The Melish Case

The final Episcopalian controversy to be discussed here has been characterized by one church-state authority, Canon Anson Phelps Stokes, as "one of the most important cases in recent years involving church-state relations."

The Melish case arose in 1948, when the Church of the Holy Trinity in Brooklyn became a political battlefield. The Rev. J. Howard Melish, rector of the parish — and one of the most warmly regarded clergymen of the Protestant Episcopal Church — became the butt of sharp criticism after taking on as assistant his son, William Howard Melish. The younger Melish had a long record of pro-communist activities. He had served as a lecturer and trustee at the Jefferson School of Social Justice, a training ground for Communist Party members; he was a frequent contributor to the communist magazine, *New Masses;* he was postwar chairman of the National Council of American-Soviet Friendship (listed by the United States Attorney General as a communist-front organization). Young Melish's association with communist-front activities continued after most Americans had become aware of the imperialistic designs of the Kremlin.

In 1947, Melish returned from a trip to Yugoslavia — on which he had been accompanied by Claude Williams, Guy Emery Shipler, and four other ministers — with favorable reports of Marshall Tito's regime. Soon after, he was invited to appear on the radio program "Town Meeting of the Air" in a discussion of "How To Combat Anti-American Propaganda in Europe." One of the participants, Major General William J. Donovan, wartime head of the Office of Strategic Services, in the course of the broadcast bitterly attacked Melish's long pro-communist record — especially his chairmanship of the National Council of American-Soviet Friendship. Shortly before the radio program, Attorney General Tom Clark had listed the same National Council as a communist-front organization.

Donovan's condemnation of Melish, heard over a coast-to-coast network, was an important factor in consolidating opposition to their assistant minister among the congregation of Holy

Trinity. By early 1948, the church's vestrymen had asked the elder Melish to dismiss his son. When their urgent advice was rejected, they called upon the Bishop of Long Island, James Pernette DeWolfe, to replace the rector with a more tractable man. The Bishop agreed, and the official papers of dismissal were delivered to Melish after the Ash Wednesday services.

Melish refused to vacate his pulpit, and the Bishop's action immediately created a storm within the denomination. Most of the congregation at Holy Trinity — which according to Melish opponents was suddenly enlarged by an influx of his supporters — came to the defense of the father and son. On March 7, 1949, a few days after the Bishop's judgment was delivered, the nine vestrymen were dismissed, at a special caucus of the congregation, by a vote of 261 to 27. The same meeting asked the rector to set a date for another session for the election of a new vestry. The retiring vestrymen issued a strong statement upholding their position. They reviewed Melish's extensive involvement in communist-front groups, and concluded:

We cannot reconcile ourselves to seeing a Christian minister appear to be an apologist for Soviet communism, when one of the creeds of communism is atheism. Nor can we believe in the independent thinking of a Christian minister who remains silent in the face of the destruction of human rights and human lives by Soviet communistic forces. Nor can we acquiesce in acts and speeches which give aid and comfort and the apparent blessing of the church to those who are endeavoring to undermine our principles of Christian life and basic American freedom. . . . We object to the use of the name of this church to give weight and prestige to the views of the assistant minister in support of Soviet propaganda.

Meanwhile, the deposed vestrymen sought a court injunction against the ministers and congregation to reinstate them in office for the rest of their normal terms; the presiding judge issued a temporary injunction to maintain the *status quo*. At the annual meeting, held soon after, the parish named a slate of five new vestrymen, sympathetic to the Melish cause, and passed a resolution instructing the incoming officers to petition Bishop DeWolfe to withdraw his judgment.

When Judge Meier Steinbrink granted a permanent injunction affirming Melish's removal, the rector appealed. His son carried on the church's activities at the request of the new vestry. Under

Episcopal canon, the younger Melish can serve as a "replacement" until the vestry asks its Bishop to supply a full-time rector.

While the appeal to restore the elder Melish went to New York's Court of Appeals, visiting preachers regularly included leaders of the denomination's extreme political fringe: Kenneth Ripley Forbes, William B. Spofford, Sr., Joseph F. Fletcher, Robert Muir, Jr., and Thomas Fletcher Opie.

When the Court of Appeals, New York's highest court, refused to review the case, Dr. J. Howard Melish acquiesced. In a public statement, he said:

> From a purely personal point of view, the termination of my rectorship, which this decision of the court makes effective, is scarcely important. I am an old man of 76, my health is impaired, and my work is done. What concerns me is not my personal vindication but what this outcome of my case represents for religious freedom in the Protestant Episcopal Church and the United States of America. . . . What these men have done in securing the injunctive power of the state to enforce an ecclesiastical decision, in direct contravention of the specific provisions of the canon law of the church, establishes a precedent of state interference in church affairs that endangers the freedom of every minister and congregation in the land, and breaches the concept of separation of church and state at the heart of the American Constitution.

He concluded with the words: "My next appeal must be to the court of heaven."

The controversy enveloped many leading churchmen of other denominations as well. In early 1951, after Bishop DeWolfe obtained the civil injunction, a brief was filed with the United States Supreme Court, on behalf of the dismissed rector. It was signed by 2,576 clergymen. Contending that the secular court had no jurisdiction in the matter, the brief asked for an overruling of the earlier New York decision which granted the injunction enforcing the bishop's ecclesiastical judgment. Their brief is believed to be the fullest expression of opinion from diverse denominational groups ever to come before the Supreme Court. Twelve bishops joined in the appeal — ten Episcopalians and two Methodists. Others included the president and past president of the General Synod of the Reformed Church of America; the moderator and former moderators of the Congregational Christian churches; numerous heads of denominational colleges, deans of theological seminaries, and editors of religious publications.

When the United States Supreme Court, without giving its reasons, refused to review the decision of the New York courts, the Melish controversy reached a stalemate. Ironically, the younger Melish — against whom the original vestry's action had been directed — today is in a position to direct all the activities of the Brooklyn parish.

Issues in dispute were interpreted differently in various quarters. To the general public, young Melish's political affiliations were the basic cause of the controversy. Some Episcopalians viewed the case as an ecclesiastical tug of war, in which less formalistic churchmen joined the Melish forces merely because Bishop DeWolfe was a symbol of the "high" church. Others saw the contest as a difficult problem of church polity where the congregation was arraigned against the vestry, and later against the bishopric. The largest number of Melish supporters came to his aid because they judged it to involve a basic issue in civil liberties.

The Fritchman Case

Within church circles one of the most interesting episodes involving pro-communist infiltration centered on Boston's staid Beacon Hill, in the offices of the American Unitarian Association, national administrative body of the Unitarian denomination.

The controversy revolved around the Rev. Stephen H. Fritchman, former editor of the *Christian Register,* official Unitarian monthly. Fritchman, a powerful personality with a wide educational background, was born in Cleveland. He served as religious news editor of the New York *Herald Tribune* from 1926 to 1928, and then left the Methodist church to assume a prominent role in the Unitarian denomination. From 1938 until January 1947, he served as director of the American Unitarian Youth; at the end of 1942 he became editor of the *Christian Register.*

The struggle which rent the denomination had two principal facets. The technical question arose from disagreement over the extent to which the officers of the American Unitarian Association should control the magazine. Underlying this surface dispute, however, was a bitter division on matters of public policy.

At the close of World War II, the Unitarian denomination

was suffering from the activities of a small but influential pro-communist fringe which had successfully infiltrated the American Unitarian Youth and the Unitarian Service Committee. Fritchman himself was director of the youth group, which had subtly aligned itself with Stalinist elements in the United States and throughout the world. The American Unitarian Youth conferences served as forums for faithful party-liners, and affiliation was maintained with the communist-controlled World Federation of Democratic Youth. Martha Fletcher, associate director of the youth group from 1942 to April 1945, during that period — according to Herbert A. Philbrick in his book *I Lived Three Lives: Citizen, "Communist," Counterspy*—was the leader of a communist cell. After the war the Unitarian Service Committee found itself with two workers — Madame Tempi at its Paris headquarters and Noel Field at Geneva — both of whom were deeply involved in communist activities. These two lost their jobs when the Rev. Raymond B. Bragg came to Boston in 1947 to head the Committee. Field, who subsequently disappeared behind the Iron Curtain and is said to be in prison there, has been called a Soviet agent; but during the 1952 Prague purge trials, Czech communists labeled him an "imperialist spy."

The storm clouds gathered at the American Unitarian Association in 1946, when objections to Fritchman's political orientation were voiced by certain political liberals, led by John Haynes Holmes and Donald Harrington, ministers of the Community Church in New York City. On September 18, 1946, the first written protest from official Unitarian headquarters was made by Melvin Arnold, new director of the division of publications; he accused the editor of creating the impression that the *Register* allowed "free criticism of every national and international policy which is also criticized by the U.S.S.R., but never the reverse."

Aroused conservatives within the denomination began to add their criticism. In October Fritchman was exonerated by the Unitarian board of directors of charges brought by Larry Davidow, Detroit lawyer. Davidow had accused Fritchman of using his positions of trust — both as editor of the *Christian Register* and as director of the American Unitarian Youth — "for a studied and deliberate campaign [of] proselytizing in behalf of the Communist Party cause."

In the wake of these accusations, the board of directors of the American Unitarian Association established a committee of four to advise Fritchman in publishing the magazine. The committee was composed of Dr. Frederick May Eliot, president of the Association; Judge Lawrence G. Brooks, chairman of the board of directors; Frank B. Frederick, the Association's legal counsel; and Arnold.

Meanwhile, others within the denomination had entered the controversy. The Rev. Edward Wilcox, minister in Lynn, Massachusetts, circulated widely his booklet, *The Strange Case of Mr. Fritchman,* accusing the controversial editor of association with twenty-four communist fronts and calling upon Unitarians to oust him from his influential posts.

Under pressure from both liberals and conservatives, Fritchman resigned as director of the youth organization on January 9, 1947, ostensibly to devote more of his time to the *Christian Register.* A year later the American Unitarian Youth took strong steps to repudiate its pro-Kremlin elements, characterizing the World Federation of Democratic Youth, from which it withdrew, as an "instrument of communist policies."

A flurry of letters involving the status of Fritchman, pro and con, reached local churches throughout the country. Homer A. Jack, liberal minister from Chicago, circulated a pamphlet called *The Threat of American Communists to the Liberal Church and Other Institutions.* A. Powell Davies, minister of the influential All Souls Unitarian Church in Washington, D. C., joined the debate with a protest against Fritchman's policies. In Cleveland, the local chapter of the Women's Alliance, Unitarian women's organization, canceled its subscriptions to the magazine until Fritchman should be replaced as editor.

A report later prepared by Friends of Democracy, at Arnold's request, analyzed the contents of the *Christian Register* for 1945-1946. It declared that the magazine had become "one-sided . . . almost invariably supporting a pro-communist line." It also noted that in answer to this charge from his fellow-ministers, Fritchman had replied that both sides of a question are not always necessary: "I knew from my reading of the one-sided Sermon on the Mount there was only one side for an honest man to take." This analysis by Friends of Democracy, an outside organization, was to contribute heavily to Fritchman's eventual defeat within the denomination.

Principal antagonist of Stephen Fritchman was Arnold. In late 1946, at the request of the board, Arnold compiled a report on the controversy in which he charged that "a high proportion of the non-Unitarian authors [of articles and book reviews in the magazine] . . . are either part of what might be termed the *New Masses-Daily Worker* coterie, or are leaders in organizations in which there admittedly is a considerable communist participation." Soon afterward the division of publications under Arnold issued a statement of policy, including this statement:

> The Division of Publications, in selecting authors and editorial contributions, is not engaged in "selling" month in and month out either the status quo or any closed system of ideas, or values, or "isms" — social, economic, political, theological — whether advocated by high, low, middle, left, or right. As an example, we are not in the business of press-agenting capitalism, socialism, communism, Marxism, Single Taxism, and so forth — or of the status quo. As a corollary to this, we in our selection of authors and articles do not have any "sacred cows" — we do not recognize any ideas, system, or countries as either above criticism or as subject only to kid-glove handling.

The controversy reached a climax in April 1947, when the May issue of the *Christian Register* was to carry an editorial by Fritchman titled "Americans Bearing Gifts." In it the editor attacked United States foreign policy in Greece, Turkey, China, Korea, and elsewhere, closely following the line then advocated by the Communist Party.

Contrary to the procedure that had been outlined by the board of directors of the American Unitarian Association, Fritchman failed to submit page proofs of the editorial to the committee appointed to work with him on magazine policies, and he departed on a nation-wide lecture tour. Just before the *Christian Register's* publication date, Arnold discovered the content of the proposed editorial, telegraphed Fritchman in Oklahoma that the committee would not accept it, and urged his immediate return to Boston if he objected to its replacement. Fritchman did not return and the editorial was removed. In a letter to Fritchman soon after, Arnold stated:

> Freedom of the press does not belong to an editor or publisher; it

belongs to the public; and the freedom of the denominational press does not belong to you or to me, but to the fellowship. One of your jobs and one of my jobs is to see that the fellowship's freedom of expression is defended against the extremists of left and right, high and low, who want to shut out those who don't follow a theological or ideological line.

On May 8, 1947, Fritchman sent a letter to all Unitarian ministers charging that the "free press" of the denomination was threatened by censorship and announcing that he would resign later the same month, at the annual meeting of the Association. Meanwhile the executive committee of the board of directors suspended him from his editorship, and Fritchman prepared to carry his case to Unitarianism's "town meeting." In a tense and emotional session of the annual meeting, Fritchman's supporters asked the Unitarian delegates to reinstate the suspended editor. Most of those who came to Fritchman's defense based their case on the issue of civil liberties. These included such conservative denominational leaders as the Rev. Palfrey Perkins, minister of King's Chapel, and the Rev. Charles E. Park, now minister emeritus of the First Church in Boston. Fritchman himself asserted that he had been suspended for refusing to publish "a few vitriolic words on the Soviet Union." At the same session Davidow, in Boston as a lay delegate, dramatically pointed to the ousted editor and shouted: "I insist that he is a communist and I invite him to start action on libel!"

But finally the delegates voted overwhelmingly to confirm the action of the executive committee of the Association's board of directors — and Fritchman was defeated. President Eliot, commenting on the action of the annual meeting, said: "The officers of the Association interpret the vote as an indorsement of their determination to preserve a truly liberal position which has been assailed from the extreme right and the extreme left."

With the dismissal of Fritchman, the *Christian Register* assumed an independent political slant, and began to include in its columns sentiments strongly critical of the Soviet Union.

That summer, Fritchman's supporters organized a Committee of 100, with headquarters in New York, which worked to rally the denomination behind the deposed editor. Their purpose was to gain control of the forthcoming biennial conference scheduled for Washington, D. C., in the fall, and to obtain Fritchman's reinstatement. In a 20-page "Letter to Unitarians," the Committee of 100 charged: "The attack on Mr. Fritchman took many forms during the years 1946 and 1947; disreputable methods were employed, such as wire-tapping, efforts to search Mr. Fritchman's apartments and files, trailing his movements, opening his office safe . . . for material to use in discrediting him." It is known that a handful of over-zealous Unitarian laymen, unassociated with the national headquarters, *were* involved.

Largely through the impact of the Friends of Democracy report, the campaign of the Committee of 100 was unsuccessful. Fritchman, resuming his earlier role of preacher, accepted a call from the First Unitarian Church of Los Angeles. Called before the House Committee on Un-American Activities September 12, 1951. Fritchman refused to answer questions about Communist affiliations on grounds of possible self-incrimination. The closed hearing testimony was released July 31, 1953.

Today, Fritchman is still minister of that church, a West Coast platform for many Soviet apologists. In September 1952, the United States government denied Fritchman a passport to visit Australia; he appealed to the American Unitarian Association to intercede, but his request was quickly rejected.

Several minor incidents would seem to indicate that, unable to reach positions of importance within the official headquarters of Unitarian organizations, the communist-liners have decided to work from the bottom up. Several chapters of the unofficial Unitarian Fellowship for Social Justice located near the large metropolitan centers in California and New York have engaged in disputes over the extremist political philosophies of some of their members. In both areas, local Fellowship groups began to join together into larger, more effective regional organizations. Fortunately, ministers of the churches involved and national officials of the Unitarian Fellowship for Social Justice have been alert to the possible danger of infiltration. Local chapters, which are chartered as inherent organizations of the local churches, must be considered by these churches to be representative of their own membership. When this seemed to be untrue in San Diego, Calif., and Hollis, Long Island, in the winter of 1952-1953, the churches abolished their Federation chapters, and the national officers backed their decision.

Three Case Studies: Phelps, Darr, Davis

The story of pro-communist activities in American Protestant-ism has taken many forms. Three case studies — representing different denominations — may serve as illustrations.

The American Baptist Convention (northern) was stirred in 1950 when the communist magazine *Soviet Russia Today* published a letter which Dr. Dryden L. Phelps — missionary to West China, and nephew of famed Yale Professor William Lyon Phelps — had written to the Rev. William Howard Melish. The letter said in part:

I am a missionary of the American Baptist Foreign Mission Society, at this University since 1921, with the exception of furloughs. Now we are having a thrilling experience of reorganizing every phase of our University life, and of Chinese society. It is the most profoundly religious Christian experience I have ever been through. I absolutely believe this to be the most comprehensive renaissance the human spirit has ever experienced: and the most dynamic change in human history. God is working alongside of these Communists.

Immediately, a cry arose from the denomination to recall Phelps from the field.

At the request of the American Baptist Foreign Mission Society, Phelps and his wife returned to America in November 1951, to "confer" about his view of the Chinese situation. They had served for thirty years in the West China mission, and for many years on the faculty of West China Union University. On January 22, 1952, they appeared before the board of managers of the Foreign Mission Society and offered their resignations.

Phelps assured his hearers that he and his wife "have never been, and are not now, Communists. . . . When, a year and a half ago, in August of 1950, I wrote that God was working along side the Communists, I did not mean — and I did not say — that Communists are religious or that they are Christians, though some of them are; nor did I mean to say that God is working only with the Communists, or with all Communists, or with all that the Communists do." Phelps said his sympathies were based on three things: first, specifically Christian activities being carried out under the "People's Republic of China"; second, "significant things . . . happening expressive of the Christian spirit and for which Christian teaching may be in part responsible"; and, third, what he described as a "turning of human destiny in China."

In accepting his resignation, the board of managers expressed the conviction that Phelps's action and beliefs were prompted by "his supreme and dominating purpose — to preach and teach the Christian faith." They also expressed satisfaction with the assurances of Dr. and Mrs. Phelps that they had never been communists.

Phelps's official connection with the American Baptist Foreign Mission Society terminated on January 31, 1952. Since that date, he has been active as a speaker at pro-communist meetings, where he consistently offers a strong defense of the Chinese communists. Occasionally he has been invited to express his views before reputable church organizations which believe that unconventional opinions should be given a fair hearing.

Operating in the center of the pro-communist sphere of Protestant clergymen has been a Congregationalist, John W. Darr, Jr., who has headed, sponsored, or otherwise co-operated with a long list of movements aimed at helping the cause of the Kremlin.

For several years, Darr carried in his vest pocket a "religious organization," the United Christian Council for Democracy, which once represented six unofficial social-action groups of major Protestant denominations. Before Darr took over leadership of the Council, it had been headed by another pastor, the Rev. Richard Morford, Presbyterian, now secretary of the National Council of American-Soviet Friendship.

Darr has been a protégé of Dr. Harry F. Ward, who from 1918 to 1941 taught future ministers as a professor at Union Theological Seminary. Darr's dubious activities through the past few years have been innumerable. In 1948, for example, he was a sponsor of the Youth for Wallace movement, the May Day Parade, and the National Youth Assembly Against Military Training — described by the *Daily Worker* as "the youth front of Gideon's Army." He also served as co-chairman of the New York Committee Against War Prop-

aganda, chairman of the Conference to Defend the Bill of
Rights, and charter member of the Committee to Enforce the
Fourteenth Amendment — all pro-communist groups. The following year, Darr represented the Young Progressives of America in Washington, D. C., served as the public-relations agent
for England's "Red Dean" when he visited the United States,
and became secretary of the American Council for a Democratic
Greece. More recently, Darr's chief efforts have been directed
toward world peace — Soviet style. He has been an important
American figure in numerous "peace" conferences in the United
States and abroad. In early 1953, when he returned from such
a conference held in Copenhagen, his passport was picked up.

The United Christian Council for Democracy, which Darr
used to head, had been formed in 1936. Among the unofficial
church groups which originally backed it were the Presbyterian
Fellowship for Social Action, the Rauschenbush Fellowship for
Baptists, and the Evangelical and Reformed Council for Social
Reconstruction. When these three disappeared during the post-
war period, the Council became the tool of party-liners. Another
early affiliate, the Unitarian Fellowship for Social Justice, withdrew in 1948. At its annual meeting that year, the Unitarian
Fellowship strongly criticized the Council:

1. [It] does not hold regular meetings of its board of directors or does
not notify all representatives of meetings that are held.
2. Through its executive secretary, [it] is represented as supporting
causes the validity of which its member groups have not had an opportunity to discuss or approve or disapprove.

Of the Council's six original supporters, therefore, only two
were left — the Methodist Federation for Social Action and the
Episcopal League for Social Action. Today the United Christian
Council for Democracy is defunct; but Darr still uses his ministerial status to lend prestige to the communist cause.

On occasion, pro-Soviet attitudes seem to have successfully
filtered into the mainstream of Protestant church literature. An
interesting example was the appearance in Methodist publications of articles by Jerome Davis soon after World War II. Davis
has been attacked as a sympathizer with a number of communist

causes — although he has not followed every variation of the party line.

Davis' career has been a colorful and tumultous one. He was in Russia during the Bolshevik Revolution, serving as YMCA secretary among prisoners of war. In 1936, he was ousted as Professor of Practical Philanthropy from the Divinity School of Yale University. Davis charged that prominent industrialists who contributed heavily to the university brought pressure upon the administration to punish him for his extreme political and economic views. The administration countered by saying that the action had been taken for budgetary reasons and because Davis' teaching ability failed to meet the faculty standards.

Later Davis was elected president of the American Federation of Teachers. In 1945, he received nation-wide publicity for the $250,000 libel suit he brought against the Curtis Publishing Company, publishers of the *Saturday Evening Post,* and against Benjamin Stolberg, labor writer. Stolberg in a *Post* article had charged Davis with being a "communist" and "Stalinist." Davis contended that this attack cost him a well-paid position with the National Youth Administration. Character witnesses for him included Harry Emerson Fosdick and Rabbi Stephen Wise, while the defense produced testimony that Davis was a "90 to 95 per cent Communist." After a hung jury, the contestants settled out of court for $11,000 — Davis the recipient.

Davis served for a brief period as a war correspondent. He continued to be intrigued with the Soviet Union and immediately after the war published *Behind Soviet Power,* considered by many to be a glorification of Russian communism. His book was sent out in May 1947 by the Board of Missions and Church Extension of the Methodist Church. An accompanying letter — signed by Bishop G. Bromley Oxnam and Dr. R. E. Diffendorfer, two churchmen who have a clear understanding of the dangerous nature of communism — suggested *Behind Soviet Power* as reading that would be helpful toward understanding the appeal communism had to many people, and recommended other writings in the field that pointed out the vicious elements in the Soviet program. A strong statement condemning communism, drafted by John Foster Dulles and adopted by the Federal Council of Churches, was included with the book. Later Davis made an attempt to distribute it to many Congregational and Unitarian ministers.

Simultaneously, his work was appearing in the *Classmate,* youth publication of the Methodist Church. An article on the life of Joseph Stalin, published in July 1947, stated:

> It would be an error to consider the Soviet leader a willful man who believes in forcing his ideas upon others. Everything he does reflects the desires and hopes of the masses to a large degree. . . . No doubt he has serious faults. He loves power; he may have been ruthless in getting it. But can we go out to serve God and the common people of America as sincerely and courageously as Stalin did for what he believed was best for his people?

Although the Methodists appear to have erred in using Davis' material, it must be recalled that many leading churchmen of the post-war period sincerely believed that friendship with the Soviet Union might be possible. Many of them, who have no sympathy for communism, still express their hope that such reconciliation might be achieved. Such proponents of friendship may prove to be mistaken; but they should not be lumped together with blind apologists for the Kremlin.

Davis has regularly spoken before pro-communist rallies. He was sponsor of a 1949 "Bill of Rights Conference" held in New York City under the auspices of the Civil Rights Congress, a communist front.

Nevertheless, Davis has strayed far from specific points on the rigid Communist Party line. He supported Franklin D. Roosevelt in 1940 — even though the Communist Party had placed its own choice on the ballot. He expressed opposition to the Nazi-Soviet pact — blindly accepted by faithful Stalinists. He withdrew at an early date from the advisory board of *The Protestant.* In 1952, at a communist-sponsored peace rally, he boldly announced his support of Adlai E. Stevenson instead of the communist-endorsed candidate Vincent Hallinan, Progressive Party nominee. He is very friendly to many non-communist, socialist groups.

Many observers believe that Davis is a sincere, idealistic Quaker who is unselfishly devoting his life to the cause of peace. Unfortunately he has become — perhaps unwittingly — a powerful ally of the pro-communist elements in the churches.

Davis' principal project at the present time is Enduring Peace, Inc., with headquarters in West Haven, Conn. Through hospitable communist and pro-communist outlets, as well as through other channels, Davis' one-man crusade distributes literature on foreign affairs, usually with a bias in favor of the Soviet Union.

In early 1952, Davis published *Peace, War and You,* which won the endorsement of Clarence Pickett, reputable chairman of the American Friends Service Committee, who wrote the book's introduction. Some observers believe that communists are making a special effort to exploit the trustful warm-heartedness of the Quakers to further the designs of the Kremlin — viewing the traditional Quaker pacifism as a potential tool in their current "peace" campaign.

Protestant apologists for the Soviet Union continue to exploit their religious faith to advance the cause of world communism. They are not numerous. They number only a tiny fraction of the total number of clergymen in the United States — and some of these are sincere but misled idealists, still unwilling to admit the proportions of the international Soviet conspiracy. By their status in the church, pro-communist ministers can work far more damage than scores of underground comrades. They can entice hundreds of innocent people, including many fellow-clergymen, who trust in their integrity into supporting "worthy causes" initiated to benefit the Kremlin. Some of these Moscow-oriented ministers camouflage their intrigue behind the cross in an attempt to aid a movement that would subvert all Protestant principles. Others openly advocate the pro-communist position. Their program, carefully pursued, is part of a long-range plan to seize even the halls of worship, wherever located throughout the world, and enlist them as arms of communist aggression.

But churchmen also must beware of the rampant hysteria that too often has destroyed the reputation of innocent men. The free pulpit must be preserved, even at the risk of its exploitation. The Christian message must not be sacrificed out of fear that it may be misunderstood. World peace — the communists should not discredit this goal of men of good-will everywhere. Those who genuinely speak for peace — especially sincere pacifists with their rigorous interpretation of the gospel of love — often have suffered at the hands of reckless vigilantes, who care less for religious ideals than for total adherence to their own line of thought. Racial brotherhood, religious understanding, economic justice, social welfare — Americans must not allow the communists to banish these praiseworthy expressions of the Christian faith.

Fortunately, communist influence among Protestants has fallen off sharply, and today church leaders are on guard against current attempts by fellow-travelers to regain lost ground.

12

God and the "Libertarians"

Economic extremists at both ends of the spectrum are vying for the endorsement of Protestant churchmen. As we have seen in the preceding chapter, the Kremlin's few followers among American clergymen seek to identify Christianity with materialistic Marxism. Simultaneously, a network of powerful religio-economic forces hopes to identify the same religious faith with materialistic "libertarianism" — a kind of economic royalism dedicated to the extreme view that no positive governmental action of any kind is justified.

The development of extreme right-wing groups under the banner of Protestantism poses a significant threat to the independence of the churches as well as to the future of democracy. These groups are well financed by big industry, endorsed by influential, sincere citizens, and intent upon establishing a firm alliance between Protestant piety and unrestrained economic individualism. Although they pay lip service to the values endorsed by American conservatives, they are not truly conservative. In the genuine meaning of the word, they are "reactionary" — eager to return to the nineteenth-century rampant individualism that long since has been outdated by the increasing complexities of modern society. The doctrinal laissez-faire which they profess is as much the enemy of reputable conservatives as it is of those who hold liberal economic views. In fact, in this naïve trust in the perfect working of an unchecked natural order are the seeds of social irresponsibility — and even anarchy.

The discussion in this chapter deals chiefly with the current attempt to inundate Protestant ministers and laymen with free literature popularizing this "reactionary" point of view. Basically each group promoting this campaign adheres to the same creed. As one of them puts it: "We stand for free competitive enterprise — the economic system with the least amount of government and the greatest amount of Christianity."

Spiritual Mobilization

The most influential of the clergy-oriented bastions of unrestrained individualism is Spiritual Mobilization. In 1935, James W. Fifield, pastor of the 4,500-member First Congregational Church of Los Angeles — Congregationalism's largest and most prosperous parish — initiated this movement in order "to arouse the ministers of all denominations in America to check the trends toward pagan stateism, which would destroy our basic freedom and spiritual ideals."

The Fifield movement early adopted a credo that reads in part: "Man, being created free as a child of God, has certain inalienable rights and responsibilities; the state must not be permitted to usurp them; it is the duty of the church to help protect them"; and that among these rights are "the liberty and dignity of the individual, in which freedom of choice, of enterprise and of property is inherent."

Although Spiritual Mobilization is not a membership organization, it boasts of 17,000 "representatives" among the nation's clergy. Meanwhile, 100,000 others, clergy and laymen, are solicited through its literature, including *Faith and Freedom,* a monthly publication conspicuous for its intellectual façade. Spiritual Mobilization also sponsors "The Freedom Story," a weekly broadcast carried by more than six hundred radio stations in all parts of the country. The organization's most recent venture has been the development of regional conferences, held "in an atmosphere of freedom and informality," to "provide an opportunity for twenty or twenty-five men to engage in some cooperative thinking."

Among the members of the select advisory committee of Spiritual Mobilization are Donald J. Cowling, president emeritus of Carleton College; Edgar J. Goodspeed, Bible scholar and lecturer; Missionary Sam Higginbottom; Author Felix Morley; Alfred Noyes, Roman Catholic poet (and only non-Protestant on the committee); J. C. Penney, department-store magnate;

and the Rev. Norman Vincent Peale of New York City. The advisors have no function other than to add their prestige; they are not held responsible for the statements of the organization.

It is doubtful that most of the advisors share such extremist views.

Many "middle-roaders" served with Spiritual Mobilization until they recognized it as a threat to all social progress. They included Charles R. Brown, dean emeritus of Yale Divinity School; President John A. Mackay of Princeton Theological Seminary; Bishop Richard Raines of the Methodist Church; Congregationalism's Dr. Douglas Horton; and President Charles S. Johnson of Fisk University.

In 1951, Fifield inaugurated an "Independence Sermon Competition" that bestowed attractive cash prizes upon clergy who preached the most eloquent Sunday messages on the topic, "Freedom Under God." A distinguished Committee to Proclaim Liberty challenged all citizens to commemorate the Fourth of July by consecrating themselves afresh "to the great spiritual foundations of our country." The effort was endorsed by a group of eminent Americans, including Herbert Hoover, General MacArthur, Harold E. Stassen, Charles E. Wilson (of General Motors), J. Howard Pew, Henry R. Luce, Jackie Robinson, Judge Meier Steinbrink, and Bishop G. Bromley Oxnam. Most of these, of course, do not endorse doctrinaire "libertarianism."

The contest was won by the Rev. Kenneth W. Sollitt, minister of the First Baptist Church in Mindota, Illinois, whose articles appear regularly in *Faith and Freedom*. It was sponsored again in 1952.

Dr. James W. Fifield, now fifty-one years old and six feet four inches tall, embarked upon his colorful career in a Chicago parsonage, the son of a clergyman. As a promising young minister of thirty-five in Grand Rapids, Michigan, Fifield was lured away by a Committee of Eleven directed by the First Congregational Church of Los Angeles to seek a resourceful pastor. He inherited a four-story concrete structure that resembled a cathedral, complete with a 176-foot tower, 108 rooms, three auditoriums, and a gymnasium. But attached to this massive plant was a membership of barely 1,500, disheartened by a $750,000 debt.

The new minister, displaying the competence of a shrewd business executive, spent his congregation out of the red. In the process of expanding the church's activities — until it could claim the "most comprehensive church program in America" — Fifield added over 3,000 members to the roster, which began to approximate a "Who's Who Among the Important and Prosperous in Los Angeles." In July 1942, the mortgage was reduced to ashes, and today the First Church functions on an annual budget of $300,000, with a corps of full-time ministers and a host of business, clerical, office, and custodial personnel.

Fifield's money-making abilities have been important in underwriting the huge budget of his nation-wide "freedom" crusade. For five years, from 1937 to 1942, Spiritual Mobilization received a substantial sum annually from the First Congregational Church. Today, Fifield claims that his movement is financed "by contributions from thousands of individuals, companies, and foundations." He welcomes gifts up to $12,500 from corporations and more from non-profit foundations.

In addition to their individual contributions, such leading business kings as J. Howard Pew (Sun Oil), E. T. Weir (National Steel), Charles M. White (Republic Steel), Frank Drake (Gulf Oil), B. E. Hutchinson (Chrysler Corporation), and others have devoted time to the raising of Spiritual Mobilization's budget.

The Los Angeles pastor has been subjected to attacks from many different quarters. Some who observe him at close range charge Fifield with personal coldness, calculated and unbounded ambition, little concern for social ills, and an obsession for "bigness" and efficiency.

He has been especially controversial within his own denomination. Many of his Congregational colleagues have resented his bitter attacks upon the church's Council for Social Action (discussed in Chapter 14). Others are angered by his fierce opposition to the proposed merger of the denomination with the Evangelical and Reformed Church to form the United Church of Christ. When the merger was being debated in 1949, Fifield dissented: "We think Congregationalism has a unique genius to contribute to the cause of freedom in the U. S. The merger will destroy that — the autonomous, free local church in contrast to the capital-C Church on the national level." Just before his view was rejected by the General Council of the denomination (vote: 757 to 172), Fifield warned dramatically: "If the merger is pushed through, the world will see the spectacle of a schism. . . . You can break our hearts and send us home." He predicted that from five hundred to a thousand churches would withdraw to form a separate group and that litigation would begin over the use of the Congregational name immediately. While the matter awaits final decision by the courts, Fifield attempts to enlist new allies in his determined battle to sabotage efforts toward the merger.

Spiritual Mobilization's rank and file have been depicted as "Protestant priests of mammon," "benefactors of the rich and powerful," and allies of groups and individuals that "nestle on the fascist fringe." For many years the organization's policy was to ignore the assertions of its many antagonists, but in the spring of 1952 Fifield categorically characterized them as "lies and misrepresentations of irresponsible journals." A few months later, Spiritual Mobilization launched *Truth in Action,* a four-page bimonthly, sent free to 100,000 clergymen and designed as "a forum for high level controversy." It tends to dismiss the most serious charges against it as communist-inspired.

The truth is that bitter criticism of Spiritual Mobilization has been made by others than communists or "irresponsible journals." The labor unions have been particularly vocal in their denunciations of the movement. The *CIO News* for January 1, 1951, for example, carried a resounding story that described Fifield as "a neo-fascist enemy of organized labor and the New Deal who has used his pastorate and his church as a springboard for spreading the gospel of big business." Such liberal anti-communist groups as Americans for Democratic Action and Friends of Democracy have attacked Spiritual Mobilization both for its extreme right-wing policies and for its complacent willingness to cooperate with any other organizations that happen to be traveling in the same direction.

Many churchmen — including astute and fair-minded conservatives — have objected loudly, too. One post-war criticism appeared in *Social Action,* challenging and highly controversial publication of Congregationalism's Council for Social Action. A special issue (May 15, 1951) was devoted to a discussion entitled "Protestant Piety and the Right Wing." It made these accusations against Fifield and Spiritual Mobilization: theological humanism, vagueness and inconsistency, distorted judgments, racism, and extreme nationalism. "Unless Protestant churches come to know themselves and the forces working on them," the article warned, "they may simply be victims of pressure groups, rather than witnesses to a gospel judging and redeeming all groups and aiding men to assess the channels through which they may serve the causes of freedom, justice, and peace."

Spiritual Mobilization termed the article "a particularly irresponsible attack" and charged the author with methods "which would have earned him an F in any journalism school." Several errors in the *Social Action* article were alleged.

In February 1952, Theologian Reinhold Niebuhr spoke out against Spiritual Mobilization's "political program," which he called "identical with that of the National Association of Manufacturers, to which it adds merely a prayer and religious unction." Fifield quickly complained that his influential critic did not manifest "any understanding of the intellectual foundations of our policies." Edmund A. Opitz, a Unitarian clergyman and regional conference director for Spiritual Mobilization, engaged Niebuhr in a brief duel in the columns of *The Reporter,* biweekly journal of liberal political opinion. "First," contended Opitz, "we have no 'political program,' and secondly, if we did have a 'political program' it wouldn't be 'identical with that of the National Association of Manufacturers.'" He charged Niebuhr with "using hearsay evidence, a failing which besets even theologians." Niebuhr countered by denouncing Spiritual Mobilization for exploiting religious ideas "to make already indiscriminate devotion to unregulated economy even more indiscriminate."

The Fifield movement has been extremely sensitive to another grave charge — racism, especially anti-Semitism — elaborated in an article by Carey McWilliams, author of *Brothers Under the Skin* and *A Mask for Privilege.* Writing in *The Nation* in early 1948, McWilliams accused Fifield of using his pulpit to promote prejudice against minorities in the Los Angeles area. To document his thesis he quoted Fifield against "the efforts of minorities to push in where they are not wanted. . . . We do not intend to turn the town over to Jews, Mexicans, and Negroes." According to McWilliams, Fifield also has expressed approval of restrictive covenants and other forms of segregation, while opposing fair-employment legislation, the Genocide Pact, and the Universal Declaration of Human Rights. While not denying the veracity of the quotations, Spiritual Mobilization's vice-president, James C. Ingebretsen, accused McWilliams of lifting them indiscriminately from their contexts, and characterized him as "known Communist sympathizer."

Whatever the truth may be, many minority-group leaders on the West Coast have become convinced that Fifield is no friend of theirs. In December 1952, for example, Rabbi Julius J. Nodel of Temple Beth Israel in Portland, Oregon, expressed the fears of many Jews and Negroes, in a sermon attacking the activities of Fifield and his cohorts. "Their spirit is antithetical to religion; there is nothing spiritual about them," charged the Rabbi. "Thousands of gullible followers are deriving sadistic pleasure at having their pet prejudices repeated and a few vested interests capitalized." Nodel documented his attack upon Fifield by a list of his words and deeds presumably implying antagonism toward minority races and religions.

Meanwhile, some of the staff of Spiritual Mobilization, genuinely embarrassed by the remarks which have given rise to these doubts, are struggling to compensate for the damage that Fifield may have done. *Faith and Freedom* for December 1952 and January 1953 carried two articles exposing the fallacious arguments of *The Iron Curtain Over America,* the dangerous piece of racist propaganda discussed at length in Chapter 4.

The Fifield movement rejects the widespread contention that it is political, maintains that it takes no position on specific proposals for social justice, and claims to be interested solely in the moral problems underlying the structure of society. "Clergymen may differ about politics, economics, sociology, and such," says Fifield, "but I would expect that in matters of morality all followers of Jesus would speak in one voice." What would they say? "All that government can do in behalf of freedom is to let the individual alone and it should secure him in his rights by making others let him alone." Why? Because any deviation from "freedom" — Fifield's favorite synonym for unregulated "laissez-faireism" — is a violation of "the natural law which inheres in the nature of the universe and is the will of God."

Therefore, Spiritual Mobilization embraces an anarchistic "libertarianism" which, in spite of Fifield's denials, generates as a corollary a well-defined political line. In fact, the Los Angeles pastor himself has clearly stated his program for America:

> First, we must see to it that no more socialistic laws are passed. We must stop the granting of special privileges to any group. . . .
> Our second step is to get rid of the socialistic laws we now have. This requires that we take away special privileges from groups who now have them. . . .
> The third step is decentralization of government. The federal government should retain only those powers which cannot be handled on the local level.

Many of the "socialistic laws" that Fifield wants repealed have been accepted by conservatives and liberals alike as part of the American way of life; they include laws, national or state-wide, providing for social security, a minimum wage, old-age pensions, veterans' benefits — in fact, welfare legislation of any kind. Taxes are decried as "tyrannical." Subsidies, of course, are opposed, and those "libertarians" who are consistent (many are not) want all tariffs abandoned also.

As a nationalist, Fifield opposes effective international co-operation. His latest drive has been directed at UNESCO. Through Freedom Clubs, Inc., which he claims is "non-partisan, non-political and serves no selfish interests," Fifield was in the vanguard of a successful campaign to purge UNESCO materials from the public schools in the Los Angeles area.

All viewpoints that diverge in any particular from the narrow "libertarianism" of Spiritual Mobilization are sharply condemned as "anti-God," "contrary to the Moral Law," and "conducive to statism." The "social gospel" is a key scapegoat, and has been characterized by William Johnson, editor of *Faith and Freedom,* as "pure socialism." One libertarian charges: "The Social Gospel has been challenged to produce its intellectual and ethical credentials — and it has none." Another accuses "social gospelers" of advocating *"socialized* covetousness, stealing, and the bearing of false witness." To combat the social action emphasis of most major denominations, Fifield urges each clergyman "to bear a courageous and worthy witness to freedom under God from his pulpit Sunday after Sunday and in all other areas of his influence." "Congregations will grow if you do it," he adds.

No creed in the history of the world, one *Faith and Freedom* writer complains, ever captured the hearts and minds of men as has the modern creed of statism. "Men may differ in their rituals, they may call themselves Americans, Englishmen or Russians (New Dealers, Socialists, or Communists), but in their adherence to the doctrine of the omnipotence of the State they are as one." Although he was somewhat encouraged by the 1952 Republican victory, Fifield has always been an alarmist, continually painting a bleak picture of the national scene. "I feel sure there is a conspiracy to destroy freedom in America," he has stated. And again:

> Infiltrations into the government and other areas of our national life have advanced to alarming proportions. A careful review by responsible historians of the pattern of infiltration in other countries behind the Iron Curtain indicates that we are moving down exactly the same road.

To the activities of Senator Joseph McCarthy of Wisconsin, the Los Angeles pastor has given his enthusiastic endorsement. When Representative Harold H. Velde hinted that the churches might be investigated, some members of the Spiritual Mobilization staff objected. Consistent with their extreme antipathy toward government interference of any kind, they proposed that communism in religion "be exposed by private citizens using privately-raised funds." But Fifield applauded the Velde suggestion. He stated: "Chairman Velde took a position in which thoughtful clergymen of the nation, who are dedicated to freedom under God, will support."

Spiritual Mobilization claims that it has had a marked influence upon the economic and political thinking of clergymen in the United States. In 1949 Fifield conducted a survey which allegedly proved that 64.2 per cent of Protestant ministers were opposed to "New Deal philosophy" and other types of "collectivism." This he contrasted with sentiment in 1934, when, according to Fifield, 82.4 per cent of the ministers were for the New

Deal "or some other impractical idealism." In a more recent poll of 2,000 pastors sponsored by *Faith and Freedom*, the findings again were said to prove that "more ministers are interested and active for our ideals today than at any time since we started." Some 65 per cent expressed alarm at big government, while only 13 per cent favored expanded state services; 84 per cent declared that there is a real danger of losing personal freedom if the government controls the nation's industry. The typical minister was found to be "intensely loyal to the concept of freedom and voluntarism."

Christian Economics?

Another organization of the far right devoted to rallying ministerial support for "libertarianism" is the Christian Freedom Foundation, Inc., publishers of the four-page biweekly *Christian Economics*. The journal adopts a pseudo-intellectual approach similar to that of *Faith and Freedom* — although it is geared more directly to current headlines and salted more liberally with Bible verses that presumably add scriptural sanction to the views espoused.

More than 175,000 Protestant clergymen in the United States and a growing list of laymen regularly receive *Christian Economics* free of charge, though an effort has been made to distribute the paper on a subscription basis at one dollar per annum. In addition to the publication, the Foundation supplies free, upon request, speakers or radio discs for use by churches, radio stations, youth groups, and other organizations interested in promoting the views of the Christian Freedom Foundation. One of the most effective devices for reaching laymen — a technique developed during the past months — is the sending of free reprints to ministers for weekly insertion in their church bulletins.

Howard E. Kershner, president of the Christian Freedom Foundation, has had a varied career, including the manufacture of leather goods and the management of a prosperous real-estate business. Before establishing the Foundation in 1950, he was respected as a Quaker humanitarian. He directed the European relief work of the American Friends Service Committee from 1939 to 1942, founded the Temporary Council on Food for Europe's Children, and served on the executive committee of

Herbert Hoover's National Committee for Food for the Small
Democracies. Kershner, however, has no sympathy with Quaker
pacifism. "Only the naive will talk of rapprochement and understanding with the present Russian government," he has declared.
And again:

World War III, in which we are now engaged, is not simply a struggle
of Russia against America, it is a battle between lies and honesty; hooli-
ganism and integrity; unprincipled gangsterism against sound worth and
accomplishment; anti-Christ against Christ. The lowest slime that ever
crawled out of the pit now challenges all that honest God-fearing men
have builded.

Kershner has long been an outspoken critic of liberalism; as
early as 1936 he wrote a volume entitled *The Menace of Roosevelt and His Policies.* In retrospect, the author recently said of
this book: "At that time I gave Mr. Roosevelt credit for being
sincere. I have long ceased to believe that, and for some years
have not encouraged the circulation of the book."

Kershner and his wife each year travel abroad, proclaiming
"freedom" — Foundation-style. The Christian Freedom Foundation appears to have a small but enthusiastic following in
Europe, especially in England.

Working with Kershner in the New York office is Percy L.
Greaves, the Foundation's consulting economist and former aide
to a number of ultra-conservative interest groups and Congress-
men. In past years Greaves worked as personal researcher for
former Senator Owen R. Brewster of Maine and Representatives
Fred A. Hartley of New Jersey and Ralph W. Gwinn of New
York. With Merwin K. Hart and other backers of the National
Economic Council (see Chapter 10), Greaves established the
Foundation for Freedom, Inc., with himself as executive director.
The Foundation lasted only long enough to publish *Operation
Immigration,* a Greaves pamphlet on proposed legislation for
displaced persons. If we Americans open our doors to the "dregs
of Europe," Greaves warned, our standard of living will be
lowered and our moral leadership undermined. He was particularly disturbed by the "alien influence" in government and labor
unions. Some observers accused Greaves of deliberately excerpt-
ing selected quotations to make it appear that only "undesirable"

elements were being brought in as D.P.'s. Others pointed out how his endorsement of rigid immigration barriers completely contradicted the tenets of his "freedom cult."

Greaves— as mentioned in Chapter 2 — took a leading role in the founding of the Constitution Party as a result of his keen displeasure with the nomination of Eisenhower. *Christian Economics* apparently shared Greaves' stout pre-convention opposition to the General. Even on October 7, 1952, an editorial began: "If one wants more socialism, he can vote Democratic or Republican this year and be sure of winning." General MacArthur, in contrast, was hailed as "a statesman of the highest order." Greaves later withdrew from the Constitution Party.

Greaves views economics as an exact science, much like mathematics, and he is inclined to excuse his critics with the brisk remark: "You simply don't know enough economics!" He is the most extreme member of the highly paid staff of the Christian Freedom Foundation, and has maintained contacts with groups and individuals of the ministry of hate.

In addition to Greaves' front-page columns in *Christian Economics,* numbered among its regular contributors are many other names that appear time and again in ultra-conservative circles: V. Orval Watts, West Coast economic consultant; former Congressman Samuel B. Pettengill; Frank C. Hanighen, editor of *Human Events;* the economic team of Fred G. Clark and Richard Stanton Rimanoczy; Alfred P. Haake, mayor of Park Ridge, Illinois; Thurman Sensing of the Southern States Industrial Council; the Rev. William R. Johnson, for thirty-six years a Methodist teacher in China; and Walter E. Spahr, professor of economics at New York University.

More than fifty clergymen — many of them distinguished — serve on the Foundation's board of directors. An executive committee, composed of the organization's officers and a selection of ministers from the Middle Atlantic states, meets from time to time to give formal approval to Kershner's policies. Among its prominent members from New York City are Norman Vincent Peale of the Marble Collegiate Church, Henry Darlington, retired rector of the Church the Heavenly Rest, and Daniel K. Poling of the Ft. Washington Collegiate Church. Samuel M. Shoemaker, formerly of Manhattan's Calvary Episcopal Church — now in Pittsburgh — is one of the Foundation's five vice-presidents.

Christian Economics is — to put it mildly — a controversial publication. While most clergymen who differ with its ideology quietly drop their free copies in the wastebasket, occasionally one will become quite excited and explode in a letter to the editor. One forceful Vermont preacher summed up what many other ministers think, in words they would be reluctant to use:

> Can't take any more of it! . . . your hypocritical "drool" that bears the misnomer of Christian economics. There ought to be a law against such travesty on two important words. . . . Your paper would be honest at least, and not deceive so many gullible clergymen, if you rightfully called it "Big Business Propaganda."

According to Kershner, about 60 per cent of the letters to his office signify strong approval, 20 per cent are disturbed, and 20 per cent are sharply critical. The Foundation has a policy of publishing few of these criticisms — and rarely any intelligent ones. Its "Letters to the Editor" column is heavily weighted with emotional bouquets. Norman Vincent Peale, for example, has written: "I read *Christian Economics* with great interest and consider it the soundest and best paper of its kind." Unfortunately, more and more ministers — apparently unaware of the implications of Foundation ideology — are voicing their approval of the paper's economic views.

The writers for *Christian Economics,* like those of *Faith and Freedom,* hold that the Christian system would be "the freest possible economic order with the least possible amount of government regulation and the greatest infusion of the Christian conscience at all points." They sum up their brief against "socialism" (equated with welfare legislation of any kind) by contending that it "dethrones God and enthrones the state. It violates the first and great Commandment and makes the state the arbiter of the affairs of men rather than God." Moreover, they say, it transgresses the eighth and tenth commandments by "forcibly taking the wealth of the more enterprising citizens for distribution to others." Because its rosy promises always fail to materialize and, instead, produce poverty and oppression, Foundation thinkers contend that "socialism" also usurps the ninth commandment, "Thou shalt not bear false witness."

Howard E. Kershner depicts the world as the battlefield of two conflicting forces. The most inclusive struggle, he suggests, is the age-old battle between God and Satan. But this struggle, according to Kershner, has many subdivisions — good vs. evil, varying degrees of freedom vs. varying degrees of slavery, individualism vs. collectivism, free enterprise vs. the welfare state, etc. "The laws of economics are part of the laws of God." The further we diverge from the principles of natural Law — meaning an untrammeled economic order — the more we rebel against the authority of God and the teachings of Christianity.

Although *Christian Economics* is moderate in its language, sometimes Kershner gives way to the jargon of the demagogue. Recently he asked an audience: "Why do we barter away our liberty and surrender freedom's birthright for a stinking mess of welfare state pottage brewed by power hungry politicians on the march to statism? Why do we let them wind the skein of controls and socialization tighter and tighter until eventually they can deliver us bound, gagged, and helpless into the toils of the omnipotent state?"

On Washington's birthday in 1953, Freedoms Foundation, Inc., of Valley Forge, Pennsylvania, included Kershner among those whom it honored for "outstanding contributions to a better understanding of the American way of life." Freedoms Foundation was chartered in 1949 as a "nonprofit, nonpolitical, nonsectarian organization" to reward those who "speak up for freedom." While it has many worthy objectives and widespread support, it has tended to promote an ultra-conservatism similar to that promulgated by Kershner's group. The most capable member of the *Christian Economics staff,* George H. Cless, Jr., received a Freedoms Foundation award in 1949 for his pamphlet *Test for Truth,* "Truth vs. Myths about Profit."

The "non-political" Christian Freedom Foundation "scares up" large contributions by painting a sinister picture of liberals among the clergy. One pamphlet apparently aimed at potential donors begins: " 'Christian Liberalism' which is so friendly to Socialism, has penetrated the Protestant Church so deeply that, throughout the country, many ministers and laymen of many denominations have become 'fellow travelers.' " With alarm, the Foundation suggests that socialism is being spread in the name of

Jesus Christ; some pastors are "deliberate, untiring supporters of Karl Marx." Clergymen like Reinhold Niebuhr and church groups like the Congregational Council for Social Action are pinpointed for special attack. The pamphlet solicits contributions to rescue those innocent ministers who have been deceived by "church reds." Bulk subscriptions are requested from "individuals and concerns who are aware of the socialist fraud and desire to promote a sane attitude toward free enterprise in our United States."

It is reported that the Christian Freedom Foundation has withdrawn this pamphlet from circulation.

Economic Education?

Some ramifications of the economic theory underlying both Spiritual Mobilization and the Christian Freedom Foundation are hatched on the banks of the Hudson River by the Foundation for Economic Education, Inc., the self-styled "intellectual arsenal" for this anarchistic crusade. The Foundation was established in 1947 by Leonard Read, ex-manager of the Los Angeles Chamber of Commerce, former executive vice-president of the National Industrial Conference Board, and a member of the advisory committee of Fifield's Spiritual Mobilization.

Read is president of the Foundation for Economic Education. Among those serving with him on the staff are Russell J. Clinchy, a Congregational minister, former director of the Christian Freedom Foundation and still a regular contributor to *Christian Economics;* Paul L. Poirot, OPA economist during World War II; and F. A. Harper and W. M. Curtiss, both ex-professors of marketing at Cornell University.

Besides their own essays, the staff circulates standard texts of economic "laissez-faireism" (e.g., Adam Smith and Herbert Spencer), speeches and tracts by certain articulate industrialists, and the writings of Frank Chodorov, associate editor of the Washington monthly newsletter, *Human Events;* the late Albert Jay Nock, author and publisher; of the French economist Bertrand de Jouvenel; of Ludwig von Mises, visiting professor of economics from Austria; of Henry Hazlitt, associate editor of *Newsweek;* of Clarence Manion, dean of the College of Law of

Notre Dame University (and on Senator Taft's list of his choices for Secretary of Labor); and many more.

Unlike Spiritual Mobilization and Christian Freedom Foundation, the Foundation for Economic Education does not aim at a mass audience. A small voluntary mailing list of 25,000, plus volume purchases by interested companies and individuals, provide the audience. The Foundation's expensive and well-planned literature avoids emotional vocabulary and seeks to present with clarity and dignity the principles of "libertarianism." Donations at the start came principally from a small group — Armour, B. F. Goodrich, Chrysler, Consolidated Edison, Du Pont, General Motors, Marshall Field, U. S. Gypsum, U. S. Steel, and the Volker Fund.

Unlike Spiritual Mobilization and the Christian Freedom Foundation, the Foundation for Economic Education has not evangelized among ministers as a specific group. Indeed, this has not been necessary, as long as their economic viewpoint reaches the clergy through the columns of *Faith and Freedom* and *Christian Economics*. But, boasts Russell J. Clinchy, "religious spokesman" for the Foundation: "Each one of the members of the senior staff at this Foundation is an active church member, and I have never seen a greater religious interest, nor a greater personal social concern, than I find among this group."

The Foundation's premises are fundamentally theological, although its religious creed is neither long nor profound. Advocates of welfare legislation, contend Foundation spokesmen, are seeking to manipulate the forces of government "to repeal the law of variation; to redesign mankind; to force their concepts of morality and economics on all other persons; in short — to play God." They violate the "economic commandments" (theft and covetousness), according to this view, and such violation "will assuredly spread to other commandments"; in this fashion, the enemies of individualism will "destroy faith in and observance of our entire basic economic code."

In the New Testament, the Foundation's "libertarians" discover that Christ "did not resort to theft in acquiring the means of material satisfaction"; moreover, the Golden Rule, when combined properly with the Decalogue, represents an endorsement of private property and the "libertarian" concept of freedom, on the one hand, and spiritual exhortation to individual charity, on the other. One Foundation economist assures us that "if the Sermon on the Mount were to appear in our day in the form of an address or publication, it would be scorned as reactionary."

Some of the writers endorsed by the Foundation — for instance, Chodorov and Nock — have advocated a "freedom" that embraces the political ingredients of anarchy. They boldly call government "the enemy of the people," and, with Henry David Thoreau, profess "that government is best which governs not at all." State administrators and functionaries are categorized as "a professional criminal class."

Many Foundation spokesmen carry their concept of freedom to these extremes, and they unanimously tend to conceive of government as a necessary evil, whose only justifiable role is as the protector of the God-given rights of the individual. Freedom is the natural birthright of man, they contend, and the state can best encourage its exercise by leaving the individual alone and compelling others to do the same.

Among the assumptions underlying the creed of economic "libertarianism" promulgated by the Foundation for Economic Education and like-minded organizations, the following are basic:

(1) *"God's Law" is the same as "natural law," which is the same as "laissez-faireism."* To let "natural law" take its course is to do the will of God. Whenever man interferes with "natural law" through economic regulation, he is fighting against God. Laissez-faire capitalism arises directly from the Christian faith. All forms of "collectivism" —i.e., government regulation of any sort — are therefore anti-Christian.

(2) *The only legitimate avenue to social betterment is through individual conversion.* Taxation rides roughshod over initiative. Taxes — which steal from men what rightfully belongs to them — prevent their fulfilling the duties of charity. If a millionaire experiences "religious conversion," some of his abundance will flow toward assuaging the needs of those poor who cannot help themselves.

(3) *There is no middle ground between "libertarian-*

ism" and communism. Everyone must either support un-trammeled laissez-faire — under which there would be no public post offices, no public highways, no public schools — or be guilty of aiding the cause of "godless, materialist communism." The difference between the "statism" of Russia and the "statism" of the United States is one of degree only. Genuine freedom lies in an absolute minimum of outside interference in the life of the individual.

Oddly enough, this "libertarianism" and Marxism have much in common. Both trace all good and all evil to economic causes. Both embrace a philosophy of extreme materialism. Both are fatalistic, in that they believe in the inevitable working of "natural law."

Stripped to its essential credo, the extreme form of "libertarianism" is a curious sibling of Marxism.

The National Council and J. Howard Pew

Exponents of these extreme economic doctrines threaten to achieve positions of power in American Protestantism. This danger became evident in 1950, at the founding convention of the National Council of Churches.

J. Howard Pew — prominent Presbyterian, Sun Oil and Sun Shipbuilding magnate — arrived at Cleveland as chairman of a "sponsoring committee" of nearly one hundred lay men and women from more than thirty states. The group included wealthy businessmen of strategic position in the world of finance and industry. Among them were Harvey S. Firestone, Jr. (of Firestone Tire and Rubber), Harry A. Bullis (of General Mills), Donaldson Brown (of DuPont), Robert E. Wilson (of Standard Oil), Edward L. Ryerson (of Inland Steel), and Colby M. Chester (of General Foods). Others in the "sponsoring committee" were well known for their middle-road positions on economic questions — for instance, Harold E. Stassen, Charles P. Taft, and Charles E. Wilson (of General Electric). A number of labor, farm, and educational leaders were also included.

Pew's group was called the National Laymen's Committee. It should not be confused with another ultra-conservative organization, the Laymen's National Committee, Inc., sponsor of

National Bible Week and National Sunday School Week. The two groups, however, have much in common, including overlapping membership. Pew's colleague Bullis, for instance, is national chairman of the Laymen's National Committee, Inc.

At the founding convention of the National Council in Cleveland, the announced program was set aside one morning in order that Pew might be escorted to the platform to deliver an address. In it he informed the delegates that "the Protestant minister differs from the layman principally in the fact that he has been relieved of the necessity of earning his livelihood." Pew deplored the destruction of "Christian liberty" — which he associated with economic laissez-faire — and exhorted his hearers to make the church a bulwark of freedom as defined in the "libertarian" credo. He mentioned the role which he and his colleagues proposed to play in formulating policy in areas in which they had "special competence and interest."

Liberals and moderates took alarm. For a generation the Federal Council of Churches had successfully resisted an alliance with big business, or any other special interest group. Its concern for social idealism had aroused the antagonism of those, who — like J. Howard Pew — equated prophetic religion with subversive ideology. But by 1950 the temper of the times had wrought significant changes. The same Mr. Pew assumed an important role in the National Council: that of money-raiser. He and the committee took on the responsibility of "obtaining $600,000 of needed new gift support for the National Council."

The *Christian Century* gave expression to doubts that troubled many Protestant churchmen. "We have no reason to question Mr. Pew's sincere belief in the principle of Protestant cooperation," said the journal, "but we cannot ignore the fact that to the American public Mr. Pew's name is virtually a symbol of ultra-conservative positions on practically all public issues."

The presence of Pew and his colleagues in high ecumenical councils has led to tension. When the oil magnate began to define the functions of his group, he suggested that it had the right to review Council pronouncements — and unofficial publications as well. At several points, the friction has nearly produced sparks. Pew views the National Council's Division of Christian

Life and Work as a promoter of "European collectivist ideas." Only through the self-restraint of all persons involved and the remarkable conciliatory powers of Samuel McCrea Cavert, general secretary of the National Council and others, has an open rupture been prevented.

Before becoming a new "angel" of the church-unity movement, Pew had been a heavy contributor to the activities of many apostles of discord. During the founding convention in Cleveland, Verne P. Kaub was "flabbergasted" to note Pew's position — because Pew had contributed generously to Kaub's own American Council of Christian Laymen, vehement critic of the National Council of Churches (see Chapter 10). Another saboteur of Protestant co-operation, Carl McIntire, once solicited $50,000 from Pew to finance one of the divisive "missionary" jaunts to the Far East mentioned in Chapter 8. Pew not only has made substantial contributions to Spiritual Mobilization and the Christian Freedom Foundation, but also has actively appealed to wealthy friends on behalf of James W. Fifield. When *Christian Economics* was launched in April 1950, Pew gave Howard E. Kershner his personal check for $50,000 to get it started. And he underwrites a major share of the budget of the Christian Freedom Foundation.

In fact, through his financial contributions to these movements, J. Howard Pew has probably been the major force behind the current revival of the archaic economic thought of the late nineteenth century. Through these "non-partisan" educational fronts, he effectively promotes his own ideology.

Disturbed by Pew's activities in the National Council of Churches, many churchmen have wondered what the ecumenical body could do about his undue influence. The Council has expanded until it stands in need of financial "angels." Its budget was originally set at $4,500,000 — a sum far larger than the combined budgets of the eight interdenominational agencies that had joined to form the Council. And Pew has aided the Council materially through his personal emergency appeals to corporations; over a thousand of them have been placed on the list of contributors. While 70 per cent of the total budget now comes from the constituent denominations, 30 per cent arrives in the form of gifts from individuals, corporations, and foundations —

many of which had been regular contributors long before Pew entered the picture.

Gratitude for the new efforts was expressed at the 1952 biennial meeting of the National Council. Speaking of Pew's National Laymen's Committee — and its sister organization, the National Laywomen's Committee — the Committee on Appraisal of Programs and Budgets reported:

We acknowledge with appreciation the helpful contributions made during the biennium by the National Laymen's Committee and the National Laywomen's Committee through recruitment and active enlistment of men and women of character, ability, and experience, most of whom were not previously related to any of the twelve bodies which formed the National Council of Churches. Today, many men and women originally recruited for the lay committees constitute the nucleus for the Business and Finance Committee. The national lay committees are largely responsible also for activating a program of special interpretation, and for securing added financial support.

Simultaneously, however, first tentative steps were taken toward disbanding the Pew faction and integrating its members into the structure of the Council. Church leaders such as Bishop G. Bromley Oxnam had proposed that members of the lay groups, as individuals, be brought into the "functioning, decision-making agencies of the Council, not in a separate, irregular body." Many felt that an impression had arisen — rightly or wrongly — that church leaders often had not consulted lay opinion adequately before issuing policy statements. To bring Pew's colleagues into the regular policy-making bodies would help to allay this criticism. Others contended that the presence of more proponents of the extreme right would serve to balance the vociferous, doctrinaire faction among the liberals.

Whatever the various motivations, the 1952 biennial assembly decided to take this step, resolving the work toward the

. . . speedy and complete integration of lay workers into the structural life of the Council . . . [so] that by June 30, 1954, there will be no need for a Lay Committee (as such) because its members will be actively working throughout the Council from top to bottom on a variety of policy, managerial, and program committees and boards where their experience and ability can be utilized to the fullest degree.

Some observers expressed concern over the 1952 selection of vice-presidents for the National Council, which may indicate that the influence of the National Laymen's Committee was beginning to be felt. Of these six vice-presidents at large, three are allied with hyper-conservative financial or political interests: Jasper E. Crane, of DuPont; Mrs. Olive Ann Beech, president of Beech Aircraft; and Mrs. Norman Vincent Peale, wife of the famed minister-author. A few, however, interpreted their election as a conscious effort to placate extremist elements by giving them figurehead positions.

What does this power struggle mean for the future of social concern among the Protestant churches? Most churchmen hope that the representatives of moneyed interests — sincere though their antiquated views may be — will be converted to less extreme views. But Pew is not surrendering. Already he has urged his allies, once they have been distributed on various National Council committees, to attend meetings without fail and to work for adoption of the "right" kind of stated policy.

Reinhold Niebuhr expressed the doubts of many when he wrote: "There are indications that a long period of 'creative tension' between the clerical leaders of American Protestantism and the American business community is coming to a close with the triumph of the business community over the churches."

Others are less pessimistic. They are confident that Pew and his friends cannot turn back the clock fifty years. The church still has progressive leaders who will neither "sell out" nor be intimidated. Behind them are thousands of Protestants across the land — ministers and laymen — who will not be silenced on matters of social justice. The "infiltration" of the National Laymen's Committee into the National Council will not succeed without a struggle.

As powerful right-wing pressure groups gain influence on the national scene, can the church remain independent? Or will Protestantism retrogress to its nineteenth-century alliance with economic privilege, when its social theories echoed the heartless notion of "survival of the fittest" — which too often meant the exploitation of the "have-nots" by the "haves"?

The "libertarians" aim to mold public opinion their way, and they view the churches as desirable instruments through which to propagate their antiquated views. They hope to convince churchmen that all welfare legislation is "tyrannical," "social-istic," and "un-American." A few may agree. Those who oppose social security, pensions for the blind and aged, veterans' benefits, laws to protect laborers from abuse and farmers from disaster, and every other legal expression of humanitarian concern — including public schools, parks, and libraries — will want to join the "libertarians" in their campaign to turn back the clock.

The overwhelming majority of American citizens, however, would view the repeal of these benefits as antithetical to the most elemental standards of justice and subversive of America's democratic way of life. There is grave danger, however, that by vague and emotional appeals to "freedom under God" — channeled through mass media that only big money can afford — Protestants will be lulled into complacency, while aggressive "libertarians" try to rob the nation of its cherished inheritance.

Proponents of unregulated laissez-faire, of course, have a right to be heard, within Protestantism as without. They should not be fought by smear tactics — the method too frequently used in the battle of ideologies. With open minds and constant alertness, keen conservatives and liberals alike should examine the obsolete "libertarian" ideology.

Measured in the scales of human welfare, "libertarianism" will be found wanting.

13

The Struggle Within Methodism

The Methodist Church — America's largest Protestant denomination, with a membership exceeding nine million — is in the midst of an ideological struggle that could reach gigantic proportions and rob Methodism of its historic concern for social justice. For many years, the spiritual descendants of John Wesley's eighteenth-century English movement had been directed by devoted and dynamic leaders and blessed with internal harmony. The emphasis upon religious experience coupled with a unique form of church government militated against the divisive forces that were causing serious conflict and schism within other major Protestant denominations.

Today, however, the situation seems to have changed. Groups of self-proclaimed "patriots" — as sincere as they are dangerous — have determined to undermine the Methodist heritage of social justice, and to substitute bigotry, blatant nationalism and economic chaos.

The roots of the present problem go back to 1907, when a small group of consecrated idealists met to establish the Methodist Federation for Social Service. Among them were some of the "grand old men" of Methodism — including the dean of her bishops, Herbert Welch. Although they held divergent views on social and economic questions, they were convinced of the moral responsibility of the Christian community and set, as their common goals, economic justice, racial and religious goodwill, and world-wide peace.

The Federation was officially recognized by the denomination in 1908, a year after its founding, when the General Conference — national governing body of Methodism — resolved: "We note with satisfaction the organization of the Methodist Federation for Social Service, composed of members and friends of our church and of the Methodist brotherhood." Four years later, the General Conference recommended that the Federation be acknowledged as "the executive agency to rally the forces of the church" in support of the denomination's social objectives.

Early Criticism of the Methodist Federation

Soon after the Federation was born, czarist Russia was overthrown and the Bolsheviks established the Soviet Union. Through the United States swept a wave of hysteria, culminating in the Palmer raids — which used the nation's fear of Marxian revolution as the excuse for an attack on philosophical anarchists and on many innocent idealists, building up in the public mind the picture of a sinister plot to overthrow the republic. The Sacco-Vanzetti case in this period was typical of the reaction against political non-conformists. In the Methodist Federation, a few persons were captivated by the vision of a Marxian classless society; they laid the cornerstone for later pro-Soviet control of the social action group. But the majority were liberal crusaders, concerned only with the abolition of social injustice and the coming of the Kingdom of God on earth.

By 1924, the first doubts about the Federation's policies were voiced in General Conference debate. Though it was again commended for "its splendid activities," a Commission on Social Service was appointed to re-evaluate the social action of the denomination and to suggest a more representative and effective organization. In 1932 — when the depression had aroused most denominations to social responsibility — the General Conference adopted a recommendation once more praising the "invaluable work" of the Federation. The Conference asked the Federation to continue as an independent group — at the same time, pointing out that it "does not speak, nor does it attempt to speak, for the Church."

A bitter controversy flared up in the middle of the 1930's, when the Federation was subjected to widespread criticism beyond any in its twenty-year history.

The Hearst syndicate headlined a series of articles, "Rid the

Methodist Episcopal Church of 'Red' Incubus," by Ralph M. Easley of the National Civic Federation. Calling upon the General Conference for rigorous action, Easley demanded that it "deal with the McConnell-Ward-Chappell aggregation without gloves." Similar action was urged by the Philadelphia *Inquirer*. At the same time, Elizabeth Dilling, author of the widely circulated book *The Red Network,* called the Federation the "spearhead for Communism in all Protestant churches."

Within Methodism, the battle raged with even greater fury. Rembert Gilman Smith, preacher of the Methodist Episcopal Church, South, organized the Methodist League Against Communism, Fascism, and Unpatriotic Pacifism, with national headquarters in Chicago. Smith produced a pamphlet, *Methodist Reds,* and a book, *Moscow Over Methodism* — both enthusiastically received by enemies of the Federation.

A Conference of Methodist Laymen was convened in Chicago in July 1935, "for renewed emphasis on the spiritual phase of the life and work of the church." Its leaders, including many prominent bankers, contended that ministers should "preach the gospel" and leave social, political, and economic problems to those who understood them. In a statement to the press, these laymen demanded "the settlement of the status of the Communist-influenced Methodist Federation for Social Service, and of Clergymen and church officials who use their positions to preach Socialism and Communism." A similar lay group was formed in Southern California "to eradicate those sinister influences that have insinuated themselves into the church."

The foes of the Methodist Federation for Social Service arrived at the 1936 General Conference insisting that the Federation be investigated and that it stop using the name "Methodist." A review commission was appointed to carry out the first demand; but a formal resolution decided that Methodism included "all those who belong to any branch of the Wesleyan family" and that the name could not be withheld from any group. On the other hand, they asked that unofficial organizations make their independent status evident at all times. The Federation thereafter carried the word "unofficial" on its letterhead.

The anti-Federationists won another partial victory the same year when the General Conference expressed its regret that "certain unofficial" agencies vigorously battling fascism and war remained "strangely silent upon such matters as class struggle and communism."

There were occasional references to the Federation's "radicalism" from 1936 until the end of World War II. For the most part, however, it waxed strong and respectable, especially after the United States joined the Soviet Union in the struggle against the Axis powers. Although the pro-communist faction contributed the top leadership, most of the members were liberals who hated totalitarianism.

Post-war Exposés

One of the earliest post-war exposés of communist infiltration into religious circles appeared in the Scripps-Howard newspapers. In October 1947, Rabbi Benjamin Schultz — later national director of the American Jewish League Against Communism — wrote three articles designed to uncover communism in Protestant, Catholic and Jewish religious organizations. Schultz attacked the Methodist Federation for Social Service for its involvement in a "pro-Soviet network." He singled out Bishop Lewis O. Hartman of Boston, Harry F. Ward, "father" of the Federation, and Jack McMichael, its young executive secretary.

Two months later, the same newspaper chain featured another series of three articles, this time aimed only at the Federation. It set the stage for a long and bitter conflict in the denomination. The author was Frederick Woltman, staff expert on native communism, who had just received the Pulitzer Prize for his revelation of communist infiltration into segments of American society. His articles focused on the Federation's 1947 membership meeting in Kansas City.

The Scripps-Howard newspapers headlined Woltman's first story: "MINORITY GROUP GIVES REDS SOUNDING BOARD FOR THEIR PARTY LINE." Woltman charged that the Federation had "for years . . . closely followed the Communist Party line on many issues" and that "if the Federation and its scheduled speakers run true to form in Kansas City, the Soviet dictatorship will be extolled, America's foreign policy will be castigated, Yugoslavia's Communist dictator will be greatly whitewashed, and Chiang Kai-Shek will be denounced."

Three days later, his second assault upon the Federation began: "The spirit of Christmas and the Sermon on the Mount were invoked here this week end as justification for an all-out attack on America's foreign policies and a glowing defense of the Soviet Union in both her foreign and domestic affairs."

A final article reported that the meeting ignored "threats of Russian imperialism, of the revived Communist International and of Communist infiltration tactics in America." But Woltman did acknowledge that most delegates had no bias in favor of communism: "The cards were stacked against the delegates. On the controversial issues of Russia, European recovery, China, civil liberties in America, they heard only one side of the story."

Rapid-fire counter-attack against the Woltman series came from Clyde R. Miller, head of the Federation's Commission for Propaganda Analysis. Miller sent a public letter to Carl W. Ackerman, dean of the School of Journalism of Columbia University. Miller stated: "I seldom have seen such deliberate distortion of facts and such malicious propaganda." He then echoed the fanciful "party-line" charge that the Scripps-Howard papers were deliberately conditioning the American people for war.

The Federation itself published a lengthy retort to the Woltman charges, and the Scripps-Howard newspapers reciprocated with *The Facts,* a pamphlet designed to reply to champions of the Federation. The pamphlet contended: "The decision to cover the Kansas City convention was based on the advance list of key speakers, . . . and on a study of their background and that of the Federation which indicated the Communist point of view on vital issues of the day would prevail."

The most resounding attack upon the organization — whose name by now had been changed to the Methodist Federation for Social Action — appeared in February 1950, when the *Reader's Digest* ran a brief article by Stanley High, one of its editors, entitled "Methodism's Pink Fringe." In this article, High alleged that the Federation's aims were "to discredit America at home and abroad, to condemn the American economic system as unchristian, to promote conclusions which give aid and comfort to the Communists." This interpretation provoked thousands of embarrassed Methodist ministers and laymen to ask the Council of Bishops to repudiate the Federation. The *Reader's Digest* refused Federation spokesmen an opportunity to answer the High charges.

Bishop G. Bromley Oxnam, one of Protestantism's most articulate spokesmen against communism, prepared a cogent reply — "Think and Let Think, A Gentle Rejoinder to Stanley High's Article, 'Methodism's Pink Fringe.' " Oxnam contended: "No one questions the right of Mr. High to attack the present leadership of the Methodist Federation for Social Action or the policies of the organization." The Bishop objected, however, to the manner in which the attack was written — "in such fashion that the uninformed reader gains the impression that bishops and prominent officials are in effect in a conspiracy to 'promote conclusions which give aid and comfort to the communists."

Oxnam scoffed at the idea that the Federation was a threat to the church and the nation:

> If after forty years of history the Methodist Federation for Social Action has 5,800 members [actually much less than that], if it is still in desperate financial straits, and if the church itself speaks its own mind as it does in the General Conference, it would appear that Mr. High might rove in more productive fields and devote his admitted and saleable talents more constructively elsewhere.

The *Reader's Digest* was assailed by other key Methodists who, like Oxnam, had long records of opposition to totalitarianism, from whatever source it came. Walter G. Muelder, dean of Boston University's School of Theology and one of High's prime targets, wrote a sharp reply in *Zions Herald,* organ of the Boston Wesleyan Society and Methodism's oldest publication. "Years of journalistic experience," Muelder said, "have taught him how to cut skilful figures of insinuation and distortion of truth on the ice of misrepresentation without passing the fringe of libel and falling into the open water of character assassination." John E. Marvin, editor of the *Michigan Christian Advocate,* ran an answer entitled "A Presbyterian Tells Us Methodists, But Not Much," in which he observed:

> In fact, if Mr. High knew the Methodist Church better, he would realize that since the last General Conference it has been working on the problem raised in his article. . . . This is mentioned here simply to

remind Methodists that their church is quite aware of the problem he mentions, but unlike Mr. High (who can do nothing about it since he is not a Methodist), the Methodists are doing something about it. They know all he knows and much more.

Reports by the House Committee on Un-American Activities

Meanwhile, the whole picture was confused by the appearance of a superficial brochure, *100 Things You Should Know About Communism and Religion,* published in 1948 by the House Committee on Un-American Activities. In addition to naming the Epworth League (extinct since the merger of three major branches of Methodism in 1939) as a *current* target for communist infiltration, the Committee described the Methodist Federation as "a tool of the Communist party." They furnished no supporting evidence whatsoever, gave no one an opportunity to answer this charge with the help of public funds. They even admitted seven days later that their survey had been made public without any investigation of the group under attack.

The Federation's reaction to the Committee's attack was equally indefensible. Clyde R. Miller accused the Congressmen involved of somehow conspiring with the Roman Catholic hierarchy to sabotage the principle of separation of church and state. "To those who have followed the work of this House Committee and who are familiar with the political policy and propaganda of the Roman Catholic Church," declared Miller, "it is *not* strange that only Protestant organizations are attacked in the report."

Such an appeal as Miller's to sectarian bigotry has been a frequent device of those who wish to divert criticism from their own conduct. It would appear preposterous to imply that the members of the Un-American Activities Committee — nearly all of whom are loyal Protestants — were servants of the Vatican.

On February 17, 1952, the same House Committee issued the 88-page *Review of the Methodist Federation for Social Action.* This self-described "careful and studied review" goes beyond any of their earlier publications in arousing doubts, in the mind of a careful reader, about the Committee's standards of judgment and its investigatory and research techniques. Since the booklet continues to receive wide circulation and fervent applause, it is appropriate to consider a few of its many inadequacies.

The most obvious weakness of the report is its deplorable dearth of factual information. The files of Friends of Democracy or *Counterattack* — or a dozen privately financed anticommunist groups or publications — could have provided considerably more data than are revealed in the Committee report. At best it has thrown together haphazardly a smattering of newspaper and magazine articles. Exhaustive materials on the history and policies of the Federation could have been obtained from a large variety of first-hand sources — including the Federation's own *Social Questions Bulletin,* of which there are complete files in many libraries.

This deficiency might not be so serious had the Committee tapped only reliable reservoirs of information. But most of its data, obtained second-hand, are highly suspect. The inclusion in full of Woltman-High attacks upon the Federation — controversial though they are — might be warranted. It is disconcerting, however, to discover that the other key sources are Robert McCormick's Chicago *Tribune,* William Randolph Hearst's Los Angeles *Examiner,* and the *National Republic* (discussed in Chapter 10) — none of them noted for fairness.

In addition to the House Committee's lack of reliable information and its unfortunate selection of biased sources, the *Review of the Methodist Federation for Social Action* is poorly organized, so that at places it becomes almost unintelligible. As one of many examples, Clyde Miller's condemnation of the House Committee report of 1948 is directly followed by a lengthy article outlining the program of study and action of the Federation. Then, without any continuity, there appears a reply to Miller's statement of five pages before.

Or consider the report's attempt at chronology. It includes a single expression of extreme pacifist sentiment in 1934 to "prove" that the Federation in 1952 was "giving aid and comfort to the enemies of our country." The "careful and studied review" completely ignores the period from 1938 to 1947, although knowledge of this decade is mandatory if the political bent of the Federation is to be evaluated accurately.

In glancing at page 43 of the report, it is logical to conclude that no informed Methodist played a role in its preparation. The Council of Bishops had once issued a statement protesting certain "un-American and unconstitutional practices by governmental authorities in the attempt to rid public offices of employees alleged to be engaged in 'subversive' efforts against our nation." The House Committee's staff, however— evidently unable to distinguish between the denomination's Council of Bishops and the unofficial Federation — asserted that the bishops' protest somehow established the sinister nature of the Federation.

The best illustration of the Committee's carelessness is its admission that "information in the files of this committee is not clear as to when the Methodist Federation for Social Service became the Methodist Federation for Social Action." A telephone call to any of a large number of Federation leaders or a quick perusal of the *Social Questions Bulletin* would have removed such a troubling doubt.

Methodism's official organ, the *Christian Advocate*, typified the unfavorable reaction of many churchmen toward the House Committee's report. In an editorial entitled "Sadly Disappointed," the *Advocate* commented: "To anyone who has read the evidence presented without becoming convinced, the review of the matter is still unconvincing. . . . The review of the House Committee on Un-American Activities adds nothing, and we are sorely disappointed. We had a right to expect more."

Haste in preparation was the chief reason for the manifest inadequacies of the *Review of the Methodist Federation for Social Action*. Methodism's General Conference had scheduled its quadrennial meeting for the following May. Enemies of the Federation — inside as well as outside of Congress — brought considerable pressure to bear upon the House Committee to produce a report as quickly as possible. The Committee apparently gathered together the sparse contents of its files, ordered them printed by the government printing office, and distributed them free of charge in large quantities.

The Battle Against "Party-Line" Control

The key to the truth about the Methodist Federation for Social Action can be found by carefully surveying the inner conflicts within the Federation itself. Its critics often have failed to recognize that such a conflict exists. Some, of course, have not been able to distinguish between various points of view left of center—all "leftists," they think, must be communist. Some journalistic critics have sacrificed integrity for sensationalism; others, including Fred Woltman and Stanley High, have told only part of the story. As a result, they have perhaps conveyed the impression that most Federationists are willing plotters in the over-all Kremlin-directed conspiracy.

But, despite these implications, the Federation at one time received support from many persons of varying political views. Many liberals, of whom Bishop G. Bromley Oxnam was a leading example, withdrew when it became evident that Federation leadership was apologizing for Moscow. Other liberal members remained, however, hoping to change the suspect policies while continuing to work for Christian social ideals. Among them have been socialists and pacifists, all as strongly opposed to communism as they are devoted to their individual interpretations of their religious faith.

Ranged against the majority is a vociferous handful of pro-communists and fellow-travelers who have successfully held the reins of leadership. This ruling clique centers around Harry F. Ward, for many years secretary of the Methodist Federation, and Jack McMichael, Ward's successor. While they are both intelligent and sincere, they follow faithfully the ideological routes charted by the Kremlin, blind alleys and all. These men represent the same point of view in two different generations — Ward, the Federation's "grand old man," a slight, soft-spoken, bespectacled scholar of seventy-eight; McMichael, a dynamic, suave young platform speaker with a Georgia accent.

Much of the controversy within the Federation has revolved around these two men — particularly around McMichael, who was in control at the New York headquarters after he succeeded Ward in 1944. One of the top youth leaders in the nation, he had from 1936 to 1938 served as chairman of the student YMCA and co-chairman of the National Intercollegiate Christian Council. Later, he worked with sharecroppers and served as a chaplain with the Maritime Service. McMichael received his formal education at Emory University in Georgia (A.B.), Union

Theological Seminary in New York (B.D.), and the Pacific
School of Religion in Berkeley, California (S. T. M.). While at
Union Seminary, McMichael was one of Ward's favorite students.

McMichael's involvement in pro-communist activities began
before World War II, when he was national chairman of the
American Youth Congress — later listed by the United States
Attorney General as a communist-front organization.

In February 1941, McMichael got nation-wide publicity when
he led six thousand members of the American Youth Congress
in a march on Washington to protest the draft act. At the time
— during the Hitler-Stalin pact — the efforts of communists in
this country were aimed primarily at undermining national defense. McMichael appeared at a Senate committee hearing to
represent the youths — many of them religious pacifists — in
their opposition to selective service.

An interesting incident occurred at the end of the testimony
heard at the morning session of February 8, 1941. McMichael,
apparently believing that the hearing was about to adjourn without allowing him to voice his objections, rose and informed the
chairman, Senator George of Georgia, that he had been sent
"to testify against this bill because it is the young people of the
country who will lose their lives if it is passed." "Senator George,
American youth has the right . . .," he was continuing when two
policemen grabbed his arms and led him quickly from the room.
McMichael's words evoked enthusiastic applause from the
partisan audience, and Senator George sternly warned that any
more "troublemakers" would be removed.

After being rushed to a guard room, McMichael was finally
released after conferring with Congressman Vito Marcantonio,
faithful Stalinist voice in the House. That evening he led a
torchlight parade which gathered near the Washington Monument to listen to McMichael and Marcantonio denounce "Wall
Street-Downing Street imperialism."

Ward and McMichael have sought to steer the Methodist
Federation straight along the narrow Communist Party line.
The mass of evidence supporting this fact is so overwhelming that
it cannot be fully covered here. The two men have long records
of past affiliation with communist fronts. This fact in itself is
insufficient to indict them. But both Ward and McMichael

continue to bolster communist causes, to address party-line meetings, to sign Kremlin-inspired petitions. Through their control of the *Social Questions Bulletin,* they seldom permit it to deviate from the Moscow version of "truth." All communist demands are fervently endorsed, from "Free the Rosenbergs" to "Stop Germ Warfare."

This may be the free expression of a genuine idealism. But its subtle and consistent pattern of part-truth and part-error has involved its adherents in the communist cause.

Many Federationists have worked to rid their organization of the Ward-McMichael influence. John M. Mecartney, a student at Garrett Biblical Institute — joined by Hiel Bollinger, secretary of the Methodist Student Movement, and others — initiated a major drive against McMichael in 1950. In a long memorandum, Mecartney charged that the Federation's executive secretary had supported or signed statements by a large number of groups with a pro-communist bias:

> Jack McMichael has had ample opportunity to learn the nature of such groups, for he was in the leadership of the American Youth Congress from 1939-41 where he saw the communists operate at close range. A person might make an occasional mistake over the years in signing wrong statements. But no one makes as many mistakes as our executive secretary unless he is naive or purposely inclined to support groups with a pro-communist bias. Either case is grounds for bringing into the executive secretaryship the type of leadership that does not make these mistakes.

Mecartney's carefully prepared memorandum established McMichael's association with the following pro-communist organizations:

American Continental Congress for Peace (1949)
American Peace Mobilization
American Youth Congress
Bill of Rights Conference (1949)
Citizens Committee to Free Earl Browder
Civil Rights Congress
Committee for a Democratic Far Eastern Policy
Conference on China and the Far East (1946)
International Workers Order
May Day Parade (1947)

> National Committee to Defeat the Mundt Bill
> National Committee to Win the Peace
> National Conference on American Policy in China
> National Federation for Constitutional Liberties
> Schappes Defense Committee
> United Defense Committee Against Loyalty Checks

McMichael has admitted his connection with all of these groups.

Mecartney added a long list of various statements and pro-communist petitions which McMichael had signed. This was in 1950 — and the number of his affiliations has grown since then. As emphasized above, the past pro-communist record of McMichael — or of any other person — should never be used by itself as a basis for applying labels today. But McMichael continues today to follow the pro-communist line.

In the spring of 1951, another major schism developed within the Federation. The Boston chapter, centered in the Boston University School of Theology, had been an ardent champion of the Federation in the face of increasingly sharp attacks upon its leadership. Gradually, however, Dean Walter Muelder of the divinity school, Emory Stevens Bucke, then editor of *Zions Herald*, and other influential Bostonians became convinced of the threat McMichael posed to the welfare of the national organization. Notice was given that the Boston chapter would withdraw if a new executive secretary were not chosen.

In a letter addressed "To Our Brethren of the Federation," the Boston chapter carefully outlined its indictments of MFSA leadership:

"(a) The organization of the MFSA is insufficiently democratic. Lack of democracy and established procedures of calling and cancelling meetings has led to excessive control of MFSA policy by the executive secretary. . . ." The letter pointed out that McMichael had controlled his tenure in office through determining the date, time, and place of committee meetings, that he had cancelled or postponed them when he thought it to his advantage, that he had utilized the national office channels for the advancement of his own views, that he had edited the *Social Questions Bulletin* in accordance with his own opinions, and that he had personally propagandized on cross-country trips at MFSA expense.

"(b) The name of the MFSA is being linked correctly with the charge of unobjectivity and untruthfulness. . . ." This was also traced to McMichael's autocratic control.

"(c) In the public mind, the MFSA, through its official mouth-pieces, the executive secretary and *Social Questions Bulletin,* is being placed in the position of seeming to support an ideology repugnant to the vast majority of its members. . . ." Muelder, Bucke, and others contended that the Federation had become, in effect, an apologist for the Soviet Union and an antagonist of the United States.

At the meeting of the Federation in September 1951, the Boston chapter's protest was voiced, but in vain; McMichael was re-elected by a vote of 50 to 6.

In the meantime, the Council of Bishops of the Methodist Church delivered another blow. On April 20, 1950, it passed a resolution about the Federation, noting apologetically that it "does not speak for the Church, and over it neither the General Conference nor the Council of Bishops has jurisdiction." Judiciously it mentioned the Federation's "notable contributions in the field of social justice," but went on to state clearly that "we deplore and sharply disagree with certain positions taken and statements published of late in the Federation's official Bulletin."

Simultaneously, the *Christian Advocate* urged that the Federation drop the name "Methodist" and move its offices out of the Methodist Building in New York City, and that a new board of social action be established "that would be responsible for studies and activities in the area of interest that has always been close to the heart of a reforming church."

The National Conference of Methodist Youth — formerly strong Federation supporters — asserted themselves in the following resolution:

We still believe in its essential worth. . . . But now we must say that until the Methodist Federation for Social Action makes some changes in its present administration, we can no longer suggest that youth leaders support it. We deplore the attempt on the part of any person or persons in church social action groups to follow the line of any outside organization.

Another fissure within the Federation appeared in the early part of 1952. The incident is a complicated one, and there are several differing interpretations. Many of the Federation's most vigorous supporters — men such as Dillon W. Throckmorton of California and Albert E. Barnett of Georgia, who publicly espouse idealistic philosophies — finally became convinced that McMichael must go. They challenged McMichael to include in the January 1952 issue of *Social Questions Bulletin* a statement of policy to make it clear that the Federation repudiated communism. They requested that McMichael, in his capacity as executive secretary, associate himself with the statement. This he failed to do.

Some of McMichael's strongest apologists now backed away. A few resigned their positions on the executive committee; others, such as Barnett, left the Federation entirely. In September 1952, Edgar A. Love, bishop of the Baltimore area, agreed to accept the presidency of the Federation, hoping that McMichael would step aside in favor of a new executive secretary.

Repudiation by the General Conference (1952)

A severe — though anticipated — blow struck the Federation at the General Conference in 1952, when delegates from Methodism throughout the world met to review the status of the denomination during the previous four-year period. There were few who still gave support to McMichael.

A small minority, however, were opposed to public reprimand of the Federation. Some, such as Bishop Love — an able leader among Negro Methodists — believed that delegates "should think twice before they single out the Federation or any one body of Methodists for adverse action. The Federation, whatever its faults, has not failed to seek to break down the barriers which deny the brotherhood for which the Gospel of Jesus calls." Others, such as Emory Stevens Bucke, contended that "the General Conference of the Methodist Church may not legislate on a matter which is not its own creation."

A strong resolution was passed by the delegates by more than a 10-to-1 vote. It asked the Federation "to remove the word 'Methodist' from its name" and "to terminate its occupancy of quarters in the Methodist Building at 150 Fifth Avenue, New York City."

By the late spring of 1953, the Federation still had failed to meet the demands of the General Conference. Membership steadily declined until it claimed only 3,000 adherents, many of whom do not support the extreme position of McMichael. On May 7, Bishop Love announced his resignation as president. "I have felt for a long time," he said, "that the Federation could not regain its prestige and power as a militant and aggressive organization for social justice under the leadership of the Reverend Jack McMichael."

In the face of widespread repudiation from such long-standing friends, the annual membership meeting, held June 1-3 in Palos Park, Illinois, approved several major changes. A new plan of leadership was adopted whereby there would be four secretaries. McMichael stepped aside as the Federation's executive secretary — but he maintains the strategic post of editor of the *Social Questions Bulletin.* The others chosen were Willard Uphaus, who is also co-chairman of the Communist-sponsored American Peace Crusade; the Rev. Mark Chamberlain of Oregon, with responsibility for membership records; and the Rev. I. DeQuincy Newman of South Carolina, field-work secretary. Dr. Loyd F. Worley of Hartford, Connecticut, was chosen president to succeed Bishop Love. The vice-presidents elected were Bishop J. W. E. Bowen of Georgia; the Rev. Edward L. Peet of California; Mrs. Mary Phillips Buckner of Illinois; and the Rev. Clarence T. R. Nelson of Ohio.

The meeting also recommended to the Federation membership that the group's name be changed to "Methodist Fellowship for Social Action" — which change, if adopted, would not comply with the General Conference request that the word "Methodist" be dropped from the title of the organization. Because of the new secretarial plan, the New York office has been vacated, and McMichael has been appointed pastor of a small church in Upper Lake, California.

Shortly after he began his new work, McMichael was subpoenaed to appear July 30 before the House Committee on Un-American Activities to answer charges of Communist Party membership — charges made before the Committee in executive session several weeks earlier. In a tumultuous two-day hearing, McMichael talked vociferously, denying the principal allegations made against him, characterizing his accusers as "liars and perjurers." The 36-year-old clergyman was called "evasive," "contemptuous," and "obtuse" by exasperated Kit Clardy, Michigan congressman. The Committee's counsel continually asked Chairman Harold H. Velde to stop McMichael from "giving asides and speeches to confuse the answers, to confuse the counsel, and to confuse the committee." When confronted by an ex-communist and two former F. B. I. agents, who had previously testified that McMichael had communist affiliations, the witness said that he could not remember having met them.

The Committee indicated that it might ask the Justice Department to study the conflicting testimonies for possible perjury action. It unanimously voted to keep McMichael under subpoena until it finishes its interrogation of him at some future date.

Harry F. Ward, who had also been accused of Communist Party affiliation, likewise flatly denied the charge. In a letter of July 25 to the New York *Times,* Ward stated that at the beginning of his ministry he had resolved to maintain "complete independence of all political parties, and I have never deviated from this position."

Meanwhile the 1952 General Conference voted to establish an official Board of Social and Economic Relations, with these functions: (1) to implement the actions of the General Conference and the Methodist Social Creed; (2) to make available to church members resource material on social and economic relations; (3) to answer local church requests for information and guidance; (4) to encourage interest and activity in the church's relation to social and economic problems; (5) to organize service projects for Methodist youth in co-ordination with church agencies.

Observers disagree on the socio-economic views of the members of the new board. Dillon Throckmorton, former stalwart of the Methodist Federation, predicts that it will "direct the life of the church in such an official manner that there can be no doubt that the Methodist Church is in the forefront of every issue that relates to the welfare of humanity." But others are not this optimistic. Lyndon B. Phifer, editor of Methodist adult materials, is one of many who has found the membership of the Board disappointing; writing in *Zions Herald* in September 1952, he expressed the fear that "the conservative mind will predominate" and "the new board will fail to accomplish its purpose." Phifer added: "More and more it looks as if the official Board of Social and Economic Relations will need to be supplemented by a vigorous unofficial group that can either rescue MFSA from McMichael's destructive leadership or start a new movement."

History alone can judge the total impact — for good or for ill — of the Methodist Federation for Social Action. However, one immediate result of the party-line parroting of its Wards and its McMichaels has been the strengthening and marshaling of groups within Methodism which are opposed to any kind of social reform. In direct response to the Federation's continued espousal of the party line, lay resistance groups have mushroomed in different parts of the nation to protest its influence within the denomination. Some of these groups have not confined themselves to a refutation of communism, but have further advocated an extreme philosophy — politically pro-nationalist, economically ultra-conservative — with frequent overtones of racist bigotry.

These belligerent apostles of conservatism, flushed with their partial victory at the San Francisco conference, have, in turn, aroused apprehension in the minds of a growing number of Methodist pastors and laymen outside the Federation. These persons fear that the reactionary groups may not desist in their "counter-revolution" until they have succeeded in robbing Methodism of its historic concern for the alleviation of social ills.

Circuit Riders, Inc.

The best-known mobilization of lay Methodists to counter radicalism in the church is the Circuit Riders, Inc., a national organization with central headquarters in Cincinnati, Ohio. In October 1951, newspapers across the country gave wide publicity to the Circuit Riders' initial meeting in Chicago, when thirty-three Methodists from many states declared their firm intention "to oppose all efforts to propagate Socialism and Communism and all other anti-American teachings in the Methodist Church."

While all members of the Circuit Riders have been in accord in their pungent denunciations of the Federation, they have not been unanimous in other matters. A few patrons of the group are moderate conservatives, and believe — as did most critics of the M.F.S.A. — that the 1952 General Conference resolution, condemning many of the Federation's attitudes, was sufficient. But the majority argue that this was only the first round in a continuing fight, and that Methodists must restore "Americanism" to their church. They purport to find sinister influences and evidence of socialism in the National Conference of Methodist Youth, in the Women's Society of Christian Service, in denominational publications and in Methodist theological seminaries. Many wish to sabotage the newly created Board of Social and Economic Relations — contending that the church has no jurisdiction in such matters.

The executive secretary of the Circuit Riders, Inc., M. G. Lowman — professional public-relations agent and partner in an air-conditioning firm — devotes half his time to the program of the group. Their treasurer is the distinguished Paul Sturtevant — member of the New York Stock Exchange, partner in the Wall Street firm of Baker, Weeks, and Harden, and former member of the National Board of Missions and Church Extension of the Methodist Church. The Circuit Riders were represented at the 1952 Conference by their president, John Satterfield — a Mississippi lawyer who had been instrumental in organizing the Volunteer Committee of Christian Laymen, one of the lay groups co-operating with the Circuit Riders. Satterfield was a strong member of the Committee on the State of the Church, which drafted and overwhelmingly adopted the resolutions on the Federation and the changes in the official Social Creed.

Satterfield interprets the amendment to the Social Creed — acknowledging "the principle of the acquisition of property by Christian processes, and in the right of private ownership thereof" — to mean that socialism in any form in the denomination is condemned. "Our complete faith should be fully restored in our leaders," the Mississippi attorney urged, "for it was demonstrated that a few radical liberals have been vocal and active and have tried to appear to speak for the Church." He stated that the San Francisco repudiation was the first time in history that Methodism had condemned an organization: "God was with us and the action was obtained by the leaders of our Church both ministerial and lay from New York to California and from Florida to Illinois." Satterfield sounded a call to future action: "The first skirmish has been won, but there is plenty more to do. But this is only a step in the right direction."

In June 1952, Circuit Riders from every section of the country again met in Chicago to weigh their success in arousing popular support and in implementing the conservative decrees passed at the General Conference. Unanimously they decided to continue for another four years — creating good-will for "right-wingism" among Methodism's clergy, laity, and youth.

The Circuit Riders gained national publicity in March 1953 when Satterfield and Lowman telegraphed to Representative Harold H. Velde, chairman of the House Committee on Un-American Activities, requesting that Harry F. Ward and Jack R. McMichael be investigated. The request, originally made in 1952, was reiterated after Velde had suggested that the churches might be a target for congressional inquiry into communism.

The Circuit Riders have been bolstered in their activities by a network of allied lay fraternities stretching across the country. The most substantial of these organizations is in Houston, Texas — the Committee for the Preservation of Methodism, which claims to have been encouraged in its formative period by Bishop A. Frank Smith, and headed by Sam R. Hay, son of another bishop.

The Houston group was created to carry out the aims of a memorial of the Texas Annual Conference adopted in June 1950. The memorial rebuked the Federation and all other organizations "that would seek to use the Methodist Church . . . for the promotion of socialism or communism." The Committee has distributed nearly fifty thousand copies of a 35-page booklet entitled *Is There a Pink Fringe in the Methodist Church?* Its most vociferous members have included Clarence Lohman, prominent Houston lawyer and vice-president of Circuit Riders, and Mercer H. Parks, former Baptist, oil engineer, and agitator against the organized ministry.

Other organizations co-operating with the Circuit Riders include the Protest Committee of Lay Methodists of Baltimore, Maryland; the Volunteer Committee of Christian Laymen, of Jackson, Mississippi; and the Committee of Loyal American Methodists, of Manning, South Carolina. The last of these,

headed by an elderly lawyer, Charlton DuRant, has widely circulated a series of four brochures entitled *Methodist Termites.*
In addition to the materials circulated by the Circuit Riders,
Methodist Termites recommends to its readers such extremist
periodicals as Walter S. Steele's *National Republic,* George Washington Robnett's *News and Views,* Lucille Cardin Crain's *Educational Reviewer,* Frank Hanighen's *Human Events,* Joseph
Kamp's *Headlines,* and Howard Kershner's *Christian Economics.*

How far do the Circuit Riders plan to carry their attacks upon
Methodism's "subversive" elements? Members seem to disagree,
but it is certain that some extremists envision the church as a tool
of ultra-nationalism, bent on destroying all effort toward social
justice, economic security, and international co-operation. There
is the danger that these extremists may succeed in infiltrating the
Methodist Board of Lay Activities. One churchman reported
that the Circuit Riders intend to have an organized chapter
in every local Methodist church — to help the pastor sympa-
thize with their point of view. Others demand that no bishop
in the church be allowed to belong to any organization other
than those that may be officially recognized by the General
Conference. Some want all liberals thrown out of the denomination.

These Methodist malcontents are a highly controversial element with the church. They are vehemently denounced by
apologists for the Federation, some of whom dismiss them as
"race-minded Dixiecrats" and "N.A.M.-influenced reaction-
aries." Other critics are aware that prolonged agitation by the
Circuit Riders will promote discord and destroy Methodism's
freedom of thought and speech as well as her traditional interest in the improvement of the social order. Many well-meaning
Methodists, less impressed by these dangers than by others,
will still contend that it is not safe to relax pressure until the
conservative temper of the 1952 General Conference has become the attitude of the Federation.

Also active in the fight against the Federation were a small
number of independent Methodist insurgents who promote
more extreme views than those of the Circuit Riders. None
of these agitators by himself could steer the denomination away
from its customary concern for social ideals or sense of fair

play; but, together, they can create confusion and destroy the harmony within the church.

"Bob" Shuler

The most important of these extremists is Robert P. Shuler, fighting pastor of the 3,000-member Trinity Methodist Church in Los Angeles and editor of the *Methodist Challenge.* "Bob" Shuler was born seventy-two years ago in Grayson County, Virginia; received his B.A. degree from Emory and Henry College; entered the ministry in 1903; and soon rose to a position of prominence in the church. Today his three sons, Bob, Jr., Jack, and Phil, have become popular traveling evangelists. The *Methodist Challenge* — formerly known as *Free Lance* and *Bob Shuler's Magazine* — reaches nearly eighteen thousand ministers and laymen in every state. It is ostensibly published "in defense of the Methodist evangelical position in matters of doctrine and to promote true Methodist evangelism."

Shuler gave enthusiastic praise to the program of the Circuit Riders. "It has done a great and noble work," he exclaimed after the 1952 General Conference, "and every loyal American Methodist should do all in his power to support its great work."

But the Los Angeles pastor had made some additional recommendations. He has suggested a loyalty oath for every Methodist editor, every president of a Methodist college, every professor in a Methodist college. "Personally,' 'he said, "in this hour of crisis I would favor requiring such an oath of every pastor in a pulpit of the Methodist Church."

Shuler also petitioned the General Conference to "reaffirm in no uncertain terms her loyalty to our form of government, to capitalism, to free enterprise, to competitive industry, and to the character of democracy that is ingrained in our constitutional system of human relationship." He urged the abolition of Methodism's historic Social Creed and the official Commission on World Peace — "a group of pacifists, appeasers and slackers, whose only justification is that they are dreaming rather than thinking in this most critical hour of human history."

Shuler maintains many dubious associations. His most controversial friend is Gerald L. K. Smith. Shuler participated in a Smith rally soon after the war, alleging that there was no proof that Smith is anti-Semitic, or that he is "not a Christian, a patriot, and a gentleman."

Leon de Aryan, editor of the cultist *Broom* of San Diego, described Shuler's invocation at the meeting as "the smoothest piece of 'reporting' to our Father that the Jews and the Communists are running the U.S.A., leaving it to the Lord to deal with them in His own good fashion."

By 1949, he conceded that "as for the Jews, I am coming more and more to feel that Smith is right." While taking exception to some of Smith's views, Shuler more recently expressed his desire "to live to see in the White House a man who has the strength, the power, the virility, the courage, the ability, the Christianity, the conviction, the personality, and the love of country which I believe Gerald L. K. Smith has." The Christian Nationalist leader, in turn, has been very amicable toward his Methodist friend, representing Shuler as "one of the greatest men of this generation."

In his regular column, "The Changing World," carried in several weekly newspapers and many other publications, Shuler has adopted a strong nationalist line similar in many respects to that of the Christian Nationalists.

Like Smith, Shuler threw his support for President in 1952 behind General MacArthur. "Douglas MacArthur," Shuler maintained, "is the last survivor of the splendid line of genuine statesmen who made and saved this nation. . . . To name any other by the side of Lincoln, Jefferson, Washington, and Teddy Roosevelt would be blasphemy. . . . Outside of God Himself, MacArthur is our hope. It's MacArthur or Chaos!"

Like Smith, Shuler condemns the United Nations as an "absurd international concoction . . . with a score of heads and many more feet all going in different directions."

Like Smith, Shuler vigorously endorses Franco Spain — where a Protestant like himself would hardly be received with reciprocal affection. If that nation were allowed in the U.N., Shuler adds, "for once we'd have a dictator on our side that we could trust."

Nevertheless, the Los Angeles pastor notes major disagreements with Smith. "In fact I am not a nationalist," Shuler wrote in 1949. "I am an internationalist. Smith opposes our activities in Europe. I believe that the only way to self-preservation and peace is by dominating Europe and Asia as well."

The contents of the *Methodist Challenge* arouse the protests of many dissatisfied readers — among them numerous pastors who receive the paper regularly through the "kindness" of some church member. Critical letters range from the mild reminder that "much of what you say is unfair" to brisk denunciations like the following: "Your *Methodist Challenge* is the foulest piece of dogmatic, biased, prejudicial writing I've ever read for some time." A Pennsylvania Methodist woman writes: "I think you are helping Stalin and his cause by attacking the Methodist Church." And from a delegate to the 1952 General Conference comes this criticism: "I have no respect for anyone who makes his living from the Methodist Church, and then turns on it as do you."

But many thousands of conscientious churchmen are convinced that Shuler was raised up by God for such an "apostate" time as this.

Referring to the Methodist leadership, Shuler contends that "the Social planners, the Pacifists, the 'one world builders,' and the modernistic theologians are in the saddle for keeps." He calls them "carpet-baggers, come to pillage and collect the booty," or "religious exploiters and profiteers, seeking to use the Methodist Church for their selfish ends." Shuler has been particularly sharp in his criticism of Methodist seminaries. "Of the ten divinity schools in the Methodist Church there is not one that lays real stress upon the original doctrines and teachings of Methodism."

Although he is a member of the National Association of Evangelicals, Shuler has had high praise for the American Council of Christian Churches, and acrid denunciation for the ecumenical movement. He considers Carl McIntire "a most courageous warrior in a day when we need soldiers of the Cross as never before."

Shuler has said of the Evangelical Methodist Church, a 9,000-member splinter sect, affiliated until recently with the American Council: "It seems to me that the Evangelical Methodist Church is a God-sent organization, if for no other reason, in that it offers tens of thousands of loyal Methodists, who cannot go with present

Methodist leadership, a church home in which they may continue to be loyal, active Methodists."

In the light of such evident dissatisfaction with his denomination, friends have pleaded and foes demanded that Shuler leave the Methodist Church. But in spite of his unhappiness there, Shuler rejects the urging of those who say, "Come ye apart."

During 1953, Shuler is retiring from his pulpit at Trinity Methodist Church in downtown Los Angeles. Although afflicted with heart disease, he hopes to continue publication of the *Methodist Challenge* for five more years.

"I have faced terrible opposition from the evil forces of the land and from my modernistic brethren," he proclaims to his followers. "My life has been a hectic, difficult journey."

Rembert Gilman Smith

A second insurgent of the far right is 74-year-old Rembert Gilman Smith of Houston, Texas, who is no novice in the ranks of Methodist vigilantes. As has been noted, he was one of the key voices in the chorus against the Methodist Federation for Social Action in 1936 when his *Methodist Reds,* an attractive pamphlet which sold for twenty-five cents, ran into two editions. It was distributed from Maine to California among units of the American Legion, Daughters of the American Revolution, and other groups — besides bishops, ministers, and laymen of the various branches of Methodism. Chagrined that "Methodist reds" were contending that "the profit motive is not morally valid" and were trying to make organized religion a "stimulant to slaughter," Rembert Smith suggested that the Federation be known as the "Marxist Federation for Social Strife."

He went farther. He memorialized the General Conference to declare "its unfeigning loyalty" to the 24th Article of Religion, which he interpreted as a categorical endorsement of laissez-faireism.

Smith, who retired in 1937, was an adamant supporter of the extreme right wing. He wrote many pamphlets attacking the New Deal, Franklin D. Roosevelt, and labor unions. Of the last, he said:

The safety and the life of this Republic require instant war on the Labor Unions. Since 1933, they have been destroying the freedom of citizens and the Constitutional powers of the forty-eight states. With the help or consent of corrupt or cowardly politicians, they have trampled under their feet the most precious of our liberties.

Unlike Shuler, however, Rembert Smith never meddled with racism. Prior to World War II, he effectively exposed Gerald Winrod and his ultra-fundamentalist friend who preached anti-Semitism and apologized for Adolf Hitler (see Chapter 3).

The Houston pastor's current campaign has four chief aims. He is circulating the 1950 edition of *Moscow Over Methodism,* two hundred pages of disorganized charges against the Federation, bound within a cover that pictures Joseph Stalin beaming happily upon an abandoned Methodist church. He is writing a "sensational and factual" book, *Bishop G. Bromley Oxnam: Prelate and Politician.* He is preferring charges against several denominational leaders — notably Bishop Oxnam — accusing them of maladministration, "un-Christian tempers, words, and actions," dissemination of doctrines contrary to the Methodist *Discipline,* and association with eleven "subversive" organizations. In November 1952, Smith filed a $75,000 libel suit against Oxnam in the U.S. District Court for the District of Columbia, accusing the Bishop of injuring his "good name." The retired Oklahoma minister has filed many libel suits against others — including bishops. He also has demanded that C. A. Bowen and Lyndon B. Phifer, editors of church-school literature, be "tried, convicted and expelled for intolerable infidelity and heresy."

Rembert Smith's final major activity, with which he has had little success, has been to organize The Society for Reforms of Methodism, whose object would be to press for the adoption of certain corrections and additions to the official Methodist *Discipline.* Smith is particularly disturbed by the Social Creed, which he wants deleted. He contends that recognition of conscientious objectors "was smuggled into the Discipline by unscrupulous or ignorant persons with the intent to deceive." To safeguard against such radicalism in the denomination, Smith asks that every parish appoint a "Vigilante Committee . . . to discover any literature or influences apt to undermine the loyalty of our children and youth to the Constitution, to warn the Church of them, and to propose prompt measures of resistance."

Blake Craft

A third pastor-publisher struggling against alleged modernism and communism within American Methodism is Blake Craft of Clayton, Georgia, editor of *One Methodist Voice*. Craft entered the Methodist ministry in 1929; in June 1953, however, the bishop of his area refused to appoint him to a charge because of Craft's divisive activities. Craft founded his monthly tabloid in 1952 for those "who believe in evangelical Methodism, Americanism, and the peculiar heritages and cherished traditions of the Southland." According to its editor, it circulates in forty-three states and "among thousands of both stewards and ministers."

Craft strongly endorses the program of the Circuit Riders, which he had helped to organize in October 1951:

As long as there is just one Bishop who has an affiliation with just one Communist front; as long as there is just one federationist editing our Church School literature; as long as there is just one member of one general board who advocates World Government; as long as there is just one piece of literature in our Church that teaches an economic ideology that is not in harmony with our Articles of Religion; as long as there is just one person in the high place of leadership who advocates a treasonable pacifism and encourages our Methodist youth to be a conscientious objector; as long as there is just one leading official who makes light of our Congressional Committees which seek to ferret out the enemies of our country; as long as there is just one person in the high councils of WSCS who tries to put any flag over Old Glory; as long as just one Communist fronter is engaged to address our Methodist Youth Assemblies — there is a need for such a publication as ONE METHODIST VOICE and an organization such as Circuit Riders, Inc.

As a thundering exponent of Southern mores, the Georgia pastor has been very disturbed by the Methodist affirmation of universal brotherhood; and he frankly lists as one of his purposes "The Preservation of the Integrity of the Races." The greatest threat to racial integrity, he contends, "is the preaching and practicing of an impractical brotherhood by certain people in the cloak of religion and under the guise of the Church."

Craft has developed a theology for advocates of white supremacy: (a) "God designed it. . . . I do not believe that God in His creative processes happened to smear a little black by mistake on some primitive man from which sprang the Negro man." (b) "Mongrelization would mean the destruction of a cherished race-history" with its "highest culture and purest faith." (c) "All of the revealed truth of God in the development of real religion has been discovered and received by the people of the white race." Craft reproaches Negro leadership for their "superlative superiority complex." He counsels them to have "a sense of gratitude for the white people who made it possible for them not to have been born in the jungles and brought up in paganism."

The editor of *One Methodist Voice* culls much of his material from the writings of Bob Shuler, Harvey Springer, Joseph Kamp, contributors to the *National Republic,* and numerous other representatives of extremism.

In vivid terms, Craft assaults a variety of stock targets. The Federation he calls "the subtle fungus that is blighting the brightest flowers of our cherished Church," "a leprosy of radical socialism that is eating into the skin of our historic Articles of Religion," and "the 'pinkish leech' that becomes more red as it sucks the blood of our freedom." Northern Methodism is pictured as "honeycombed with the Pink Fringe, socialism, pacifism, and modernism," while "in the bounds of the lamented and late Methodist Episcopal Church, South, is the most vigorous group of Wesley's followers in the world." "Treasonable and un-American" pacifism, says Craft, "is praise for Joe Stalin and all of his American stooges," while one-worlders "seek to tear Old Glory down and trample her under the feet of those marching as an army which is hell bent on wrecking the foundations on which everything we call sacred in America rests." According to the Georgia pastor, Methodism will never attain that glory that God has in store for her if she becomes a "theological monstrosity" by "trying to incorporate into her ecclesiastical body the formalism of the Mother Church, the so-called intellectualism and perverted theology of the Unitarian Faith, and the economic ideologies of Marxism."

Although Craft has been repudiated by his bishop, and condemned by the North Georgia Conference, of which he is a member, his influence among some segments of southern Methodism should not be underestimated. The Georgia minister, a close friend of Gov. Herman E. Talmadge, has served as a member of the

Veterans Service Board of the State of Georgia and in other official capacities. While "delighted" that the Federation was rebuffed and the Social Creed amended by the 1952 General Conference, Craft announced: "The war has not been won. . . . It is no time to rest our oars." He interpreted the General Conference action to mean that liberalism of any sort must be fully uprooted, and envisioned himself as an expert suited to the task.

The Circuit Riders and the more extreme Methodist malcontents pose a threat to freedom of the pulpit. It is undeniable that the Methodist Federation for Social Action has been in need of constructive, dispassionate criticism and the purging of its pro-communist elements — but professional vigilantes have failed to serve this function. Instead, there is a real danger of their establishing their own "party line" and employing a smear technique against those who dare to defy them. Many of Methodism's malcontents of the right wing represent an extreme economic philosophy; others are fanatically opposed to any form of international co-operation; a few revert to the racist theories of blind bigotry. Often, they are not as concerned with the elimination of the communist element as with thwarting any consideration of social or economic reform by the denomination.

Because they operate in a time of fear, exploiting a genuine anxiety over communist conspiracy, they are gaining strength. But they are dangerous allies. To the Methodist heritage they pose an actual and potential threat which may surpass the present danger of communist infiltration.

14

Denominational Dilemmas

A Congregational parishioner picks up his phone. A cultivated voice, obviously that of an educated young man, requests an opportunity to discuss "important church matters." A tall stranger arrives at the spacious suburban residence to inform the expectant layman of a "plot afoot" to exploit the Congregational church for the advancement of "socialism."

The target of his insinuations is the denomination's Council for Social Action, which since 1934 has attempted to "make the Christian gospel more effective in society, national and world-wide, through research, education, and action." But to some of its critics the same C.S.A. appears as part of a radical scheme engineered by shrewd clergymen who resent the material success of prosperous members of their congregations.

The stranger suggests several techniques for "resisting" the attempt of the Council for Social Action to impose its "leftish" dogmas upon rank-and-file churchmen: Withhold all funds from the C.S.A. Contribute generously to special programs to halt "hierarchical" attacks upon "the American way." Scrutinize closely any suspicious civic activities of the local minister. Organize an "investigating committee" to inquire into policies of the Council for Social Action (thus necessitating expense and time-consuming efforts on the part of its staff). Support the national endeavors of aroused laymen organized into the Committee Opposing Congregational Political Action.*

This Committee also has flooded laymen with literature aimed

---

* Since Chapter 14 was set in type, the name of this committee was changed to the League to Uphold Congregational Principles.

at arousing them against the Council. Formed in 1951, the "resistance" movement was set up by eighteen prominent men from seven states. One of their immediate projects was to distribute widely the alarmist booklet *They're* USING *Our Church to Play Politics!* This unfortunate propaganda piece — known throughout the denomination as the "Black Book" — became the center of widespread controversy. Immediately, influential churchmen were disturbed, some joining the growing opposition to the Council, others rushing to its defense.

The booklet charged that the Council for Social Action "stands for things most Congregationalists don't believe in and would strongly disapprove." The C.S.A. was described as "the idea of some people who . . . thought our system of government was outmoded, [who] disliked the American way of doing business . . . [and] did not like people to make profits." Particular disapproval was shown for the legislative work of the Council: "Whenever CSA makes a Washington appearance — and it does so frequently — it is trading on the dignity of our Congregational name and the strength of the numbers of Congregationalists." The booklet concludes: "CSA wants the government to have more power to control all our lives. . . ."

How much truth is there in these extensively circulated accusations? The answer must be sought in the history of the Council. Its spiritual "father" was Professor Arthur E. Holt of Chicago Theological Seminary, who followed in the train of many earlier Congregational social prophets: Horace Bushnell, Washington Gladden, Newman Smyth, Josiah Strong, Graham Taylor, and others. Under their leadership, Congregational churches, working co-operatively, had established occasional committees and commissions in such fields as labor-management relations, racial problems, and international affairs. By 1927, the denomination had an official department of social relations.

Seven years later the Council for Social Action was established by an overwhelming vote (130 to 17) of the General Council, Congregationalism's guiding body. The C.S.A., in its relations with the churches, was handicapped from the outset by its alleged connection with the so-called "resolution against the profit motive," also passed in 1934. This has been used to attack the agency from its infancy, even though, as a matter of record, the first C.S.A. disassociated itself from any doctrinaire position on economic matters by stating in an early message to the churches: "The Council is committed neither to Communism nor Socialism nor Capitalism nor to the New Deal."

The C.S.A. has not always followed a policy that would help it to win friends. For example, in the May 15, 1951 issue of *Social Action,* its small and well-edited — but very biased — periodical, appeared a sharp critique of "Protestant Piety and the Right Wing." The issue dealt with such ultra-conservative groups as the Committee for Constitutional Government and the National Economic Council (see Chapter 10), Spiritual Mobilization, the Foundation for Economic Education, and the Christian Freedom Foundation (see Chapter 12). Several of these groups lodged strong protests at Congregational headquarters, and opponents of the Council for Social Action gained additional support.

While some critics of C.S.A. accuse the social-action group of promoting a collectivist point of view, others have expressed the opinion that the Council's principal shortcoming has been its failure to give adequate representation to the high percentage of Congregational membership which, in view of its economic well-being, tends to be conservative. Still others, liberals included, believe that the Council has erred in trying to speak on behalf of the "Congregational Church" — which, they argue, does not exist as such. Congregationalism has always emphasized the full autonomy of the local parish.

Organized opposition to the Council for Social Action has centered principally in two groups. One is an independent group of laymen in Minnesota, where criticism had arisen soon after the C.S.A. came into existence. The opposition finally consolidated, with main support coming from the wealthy Plymouth Congregational Church in Minneapolis. Among the chief critics from that parish have been U. S. Representative Walter Judd; F. A. Bean, prosperous flour-mill executive; and Gideon Seymour, liberal editor of the Minneapolis *Tribune.* An attempt to mediate the differences between this Minneapolis lay group and the Council for Social Action has been made by the Rev. Howard Conn, pastor of the church to which these three opposition leaders belong.

In the background in Minnesota stands Donald J. Cowling,

president emeritus of Carleton College. Until 1948, Cowling tolerated the activities of the Council for Social Action. But in that year C.S.A. spokesmen testified in Washington on behalf of federal aid to education. Cowling took sharp exception to the C.S.A. position — in spite of the fact that the denomination's General Council had endorsed the same principle. Shortly afterward, when Ray Gibbons, C.S.A. director, visited the Minneapolis area, Cowling summoned him into his office and asked for an about-face on the issue — "retract or else." With characteristic emotion, he expounded his devotion to the "American individualism" which had spurred him on from youth through his intensive academic training at Yale to his steady climb in the educational world.

Some observers sense a contradiction in Cowling's attitude on social problems. He has been a vigorous proponent of local and state efforts on behalf of social improvement and a life-long internationalist — even a staunch World Federalist. Nonetheless, Cowling has served for many years as chairman of the advisory board of Spiritual Mobilization.

Spiritual Mobilization's executive director, James W. Fifield (discussed at length in Chapter 12), has been the dynamo behind the second lay opposition group. His organization — the Southern California Committee for Inquiry into the Council for Social Action — has been maneuvered overtly by James C. Ingebretsen, executive vice-president of Spiritual Mobilization and Fifield's urbane "trouble shooter." Other leaders of the West Coast group include Norris Poulson, U. S. Congressman from California, and Robert A. Millikan, well-known Pasadena physicist — both advisors to Spiritual Mobilization.

While the Congregational struggle involves many who take a middle-of-the-road position on social and economic matters, leaders of the Spiritual Mobilization "school," which opposes all constructive social legislation whatever, appear to have given the major impetus to the movement against C.S.A.

The initial attack circulated by the Fifield group was an anonymous undated "study" designed to discredit the C.S.A. Later, John Payne, a public-relations expert of Covina, California, was solicited to "do a very thorough research job" on the Council for Social Action. His analysis was given limited circulation among "trustworthy" laymen, with instructions that it should be withheld from ministers. More recently, Payne has modified such "anti-clerical" policies and occasionally seeks to obtain from ministers lists of their most affluent laymen. On several occasions, such forays into local congregations have aroused the ire of the pastors.

Although Payne has assumed an important organizing role in the Committee Opposing Congregational Political Action — which united the Minneapolis and Los Angeles groups — most of his efforts today involve the preparation of long "analyses" of C.S.A. literature and coast-to-coast expeditions to persuade laymen to support the movement against the Council.

Perhaps the most nefarious of his "analyses" attempts to connect leaders of the Council for Social Action with alleged communist fronts (as labeled by the House Committee on Un-American Activities). Principal target has been the Rev. Herman F. Reissig, international-relations secretary of the Council since 1948, whom "researcher" Payne has accused of affiliation with twenty-one subversive organizations. Reissig has denied most of the charges and explained others. He was, for example, executive secretary of the Spanish Refugee Relief Campaign (as of its two predecessor organizations). But he led the struggle within this group that resulted in the eviction of the communists. In 1939 he resigned as chairman of another front — the American Committee for the Protection of the Foreign Born — following a national convention during which it became evident that the communists were exercising considerable influence over the organization. Today, Reissig is one of Protestantism's keenest critics of communist theory and practice.

Such charges by the Committee Opposing Congregational Political Action have become more and more careless. It has adopted the methods used by professional "vigilantes" (such as those discussed in Chapter 10) by confusing the facts and by ignoring completely the innumerable factors that must be weighed before it is fair to categorize the political views of anyone.

Other targets have included Dwight J. Bradley, director of the C.S.A. from 1938 to 1941; the late Eduard C. Lindeman, noted sociologist and occasional contributor to *Social Action;* and

Alfred W. Swan, pastor in Madison, Wisconsin, and one of the C.S.A.'s founders.

Other analyses have attacked various aspects of the C.S.A. program. One 10-page document, for example, discussed *Social Action,* concluding that the content of the bimonthly magazine "has been both predominantly political and overwhelmingly one-sided"— a charge which has been too often true. In an "analysis" of *Labor Letter,* edited in Chicago by Francis W. McPeek, Payne concluded that it "is not a proper or a worthy publication for any agency bearing the Congregational name." Recently Payne has scouted far afield from his own denomination to launch an attack on Christian Action, a new interchurch organization dedicated to the interests of social concern among Protestants.

In June 1952, a thousand delegates from Congregational churches across America assembled for their biennial meeting in Claremont, California. One of the most important issues to be considered — second only to the problem of merger with the Evangelical and Reformed denomination — was the activities of the Council for Social Action. The Committee Opposing Congregational Political Action (C.O.C.P.A.) produced a "statement of grievances," summing up their objections to the social action group:

a. Rather than being broadly representative of our membership, the Council for Social Action has been dominated by a particular point of view and has asserted that its greater spiritual insights relieve it from responsibility to the churches themselves.

b. The Council for Social Action has been manifestly partisan in its approach and has, therefore, not functioned as a research agency.

c. The Council for Social Action has openly advocated socialist doctrines and measures in its publications, through its Washington lobby, and in addresses of its staff members.

d. It has at times presumed to speak for all Congregationalists, and has necessarily left the opinion that it represented a substantial body of opinion within the church membership.

e. The Council for Social Action has expended nearly a million dollars that would otherwise have been used to further the missionary program of the churches.

f. The Council for Social Action has struck a divisive and discordant note in our fellowship, which has set brother against brother, and threatens to undermine the church's great mission of good works.

One afternoon of the session was devoted to a hearing on the Council for Social Action, conducted by the denomination's Board of Review — established in the spring to examine the criticisms made by C.S.A. opponents. Four speakers for the C.O.C.P.A. presented their case, recommending that the C.S.A. be stripped of its power to act, be given a status independent of the denomination, be dropped from the budget, and thereafter be known as the Commission for Social Education.

Numerous persons spoke up in defense of the Council for Social Action. Their chief criticism was aimed at the methods employed by Payne in his campaign to discredit the C.S.A., especially his circulation of the "Black Book." Said a Minnesota layman, Gordon Mikkelson: "While devoted laymen are searching for reasonable adjustment of differences, this propaganda appeals to our emotions, to our fears, to our hates, and to our prejudices." A Massachusetts pastor, the Rev. Bedros Baharian, inquired, "Who wrote this book? Why aren't the authors here to speak for what they sent through the mail. . . . If those who wrote it do not care to defend it, can we not put it in the same class as the infamous Protocols of Zion that were declared illegitimate in 1924?"

The results of the conflict so far are not totally clear. On the one hand, the pressure of the conservatives has led to the disclaiming of the 1934 "profit-motive resolution," and their activities have made some inroads into the finances of the C.S.A. and have caused it to revamp some aspects of its program. On the other hand, the Council for Social Action was gratified by a General Council resolution approving its report "with commendation," passed by an overwhelming vote of 689 to 34 (19 abstaining). The Board of Review continued to study the situation, and is expected to render its report in the fall of 1953.

But the C.O.C.P.A. has continued to publish and distribute its attacks unabated. It is aiming much of its fire at the denomination's General Council itself, hoping to discredit it as in "complete violation of the most basic principle of Congregationalism." The chief complaint is that a large percentage of the members of the General Council are clergymen — a symptom of the growing "anti-clerical" sentiment developing in some Protestant circles. The C.O.C.P.A. has charged that "in the

General Council, a minister has 250 times the voting power he has in the local church. . . . In matters controlled by the General Council, the voting rights of the 5000 ministers and professionals of the denomination are equal to those of the 1,250,000 laymen."

The situation remains fluid. The Committee Opposing Congregational Political Action has several meritorious arguments. It has been a valuable corrective — and it can continue to perform service as a balance against those among the liberals who consistently seek to identify their own particular economic and political creed with the Christian faith. But the struggle must be kept within bounds. The danger today is that the more rabid elements of the C.O.C.P.A., encouraged by their success in arousing a well-organized opposition, will seek more and more power until they threaten to sabotage the entire social concern of the denomination.

In early 1953 a new and widely circulated book, *Destiny for Congregationalism,* made fresh attacks upon the Council for Social Action. It was written by Malcolm K. Burton, pastor of the first Congregational Church of Pontiac, Michigan.

This battle within Congregationalism has obvious bearing upon the future of the ministry of disruption. In fact, by exploiting such controversies as this, apostles of discord can move from the periphery of church life into its center. Clergy and laymen must be aware of such dangerous infiltration, stemming from either extreme right or left, lest their churches become instruments for the promotion of ideologies that contradict the basic tenets of their Christian faith.

The Northern Baptists: Schism and Secession

Far removed from the political-economic conflicts in which Methodism (see Chapter 13) and Congregationalism have become embroiled are the Baptists. They face a bitter and perennial battle centered on the "modernist-fundamentalist" controversy — which in most major Protestant denominations had lost its impetus by the mid-1930's. The situation is complicated by confused battlelines; the fight has hinged on a conflict of personalities as well as a clash of doctrines. Although nearly all Baptists are far removed from the ministry of disruption, a few controversial figures flirt with spokesmen of hate and disruption and borrow from time to time their techniques of smear — including such epithets as "communist" and "modernist."

Today Baptists in the United States number almost eighteen million — by far the largest of the "communions" of Protestantism — but they are sharply divided. Seven million are in the Southern Baptist Convention, founded in 1845 when it broke away from the national movement, partly over the issue of slavery. Another seven million belong to two Negro groups, the National Baptist Convention, U. S. A., Inc. (4,467,779), and the National Baptist Convention of America (2,645,789). A million and a half are represented in the American Baptist Convention — known until 1950 as the Northern Baptist Convention. Of these four major groups, all but the Southern Baptists have entered the National Council of Churches — although more than twenty small Baptist splinter groups have also failed to join the ecumenical organization.

Directly after World War I, Baptists, particularly in the North, were enveloped in the modernist-fundamentalist controversy that swept through all American Protestantism. In fact, it was a New York Baptist weekly, *The Watchman-Examiner* — still a key spokesman for fair-minded fundamentalists — that coined the term *fundamentalist*. The word was designed to describe those "who mean to do battle royal for the fundamentals." Their grievances were many. The "social gospel" was said to be replacing religious faith. The Northern Baptist Convention, founded in 1907, was criticized for "ecclesiasticism." Seminary professors were accused of promoting "heresy." Strong objection was voiced to Baptist participation in the Federal Council of Churches and the postwar Interchurch World Movement.

To combat these trends the Fundamentalist Fellowship was launched in Buffalo in 1920. But three years later, at a regular meeting of the Convention, it met decisive defeat in a battle to impose a rigid creedal test upon fellow Northern Baptists — a battle which demonstrated that the fundamentalists, while very strong, were hopelessly divided. The less extreme, led by J. C. Massee, showed interest in preserving the Convention even if it entailed compromise in non-essentials by all the contending factions. The more virulent, led by W. B. Riley (whose association with Gerald Winrod in the promotion of the fraudulent *Protocols* was described in Chapter 3), were unwilling to accept anything they had not themselves proposed. This second group took such offense at the convention's action that in May 1923 — convinced that "modernism" was in the saddle — Riley (while not a "separatist") helped establish the Baptist Bible Union of North America. The Union sought to unite northern extremists with those in Canada and in the South as well.

Meanwhile, the patience of the fundamentalists in all denominations was severely tried when Harry Emerson Fosdick, a Baptist (though then serving as pastor of New York's First Presbyterian Church), delivered his famous sermon "Shall the Fundamentalists Win?" He denied the inerrancy of the Bible and regretted the emphasis upon the doctrines of the Virgin Birth and the Second Coming of Christ. His closing words were tense:

And now in the presence of such colossal problems in Christ's name and for Christ's sake the fundamentalists propose to drive out from the Christian churches all the consecrated souls who do not agree with their theory of inspiration. What immeasurable folly!

Fosdick's sermon was accepted by fundamentalists everywhere as a clarion call to battle.

At first the Baptist Bible Union seemed to prosper. Dr. T. T. Shields, fiery pastor of the Jarvis Street Baptist Church in Toronto, was chosen first president. In addition to Riley, the Union's ruling triumvirate included J. Frank Norris, Fort Worth pastor and incessant agitator within the Southern Baptist Convention. Early in 1926 the Union published a series of Sunday-school lessons in competition with those sponsored by the American Baptist Publication Society. The next year it accepted responsibility for Des Moines University, with the understanding that it would also assume the Baptist institution's $300,000 debt. The three strong-minded Baptist Bible Union leaders quarreled, however, while expected support from the reputable Massee faction did not materialize. In the spring of 1929, amidst a myriad of charges, Des Moines University students rioted against their new administration. Perhaps the most offensive practice of Shields, a Canadian, was to insist that students rise when "God Save the King" was played. When the Ku Klux Klan, strong in Iowa at that time, showed displeasure with his "America-second" attitude, Shields and his trustees quickly packed and walked away. This incident brought sudden death to the Baptist Bible Union.

But a small extremist faction sought to preserve the Union's remains. One offspring was the General Association of Regular Baptist Churches, organized in May 1932, "to raise a standard of Biblical separation from worldliness, modernism, and apostasy." Thirty-two churches initiated the Association; today it boasts of more than 650 local congregations with over 130,000 members. In Canada, T. T. Shields formed a parallel group, the Union of Regular Baptist Churches of Ontario and Quebec. In 1949 he was ousted from leadership of the group and organized still another splinter, the Conservative Baptist Association of Canada (see Chapter 8).

The Fundamentalist Fellowship still hoped to win control of the Northern Baptist Convention, only to suffer new and humiliating defeats. Meanwhile, within the Fellowship itself, younger and more fanatical elements gradually seized the reins, until it became a smooth-working pressure group organized to plot strategy against the "modernist" bogey. The original leadership of the Fellowship — fervent but usually fair-minded — was pushed aside. In 1943 the first major explosion occurred when an alleged "liberal" was selected as one of the administrative secretaries of the Northern Baptist Convention's regular missionary society. Long-smoldering dissatisfaction came to the fore; within a few months an independent group was founded — the Conservative Baptist Foreign Mission Society. Attempts by the Northern Baptist Convention to reconcile the differences were fruitless, and the new Society today claims regular support from 1,500 churches. Fundamentalist leaders who had been unable to wield power within the denomination could now rejoice in the opportunity of running their own show.

By 1946 the Fundamentalist Fellowship had made careful plans to challenge "modernist control" of the Northern Baptist Convention at the forthcoming Grand Rapids meeting. The Fellowship asked for a doctrinal test that many believed would nullify traditional Baptist emphasis on freedom, and consequently keep out all who did not conform exactly to the fundamentalist position. People were alerted on both sides. When two rival slates of officers were presented, the conservatives suffered a stinging rebuff.

Dejected by such an overwhelming defeat, the Fellowship named a Committee of Fifteen to chart a future course of action. Two groups finally emerged: the Conservative Baptist Fellowship and the Conservative Baptist Association. The first now is exclusively engaged in propaganda efforts. The second has set up a "convention" that seeks to woo churches from the American Baptist Convention — new name for the former Northern Baptist Convention. The Conservatives claim major gains; today their Association boasts of over 650 churches with a combined membership exceeding 150,000. Actually, of the 650 churches claimed, only 250 have withdrawn from the American Baptist Convention. Such success as the Conservatives have achieved can be traced in part to a certain amount of duplicity. To "separatists" it presents itself as a "separatist" body; to "anti-separatists" it implies that a church can be a member both of the American Baptist Convention and of the Conservative Baptist Association at the same time.

The Conservatives have demonstrated particular strength in several traditional centers of Baptist advance. In Minnesota, disrupted for years by Riley-led heresy hunts, Richard B. Clearwaters of the Fourth Baptist Church in Minneapolis — Association president in 1952 — succeeded in bucking American Baptist Convention supporters and capturing the state convention machinery. This fundamentalist victory was made possible by support from delegates from dozens of small rural churches pastored by alumni and students of the Northwestern Bible Schools, which Riley had founded. Nearly two-thirds of the Baptist constituency in Minnesota, however, remained loyal to the denomination, Riley's own 3,500-member First Baptist Church of Minneapolis refused to withdraw — in spite of their minister's leadership in the dissident movement. As a result, just before his death in 1947, Riley sought to have his own name dropped from the rolls of the Convention. "I should be ashamed to die in the fellowship that seemed to me un-Biblical, and consequently un-Baptistic," he wrote.

An interesting sidelight of the Minnesota episode was the

position taken by Billy Graham, a Southern Baptist, who had succeeded Riley as president of the Northwestern Bible Schools in December 1947. Graham, refusing to lend his influence to the cause of the extremists, became the butt of their criticism. In March 1952 Graham resigned in order to devote full time to his evangelistic efforts. Some observers believe, however, that he was sensitive to the pressure of his critics.

In Arizona, Richard S. Beal, vociferous pastor of the First Baptist Church in Tucson, persuaded the old state convention to withdraw from the American Baptist Convention, carrying with it more than half of the Baptist churches of the state. Today Beal appears to have his sights set upon the Southern Baptist Convention, where he hopes to find new fields to disrupt.

In Oregon, the Rev. Albert Johnson of Portland led a faction out of that state's Baptist convention. The extremists had made careful plans to take over the convention machinery, as they had in Minnesota and Arizona. Laymen were alerted. The rebel program was overwhelmingly rejected — partly because the convention decided at the outset that no church could participate in its proceedings if it had not supported official denominational agencies. A strong bloc of fifty churches then left the American Baptist Convention to rally with the insurgents.

The Conservatives appear to be well entrenched. They have seized control of the Western Baptist Theological Seminary at Portland, Oregon (now Western Conservative Baptist Theological Seminary); and they have established the new Conservative Baptist Theological Seminary at Denver, Colorado. They have failed in their efforts to capture other conservative strongholds that maintain affiliation with the American Baptist Convention —notably the Eastern Baptist Theological Seminary in Philadelphia, and the Northern Baptist Theological Seminary in Chicago.

Although the chief issues between the American Baptist Convention and the Conservative Baptist Association hinge on personalities and on doctrines, the Association has also attempted to sabotage all progressive social policies of the Baptists and of the ecumenical movement. Its attractive-looking "Case Series" booklets, prepared by Chester E. Tulga and circulated by the Conservative Baptist Fellowship, have sold over 150,000 copies at twenty-five cents each. Their titles illustrate the negative attitude of many Conservatives. Six of the first seven of the series are called:

> *The Case Against the Federal Council of Churches*
> *The Case Against Modernism*
> *The Case Against the World Council of Churches*
> *The Case Against the Social Gospel*
> *The Case Against Modernism in Foreign Missions*
> *The Case Against Neo-Orthodoxy*

Tulga also circulates a "history" of the American Baptist Convention entitled *How a Simple Democratic People Built an Ecclesiastical Machine.*

The charges in these booklets echo many that have been cited in previous chapters; in many instances the opinions of professional disrupters of Protestantism are quoted as facts. Witness this typical misrepresentation of the World Council of Churches:

> The World Council of Churches, like the Federal Council of Churches, was formed as a vehicle for the social gospel, which aims at the socialization of the world rather than the salvation of souls.

Elsewhere in the pamphlet the tenor is the same. For example:

> The World Council was dominated by the clerical mind, represented on the one hand by the ecclesiastics of the state churches and on the other by the utopian dreamers of socialistic American Protestantism. The election of the leftish Bishop Oxnam as the American President was an indication that world socialism is congenial to the ecumenical mind of the Council.

The Conservative Baptist Association must take its place in the ministry of disruption for its negativism, its schismatic methods, and its unfair attacks on other Protestants. How much success will this faction achieve? A few observers predict that the battle has just begun, and that before it is over the Conservatives will tear away half of the northern convention. Denominational leaders, however, on the basis of their contacts over the entire area, believe that the greatest crisis has passed — and that the Conservatives have failed.

J. Frank Norris and the Southern Baptists

While temperate northern Baptists were struggling to keep their denomination free from control by extremists, the massive

Southern Baptist Convention, bringing together nearly 30,000 local congregations, likewise was confronted by bitter vilification from a handful of fanatical fundamentalists. The ringleader of the extremists, J. Frank Norris, died on August 20, 1952; but his efforts to disrupt the Southern Baptist Convention have been pushed by his disciples. It is fitting — even imperative — that a brief summary of his dramatic career be recounted here. He will go down in history as the most colorful figure in the entire history of the "modernist-fundamentalist" controversy.

Alabama-born J. Frank Norris was a man of powerful physique, craggy features, swift-moving, deep-set eyes, and a picturesque and violent vocabulary. In private conversation he seemed well educated and well read, and he talked with flawless diction. But as soon as he had an audience, he would "rant and rave," purposely mispronouncing words and reveling in homely colloquialisms. Sensationalism, excitement, battle — these characterized the life of the man who was variously dubbed "Texas Cyclone," "Texas Tornado," or "Stormy Petrel of the Southwest." To his enemies he was a "self-centered tyrant" with a flair for publicity.

Many people remember Norris as the "pistol-packing parson" who shot and killed a political opponent, D. E. Chipps, more than twenty-five years ago. There are several conflicting accounts of the incident. In retrospect, *Time* magazine summarized the event in this fashion: "In his church study at Fort Worth in 1926, the Rev. Mr. Norris killed an unarmed political enemy by shooting him four times in the belly and was acquitted on grounds of self-defense." Throughout the rest of his life, Norris was hyper-sensitive about the episode, and he made it clear to those "careless" enough to refer to him as the "pistol-packing parson" that there was no evidence that he carried or "packed" a pistol. The evidence, contended Norris, was that he obtained a pistol from the watchman after a police officer had informed him of a "threat" by Chipps.

A few years later, another jury acquitted the Fort Worth pastor of a new charge — burning down his church. Norris had succeeded from the start in drawing a giant crowd. The old First Baptist building became too small and he demanded a new church; when he met with resistance the building was consumed in a blaze. Norris was indicted when detectives looked into the cause of the fire, but he capitalized on the indictment to obtain sufficient funds for the erection of the new First Baptist Church — a huge auditorium that is more noted for its capacity than for its architectural beauty.

"Bigness" was a key word in Norris' struggle for power among fundamentalists. During his term as pastor of the First Baptist Church, its membership climbed from 1,000 to 12,000, and the church property grew from one building to real estate valued at $2,300,000. In 1935 Norris branched out from Fort Worth to take over, in addition, the 800-member Temple Baptist Church in Detroit, Michigan. By 1950 he boasted that he was ministering regularly to 22,000 church members — the largest combined membership under one minister in the world. Norris managed to preach in each of his two churches on alternate Sundays, and he earned for himself the title of "flying parson." During the week he would fly to fundamentalist conferences throughout the country, "promoting real old-fashioned New Testament revivals."

In addition to his vast pastoral enterprises, Norris published a weekly 8-page newspaper, *The Fundamentalist,* and directed the activities of the Bible Baptist Seminary in Fort Worth, which, at the time of Norris' death, could boast over five hundred students, a faculty of seventeen, and property valued at $2,000,000. *The Fundamentalist* proclaimed that the Seminary had "higher standing than any other seminary on the American continent. . . . It is the only seminary on the American Continent where the highest degree given is based solely and wholly and only on the English Bible. . . . The Bible Baptist Seminary stands out like a tall giant oak among the forest of smaller trees."

The Southern Baptist Convention was the chief target of Norris' attacks. For a quarter-century he assailed nearly every important Southern Baptist leader. He once complained: "The Baptist 'leaders' are trying to do to the Baptist people what the Methodist bishops have already done to the Methodist people. *The Fundamentalist* will see to it that they will fight for every inch of ground they take." Norris pointed to alleged "modernism" among Southern Baptist leaders, in Southern Baptist theological seminaries and Sunday-school literature.

May 6, 1947, was a memorable day in the life of the Fort

Worth pastor — and of other Southern Baptists as well. Louie D. Newton, then president of the Convention, climbed to the rostrum in St. Louis Second Baptist Church to report to 1,000 pastors, gathered for a pre-convention assembly, on his recent trip to the Soviet Union. Suddenly Norris arose — with a list of seventeen questions. Outcries from the audience interrupted him as he started to read from the list. But Norris persisted. Newton signaled with an upraised arm for the start of a hymn. The entire gathering rose to join him in "How firm a foundation." Norris chimed in on the second verse. When the grey-haired Texas pastor again started to read from his list, a knot of young minister-veterans gathered around him amid cries of "Throw him out!" By the time four policemen arrived, Norris had resumed his seat. This was the last Southern Baptist Convention he attended.

To Norris, Louie D. Newton was a "red." "Every preacher and every layman in the Southern Baptist Convention hold their noses when they think of Louie Newton's record," cried *The Fundamentalist*. "They can't ignore Norris when the president of the Southern Baptist Convention is cheek-by-jowl with Bishop G. Bromley Oxnam, who is one of the main fifth columnists of Joe Stalin in America." But many other Southern Baptists were maligned in Norris' paper, too. Joseph M. Dawson — who serves as executive secretary of the Baptist Joint Conference Committee on Public Affairs — was another target. He was charged with denying "every fundamental of the faith." Norris complained bitterly: "Every time the Baptists of Texas give one dollar a part of it goes to support 'Jodie's' [Dawson's] $10,000-a-year salary, high-powered secretarial force and fine offices with mahogany furniture." Even hyper-conservative leaders of the Convention — all who refused to follow Norris' suggestions — were assailed as "the chief enemies of the Christian faith."

Norris constantly predicted that the Southern Baptists would be "ensnared" by the ecumenical movement. In 1950 he warned his congregation: "The Northern Baptist Convention went over boots, bag and baggage to the Federal Council and now the leaders of the Federal Council have put their fangs into the Southern Baptist Convention. . . . They are infiltrating just like the Communists." Earlier he had written in *The Fundamentalist:* "The Federal Council of Churches denies every fundamental of the faith held by New Testament Baptists." When he no longer attended meetings of the Convention, Norris gave fervent support to the efforts of the late E. P. Alldredge to "expose" ecumenicalism on the convention floor and through the booklet *Unionizing Southern Baptists* — in which Alldredge claimed to "unmask" intrigue between certain Southern Baptist leaders and the Federal Council of Churches.

Norris favored a society based upon white supremacy, and he sharply attacked any Southern Baptist leaders who dared express other ideas. Curiously enough, however, he took issue with many of his anti-Semitic friends. In a pre-war exposure of the *Protocols of the Learned Elders of Zion* (the forgery discussed in Chapter 3), he wrote:

> My plea is not for the sake of the Jew, but for our own sakes; and the strangest of all strange things is that any Christian should lift his hand against the Jew, knowing the Bible pronounces a severe curse on every hand that has been lifted against this peculiar people, and pronounces a blessing upon every hand that blesses this people.

Norris' particular interpretation of the Bible led him to champion Zionism. When the Southern Baptists at their 1948 convention failed to pass a resolution congratulating Truman upon his prompt recognition of Israel, Norris falsely accused them of anti-Semitism in an oration in a near-by hall.

But Norris found it easy to associate with a number of flagrant racists — though any one of his "friends" could suddenly become the object of his venom. During the nation-wide fundamentalist-modernist controversy, he was a colleague of W. B. Riley, peddler of the forged *Protocols,* and a close friend of Gerald Winrod and Elizabeth Dilling (see Chapter 3).

Because of Norris' pre-war espousal of the interventionist cause, however, he broke with most nationalists and became the butt of their sharp criticism. Riley described Norris in January 1941 as "a moral leper and the most inordinate liar living. No crime he has not committed — murder included." Mrs. Dilling summed up her case against the Fort Worth pastor in a 12-page brochure entitled *Trigger Norris.* She accused him of "making peace" with the New Deal, the Federal Council of Churches, and the "anti-Christian, pro-Red B'nai B'rith."

Up until his death in 1952, Norris worked close to "Colorado

Cowboy" Harvey Springer (see Chapters 7 and 8), Louisville Evangelist Mordecai Ham, and a long list of others who promoted hatred for Jews. He even briefly courted the friendship of Gerald L. K. Smith (see Chapter 4); but in 1947 — after Smith had spoken in his church and Norris reportedly had introduced the Christian Nationalist leader to the Governor of Texas — he repudiated Smith on the grounds that the latter had little genuine interest in the gospel. Smith, in turn, vigorously attacked Norris for his attitude toward Israel. "How can you be so critical of Dr. Louie Newton, the leader of the Southern Baptist Convention," wrote Smith, "when you, Dr. Norris, send a telegram congratulating one of the most obnoxious Communist Jews on the face of the earth?"

J. Frank Norris was also much more tolerant of Catholicism than most of his friends. During his early ministry, Norris generally became known as a zealous anti-Catholic for hammering relentlessly at the papacy and the American hierarchy. By the middle of the 1930's, however, he claimed to have stopped attacking the Roman Catholic Church in the interests of better understanding between faiths.

During the summer of 1947 Norris made a trip to Europe and the Near East with three of his colleagues — Beauchamp Vick of Detroit, Luther Peak of Dallas, and Wendell Zimmerman of Kansas City. In Rome they had a fifteen-minute interview with Pope Pius XII and hailed him as "the only power in Europe standing like Gibraltar against communism" — a statement that aroused immediate and explosive reaction. T. T. Shields — a long-time friend of Norris, and his former associate in the Baptist Bible Union — "deplored" his conduct. The Canadian Baptist wrote in his *Gospel Witness and Protestant Advocate:*

> We repudiate his whole action as being, not only unworthy of any minister of the gospel, who calls himself Protestant, but as an outstanding example of the very principle enunciated in the remark in this article, that we know of no living man who can talk more nonsense in five minutes on world affairs than Dr. Norris. His action in Rome, while it will serve the purpose he had in view, namely spreading himself in the public press, in our judgment was the essence of folly.

In turn, Norris regularly attacked Shields for defending the Soviet Union.

On his many trips abroad, Norris made friends in high places. He was the guest of three prime ministers of England, two presidents of France, the Grand Mufti of Jerusalem, the high commissioner of Palestine, and the president of Hebrew University. Once he carried with him commendation from such leading Americans as Wendell Willkie, Frank Knox, and Cordell Hull.

In 1950 Norris, joined by Mordecai Ham, by Bob Ingle (pastor of the 2,000-member Berea Baptist Church in Jacksonville, Florida), and by Jim Norwood (another close associate of the Fort Worth patriarch), went to Geneva, Switzerland, to attend a conference of the International Council of Christian Churches (see Chapter 8).

About the time that Norris and his circle were joining forces with the International Council of Christian Churches, his World Baptist Fellowship — which included several hundred independent Baptist churches in the North and South — was rocked by a bitter struggle within its own ranks. Norris had witnessed numerous splits during his long reign at the First Baptist Church, but this particular schism proved to be the most serious of his career. When the World Baptist Fellowship met on May 15, 1950, Beauchamp Vick, co-pastor of the huge Temple Baptist Church in Detroit and president of the Bible Baptist Seminary, led an open rebellion against Norris' leadership. Many members of the Fellowship were determined to free themselves from the paternalistic control of the "Texas Tornado." *The Fundamentalist* venomously attacked Vick as "boastful and conceited in his imaginations . . . who believed that he could step in and set aside God's servant and take over a movement that God himself established."

Norris launched into a scurrilous smear campaign against all those who resisted his iron hand. He charged them with every form of vice, including financial manipulations, marital infidelity, sexual perversion, and religious racketeering. Most of these attacks were vividly portrayed in *Fundamentalist* cartoons.

Vick and his supporters organized yet another splinter group, the Baptist Bible Fellowship, which now boasts of more than three hundred affiliated churches. The new Fellowship opened the Baptist Bible College in Springfield, Missouri, and initiated its own newspaper, the *Baptist Bible Tribune,* edited by Noel

Smith, former editor of *The Fundamentalist*. Smith was never at a loss for epithets to toss back at Norris; one of his favorites was "the corny old egotist."

But the Baptist Bible Fellowship has proved to be as much an ally of the apostles of discord as the Norris faction — perhaps more so. Noel Smith circulates his dishonest denunciations of the Southern Baptist Convention in booklet form, under the title *Should a Bible Believing Baptist Support the Cooperative Program of the Southern Baptist Convention?* He takes the usual liberties in attaching the labels "modernist" and "communist" to any ideas with which he disagrees. According to Noel Smith, Riverside Church in New York "is a pagan temple"; Dr. Louie D. Newton is a "radical"; Southern Baptist seminary faculties are overrun by "liberals"; the Revised Standard Version of the Bible "is an attack on the Deity of Christ"; the entire program of the Southern Baptist Convention is "the product of a little coterie of self-chosen and self-appointed Southern Baptist ecclesiastical politicians."

Noel Smith's *Baptist Bible Tribune* expresses itself in similar terms on a wide variety of issues. The newspaper characterizes Billy Graham as "one of the most compromising, irresponsible evangelists this country has ever produced"; *Christian Life,* a popular, reputable fundamentalist monthly, has "set itself up as the tin-horn pope of American Christianity"; the National Conference of Christians and Jews is "an anti-Christian organization"; the United Nations is synonymous with "organized greed, atheism, and materialism," and its "Mother Superior" is Eleanor Roosevelt, "Madonna of the Crooked Deals"; the National Council of Churches is the "devil's religious department of the United Nations," controlled by a "crowd of arrogant, irresponsible, smart alecks, upstarts and radicals!"

Attempts have been made — thus far without success — to effect a union between the World Baptist Fellowship, now headed by Harvey Springer, and the Baptist Bible Fellowship. Luther C. Peak, pastor of the Central Baptist Church in Dallas, former president of Norris' Bible Baptist Seminary in Fort Worth, has taken the lead in this effort. In his *Evangelist and Bible Teacher* (once described by Noel Smith as "the step-calf of Norris' dried-up cow") he has pleaded: "The controversy between the two is over. Let us all be through with it." But Smith's response was sharp:

It is with no satisfaction that I have to tell you that Mr. Peak's public responsibility is about the same as a 10-year-old boy. The "controversy" between The Tribune and his brethren ended the day they called in their dogs. We left them because their proposition was that J. Frank Norris' emotional whims superceded the laws of God and man. They now want us to come back and get their properties out of hock. We did it once. We don't intend to do it again.

Meanwhile, reputable fundamentalists in all Baptist camps have tired of the self-styled "Bible Baptists." Their attitude was well expressed by John W. Bradbury, editor of *The Watchman-Examiner:*

This practice of separating Bible-believing people under the assumption that some have a particular blessing from the Lord which sets them apart from their cobelievers is one of the strangest doctrines afflicting our time. It cannot produce a great united body of witnesses to the truths of the Word of God. Rather, it conveys the impression that evangelical truth divides those who mutually believe it.

The reaction of the apostles of discord to Bradbury's rational appeal was typical. Wrote Noel Smith:

The Watchman Examiner is to the compromisers, inclusivists and "conservative" Modernists what Dean Acheson is to the internationalist set. . . . We have been saying that a British Israelite was the only thing on earth that can stand on its head longer than a Christian Scientist. But since reading Dr. Bradbury, we are in doubt.

Bradbury has been joined by many other leading fundamentalists in repudiating the "spiritual heirs" that J. Frank Norris left behind. But the World Baptist Fellowship and Baptist Bible Fellowship continue true to the "traditions" of their late patriarch.

Symptoms of Denominational Strife

The survey, in this and the preceding chapter, of controversies among Methodists, Congregationalists, and Baptists has shown how these major Protestant denominations are harassed by the ministry of discord. But in other churches also, malcontents sow the seeds of trouble. Ministers of discord in these churches answer various descriptions. Some seek to muffle those who boldly preach the gospel of justice, peace, and brotherhood. Others noisily raise the banner of theological exclusiveness as a façade behind which to promote quarrelsome divisiveness. Still others exploit religious faith to bolster bigotry against minority races and creeds.

Briefly spotlighted, here are a few of the danger areas among Presbyterians, Episcopalians, Disciples of Christ, and others — disputes that threaten their harmony and effectiveness. The malcontents in these denominations are not of such a character that their inclusion in this survey is automatic — but continued agitation on their part could well "merit" them an important place among the apostles of discord before long. One purpose of this study is to focus attention on approaching thunderclouds in the hope that they might be dispersed before the storm.

PRESBYTERIAN, U. S. A.

Within the Presbyterian Church in the U. S. A. (northern), as with the Methodists and Congregationalists, conflict has been agitated by vigilantes of the extreme right wing, whose attacks have been centered on official denominational publications. Much of this dissension may be traced to one of its ex-ministers, Carl McIntire, who fathered the splinter Bible Presbyterian Church after he was unfrocked in 1936. (He was discussed in Chapter 8.) On February 26, 1953, the western section of the World Presbyterian Alliance, representing nine Calvinist bodies with over 5,000,000 members, publicly censured McIntire's "disruptive and deceptive" assaults on the integrity of the ecumenical movement and co-operating denominations. "We encourage our brethren to bear with patience and judge with charity these unhappy attacks upon their faith and ministry," the Alliance declared.

While McIntire has focused his blasts upon Presbyterian "modernism," he has also been a factor in confusing some well-meaning Presbyterians by his persistent cry, "Red!" One of several brochures that have incited disharmony is entitled *Is There a "Red" or "Pink" Cell Operating in Our Own [Presbyterian] Church?* This twelve-page indictment has been distributed by the men's bible class of the First Presbyterian Church in Sapulpa, Oklahoma — most members of which since have affiliated with the McIntire splinter. The brochure's compiler is a prominent lawyer, Glenn O. Young, who served as ruling Elder in the U. S. A. denomination and as teacher of the sponsoring Sunday-school class.

Young's discussion begins with the proposition that "the Devil himself is the world's foremost 'liberal.' " From there, he launches into a bitter condemnation of *Crossroads*, denominational student quarterly, because it has expressed allegedly "subversive" ideas — as in its liberal viewpoint on the race question. Young explains: "Generally negroes [*sic*] are mindful of the debt they owe to the innate sense of justice and right that characterizes Christian Americans." He criticizes the journal's use of the word "democracy" and charges that *Crossroads*' support of the World Council of Churches implies endorsement of its "cosmopolitan religion." Most right-wing extremists like Young accuse any who speak of "democracy" of communist tendencies.

Young's other targets are *Presbyterian Life* and Paul Calvin Payne, prominent religious educator. Young was annoyed at Payne's defense of former Assistant Secretary of Defense Anna Rosenberg, whom Young castigated as a "foreign-born, non-Christian woman"; and at Payne's condemnation of Gerald L. K. Smith — who in Young's terminology is a patriot who is "making commendable efforts to help ferret out spies."

Writing recently in Smith's *The Cross and the Flag*, Young characterized the United Nations as "born in a witches' cauldron of intrigue, syndicalism, treason, and treachery."

PRESBYTERIAN, U. S.

The problem within the Presbyterian Church in the U. S. (southern) is different and more disruptive than that of its Yankee sister. The malcontents are numerous — some properly belonging in the ministry of disruption while others are fair-minded conservatives. They oppose the plan of merger with the northern Presbyterians; they hope to pull the southern denomination out of the National Council of Churches and the World Council of Churches; they constantly complain that "modernism" and "ecclesiasticism" thrive in their own ranks. Though the dissenters are a minority in the denomination, they have rallied vociferous and widespread support for their point of view.

The *Southern Presbyterian Journal,* published in Weaverville, North Carolina, states the case for the most extreme faction. Its editor, the Rev. Henry B. Dendy, is a pastor in Weaverville; its associate editor, L. Nelson Bell, affiliated with the College of Surgeons in Asheville, was for many years a medical missionary in China. Nearly fifty ministers and laymen, some highly influential, serve as sponsors or contributing editors. The *Journal* carries its credo on its cover: "A Presbyterian weekly magazine devoted to the statement, defense, and propagation of the Gospel, the faith which was once for all delivered unto the saints." (It has no official connection with the Presbyterian Church in the U.S.)

In combatting merger with the U. S. A. church, which is the *Journal's* principal mission at present, the extremists cite the 1939 Methodist union: "The plight of Southern Methodists who were unorganized and who were swept into merger with the Northern Methodists [is] a tragic example of the harm which such mergers generate." One elder warns denomination leaders: "We do not have the least intention in the world of merging with the heresy-tainted Northern Presbyterian Church. If merger does take place, we intend to sever our connection with the Presbyterian Church." The *Journal* has been aided in its battle against "reunion" by several resistance groups, including the Continuing Church Committee — now the Association for the Preservation of the Southern Presbyterian Church.

Strong objection both to the merger plan and to continued affiliation with the National Council of Churches can be traced, in part, to the race question. Writing in the *Southern Presbyterian Journal,* one apostle of bigotry advances the traditional arguments of those who seek to "guard" white supremacy:

1. In the first place I believe that segregation is in harmony with the plan and purpose of the Almighty Himself, as the best means to prevent amalgamation of the races.
2. In the second place I believe in segregation because, it is not only in the plan of God but it is in harmony with a well known law of nature, stated in the proverb, "Birds of a feather will flock together." . . . The Negro, if let alone by these ceaseless agitators, feels more at home and happier among his own people. . . .
3. In the third place I believe in race segregation because it contributes to the harmony and peace among the races. . . . This is one reason

362 Apostles of Discord

why the Christian white man in the South wants race segregation, for the protection of the Negro.

The northern Presbyterians and the National Council of Churches have both gone on record against segregation as "a denial of the Christian faith and ethic." Opponents of merger and ecumenicalism have been quick to point out this fact.

The success of the southern Presbyterian dissenters will depend upon the controversy they can arouse and their ability in exploiting traditional rivalry between the North and the South.

DISCIPLES OF CHRIST

The Disciples of Christ, with nearly two million members centered in the midwestern, southwestern, and border states, is another Protestant body that has suffered from internal tumult. Its principal disrupting elements have directed their blasts at the denomination's leadership, its participation in the ecumenical movement, and its present endorsement of a moderate program of social reform.

At the turn of the century, a strong faction of the original movement, involving several hundred congregations, left to form the million-member Churches of Christ. Since then the Disciples have made steady progress, but not without scars from intramural battles. Soon after the denomination's United Christian Missionary Society was organized in 1919, a large segment of fundamentalists were charging that "modernists" were dominating the new group. A second split threatened the Disciples; one result was the establishment of the North American Christian Convention — rival to the regular International Convention of Disciples of Christ.

The dissenters' most important journalistic voice is the *Christian Standard*. Founded in 1866 to represent a "progressive" viewpoint, the *Standard* today expresses a bias in favor of narrow denominationalism and against interchurch co-operation. When the National Council of Churches was established in 1950, the journal commented:

It is quite evident from the wide range of activities covered by the merging organizations and the intricate and complicated structure of the new Council, that the aim is nothing less than the control of every phase of congregational activity of every local church. . . . In our opinion, with the formation of this ecclesiastical monstrosity, and what will be its parent body, the World Council of Churches, the Reformation has been set back several hundred years.

Protestantism's malcontents are supported even more enthusiastically by the *Restoration Herald,* sponsored in Union City, Indiana, by the 27-year-old Christian Restoration Society. First editor of the *Herald* was James DeForest Murch, who now directs the publication of *United Evangelical Action,* journal of the National Association of Evangelicals (see Chapter 8); its editor since 1928 has been bitter-tempered Robert E. Elmore, formerly a minister in Phoenix, Arizona. Elmore complains caustically about the organization and leadership of the Disciples:

> Thus, in the midst of the free churches of Christ, the Disciples denomination arose. Clothed in the robes of Pharasaic self righteousness and deception, pious, persuasive, super saintly, the Disciples Rabbis set aside the Son of God, nullify the Holy Bible, and repudiate the divinely instituted Church of Christ.

The *Herald* editor characterizes the Disciples as a "subversive sect set up in the midst of the free churches of Christ"; he has called the United Christian Missionary Society "a centralized syndicate, or ecclesiastical monopoly, completely controlled by so-called modernist or 'liberal' officers." Elmore adds: "The Disciples rulers and elders and scribes have led their blind and ignorant and docile followers deeper and deeper into the mire."

The "independents" have demonstrated increasing strength. They have sent out many missionaries; they have been vigorous in recruiting large numbers of young men for the ministry; they had established nearly thirty-five Bible colleges by the spring of 1953 — most of them small and non-accredited. While they technically remain aligned with the Disciples of Christ, they have gone increasingly their separate way.

Fundamentalist withdrawal from the Disciples — as in the case of the Baptists — could carry away half of the denomination; indeed, in effect, two bodies already exist within the framework of the one denomination. But it is unlikely that all the obstructionists — often characterized as "independents" — will find it possible to agree on a basis for unity. Elmore reveals his contempt for many ultra-fundamentalists in terms like these:

> Some of our "independent" friends are a bit handicapped with egoinflatus, ambition-expansissimus, popularitus, high pecuniary blood pres-

sure, gimcrackery, Pecksniffian piety, Barnum and Bailey jumboism, and showmanship, or something. The only independents the Disciples Sanhedrin fears are the self-effacing, Christ exalting, Bible believing fanatics.

PROTESTANT EPISCOPAL

The 2,500,000-member Protestant Episcopal Church has been embroiled in a family quarrel quite unlike that of any other denomination. Among Episcopalians there has been, on the one hand, a small but influential pro-communist element (cited in Chapter 11); and, on the other, strong clerical and lay support for the extreme right, through organized "libertarianism" (cited in Chapter 12). The deepest source of controversy within the denomination, however, is the disagreement on matters of ceremony, doctrine, and ecclesiasticism. Contenders in this fray are sometimes facetiously categorized as "the high and crazy, the low and lazy, and the broad and hazy." The first of these, the "high," warrant brief mention in this particular study because of the disruptive activities of a vociferous minority among them — particularly in their bitter opposition to co-operation with other Protestant denominations.

Extreme "high-church" sentiment is represented by the militant American Church Union, founded in 1937 for "the furtherance and defense of Apostolic faith and practice" and today claiming the support of thirty bishops as well as one of every six Episcopal priests. There are cogent arguments for omitting the Union from a survey of the apostles of discord. In the first place, its adherents are recognized for their piety, their scholarship, and their individual social concern. Second, the struggle is primarily over matters of doctrine — with which this study is not concerned. Technically, moreover, few of these "high churchmen" deem themselves Protestants — in the generally accepted sense — and many Protestants likewise fail to acknowledge their right to the name. Episcopalians oriented toward the American Church Union usually feel closer kinship with Roman Catholicism than with American Protestantism. The English Reformation, many of them contend, arose from political and ecclesiastical rivalry between the Church of England and the Church of Rome; in contrast, Luther, Calvin, Knox and other Protestant "reformers" took issue with basic Roman Catholic doctrines.

Although traditionally the ceremonial emphasis of the "high" church has offended "low" churchmen — who refer to the ritualists as "highfliers," "tractarians," and "Romanizers" — today the principal battle is being waged between "high" and "broad" churchmen. The American Church Union accuses the "broad" element of "humanism." One writer in the highly reputable and pro-ecumenical *Living Church,* influential journal allied to the "high-church" cause, has declared: "Humanism leads eventually to a dilemma, Western materialism or Communism. . . . It is too 'broadminded' to smash altars with axes and hammers; it is too subtle in its iconoclasm; it causes men to ignore them."

The replies of the "broad" churchmen, especially those in the Episcopal Evangelical Fellowship, have been fully as acrid. Warned one critic of the American Church Union in an article called "Mediaevalism Rapidly Returning":

Many of us are unwilling to have the hierarchy reestablished, and the whole of the life, authority, and power of the church vested in the ministry, without regard to the whole body and the priesthood of the laity. But, due to a policy of appeasement on the part of bishops, an unwillingness on the part of the clergy to seem intolerant in a positive stand, and a lack of historical background on the part of the laity, the Anglo-Catholics, organized and well-financed, are making rapid headway. If the laity understood what is taking place they would be making far more protestations in true Protestant form and spirit. . . .

They should be awakened to the fact that Anglo-Catholics are taking advantage of liberalism to establish their own position and eliminate all others.

The American Church Union is opposed to close co-operation with organized Protestantism, especially through the ecumenical movement. It finds a "deep and thoroughgoing contradiction and opposition between the teachings and beliefs of the Protestant Churches and the Anglican Church." At the Episcopal General Convention in 1952, the Union sought to injure the cause of ecumenicalism by slicing from the budget funds designated for the National Council of Churches. The convention issue of the *ACU News* demanded: "Let's Reduce the Budget — Over Half Million Dollars Will Go Outside Church." Interdenomination activities, said the newssheet, are often "highly antagonistic and destructive to the Episcopal Church." Phrases like "extracurricular extravagancies," "Santa Claus for Pan-

Protestantism" and "spendthrift giving" were used. The paper referred to the National Council of Churches as having "its hands in our pocket." But when the vote was taken, American Church Union "isolationism" was soundly rebuffed.

The future of Protestant co-operation will depend in large part upon the continued participation of the Episcopal Church. So far, it has been a pioneer in the church-unity movement, both in this country and abroad. But there is a possibility that growth of "high-church" sentiment, if channeled through such groups as the American Church Union, might work havoc with the ecumenical movement and lend powerful assistance to those in the ministry of disruption who — for entirely different reasons — share a distaste for co-operative Protestantism. At the present time, however, most Episcopalians — "high," "low," or "broad" — intend to continue their fellowship with Protestants of other denominations.

Other major Protestant denominations not mentioned above have suffered from internal discord as well. Often the battles have been restricted to the realm of doctrine. Occasionally they have stemmed from attempts to capture the church on behalf of one or another social or economic viewpoint. At times "hyper-denominationalists" have sought to wreck all efforts to achieve interchurch co-operation. In some cases, malcontents have succeeded. Vociferous religious "nationalists" in the powerful Missouri Synod of the Lutheran Church, for example, have been partly responsible for the failure of that body to join with other Protestants in the ecumenical movement. In other cases, malcontents have failed. The Church of the Brethren, for example, found it necessary to ask several of its ministers and congregations to disassociate themselves from its fellowship after they had provoked sharp discord within the denomination.

Most Protestant denominations pride themselves on a freedom that allows for the co-existence of different and sometimes contradictory viewpoints. This is a healthy situation so long as this freedom is not exploited by malcontents who wish to destroy the constructive leadership that has won control of nearly every major Protestant denomination. The way of preventing an insurgent victory is not through "purges" by which unanimity might be compelled. Clergy and laymen must be informed and vigilant to the threat of dissident movements.

While the major denominations have been moving toward a more co-operative relationship, many are experiencing internal tensions which occasionally have erupted into the open. Among Methodists, Congregationalists, and northern Presbyterians, political issues have been the most important cause of factionalism. Among Baptists, Disciples of Christ, and southern Presbyterians such political issues, reinforced by theological disputes, have led to bitter conflict. The case of the Episcopalians as seen in this chapter, has been unique.

Today creative Protestantism is being challenged. This survey has sought to examine destructive forces that promote hate and discord in the churches. The denominational conflicts are an important part of the over-all picture; they add another dimension to the ministry of discord. Will these malcontents succeed in obscuring the moral demands of the Christian faith?

15

Conclusion: Swords Into Plowshares

This survey has attempted to bring to the reader a factual account of various groups and individuals, on the fringes of Protestantism, which promote hate and disruption. To analyze and interpret this material adequately would require a different and longer study. Many important questions can only be raised: What sociological phenomena account for the growing strength of Protestantism's militant apostles of discord? What are the psychological roots from which the ministries of hate and disruption have sprung? To which economic, theological, geographical, political, and cultural groups do they have greatest appeal — and why? What concrete steps can be taken to resist their growth?

One encouraging aspect of the total picture is the fact that the apostles of discord have rallied partly to protest against the increased dedication of mainstream Protestantism to the advancement of Christian social ideals. The dogmatic tenor of the "white supremists," for example, has been strengthened by their realization that racism — its theory and its practice — is being repudiated by all major denominations.

The first part of this survey, "The Ministry of Hate," sought to show how promoters of racial and religious bigotry flagrantly exploit the Christian faith. Even though the problems arising from latent prejudice in Protestant circles are more subtle and more extensive, the role of the "crackpot" — as the crude bigot appears to most Americans — continues to be important. The professional bigot has occasionally succeeded in disrupting, by dishonorable means, efforts to achieve racial and religious

368

harmony; in periods of hysteria he offers up convenient scape-goats as a sacrifice to public anxiety. Though these bigots, these "poison peddlers" are widely discredited, in times of tension they threaten to reap a harvest of hate.

The danger of an alliance between flagrant racists and right-wing extremists further complicates the situation, for some of those who are disgruntled with the growth of social reform charge that "alien" forces are seeking to undermine traditional American freedoms.

In direct contradiction to the doctrines of the ministry of hate, every major Protestant denomination has taken important steps to remove patterns of racial discrimination in its churches and in society as a whole. Illustrative of this progress is the firm stand on segregation of the National Council of Churches, which represents thirty denominations with a total membership of more than 35,000,000. In June 1952 its General Board included this statement in a lengthy resolution:

> The National Council of the Churches of Christ in the U.S.A. in its structure and operation, renounces and earnestly recommends to its member churches that they renounce the pattern of segregation based on race, color or national origin as unnecessary and undesirable and a violation of the Gospel of love and human brotherhood. While recognizing that historical and social factors make it more difficult for some churches than for others to realize the Christian ideal of non-segregation, the Council urges all of its constituent members to work steadily and progressively towards a non-segregated church as the goal which is set forth in the faith and practice of the early Christian community and inherent in the New Testament idea of the Church of Christ. As proof of our sincerity in this renunciation, the National Council of Churches will work for a non-segregated church and a non-segregated community.

Quite different from the problem of segregation within Protestantism itself is the question of anti-Semitism — involving relations with adherents to a different faith. Nearly every major Protestant denomination has expressed itself clearly on this issue, as well. Representative of their attitude was a resolution passed by the World Council of Churches, assembled in Amsterdam in 1948:

> In many lands virulent anti-semitism still threatens and in other lands the Jews are subjected to many indignities. We call upon all the churches

we represent to denounce anti-semitism no matter what its origin, as absolutely irreconcilable with the profession of practice of the Christian faith. Anti-semitism is sin against God and man.

Among Protestants, there are divergent views on appropriate ways to improve relations between Christians and Jews. One traditional viewpoint, especially strong among fundamentalists, is that the only certain solution to the problem lies in the conversion of Jews to Christianity. This approach has been exemplified in the activities of such organizations as the American Board of Missions to the Jews. A second solution is offered by the National Conference of Christians and Jews — whose philosophy is "live and let live." Two other attitudes are represented by small but articulate groups: the first by the American Christian Palestine Committee, pro-Zionist in outlook; the other by the American Council for Judaism, often hostile to Zionism, which emphasizes Jewish religious and cultural contributions.

The Catholic question poses still another problem for Protestants. Most of the original bitterness once directed at individual Roman Catholics has disappeared, with the gradual assimilation of immigrants who came to America in the nineteenth and twentieth centuries. Today, legitimate controversy rages over the religious teachings of the Church of Rome and Catholic "political power." Protestants disagree sharply on the cure for this latter problem. Many, taking an uncompromising stand in support of a "wall of separation" between church and state, view the Roman Catholic hierarchy as the chief enemy of their principle. Others, agreeing with Catholic opposition to a completely "secular" state, yet fear that Protestantism's historic rival would gain the most from any full-scale abandonment of the separation of church and state. An important factor tending to reduce Catholic-Protestant antagonism today is the feeling of co-operation against a common enemy — communism.

The second half of this study has been concerned with various branches of "The Ministry of Disruption." The saboteurs of good-will among Protestants direct their principal blasts at the ecumenical movement, which seeks to develop interchurch co-operation. They describe it as "a master stroke of the devil" and depict the World Council of Churches as an ecclesiastical octopus with tentacles aimed at drawing the churches into apostasy, radicalism, and a "trek back to Rome."

Of course, the ecumenical movement is not — nor does it pretend to be — a panacea for all the ills of Protestantism. Within its framework there are wide differences of opinion as to its proper functions and its future. Some Protestants advocate a federal union modeled upon the American system of government — the denominations keeping their identity within an organization to which powers are clearly assigned. Others contend that a co-operative agency loosely organized, as at the present time, is the only legitimate goal toward which Protestants should work. Only a few now desire the organic union of all important Protestant denominations.

The major groups that still have not been brought into the ecumenical movement include large reputable fundamentalist denominations, such as the Missouri Synod Lutherans and the Southern Baptists, whose interest in co-operative efforts, however, is growing; a number of smaller fundamentalist sects, who genuinely fear the theological inclusiveness of the ecumenical movement and predict its development into a "superchurch"; and a small segment of "religious liberals," notably the Unitarians and Universalists, who have been excluded because of their refusal to accept a doctrinal statement professing "Jesus Christ as Lord and Saviour." This study has not dealt extensively with any of these.

Other more vociferous critics allied with the ministry of disruption spread false and irresponsible charges, hoping to divide Protestants and to secure for themselves a large following. As the survey has shown, these saboteurs of interchurch co-operation accuse ecumenical leaders of flagrant disregard for traditional Protestant doctrines and wholesale acceptance of pro-communist ideologies. The influence of virulent anti-ecumenicalists is slight and constantly weakened by serious schisms within their own circles. Their success or failure will depend upon their ability to exploit the anxiety of the times and the formidable barriers that have separated Protestants in the past.

Within the ministry of disruption, a powerful weapon wielded by opponents of Protestant leadership has been the "Red" smear. This name-calling, directed recklessly against liberals and conservatives alike — many of whom have been in the forefront of the fight against communism — demands the careful attention of Protestant churchmen. None of these professional vigilantes have shown themselves competent to discern the real differences between the actual Moscow collaborator and the non-communist — or even the anti-communist. Such insight is not demonstrated by equating social reforms with communism, nor social reformers with communists — as the apostles of discord usually do. This insight can be achieved only through persistent and thorough study of communist policy, as described in actual party literature, and through development of the ability to recognize the communists' distinctive methods of expression — including the vocabulary, popular party clichés, slogans, and treatment of issues, both major and minor ones.

At the same time, responsible Protestant leaders cannot ignore the real problem of infiltration into their churches. Where it can be established that ministers are actually serving as agents of a foreign power, the problem should be handled swiftly by the government, through the Federal Bureau of Investigation and the Department of Justice. Only a handful of pro-communists are active in Protestant circles today, but the churches have become a key target for communist subversion and must be on guard.

Many other questions involved in the communist issue require difficult decisions: When ministers champion pro-communist propaganda, can their right to preach be challenged without violating basic American tenets or civil liberties? Should a congregation tolerate pro-communist expression or pro-communist affiliation on the part of its pastor? How should churches weigh the charges of "affiliation" with "Red" fronts brought against many Protestant leaders? Can they adequately distinguish between the churchmen who joined many now-suspect organizations in the years before the Hitler-Stalin pact of 1939; who during the 1930's gave innocent support to groups that later became dominated by communist minorities; who lent their names and energies to Soviet friendship groups during World War II when it was considered patriotic to do so — and those few others who stuck with the Communist Party line at every turn and still stick with it today? Should a church ever allow communist groups or individuals to use its facilities? Should Christians co-operate on any specific projects with communists? What treatment should a denomination accord to a small, vociferous pro-communist faction within its own ranks — as in the case of the present leadership of the Methodist Federation for Social Action or the Episcopal League for Social Action? How can church groups avoid capture by a well-disciplined communist minority?

One important factor contributing to the growing lay concern about charges of "left-wing" domination of the churches has been the unfortunate tendency of some Protestant leaders to identify Christianity with a specific and dogmatic variety of "liberalism." While denominational leaders have a responsibility to keep the vision of Christian ideals before their people, liberals among them have sometimes tended to ignore the opinion of those more conservative than themselves. In some denominations, apostles of discord have successfully enlisted intelligent and sincere laymen who resent what they consider the clergy's continued monopolization of leadership and its reluctance to share the policy-making role.

Among the groups in the ministry of disruption are the best-organized enemies of forward-looking Protestantism — the well-financed groups dedicated to the promotion of "libertarianism." In place of the social ideals of Christianity they would substitute the narrow dogma of extreme laissez-faireism, in an attempt to identify Christianity with selfish economic interests. Their efforts have met with great success, and there is a real danger that "libertarianism" will diminish Protestantism's concern for human justice. Many unwitting churchmen are being drawn into their ranks.

The influence of organized "libertarianism" — as this study has attempted to show — not only reaches into denominational groups but also represents what is perhaps the most concerted effort of the extreme right to infiltrate the core of Protestantism through the National Council of Churches. Another important question faces American Protestants today: Can the proponents of co-operative activity, who have guided the social politics of the ecumenical movement for nearly half a century, withstand this new concerted drive to identify Protestantism with an antiquated economic philosophy?

American Protestantism today is challenged by the apostles of discord. Can it escape identification with the narrow viewpoints that emanate from the ministry of hate and from the ministry of disruption? It is unlikely that protagonists in this battle for the Protestant mind will yield without a struggle. So far, the conflicts among clergy and laymen have not succeeded in destroying the basic harmony of most of the churches. Occasional explosions, of course, have disturbed many Protestant circles. But wise leadership, dedication to common religious traditions, and adherence to the principles of conciliation have militated against divisiveness and schism, against defamation and unjust accusation.

Can the forces of justice and brotherhood within Protestantism successfully defeat the bid for power of these apostles of discord? The future of the Christian faith in America will depend, in large measure, on the answer to this question.

Notes

Chapter 2
The Protestant Underworld vs. Dwight D. Eisenhower

PAGE 11. The first two quotations are from *The Broom*, published in San Diego by C. Leon de Aryan. The first is from the issue of Dec. 1, 1952, p. 1; the second, from the issue of Dec. 8, 1952, p. 2.

Such characterizations of Eisenhower appointees as appear on this and the following page have continued to fill the extremist press. They are especially crude in the literature distributed by Gerald L. K. Smith (discussed in detail in Chapter 4). But there are other sources for such statements. The characterization of John Foster Dulles as "an effective tool of extremely radical and pacifist church leaders" was made by the American Council of Christian Churches (see article by George Dugan in New York *Times*, Oct. 30, 1948; see also *Christian Beacon*, Nov. 6, 1952, p. 8). The Catholic-edited fortnightly *Common Sense*, which features much of the material promulgated by the Protestant underworld, recently referred to Dulles as a "Red International Conspirator." Said the article (March 15, 1953, p. 1): "John Foster Dulles is thought by some to be a Communist because of his long association with the Federal Council of Churches of Christ, a Communist-front group."

PAGE 12. The midwestern nationalist sheet is the Dayton *Independent* (Nov. 20, 1952).

The New Jersey fortnightly is *Common Sense* (Jan. 15, 1953).

PAGE 13. Mrs. Waters' views were given to the writer during a visit to her home in Washington, D. C., in the autumn of 1951.

PAGE 14. Kamp's special Eisenhower edition of his publication *Headlines* was dated March 15, 1952. The quotations are taken from that issue.

PAGE 15. The quotations from the *Williams Intelligence Summary* are from the "Special Eisenhower Edition, 1952." The three quotations are from pages 8, 2, and 4 respectively.

Smith's description of Willkie's "plot" is from *The Cross and the Flag*, June 1952, p. 9. His reference to Eisenhower's "buildup" is from the issue of Feb. 1952, p. 10. His reference to Dewey is from the issue of April 1952, p. 11.

PAGE 16. The writer attended the Republican convention in Chicago in 1952; he arrived several days early in order to cover the activities of the nationalists as well. Much of the material in Chapter 2 (and later chapters, also) is based on personal observation.

Mrs. Van Hyning announced her "Crusade" in *Women's Voice* for Feb. 28, 1952 (see pp. 1, 2).

PAGE 18. Beauharnais announced his convention in his issue of his irregular bulletin to "Dear Fellow American Patriots" circulated in June 1952. His conviction under Illinois' group-libel law is discussed in that issue.

Taft's repudiation of bigotry was quoted in several newspapers across the country; e.g., the Chicago *Sun-Times*, July 2, 1952, p. 3.

PAGE 19. Smith explained his GOP convention failure in a letter to "Dear Precious Friend," dated July 1952, p. 1. It was entitled: "The Iron Curtain Is Being Lowered Over America — What Is the Answer?"

PAGE 20. Smith's characterizations of the chief Democratic contenders are from *The Cross and the Flag* of the following dates: Harriman, Barkley, and Russell, Aug. 1952, p. 16; Kefauver, June 1952, p. 18; Stevenson, Sept. 1952, p. 8. The reference to the Stevenson divorce is from Smith's letter to "Dear Loyal Friends," Aug. 19, 1952, p. 4.

PAGE 21. The West Coast Methodist quoted is Robert P. Shuler of Los Angeles, discussed in more detail in Chapter 13 (especially pp. 329-32). His description of the vice-presidential candidates is from his monthly, *Methodist Challenge,* Oct. 1952, p. 6.

PAGE 22. Williams had referred to Eisenhower as "the man most wanted by the Zionists" in his "Special Eisenhower Edition" of the *Williams Intelligence Summary,* p. 3. He discussed his switch to the GOP in *Common Sense,* Oct. 1, 1952, pp. 3-4.

The quotations from de Aryan's *The Broom* are from the following issues: concerning the "write-in" of Jesus Christ, April 21, 1952, p. 2; concerning Stevenson and Eisenhower, Oct. 13, 1952, p. 2; concerning MacArthur, May 4, 1952, p. 2.

PAGE 23. The two de Aryan attacks against Eisenhower are from *The Broom* for May 4, 1952 (p. 2) and July 7, 1952 (p. 2), respectively.

Mrs. Van Hyning's advice to her Illinois following was given in *Women's Voice,* Oct. 30, 1952, p. 2.

The two Gerald L. K. Smith quotations are from his letters of Aug. 10, 1952 (p. 3) and Aug. 22, 1952 (p. 1).

PAGE 24. Tenney's statement is from *The Cross and the Flag,* Oct. 1952, p. 3.

Smith's post-election letter announcing his "lobby" in Washington was dated Nov. 10, 1952.

The following is the official tabulation of the MacArthur vote garnered by the two principal nationalist parties:

	Constitution Party	Christian Nationalist Party
Arkansas	....	169
California	178	3,326
Colorado	2,181	....
Missouri	....	302
New Mexico	....	220
North Dakota	751	....
Tennessee	....	379
Texas	730	833
Washington	....	7,290
	3,840	12,519

MacArthur received some additional votes in those states where write-ins were permitted. In New York, for example, the efforts of the Constitution Party must have produced some MacArthur support; but the results were reported under the heading of "scattered votes" and not tabulated according to individual candidates. MacArthur received 233 votes in Missouri on the America First Party ticket. (These figures are taken from the March 1953 issue of *The Facts,* a publication of the Anti-Defamation League of B'nai B'rith.)

PAGE 25. Mrs. Van Hyning's comment on the election is from *Women's Voice,* Nov. 27, 1952, p. 1.

Chapter 3
The Plot Against the Jews

PAGE 27. The granting of the honorary doctorate to Winrod is reported by Donald C. Strong in *Organized Anti-Semitism in America* (pp. 71-72). This volume was published in 1941 by the American Council on Public Affairs.

PAGE 28. The statement of Winrod's secretary is also from page 72 of Strong's book.

Winrod's early characterizations of Roman Catholics and Jews are from *The Defender Magazine,* April 1930, p. 12, and Nov. 1934, p. 4.

PAGE 29. Winrod's reference to "Jewish control" is from *The Defender Magazine,* Dec. 1933, p. 5.

Rembert Gilman Smith's pamphlet was published in Tulsa, Oklahoma (no date). The quotation is from page 7.

PAGE 30. Winrod's characterizations of Jung and True are from *The Defender Magazine,* Nov. 1937, p. 3, and March 1935, p. 4, respectively.

PAGE 31. The letter of the Asheville "secessionists" was printed, in part, in the Asheville *Times,* Aug. 14, 1936, p. 3.

Winrod's alleged boast with regard to his Senate ambitions was cited in an article, "Keep Them Out," by Will Chasan and Victor Riesel in *The Nation,* July 4, 1942, p. 8. The repudiation of Winrod by Hamilton was carried in many newspapers; e.g., the Kansas City *Star,* July 23, 1938.

PAGE 32. Winrod's slogans are from his campaign leaflet *Viewing the Facts,* dated July 14, 1938. The New York *Times* comment is from its issue of July 23, 1938.

Mrs. Winrod's statements are from the Wichita *Beacon* of late May and early June, 1940.

PAGE 33. The 1942 attack on Judaism is from *The Defender Magazine,* March 1942, p. 16.

PAGE 34. Winrod's former ally is Jonathan Ellsworth Perkins, who accused him of a "miser complex" in his booklet *Gerald L. K. Smith Unmasked,* 1949, p. 138. Winrod's financial condition is mentioned in the Wichita *Beacon* of Nov. 29, 1950, and Dec. 11, 1949.

PAGE 35. The Wimbish letter was dated Nov. 13, 1951; the Beal letter, Nov. 7, 1951.

PAGE 36. The Sunday-school lesson is quoted almost *in toto* from *The Defender Magazine,* Jan.-Feb. 1950, pp. 31-32.

PAGE 37. The Talmud student quoted is Israel Abrahams, researcher in Talmudic and Rabbinical Literature at the University of Cambridge. His discussion of the Talmud may be found in the Hastings *Encyclopedia of Religion and Ethics.*

Winrod's statement about the Talmud is from his pamphlet *Jewish Assault on Christianity* (Defender Publishers, 1934), p. 18.

PAGE 38. The Talmudic passage quoted — or, rather, misquoted — is allegedly from Shulhan Aruk, Orah Hayim, Paragraph 539. Ben Zion Bokser's pamphlet *Talmudic Forgeries* is reprinted from the *Contemporary Jewish Record,* July-August 1939.

The Defender Magazine for Aug. 1952 (p. 16) traces "Modernism, Higher Criticism," etc., to the Talmud. Judaism has been defined by Winrod as "an opposition movement to Christianity" on many occasions; e.g., *The Defender Magazine,* Dec. 1952, p. 19. The Winrod references to the Revised Standard Version of the Bible are from *The Defender Magazine,* Nov. 1952, pp. 8-9.

PAGE 39. Sanctuary's characterization of the Pranaitis "Talmud" is from an "editor's note" appended to the Pranaitis edition which Sanctuary circulated entitled *The Talmud Unmasked.*

PAGE 40. Michelson's statement regarding Winrod was made in a letter of Jan. 14, 1953.

PAGE 41. Mrs. Dilling discussed alleged Talmudic sanctions in *Common Sense,* Aug. 1, 1952 (especially p. 3). She stated her intention of studying ancient forms of paganism in her bulletin of Sept. 1952.

PAGE 43. The apology of Henry Ford, Sr., was sent to one Earl J. Davis of Detroit — and a copy to Louis Marshall, then president of the American Jewish Committee. (For further details, see *The International Anti-Semitic Conspiracy,* a pamphlet by George J. Mintzer and Newman Levy, published in New York in 1946 by the American Jewish Committee.) Smith's contention that Ford's signature was forged is repeated often in *The Cross and the Flag;* e.g., Nov. 1951, p. 15, and July 1952, p. 14. The establishment of the "Henry Ford I, Memorial Award" was announced in *The Cross and the Flag,* March 1953, p. 13.

PAGE 44. Curtiss' *An Appraisal of the Protocols of Zion* was published by the Columbia University Press in 1942. Fourteen prominent historians endorsed its findings (p. vi). The New York *Herald Tribune* editorial appeared in its issue of May 10, 1942.

Winrod's statements starting at the bottom of page 44 (and continuing to the middle of page 45) are from the pamphlet *The Hidden Hand* (Defender Publishers, 1933), pp. 8, 23, 28, 31.

PAGE 45. The quotations from *The Jewish Assault on Christianity* (Defender Publishers, 1935) are taken from its preface and from page 24.

PAGE 46. The quotation from Riley's *Protocols and Communism* (no date; distributed by L. W. Camp, Minneapolis) is found on page 21 of that pamphlet. Riley withdrew *Protocols and Communism* from circulation after it had created division among his fundamentalist colleagues, but he continued to insist that the *Protocols* were genuine. His statement regarding *The Defender Magazine* was printed on several occasions by the Winrod monthly; e.g., Nov. 1947, p. 6. His endorsement of Mrs. Dilling's *The Red Network* was carried on the back of the book's jacket.

PAGE 47. Riley's *At Sunset or After 80* was published in 1943 by the Higley Press in Butler, Indiana.

The Conflict of the Ages was copyrighted by Arno C. Gaebelein, Inc., New York, in Oct. 1933; the quotation is from page 100.

In addition to Arno C. Gaebelein, many other leading fundamentalists were among the sixty-eight who signed Brooks' "Manifesto to the Jews." They included Donald Grey Barnhouse, Charles E. Fuller, Dan Gilbert, Will H. Houghton, H. A. Ironside, Alva J. McClain, J. Fred Meldau, Louis T. Talbot, and Charles G. Turnbull.

PAGE 48. The "religious" atmosphere at the meetings of the Christian Medical Research League was described in the *Eleventh Hour,* organ of the Lutheran Research Society, June-July 1949, p. 8.

PAGE 49. For a thorough discussion of Koch and the Koch treatment, see (among other sources) the following: the *Journal* of the American Medical Association, Aug. 27, 1949, p. 1352; "Cancer Quacks" by Bill Fay, in *Collier's,* May 26, 1951; Norma Lee Browning's articles in the Chicago *Tribune,* Aug. 1, 1949, and in *Reader's Digest,* April 1950; "Cancer Quackery Spreads Over Nation," by Ellis Moore, in the New York *World-Telegram,* March 11, 1950, p. 13.

Reilly's charges of a "plot" to make the American Medical Association "a Jewish profession" were quoted in *The Defender Magazine,* Jan. 1949, p. 14.

The Birth of a Science was written by Albert L. Wahl, Bessie L. Rehwinkel, and Lawrence Reilly (Lutheran Research Society, 1949). Reilly's tribute to Koch is on page 15.

Langer inserted Reilly material in the *Congressional Record* for Oct. 1, 1951; reprints of this material were distributed by Reilly — not at government expense. Langer regularly comes to the defense of fringe groups — sometimes of the extreme left as well as of the extreme right.

Reilly told his life story in the *Eleventh Hour* for Sept.-Oct. 1949, pp. 12-14. He wrote of his honorary degree in a mimeographed letter dated Oct. 1949 and entitled "My Answer to Mrs. Roosevelt's Attack." Mrs. Eleanor Roosevelt had attacked Reilly in her column of Sept. 9, 1949. Unfortunately, she sought also to discredit the late Dr. Walter A. Maier of the "Lutheran Hour" — for which she later made public apology.

PAGE 50. *Moscow's Master Plan for Sovietizing America* was published in 1948 by the Lutheran Research Society, Detroit; the quotation is from page 9. Winrod favorably reviewed the booklet in *The Defender Magazine,* Jan. 1949, p. 20.

The repudiation of the Lutheran Research Society by the Lutheran Church-Missouri Synod is undated. It was signed by J. W. Behnken, president of the synod, and distributed from his office in Oak Park, Ill.

PAGE 51. Mrs. Dilling's comments on Reilly were included in her regular letter dated Aug. 1949, p. 1.

The first comment on Swain is from the American Medical Association's *Journal,* Aug. 27, 1949, p. 1352. The opinion of the Akron Ministerial Association spokesman is recorded in the same place.

The material on Trinity College (Clearwater, Fla.) is taken from the college's current catalogue. Trinity College has been affiliated with the World's Christian Fundamentals Association, which was organized in 1918 by W. B. Riley (who is discussed in Chapters 3 and 14). Riley apparently met Billy Graham at Trinity; and as a result of this friendship, Graham succeeded Riley in 1947 in the presidency of the Northwestern Bible Schools in Minneapolis (from which he resigned in 1952). The World's Christian Fundamentals Association never became an influential faction in the religious world.

Its activities are now merged with those of the Slavic Gospel Association, with headquarters in Chicago.

PAGE 52. Baxter's statement near the bottom of this page appeared in his *King's Gazette,* Aug. 1949, p. 2. (The name of this periodical was later changed to *Protestant Newsletter.*)

PAGE 53. Baxter's statement near the top of this page is from his publication for March 1949 (p. 2). His article in *The Defender Magazine* appeared in the Dec. 1949 issue.

For further information on R. C. Hoiles, see (among other sources) *Time,* Aug. 30, 1948; *The Facts* (Anti-Defamation League), Nov. 1952; and *McCall's,* Sept. 1952.

PAGE 54. Herrstrom's remarks about his booklet were taken from his *Bible News Flashes,* Jan. 1950, p. 22. Quotations are from pp. 1, 7, 8, 9, 14, 20, and 21 of this booklet.

PAGE 55. Herrstrom's remarks are quoted from *Bible News Flashes* of the following dates: the reference to "Kommunist Kikes," Jan. 1948, p. 1; the reference to the anti-Christ, Jan. 1949, p. 3; the reference to discrimination, Feb. 1949, p. 2; his warning about a "sea of blood," from the same issue. Herrstrom calls the civil-rights program "the universal raping of American womanhood" in *Bible News Flashes,* May 1948, p. 3. The reference to "godless communists" is from the issue of Jan. 1949, p. 5.

PAGE 56. Remarks regarding the outburst of anti-Zionism in the Soviet Union still fill the hate press. Those quoted are dated as follows: *The Defender Magazine,* Jan. 1953, pp. 16-17; *Common Sense,* Dec. 1, 1952; *The Broom,* Dec. 15, 1952, p. 2; *Women's Voice,* Dec. 25, 1952, p. 1.

PAGE 57. Foster's statement was quoted in *Women's Voice,* March 26, 1953, p. 5. Madole's statement was made to his street-corner audience in Jan. 1953.

Chapter 4
Hitler's Ghost in American Garb

PAGE 59. The introductory quotation is from *The Cross and the Flag,* Dec. 1952, p. 9. The second statement by Smith is from his leaflet *Names of Jews Running the United Nations,* p. 1. Smith had originally scheduled his Washington pilgrimage for early June. In his letter dated May 1953 he set June 29 as a new date. (In the same letter he announced that the national headquarters of the Christian Nationalist Crusade were being transferred to California.)

PAGE 61. The Pelley platform was quoted in Roy Tozier's *America's Little Hitlers* (a Haldeman-Julius publication), p. 46.

The quotation from Smith's oration at Long's funeral was included in Thorp McClusky's article, "Huckster of Hatred," in the *Christian Herald,* Feb. 1950, p. 17.

PAGE 62. Smith's defense of Huey Long is from *The Cross and the Flag,* Sept. 1952, p. 2. His statement on Father Coughlin is from the same issue, same page.

The Defender Magazine of June 1937 (p. 4) discussed Smith's Committee of One Million.

PAGE 63. Smith's wartime platform may be found in *The Cross and the Flag*, Oct. 1944, pp. 453-60. His statement on the Methodist action is from the issue of May 1944, p. 386. His condemnation of World War II is from the issue of Sept. 1952, p. 15.

PAGE 64. The organization of the Christian Nationalist Crusade is described in *The Cross and the Flag*, July 1946, pp. 788A-788D. Smith's estimate of the strength of his new organization is from a letter dated June 30, 1947. He discusses his southern expedition in *The Cross and the Flag*, June 1947. His break with Winrod may be detected in *The Defender Magazine*, Aug. 1947 (p. 13) and Dec. 1947 (p. 16).

PAGE 65. For the 1948 platform of the Christian Nationalist Party, see *The Cross and the Flag*, Sept. 1948, p. 8 Smith's comments on his magazine are from the issues of March 1952 (p. 3) and April 1952 (p. 2). Arnold Forster, in *A Measure of Freedom* (Doubleday, 1950), p. 230, estimated that *The Cross and the Flag* has 23,000 subscribers. McClusky reported that in 1946 Smith testified "something around 90,000" before a congressional committee.

PAGE 66. Smith's five "big issues" were outlined in *The Cross and the Flag*, Dec. 1950, p. 20.

PAGE 68. The article about "interbreeding" is from *The Cross and the Flag*, Aug. 1947, p. 7. Smith refers to the Negro as a "child race" in the issue of Aug. 1947, p. 14; his reference to "Miami tan" is from the issue of March 1947, p. 905. The "campaign of mongrelization" is discussed in the issue of July 1952, p. 9.

Smith's report on Atlanta is from the "Nationalist News Service" bulletin of Sept. 8, 1947, p. 2. The "Kill Him!" letter was dated Aug. 1945.

PAGE 69. "The Forbidden Letter" was dated Jan. 1946. The alleged desire to "murder" Smith is from his letter of Jan. 19, 1952.

Smith's characterizations come from the following sources: Eleanor Roosevelt, quoted in McClusky, p. 64; Eisenhower, in McClusky, p. 64; Dewey, *The Cross and the Flag*, May 1951, p. 10; Stassen, *ibid.*, Nov. 1951, p. 14; "Jewish" dominated . . .," *ibid.*, Aug. 1951, p. 8; Pearson, in McClusky, p. 64; McGill, *The Cross and the Flag*, Aug. 1951, p. 8.

PAGE 70. Smith's remark regarding the "religious" aspect of his work is from *The Cross and the Flag*, June 1948, p. 2. The "religious requirements" are from the issue of March 1948, p. 2. His motivation is put forth on the same page.

PAGE 71. Smith's denunciation of "timid men" is from *The Cross and the Flag*, Dec. 1949, p. 28. He warns against dividing Catholics and Protestants in the issue of Dec. 1949, p. 12. The quotation describing the pamphlet *The Popes and the Jews* is from the issue of March 1948, p. 8. This pamphlet also has been circulated under the title, *The Jewish Problem as Dealt With by the Popes*.

Smith circulates a leaflet, *The Physical Appearance of Jesus*, to promote the falsehood that Jesus was not of Jewish heritage. The quotation beginning at the bottom of the page is from that leaflet.

PAGE 72. Smith's remark is from *The Cross and the Flag*, Jan. 1948, p. 2. *Jesus vs. the Jews* by Gerald L. K. Smith is undated; the quotation is from page 4.

The fundamentalist scholar is Robert L. Evans; his remark is from his book, *The Jew in the Plan of God* (Loizeaux Brothers, 1950), p. 127. The statements of Frederick C. Grant are from *An Introduction to New Testament Thought* (Abingdon-Cokesbury, 1950), pp. 94, 97, and quoted by permission of the publisher.

PAGE 74. Smith's attacks upon interfaith co-operation are from *The Cross and the Flag*, Feb. 1950, p. 24, and Dec. 1949, p. 19. His criticism of the N.C.C.J. is from the issue of Dec. 1950, p. 13. The Talmudic distortions are endorsed in the issue of June 1952, p. 18; the *Protocols*, in the issue of May 1952, p. 10.

PAGE 75. Lohbeck's remarks on this and the following page are from his booklet, *Racial Aspects of the Coming Political Struggle*, especially pp. 10-11, 24, 28. The letter is from the St. Louis *Post-Dispatch* of Oct. 16, 1950, p. 2E. It was signed by Armin Roehrig of Munich and Joachim von Wangenheim of Wiesbaden.

PAGE 77. Beard is quoted on page 9 of the pamphlet, *Benjamin Franklin Vindicated* (American Jewish Committee, no date). The president of the Franklin Institute, Henry Butler Allen, is quoted on page 10.

PAGE 78. Sammons' characterizations are from his 16-page pamphlet, *The Mysterious Power of Communism*, as follows: Smith, p. 11; Coughlin, p. 9; Pelley, p. 13; Kamp, p. 14; Rankin, p. 14.

Sammons' undated letter was headed "Open Letter to Christian Churches of All Denominations." The same letter was printed above his signature in *Women's Voice*, July 31, 1952, p. 4.

PAGE 79. The granting of the "award" to Armstrong was reported in *The Cross and the Flag*, March 1953, p. 13.

PAGE 80. Armstrong described his personal background in *The Truth About My Alleged $50,000,000 Donation* (1950), p. 4. His call for the repeal of the 14th and 15th amendments is from *The March of Bolshevism* (1945), p. 71. His boast of superiority is from *The Truth . . .*, p. 13. The remaining quotations beginning on page 80 are from *Third Zionist War* (1951), pp. 52, 53, 55; *Zionist Wall Street* (1949), pp. 20, 94; *The March of Bolshevism*, pp. 6-7.

PAGE 81. Armstrong endorsed the Talmudic distortions and the *Protocols* in *World Empire* (1945), pp. 14-15, 19.

Moseley's reported remark is from Armstrong's *The Truth . . .*, p. 6.

PAGE 82. The chairman's remarks were quoted in *The National Jewish Monthly*, Jan. 1950, p. 154 ("The Inside Story of Jefferson College," by Harold M. Case).

Armstrong reprinted the correspondence with Lee and Boaz in *The Truth . . .*, pp. 14-16.

PAGE 83. Armstrong's invasion of Piedmont College has been recounted in *The Reporter*, May 13, 1952 ("Freedom of Conscience at Piedmont College," by Harold C. Fleming), and in *The Nation*, Oct. 6, 1951 ("How to Buy a College," by Hoyt E. Bowen).

PAGE 84. The Congregational statement of policy was issued in June 1952.

Beaty's book was published by the Wilkerson Publishing Co. of Dallas, Texas. His "motto" is from p. xiii. The "self-description" is from the book's jacket.

PAGE 85. The Beaty remarks are from the following pages: "mixed stock," p. 15; "quadruple aims," p. 25; "friendly relationships," p. 9; "the defeated country," p. 10. The summations of the "three-pronged" purpose are from pages 72, 74, 77.

PAGE 86. The Beaty remarks are from the following pages: "only logical conclusion," p. 148; "Socialistic controls," p. 170; "evolve some method," p. 197.

PAGE 87. Beaty's description of his own book is from p. xii.

The arguments used in this discussion of Beaty's fallacies were formulated in two excellent articles by Orval Watts, West Coast economist. They appeared in *Faith and Freedom,* Dec. 1952-Jan. 1953. *Faith and Freedom* is the organ of Spiritual Mobilization, an organization discussed below (Chapter 12). The quotations are from the two Watts' articles.

PAGE 89. Endorsements of the Beaty book are from the following sources: Smith, *The Cross and the Flag,* April 1952, p. 16; Winrod, *The Defender Magazine,* Feb. 1952, p. 5; *Williams Intelligence Summary,* Feb. 1952, p. 4; *Women's Voice,* Feb. 28, 1952, p. 13; Zoll, quoted in *The Facts,* Feb.-Mar. 1952, p. 4; Shuler, *Methodist Challenge,* June 1952, p. 12; Owsley, quoted in *National Christian Journal,* Summer 1952, p. 5; Hazlitt, *ibid.;* Hopper, her column in the Los Angeles *Times,* Feb. 18, 1952. (Hedda Hopper was also quoted in Smith's *The Cross and the Flag* of April 1952 and May 1952. She later repudiated Smith, but not the Beaty book.)

PAGE 90. Both Darlington letters are on file in several New York offices.

Since J. Russell Maguire gained control of *American Mercury,* it has become the mouthpiece for a score of irresponsible "political analysts." J. B. Matthews is an outstanding example. In the issue of May 1953, Matthews, heralded by his admirers as "Mr. Anti-Communist," attacked as "top collaborationists" such reputable churchmen as James Luther Adams of Chicago University; Georgia Harkness of the Pacific School of Religion; Halford E. Luccock of Yale University; Walter M. Horton of Oberlin College; John A. Mackay of Princeton Theological Seminary; and others. In the June 1953 issue he blasted Reinhold Niebuhr, one of the most forceful anti-communists among Protestant leaders. Matthews' July 1953 piece, "Reds and the Churches," created a nation-wide storm that led to his dismissal July 9 as research assistant to Joseph McCarthy's Senate Subcommittee — after President Eisenhower had condemned his unfair charge that "the largest single group supporting the Communist apparatus is composed of Protestant clergymen."

PAGE 91. The remark of *The S.M.U. Campus* is from the issue of Jan. 11, 1952, p. 4.

Chapter 5

The Self-Anointed ''Chosen People''

PAGE 93. Comment on the origin of Anglo-Israelism is from *Destiny,* Nov. 1949, p. 390. A history of the "rediscovery" of Israel, from an Anglo-Israelite viewpoint, was presented in *Destiny,* Jan. 1946, pp. 17-20.

PAGE 95. *The Pattern of History* was published by Destiny Publishers in 1942; the quotations are from pages 11, 13, 16, 17, 21. Thirty-two "marks of Israel" are listed on pages 25-26. Other Anglo-Israelites find many more evidences. For example, Destiny Publishers have circulated a pamphlet by the Rev. R. G. F. Waddington entitled *One Hundred Reasons and More Why the British Are Israelites.* From Washington, D. C., Charles O. Benham distributes his pamphlet *101 Evidence Proving the Divine Origin and Destiny of the English-Speaking Peoples.*

PAGE 97. *Palestine: Center of World Intrigue* was published by Destiny Publishers in 1949 (reprinted from *Destiny*, May 1949). The quotations are from pages 17 and 22.

Sawyer's pamphlet *The Jewish Question* (no date) was distributed by the Anglo-Saxon Federation of America with headquarters in Detroit. The quotation is from page 3.

PAGE 98. Allen's remark is from page 71 of *Judah's Sceptre and Joseph's Birthright* (A. A. Beauchamp, Boston, 1943).

Detailed accounts of the "Boake Carter incident" appeared in two Grand Rapid (Mich.) papers, the *Press* and the *Herald*, Oct. 18 and 19, 1941, respectively. Carter's accusation and Rand's reply were included in both accounts. Rand's more recent remark is from a letter dated Sept. 19, 1951.

PAGE 100. The 1953 predictions were noted in the *Kingdom Digest*, Dec. 1952, pp. 6-7.

PAGE 101. The Lovell statements are from the following sources: "God wants to destroy," *Aufbau*, a German-language newspaper published in New York, Dec. 24, 1943; "One Worlders," *Kingdom Digest*, Aug. 1952, p. 6; "Kingdom Age," *Kingdom Digest*, Oct. 1951, p. 14.

Jeffers' boast was made in a letter, Aug. 18, 1952. He outlines his "theology" in the leaflet *The Creator's True Name.*

PAGE 103. The report that Jeffers was picked by the Nazi Bund to promote anti-Catholicism was carried in the Los Angeles *Examiner*, March 22, 1939, p. 1; John Roy Carlson, in his book *Undercover* (Dutton, 1943, p. 173), charged that Jeffers' Kingdom Temple was used to recruit Silver Shirts.

PAGE 104. Smith praised Swift in *The Cross and the Flag*, Dec. 1949, p. 24. Swift's remarks are from the preface to his published sermon, "Thy Kingdom Come," over Station KGER, Long Beach, Feb. 26, 1949.

PAGE 105. Kullgren's remarks on pages 105-06 are from the following sources: "Seventy-five per cent," *Beacon Light Herald*, May 1952, p. 15; "Democracy," letter, Oct. 1, 1944, p. 3; "we have no use for it," *Beacon Light Herald*, Aug. 1951, p. 10; "only a fraction," *Beacon Light*, Aug. 1936, p. 18; "largely through annihilation," *ibid.*, May 1940, p. 26; "civil war," letter, Feb. 1, 1944, p. 1; defense of Jeffers, *Beacon Light*, June 1939, p. 39; "it would be pretty hard," *ibid.*, Oct.-Nov. 1945, p. 12.

PAGE 107. Greene's remarks are from his leaflet *Civil Rights;* Gaard's from *The Broadcaster*, Jan. 1951, p. 11; Schiffner's from the *Prophetic News Herald*, May 1952, p. 2.

PAGE 108. Smith's three references to Miss Allen are from *The Cross and the Flag*, June 1950, p. 20; Sept. 1946, p. 823; May 1950, p. 10. She discusses the Negro in her pamphlet *My Country Right or Wrong, My Country* (1949), p. 21. She complains of the "destruction" of the white race in *Calling All Christians* (1951), p. 8.

PAGE 109. Miss Allen circulates her poem "Ride, Clansman, Ride!" She reports that it is based on "The Clansman," by Thomas Dixon.

Miss Allen's other remarks are from the following sources: "The anti-Semites," *Calling All Christians*, p. 12; "Our Messiah," *Zionist War-Mongering in the U. S. A.* (1948), p. 41; "The White Cross" and "by permitting Jew Professors," *Operation "Scuttling of America"* (1947), p. 33; "Only the ideals," *The Dumb, Ungrateful American Public* (1947), p. 7.

PAGE 110. Miss Allen's attack on pacifism is in *Calling All Christians,* p. 12. She dedicated *My Country Right or Wrong, My Country* to the "true Israelites," etc.

Smith commended Flenner in *The Cross and the Flag,* Jan. 1948, p. 3. Miss Allen's remark is from the *Ohio Pioneer,* Jan. 1948, p. 1. An announcement of Dayton Theological Seminary (with references to "Russian Yiddish speaking people . . .") appeared in *Kingdom Digest,* Aug. 1947, p. 30.

PAGE 111. For a typical Flenner tirade against the Jews (including the specific reference to "Esau-Amalekite International Bankers"), see *Kingdom Digest,* June 1952, pp. 41-44. Flenner's speech was quoted in *The Facts,* Sept. 1948, pp. 12, 13.

PAGE 112. Record's remark about foreigners is from *Truth and Liberty Magazine,* April 1951, pp. 2, 3.

Smith praised Stadsklev in *The Cross and the Flag,* April 1944 (p. 399) and June 1948 (p. 6).

PAGE 113. The brief remarks at the top of the page are from *Truth and Liberty Magazine* of Oct. 1947, p. 20, Jan. 1949, p. 14, and July 1945, p. 11.

Luke Rader's funeral was reported in the *Sunshine News,* July 24, 1952. His contention that the Jews are Chaldeans appeared in the *Sunshine News,* June 16, 1949, p. 1.

PAGE 114. Perkins' remarks in *Gerald L. K. Smith Unmasked* are from page 25.

PAGE 115. Perkins' remarks in *The Modern Canaanites or the Enemies of Jesus Christ* are from pages 7, 9, 38, and 40, respectively.

PAGE 116. Tappert's review was distributed in March 1948. Earlier Perkins had sent notices to all Lutheran pastors announcing his publication of Luther's book.

Chapter 6
Fiery Crosses, the Shame of America

PAGE 118. The sessions of the Beauharnais "convention" were attended by the writer.

PAGE 120. Simmons' boast is quoted in Gustavus Myers' *History of Bigotry in the United States* (Random House, 1953), p. 273.

PAGE 121. Simmons' "religious experience" is quoted in Jones' *Knights of the Ku Klux Klan,* pp. 75-76.

PAGE 122. The *Kloran* to which reference is made was copyrighted by Simmons in Atlanta, Ga. (no date). The quotation is from page 40 of the sixth edition.

PAGE 123. *America for Americans* is a brief undated leaflet; the quotation is from page 4.

Shuler's remarks were published in *The American Klansman,* July 1950, p. 2. His attack on Southern Baptists is from the issue of Aug. 1950, p. 3.

PAGE 125. Johnston's remarks concerning his new party are from the *Georgia*

Tribune, Sept. 11, 1947, p. 1. The fate of the Klan is lamented in the issue of March 13, 1952, p. 3.

PAGE 126. Johnston's remarks are from the *Georgia Tribune,* March 27, 1952, p. 3; Hamilton's from page 2 of the same issue. The telegrams from Wood and MacArthur were reported in the Dayton *Independent* of March 13, 1952, p. 1. The same issue carried the account quoted at the bottom of page 126, as well as the reference to Klan-Catholic co-operation.

PAGE 127. Kurts' statement was reported in the Dayton *Independent,* March 13, 1952, p. 1. Hendrix's pro-Catholic remarks are from his "Newsletter of the Imperial Council," No. 4, and from page 5 of his pamphlet *The Ku Klux Klan and Its Story* (no date). He attacks the Jews and the National Council of Churches on page 6 of the same pamphlet.

PAGE 128. Hendrix commends the Conservative Baptist Association, etc., in Newsletter No. 2.

The *Principles and Purposes of the Knights of the Ku Klux Klan* were outlined "by an exalted Cyclops of the Order" (no date). The quotation is from page 10.

PAGE 130. Beauharnais criticized Frankfurter in the Summer 1952 issue of *White Circle News.* He attacked the Jews in the issue of Sept. 11, 1952, p. 1.

PAGE 131. Stoner's remarks concerning the Jews are from an ad in *Women's Voice,* Sept. 30, 1948, p. 4. He attacked the NAACP in a flyer headed: JEWS BEHIND RACE MIXING.

Hamilton's remarks on his conversion are from pages 26-27 of *I Was Branded With the Number 666.* His other statements are from a flyer headed: HOW DO YOU LIKE?

PAGE 132. Hamilton's remarks are from the following sources: "the Bible very clearly," 1952 letter to "Dear Fellow Americans"; "Preserve the white stock," flyer entitled "The Kiss of Death"; "Dr. Malan's splendid victory," *White Sentinel,* April 1953, p. 3.

PAGE 133. Mrs. Jenkins' remarks (on this and the following page) are from pages 14-15 of her pamphlet, *Your Pocket Atom Bomb* (no date).

PAGE 134. The quotation from *Alien Minorities and Mongrelization* (Meador Publishing Co., Boston, 1949) is from page 32.

PAGE 135. Polk's remarks are from page 18 of *The Negro and the Constitution* and pages 7-8 of *Everything After Its Kind* (both without dates).

Blessing's *White Supremacy* was published in 1952 by the House of Prayer for All People. The quotation is from page 1. He calls for a KKK-like organization in *Showers of Blessing,* June 23, 1950, p. 15. His attack on "the modernistic preachers," is from the issue of April 1952, p. 17.

PAGE 136. Blessing's remarks concerning his background are from *Showers of Blessing,* Nov. 24, 1950. His criticism of Smith and Winrod is from the "Blessing Letter," March 1951, pp. 4-5. "God is white . . . " comes from *White Supremacy,* p. 31.

Howard's "crusade" was announced in *The Cross and the Flag,* March 1948, and Smith's letter No. 155.

PAGE 137. Perkin's statement is from page 16 of *White Man Awaken!*

The program of the United African Nationalist Movement is outlined in a 1951 "Open Letter" signed by C. A. Thornhill.

PAGE 138. Rogers' statement is quoted in *The Troublemakers* by Arnold Forster and Benjamin Epstein (Doubleday, 1952), p. 163.

PAGE 139. Bilbo's remarks are from page 116 of his book, published in 1947 by the Dream House Publishing Co., Poplarville, Mississippi; Murray's from page 14 of his book, published in 1948 in Tishomingo, Okla.

PAGE 141. The quotations are from *Militant Truth,* July-August 1950 (p. 1), and April 1950 (p. 3).

Chapter 7
"No Popery!" — Bigotry's Battlecry

PAGE 147. All quotations are from the POAU manifesto.

PAGE 150. Sugrue summarized the attacks upon him in an article, "What Happens when a Catholic Speaks His Mind?" in *Advance* (Congregational biweekly), May 26, 1952, p. 6.

PAGE 151. POAU's statements are quoted in Luke Ebersole's *Church Lobbying in the Nation's Capital* (Macmillan, 1951), p. 105. Ebersole's source was a speech by Glenn Archer, POAU's executive director, "The Church Press and Separation of Church and State."

PAGE 152. POAU's stated policy with regard to party platforms is quoted in Ebersole, p. 75. His source was the *Church and State Newsletter,* Aug. 1948.

PAGE 153. McNicholas' remarks were reported in the daily press and published, in large part, in the *Our Sunday Visitor* pamphlet, *Whose Friends are They — America's or Russia's?* by F. A. Fink, pp. 35-38. In answer to McNicholas, E. H. DeGroot, Jr., POAU treasurer, made a lengthy reply by way of an "Open Letter." DeGroot charged that McNicholas' statement was "manifestly misleading," that hierarchial action contradicted its words, and that the Roman Catholic Church is particularly intent upon securing aid for her parochial schools.

Cushing is quoted in the same *Our Sunday Visitor* pamphlet, p. 40. He was answered by Bishop Oxnam, who charged him with misrepresenting the aims of POAU and the position of the Catholic Church on the separation of church and state.

Murray's discussion of POAU was carried in *Commonweal,* Feb. 8, 1948; the quotations are from pages 515-16.

PAGE 154. *Our Sunday Visitor,* with a circulation exceeding 700,000, frequently embarrasses intelligent, fair-minded Catholics by its flagrant attacks upon Protestantism and Protestant leadership. For example, the pamphlet, *Whose Friends Are They — America's or Russia's?* is actually more of a diatribe against Protestantism, especially the Federal Council of Churches, than against POAU. *Who's Who in the POAU?* is filled with misrepresentations, serious errors, and irrelevant data. When boiled down, its content furnishes almost no factual information about POAU or its principal figures. Most POAU leaders are dismissed as pro-Communist — a charge that is, of course, false. *Who's Who in the POAU?* even quotes vigorous anti-Catholics to establish its case. For example, a long letter against the Federal Council of Churches from William Harllee Bordeaux is included to prove that "all Protestant groups do not see alike." Bordeaux is executive secretary of the fanatically anti-Catholic American Council of Christian Churches. The authors of *Who's Who in the POAU?* appear to have little regard for the reliability of their sources of information.

The attitude of the National Liberal League toward POAU was stated in a letter from Charles Smith, a League executive committee member, March 7, 1952. Carl McIntire, strong man of the American Council of Christian Churches, has attacked POAU on several occasions; e.g., *Testimony of Separation* (1952), p. 96. Christ's Mission commented on POAU in a letter from Miss Eleanor M. Jones, March 14, 1952.

PAGE 155. Peak's remarks are published in *Whose Friends are They — America's or Russia's?* (p. 43); Kiroack's are from page 41 of the same booklet. Bennett's comment is from *Christianity and Crisis,* Feb. 2, 1948 (p. 2). Niebuhr was quoted in the Brooklyn *Tablet,* July 19, 1947 (p. 1).

PAGE 156. The story of James A. O'Connor, from Christ's Mission's viewpoint, is included in the pamphlet, *Father O'Connor,* edited by L. H. Lehmann. The excerpt from the incorporation papers is given on page 14 of the pamphlet.

PAGE 157. Lehmann's reasons for leaving Roman Catholicism are given on page 5 of *The Trek from Rome,* a leaflet by Jeanne Kellar, published originally as an article in *World Outlook. Behind the Dictators* was first published in 1942 by the Agora Publishing Co., New York. The quotations are from the 1944 edition, pages 79, 33, and 12-19, respectively.

PAGE 160. The *Converted Catholic Magazine's* claim to avoid "mud-slinging" comes from its issue of Jan. 1949, p. 33. Montano's remark is from page 79 of the issue of March 1952. The attacks upon Roman Catholic morality are from an article, "Catholic Invasion of Rural America," Feb. 1949, pp. 36-39.

PAGE 161. *The Priest, the Woman, and the Confessional* (45th edition) was published by the Gospel Witness of Toronto, Canada, operated by T. T. Shields (discussed elsewhere in this chapter, and in Chapters 8 and 14). The quotations are from pages 87 and 73-74, respectively. It should be noted that many supporters of Christ's Mission do not approve of the circulation of this type of literature. Recently, for example, through the efforts of several on the staff, the hyper-sensational jacket of *The Priest, the Woman, and the Confessional* was abandoned.

PAGE 162. *Exposé* attacked Christ's Mission in its issue of April, 1953, pp. 3-4. The *Our Sunday Visitor* pamphlet was published Jan. 15, 1952; the quotation is from page 36. Mrs. Dilling's remarks are from her letter of July 1949, p. 13. Goff's comments were carried in *Common Sense,* March 1, 1952, p. 4.

PAGE 163. The *Converted Catholic Magazine* of Jan. 1949, for example, carried material from the Soviet *New Times.*

The commendation of the American Protestant Defense League is from the *Converted Catholic Magazine* of April 1949, p. 128.

PAGE 164. The A.P.D.L. leaflet quoted is *Who is Driving Us to War?* (p. 4). It was reprinted from *American Protest,* June 1947. *Will the Vatican Plunge Us Into a Third World War?* was written by G. J. Morgans, an Australian who visits the United States to arouse sentiment against Catholicism. His pamphlet was published by the United Protestant Action Movement in Melbourne (no date). Quotations are from pages 9 and 12.

PAGE 165. The quotation is from the March 1953 issue of *American Protest* (p. 7). McGinlay's remarks were made at an evening talk on Feb. 20, 1953.

PAGE 166. McIntire's remarks are from the *Christian Beacon,* Sept. 6, 1945, p. 8. Springer attacked anti-Catholicism in *Western Voice,* July 18, 1944, p. 2.

The two doggerel verses are from *Western Voice* of March 23, 1951, p. 3, and June 22, 1951, p. 3.

PAGE 167. POAU's warning is from the *Church and State Newsletter,* Nov. 1951, p. 5. Shields is discussed in an article in *Maclean's Magazine* (Canadian), June 15, 1949; the quotations in parentheses are from page 15 of that article. Shields's comments on Roman Catholicism and the war are from the *Gospel Witness and Protestant Advocate,* Aug. 9, 1945, p. 3.

PAGE 168. Shields's description of the papacy is from the *Gospel Witness and Protestant Advocate,* July 26, 1945, p. 1. His recent address was quoted in the *Christian Beacon,* July 31, 1952, p. 8; it was made at the so-called British Regional Conference of the International Council of Christian Churches.

King's remarks on his "mission" and "the thousands of white slaves" are from his "Tract No. 6 1952 Issue" (entitled "Abolish the Nunneries and Save the Girls").

PAGE 169. King's description of the confessional is from page 11 of *House of Death and Gate of Hell* (Protestant Book and Bible House, Toledo, 1948).

For ads such as quoted on this page, see *Christian Beacon,* Dec. 25, 1952, p. 7; *United Evangelical Action,* May 1, 1953, p. 7; and *Western Voice,* Dec. 5, 1952, p. 4.

Junior's description of his book selection is from a current flyer advertising the Book and Bible House.

PAGE 170. Ads of the Gospel Art Shoppe were carried in *The Defender Magazine,* April 1953, p. 24, and *Converted Catholic Magazine,* April 1953, p. 118; in both of these publications it advertises as the Old Authors Shoppe. The *Maria Monk* ad has appeared in such ultra-fundamentalist sheets as *Western Voice,* Nov. 21, 1952, p. 2.

Stone's testimony is currently circulated by the Paulist Press of New York in a pamphlet, *The True History of Maria Monk.* The story of Maria Monk — and many other interesting aspects of rabid anti-Catholicism in United States history — has been recounted in *The Shadow of the Pope* by Michael Williams (McGraw-Hill, New York, 1932).

PAGE 171. For one of the most interesting episodes in Smythe's career, see the discussion of the United Christian Church of America (page 198 and note). Smythe's remarks are quoted in a report of Friends of Democracy, May 1948, p. 13.

PAGE 172. Smythe's slogan is from *Protestant War Veterans,* August 1946.

PAGE 173. Smythe characterized the Roman Catholic hierarchy as a "dead duck . . ." in an undated issue of *Protestant War Veterans* headed "12 O'Clock Is Striking for All Free Americans!" On this occasion, Smythe described himself as "America's Most Fearless and Courageous Protestant War Veterans Leader." He warned of the "Thousands of Priests and NUNS" in another undated bulletin headed "To Hell With Racial Equality." He connects the Rothschilds to the Vatican in "Vol. 107, No. 58," headed "Roman Catholic Facism [*sic*] has Declared War on American Protestantism." In this issue he described his periodical as "The Voice of Protestant America." Smythe's characterizations of "nationalist leaders" are from the following sources: Winrod, *Publicity,* Aug. 1, 1940, p. 2; Smith, *The Protestant Veteran* (Vol. 107, No. 58), entitled "Gerald L. K. Smith, Patriot or Scoundrel?" by Edward James Smythe, "America's Leading Crusader Against the Menace of Communism and Fascism"; Mrs. Dilling, *Publicity,* March 13, 1941, p. 3. Mrs.

Dilling denounced Smythe in a letter dated June 1943. Smythe attacks the preachers, etc., in an issue of his publication (Vol. 107, No. 58), entitled "The Nationalist Movement." Smythe decries the Federal Council of Churches in *Publicity,* Jan. 9, 1941, p. 3. His endorsement of the American Council of Christian Churches is from his letter to Carl McIntire, Jan. 3, 1953.

PAGE 174. The story of Harrison Parker and the Puritan Church has been told before — by the National Catholic Welfare Conference in a mimeographed brochure; and by the Anti-Defamation League in *The Troublemakers,* pp. 114-26. Much of the background information used here comes from these two sources.

Parker's remarks regarding the "Vatican Embassy" are from *Liberty Bell,* March 18, 1950, p. 9.

PAGE 176. Parker's statement against fighting in "World War III" is from *Liberty Bell,* March 18, 1950, p. 14. He advises Protestants and Jews "to keep arms" in the "Coming Issue" for 1950, p. 3. The Smith Act is invoked on page 2 of the same issue; the demand that the Pope be tried is from page 1. Parker's warning that the Vatican seeks to recast the government of the United States is from *Liberty Bell,* identified only as "No. 25, Vol. II."

Chapter 8
Saboteurs of Protestant Co-operation

PAGE 181. The initial remarks were made by J. Harold Smith, an evangelist with headquarters in Fort Smith, Arkansas. They were carried on page 1 of the *Christian Beacon,* May 9, 1946.

PAGE 182. The twelve agencies that merged into the National Council of the Churches of Christ in the U. S. A. were as follows:

Federal Council of the Churches of Christ in America
Foreign Missions Conference of North America
Home Missions Council of North America
International Council of Religious Education
Missionary Education Movement of the United States and Canada
United Council of Church Women
United Stewardship Council
Church World Service
Interseminary Committee
National Protestant Council on Higher Education
Protestant Film Commission
Protestant Radio Commission

The denominations affiliated with the National Council of Churches and the membership of each are as follows:

National Council Denominations	*Membership*
African Methodist Episcopal	1,166,301
African Methodist Episcopal Zion	728,150
American Baptist Convention	1,554,304
Augustana Evangelical Lutheran	465,062
Church of the Brethren	186,358
Colored Methodist Episcopal	392,167
Congregational Christian	1,241,477

National Council Denominations	*Membership*
Czech-Moravian Brethren	4,090
Danish Evangelical Lutheran	19,899
Evangelical and Reformed	735,941
Evangelical United Brethren	720,544
Friends-Five Years Meeting	68,612
Friends of Philadelphia & Vicinity	5,743
Greek Orthodox Church in America	1,000,000
International Convention of Disciples of Christ	1,792,985
Methodist	9,065,727
Moravian	43,856
National Baptist Convention of America	2,645,789
National Baptist Convention U. S. A., Inc.	4,467,779
Presbyterian U. S.	702,266
Presbyterian U. S. A.	2,364,112
Protestant Episcopal	2,417,464
Reformed in America	187,256
Romanian Orthodox of America	50,000
Russian Orthodox of America	400,000
Seventh Day Baptist	6,187
Syrian Antiochian Orthodox	75,000
Ukranian Orthodox of America	40,250
United Lutheran	1,925,506
United Presbyterian	219,027
	34,681,852

The constituent denomination of the National Council of Churches include 143,418 churches and 123,109 pastors having charges.

PAGE 183. The thirty-six denominations affiliated with the National Association of Evangelicals (N.A.E.) as of Feb. 1953 are listed below with the approximate membership of each:

N.A.E. Denominations	*Membership*
Assemblies of God	318,478
Association of Fundamental Ministers and Churches	900
Brethren in Christ Church	5,680
The Church by the Side of the Road	5,500
The Church of God (Cleveland, Tenn.)	121,706
Churches of Christ in Christian Union	5,740
Conference of Mennonite Brethren Church of North America	10,262
Congregational Methodist Church	11,189
Conservative Congregational Conference	no report
Elim Missionary Assemblies	4,000
Evangelical Free Church of America	12,000
Evangelical Mennonite Brethren Church	2,079
Evangelical Mennonite Church of North America	1,907
Evangelical Methodist Church	9,000
Evangelistic Tabernacles	260
Free Methodist Church of North America	48,575
General Six Principle Baptists	280
Grace Gospel Evangelistic Association	15,000

N.A.E. Denominations	*Membership*
Holiness Methodist Church	650
International Church of the Foursquare Gospel	64,109
International Pentecostal Assemblies	10,000
Krimmer Mennonite Brethren Church of North America	1,593
Missionary Bands of the World	203
Missionary Church Association	6,175
Missionary Methodist Conference	741
National Association of Free Will Baptists	400,000
New England Christian Conference	no report
Ohio Yearly Meeting of Friends	5,987
Open Bible Standard Churches	25,000
Oregon Yearly Meeting of Friends	4,582
Pentecostal Holiness Church	41,808
Primitive Methodist Church of the U. S. A.	12,295
Reformed Presbyterian Church of North America	5,280
United Fundamentalist Church	1,000
Wesleyan Methodist Church of America	34,493

The figures quoted are principally from the 1952 *American Yearbook of the Churches.* Several not listed in the *Yearbook* are from *"Separation" — Is Separating Evangelicals,* by President Stephen W. Paine of Houghton College, a former N.A.E. president. Paine's pamphlet was published in 1951. The Missionary Methodist Conference reported its membership by correspondence in May 1953; on May 15, 1953, the Rev. Lucian Smith, General Superintendent of the Eastern Area of the Evangelical Methodist Church, estimated that denomination's membership between 8,000 and 10,000.

In addition to the thirty-six affiliated denominations, the N.A.E. embraces eight small conferences of other denominations. Members of affiliated schools, associations, mission boards, and other organizations — or individual N.A.E. members — are not counted in this survey. They have been estimated by N.A.E. spokesmen at 10,000,000.

PAGE 184. The best account of the N.A.E.'s attitude toward education is contained in Frank E. Gaebelein's *Christian Education in a Democracy* (Oxford University Press, 1951). Gaebelein, headmaster of the Stony Brook School in Long Island, served as chairman of a special N.A.E. committee to study the philosophy and practice of Christian education.

Gordon's *An Ecclesiastical Octopus* was published in 1948 by Fellowship Press (Boston). Murch's *The Growing Super-Church* was copyrighted by its author in 1952; it is currently distributed by the N.A.E. His article, "International Rot," appeared in *Action,* June 1, 1952. The activities of N.A.E.'s Washington office were described in *Action,* May 1, 1952.

It is important to note that *United Evangelical Action* carries the following statement under the masthead of each issue: "All editorials, sermons and articles appeared in United Evangelical Action represent the personal views of the authors. They do not necessarily reflect the policies of the National Association of Evangelicals, of its constituent groups, or the convictions of their individual members." Many Evangelicals strongly disapprove of Murch's strong biases and their constant injection into *Action.*

PAGE 186. The predictions are from the *Christian Beacon,* Sept. 18, 1941, p. 1. The creedal basis is stated in the preface of the Constitution of the American Council (A.C.C.C.).

PAGE 188. The charges against McIntire are from the *Minutes of the General Assembly of the Presbyterian Church in the U. S. A.*, 1936, Part I, p. 92.

PAGE 189. An official church statement, entitled *A Statement*, was circulated in 1936. The *Christian Century* editorial is from its issue of June 17, 1936, p. 878.

PAGE 190. The *Presbyterian Banner* commented on June 11, 1936, p. 3. McIntire's account is from page 23 of *The Truth About the Federal Council of Churches and the Kingdom of God* (1950).

PAGE 191. A.C.C.C. sums up its "early years" in a leaflet, *A Great Work!* Its international conference was heralded as "the most important meeting," in the *Christian Beacon*, May 13, 1948, p. 1. The "Call" was framed in Detroit, Oct. 18, 1947. It was included in the booklet, *Presenting — An International Council of Christian Churches*, p. 10. The *Christian Century's* memo to the press is from its issue of Aug. 4, 1949, pp. 774-75; McIntire's reaction was voiced in the *Christian Beacon*, Aug. 12, 1948, p. 4.

PAGE 192. Barnhouse's account was quoted in the *Christian Beacon*, Nov. 18, 1948, p. 2. McIntire termed it "manifestly contrary to fact." "When God Rebukes" appeared in the *Christian Beacon* of Sept. 23, 1948, p. 1. McIntire complained about the press in the issue of Sept. 2, 1948, p. 1. He discusses the World Council and its Amsterdam founding in his book *Modern Tower of Babel* (Christian Beacon Press, 1949).

PAGE 193. On March 23, 1949, the A.C.C.C. circulated a brochure, "We Protest One Great Hour," signed by Garman, then A.C.C.C. president, and McIntire, I.C.C.C. president. The quotations are from that brochure. The *Christian Century's* comment is from its issue of April 8, 1949, p. 420.

PAGE 194. The *Christian Beacon* headline is from page 1 of its issue of June 23, 1949. McIntire writes of his "mission" to Latin America in his collected letters, *The Struggle for South America* (subtitled "First Missionary Journey"). They were written from between July 12 and Aug. 30, 1949.

PAGE 195. The A.C.C.C.'s objective in traveling to Bangkok was reported by the Religious News Service, Nov. 15, 1949. Mackay's retort to McIntire's attacks was carried in the *Christian Beacon*, Jan. 5, 1950, p. 5. The first part of Mackay's statement was reported by the Religious News Service, Dec. 4, 1949; the reference to "Jesuitical ethic" was omitted.

The McIntire "line" on the National Council was presented in the *Christian Beacon* of June 19, 1948, p. 8.

PAGE 196. The A.C.C.C.'s attacks upon the first session of the National Council were reported in the New York *Times*, Nov. 27, 1950. His comments on the snowstorm and Taft are from the *Christian Beacon*, Dec. 7, 1950, p. 1.

PAGE 197. Wright's challenge continued: "I will even concede your right to count churches outside these fifteen bodies which, by legal action as individual churches, applied for associate membership and were received up to February 19, 1948, and also individuals who made application for membership and were duly admitted by action of your Board. This offer will be good until August 1, 1948."

PAGES 197-198. Since the McIntire faction consistently makes impressive claims as to its influence and its number of denominations and followers, it is important to examine with some care the churches affiliated with this "Twentieth Century Reformation." Very little has been published about most of these sects; in fact, it is impossible to obtain full and accurate information. The A.C.C.C. withholds all data from the *Yearbook of American Churches* (published by the National Council), although a few of its constituent denominations do submit reports.

In the first place, it is important to realize that the A.C.C.C.'s member denominations fluctuate from day to day. For example, on March 11, 1953 — according to the New York *Times* — the American Council reported sixteen denominations. Three days later, on March 14, 1953 — again, according to the New York *Times* — fourteen were claimed. The same discrepancies exist with regard to the claims of the International Council.

In the following brief survey, the names of the denominations currently affiliated with the American Council are capitalized.

As noted in the text, the BIBLE PRESBYTERIAN CHURCH was McIntire's creation following his break with J. Gresham Machen due to doctrinal differences and personality conflict. The institutions connected with the Bible Presbyterian Church include Faith Theological Seminary of Elkins Park, Pa., Shelton College (formerly National Bible Institute) of New York City, and Highland College of Pasadena, California. In 1950, the Bible Presbyterians reported 7,425 adherents in sixty-nine congregations. McIntire's church in Collingswood, N. J., is by far the largest, claiming 1,600 members. The *Christian Beacon* serves unofficially as the mouthpiece of the Bible Presbyterian Church and the American Council. It has claimed a paid circulation of approximately 25,000.

The BIBLE PROTESTANT CHURCH is a small segment of the old Eastern Conference of the Methodist Protestant Church, which joined with two other branches of Methodism in 1939 to form the Methodist Church. The approximate membership of the Bible Protestant Church is 2,100. It publishes a monthly, *Bible Protestant Messenger*. One leader of the sect, Newton C. Conant, wrote the 100-page, paper-bound book, *Present-Day Methodism and the Bible* (Sword of the Lord Publishers, Wheaton, Ill., 1949). Conant's book is a favorite text among ultra-fundamentalists; Gerald Winrod, for example, has stated: "It should be read, and studied by professing Christians of all denominations" (*The Defender Magazine,* March 1950, p. 12).

Three other A.C.C.C. affiliates stem from the Methodist merger. One, the "METHODIST PROTESTANT CHURCH" has no legal existence, since that denomination joined the Methodist Church. Its membership has been estimated at 6,000, most of whom reside in Mississippi. The ASSOCIATED GOSPEL CHURCHES, INC., includes about twenty-five congregations that broke with the Methodist Protestant Church in 1939. First known as the American Bible Fellowship Association, the sect now has about 3,000 members. A third denomination, the SOUTHERN METHODIST CHURCH, with scattered congregations mainly in the Carolinas, Tennessee, and Georgia, claims 8,500 members.

In 1946, a group of ministers met in Memphis to organize the Evangelical Methodist Church, which soon joined the American Council. In 1952 it withdrew, however; said *United Evangelical Action* (Nov. 1, 1952, p. 18): "After years of 'boss rule' by an American Council minority the Evangelical Methodist Church voted at its seventh annual conference . . . to join the National Association of Evangelicals.

"Dr. W. W. Breckbill of Altoona, Pa., president of the American Council of Christian Churches, led his faction out of the meeting in a dramatic finale to the conference sessions, Dr. Breckbill said his group would organize an 'Evangelical Congregational Methodist Bible-Believing Church.' " Breckbill still claims the name, Evangelical Methodist Church, and both sides have threatened legal action. According to Lucian Smith, one of the two General Superintendents of the majority group (led by J. H. Hamblen of Abilene, Texas), the Breckbill faction includes only four churches: "one was a rural church in the Tennessee mountains, one city church and the church in Altoona, and a church of 17 members in Mississippi" (letter, May 15, 1953). Smith added: "Our loss is hardly realized numerically, financially, or spiritually."

The largest of the A.C.C.C. affiliates is the GENERAL ASSOCIATION OF REGULAR BAPTIST CHURCHES, founded in 1932 (see Chapter 14, p. 347). In 1942 it joined the A.C.C.C.; today it accounts for more than half of the members in the A.C.C.C.'s constituent denominations. The sect claims over 135,000 members and 650 churches — figures considered by many observers to be grossly exaggerated. Its denominational publication is the *Baptist Bulletin.* *United Evangelical Action* has reported that as of Jan. 1, 1950, a high percentage of the Regular Baptist congregations had not approved membership in the A.C.C.C.

A union of various autonomous churches in 1940 produced the INDEPENDENT FUNDAMENTAL CHURCHES OF AMERICA which, in 1946, claimed 65,000 adherents in 650 churches. Its publication is *Voice.* Garman, former A.C.C.C. president, is one of the sect's leaders. (Note: The sect withdrew on April 27, 1953.)

Three other denominations in the United States are listed as A.C.C.C. affiliates: CONFERENCE OF FUNDAMENTAL CHURCHES with approximately 4,000 members; FUNDAMENTAL CONFERENCE OF AMERICA, reporting 54 members [it did not specify whether this meant churches or persons]; TIOGA RIVER CHRISTIAN CONFERENCE with 1,500 members. The last of these refused to join the Congregational-Christian merger in 1931.

In Canada, the American Council claims two affiliates. The UNION OF REGULAR BAPTIST CHURCHES OF ONTARIO AND QUEBEC has a membership approximating 5,000. In 1949, its founder T. T. Shields was not re-elected as its president and, in a huff, departed with about 1,500 followers. The larger group may withdraw from the A.C.C.C., as plans are being worked out for a merger with the Fellowship of Independent Baptist Churches in Canada. Meanwhile, Shields has formed a Conservative Baptist Association of Canada. With his assistant, H. C. Slade, and McIntire, he has established the Canadian Council of Evangelical Protestant Churches.

The National Fellowship of Brethren Churches refuses to join the American Council, and it has allowed itself to be represented in radio matters only. As noted in the text, the Old (Evangelical) Catholic Church appears to be defunct; the Iowa Eldership of Churches of God in North America has withdrawn.

McIntire has referred to the 250,000-member American Baptist Association (with headquarters in Texarkana, Ark.-Tex.) as an "auxiliary" member of the American Council. This assertion is false. The American Baptist Association does not subscribe to what it refers to as the A.C.C.C.'s "universal church idea." In 1949, the "messenger body" of the American Baptist Association adopted a resolution expressing sympathy for the A.C.C.C.'s opposition to the Federal Council; otherwise, however, there has been no connection whatsoever between the two groups.

Two other "denominations" deserve special attention because their association with the American Council graphically illustrates A.C.C.C.'s irresponsibility in checking the merits of its "constituent" members before they are admitted.

(1) The *Christian Beacon* twice reported the admission of the American Episcopal Church (Evangelical) into the American Council (May 18, 1944; Oct. 12, 1944). Leader of the new affiliate was "The Rt. Rev. D. Scott Swain, L. L. D., S. T. D., Bishop, and President of Temple Hall College and Seminary, in Chicago." In Swain's *Evangelical Churchman* for Oct.-Nov. 1944 the good Bishop proudly announced the association of his "denomination" with the McIntire faction In "Bishop Swain's Episcopal Letter to the Faithful," he notified his "followers" that: "We by Divine Providence Bishop in the Church of God, Overseer in the Flock of Christ, desire to inform the Faithful Evangelical Christians in Our jurisdiction that the American Episcopal Church is in full and complete harmony with the witness and testimony of the American Council of Christians." The same issue highlighted a message from Robert T. Ketcham, then A.C.C.C. president, who was described by Swain as "without doubt the most outstanding preacher in America today."

According to Elmer T. Clark's *The Small Sects in America* (Abingdon-Cokesbury, 1949, p. 173), Swain was ordained in 1942 by an Archbishop Carfora of the North American Old Roman Catholic Church; within a year, however, he was suspended "because he obtained his ordination through misrepresentation." Swain reported numerous churches and a membership running up to 100,000. At one time, he was listed in *Who's Who in America.* It noted that he received a degree of Doctor of Laws from an unlocated college at the age of nineteen, and that in 1936 he received a degree of Bachelor of Divinity from an unknown St. Paul Theological Seminary. Swain claimed to have entered the ministry and received ordination as bishop both in the same year.

As president of Temple Hall College and Seminary, one of Swain's chief responsibilities was to operate as successfully as possible a prosperous diploma mill. On one occasion, when in New York City, the good Bishop became uproariously drunk and distributed free Ph.D.'s to the entire audience. Several "apostles of discord" received their Ph.D.'s from Temple Hall. One of them was Allen Alderson Zoll of the National Council for American Education.

Swain's training for the bishopric included a four-year penitentiary term (1934-38) for running a confidence game. During 1936 he was paroled, but when he passed a bogus check he was sent back to prison. A writer in the *American Lutheran* (Nov. 1947) refers to Swain as a "several times married ex-convict."

In Nov. 1944, *after* his American Episcopal Church had been welcomed into the American Council, Swain sent messages on "denominational" stationery to hundreds of ministers, urging them to sign a petition which requested that the Illinois attorney general refrain from interfering in the work of the so-called Gentile Co-operative Association, headed by Eugene R. Fitcraft, who published the flagrant *Gentile News.* In Jan. 1945, Swain formed the American Christian Civil Liberties Institute "to protect Gentiles from the Jews."

Finally, on May 2, 1945, the American Council dropped Swain and his American Episcopal Church (Evangelical) from its rolls. The episode serves, however, to demonstrate the carelessness of the McIntire faction in admitting new denominations.

(2) A second suspect denomination remains on A.C.C.C. rolls, the UNITED CHRISTIAN CHURCH OF AMERICA. Its late "Presiding Bishop" was the "Rt. Rev." Alexander A. Lowande; its current top "Bishop" is the Rev. Herbert J. Elliott, Th.D., D.D. Unlike the American Episcopal Church (Evangelical), the

United Christian Church of America appears to have a few legitimate churches, though "Bishop" Elliott does not seem to be quite sure how many members there are in his denomination. "Several thousand," he has suggested.

"Bishop" Alexander A. Lowande appears to have founded the sect, although here again there is considerable doubt. In the denominational handbook, "Edited and Published by Authority of the General Council," it is suggested that the history of the group "seems to have commenced at Baltimore City in 1893." In any case, it appears to have been reorganized in the 1940's. Like Swain, Lowande had an unusual preparation for his high calling: he was a former bare-back rider in a small circus who one day took to religion. In 1932, claiming to be an "investigator," he was indicted for carrying a concealed weapon. In 1936 he served three and one-half months in the New York County jail for attempting to "arrest" persons under false pretenses.

Lowande played a leading role in a religious fraud perpetrated with the assistance of Edward James Smythe, frequently intoxicated racketeer whose lengthy record is summarized in Chapter 7. Among other dubious accomplishments, Smythe's Protestant War Veterans has been included on the official list of subversive organizations prepared by the United States Attorney General. "Bishop" Lowande headed Smythe's Protestant Chaplains' Association, which had been incorporated by Smythe, Donald Shea, leader of the National Gentile League, and a Wilson Pumphrey. In 1944, Smythe — then under indictment for alleged sedition against the United States government — joined Lowande in promoting a "National Day of Prayer." Smythe secured the co-operation of numerous governors, congressmen, and even the White House in pushing his hoax. The Smythe-Lowande plot fell through, however, when the records of the two men were exposed. Throughout this episode, Lowande's denomination appears to have remained as an A.C.C.C. affiliate.

More recently, "Bishop" Elliott's United Christian Church of America has been attempting to exploit the reputation of a legitimate sect in Pennsylvania, the United Christian Church, which broke from the United Brethren Church in Christ in 1864. On many occasions, Elliott intentionally has sought to convey the impression that the two denominations are the same. Actually, there has never been any association whatever between them; for example, the reputable United Christian Church has no bishops.

In spite of these facts — of which the American Council is aware — the United Christian Church of America remains on the A.C.C.C.'s rolls. Moreover, it is listed in A.C.C.C. literature as the United Christian Church — hence, giving many people the impression that the Pennsylvania group is a constituent member. Meanwhile, "Bishop" Elliott directs the activities of his flock from his hardware store in Brooklyn.

In summary, therefore, the following table presents an approximate picture of the denominations affiliated with the American Council:

Associated Gospel Churches, Inc.	3,000
Bible Presbyterian Church	8,000
Bible Protestant Church	2,300
Conference of Fundamental Churches	4,000
Fundamental Conference of America	no report
General Association of Regular Baptist Churches	130,000
Methodist Protestant Church	6,000
Southern Methodist Church	8,300
Tioga River Christian Conference	1,300

Conservative Baptist Association of Canada	1,500
Union of Regular Baptist Churches of Ontario and Quebec	5,000

If the claims of the constituent denominations are accepted at face value, these figures total approximately 170,000.

After this book had gone to press, the Independent Fundamental Churches of America voted to withdraw from the American Council. Many observers see in this action further evidence that the American Council is rapidly losing strength.

The International Council includes one more American denomination, the Free Magyar Reformed Church in America, with a membership of about 7,000. The Orthodox Presbyterian Church, founded by J. Gresham Machen, withdrew from the International Council in July 1952.

When confronted with the facts, McIntire contends that the balance of his 1,500,000 followers are accounted for by the other types of membership (none of which, incidentally, have voting privileges) — (1) members of individual constituent churches; (2) individual members; (3) members of local auxiliaries; (4) individual auxiliaries. If McIntire's contention is true, the A.C.C.C. should produce the sources of its membership, as all reputable groups are willing to do.

Finally, the size of any group of course does not determine the merit or demerit of its cause. The statistics of the McIntire faction are important here only to expose the exorbitant claims which it has made.

PAGE 199. Winrod's remarks are from the pamphlet *Persecuted Preachers* (Defender Publishers, no date).

PAGE 200. Springer's diatribes against Judaism in 1940 were reported in *The Defender Magazine*, Nov. 1940, p. 3. The seventh printing of *Termites* (1940) is being circulated at the present time; over 27,000 have been sold. The quotations from it are from pages 9 and 48. In *Termites*, Springer quotes liberally from Winrod (who wrote the introduction), Elizabeth Dilling, W. B. Riley, Robert Edmondson, and E. N. Sanctuary (all discussed in Chapter 3). Springer referred to Smith in *Western Voice*, June 17, 1943, p. 1.

McIntire's remarks are from the *Christian Beacon*, April 8, 1948, p. 3.

PAGE 201. Garman's deposition was carried out by the Presbytery of Conemaugh of the United Presbyterian Church upon the recommendation of a special commission appointed to study his case. The denunciation of Garman by the O.D.T. was noted in a release of the Religious News Service, June 7, 1945.

Breckbill's break with the Evangelical Methodist Church is discussed in the note for pages 197-198.

Shields's divisive career was summarized in *Maclean's* magazine, June 15, 1949.

Chapter 9

"Modernism"— and the "Battle of the Bible"

PAGE 203. The Rocky Mount "Bible-burning" was reported in newspapers across the nation; e.g., the New York *Times*, Dec. 1, 1952, p. 13.

PAGE 204. The comments of the *Christian Standard* are from its issue of Dec. 6, 1952, p. 2. The McIntire remarks were quoted in the Denver *Post*, Dec. 10, 1952, p. 29.

PAGE 205. McIntire's reference to Isaiah 7:14 is from his pamphlet *The New*

Bible: Why Christians Should Not Accept It (p. 4) Weigle's explanation was quoted in several papers; e.g., the Washington *Post*, Oct. 1, 1952. McIntire contended that the R.S.V. was designed to weaken his "movement" in the *Christian Beacon*, Nov. 6, 1952, p. 8.

PAGE 206. McIntire condemned Orlinsky's co-operation in the *Christian Beacon*, Oct. 9, 1952, p. 4. He charged "modernism" in the *Christian Beacon*, Oct. 23, 1952. He accused the National Council of monetary concern in *The New Bible . . .*, p. 12. He advised his readers against purchase in the *Christian Beacon*, Sept. 25, 1952, p. 1.

PAGE 207. Ecumenical leaders were maligned in the *Christian Beacon*, Sept. 25, 1952, p. 8. McIntire outlined nine steps in the issue of Oct. 30, 1952, p. 1.

PAGE 208. The statements quoted are from the following sources: *Baptist Bible Tribune*, Feb. 15, 1952, p. 6; *Militant Truth*, Vol. 11, No. 3-11-52-55, p. 1; *Evangelist and Bible Teacher*, Jan. 15, 1952, p. 3; *Western Voice*, Dec. 5, 1952, p. 3; Winrod, *The Defender Magazine* of Oct. 1952, p. 7, and Nov. 1952, p. 8. *The Defender Magazine* praised the McIntire faction in its issues of March 1947 (p. 22) and Dec. 1946 (p. 22).

PAGE 209. Grube contributed to *The Defender Magazine*, Dec. 1952, pp. 7-9. Smith admired McIntire's work (while criticizing his "softness" toward Jews) in *The Cross and the Flag*, June 1948, p. 5. He offered McIntire's pamphlet in his letter of Feb. 7, 1953.

The Methodist clergyman is Paul Beck, Jr.; his letter was dated Oct. 19, 1952.

PAGE 210. Murch's comments were from *United Evangelical Action*, Nov. 15, 1952, pp. 8-9. The same periodical carried six articles by Oswald T. Allis against the R.S.V., two in favor of it. Greenlee's review appeared in the issue of Dec. 1, 1952. Bradbury's comments are from *The Watchman-Examiner*, April 30, 1953.

PAGE 211. *The Fundamentalist's* comment was in the issue of Dec. 19, 1952. (Soon thereafter, *The Fundamentalist* became the organ of the World Baptist Fellowship, headed by Harvey S. Springer.)

McIntire's remarks are from *Modern Tower of Babel*, p. 133: J. Harold Smith's are from the *Christian Beacon*, May 9, 1946, p. 1.

PAGE 212. Smith's more frantic charge was quoted in *Harper's Magazine*, Aug. 1949, p. 72 ("J. Harold Smith and the Dogs of Sin" by James Rorty).

The "Edinburgh Affirmation of Unity" is used frequently in ecumenical circles today. On Pentecost, 1952, for example, it was printed on the back of a special program brochure distributed by the World Council of Churches.

PAGE 213. Attempts have been made to change the theological basis for admission into the National Council, both in the direction of a more inclusive fellowship and a less inclusive fellowship (see, for example, the *Workbook* of the Second General Assembly of the National Council, p. 120). The ousting of the Unitarians from the United Council of Church Women was reported in the *Christian Register*, March 1952, p. 23.

PAGE 214. The anonymous fundamentalist protest is frequently employed.

PAGE 215. Barth's debate with Niebuhr was reported in *Time*, Dec. 20, 1948, and Jan. 10, 1949.

United Evangelical Action's remarks are from its issue of May 1, 1952, p. 17; McIntire's from the *Christian Beacon*, Oct. 2, 1952, p. 4.

PAGE 216. Schaeffer's remarks are from his address, "The New Modernism," delivered at the Second Plenary Congress of the International Council, Aug. 16-23, 1950.

McIntire's remarks are from *Twentieth Century Reformation* (Christian Beacon Press, 1946), p. 99.

PAGE 217. The World Council statement is from its *Findings and Decisions* (in pamphlet form), p. 53.

McIntire's remarks are from *Twentieth Century Reformation,* pp. 123, 131, and 111, respectively. The A.C.C.C.'s 1948 and 1951 resolutions were reported by the Religious News Service, Oct. 29, 1948, and Jan. 8, 1951. Garman's statement is from his pamphlet *What Is Wrong With the Federal Council?* (1950 revision), p. 9.

PAGE 218. The A.C.C.C.'s resolution on U.M.T. and investigation of the clergymen were reported by the Religious News Service on April 6, 1948, and Aug. 11, 1948, respectively. It is interesting that the N.A.E. sharply takes issue with the McIntire faction on methods of preparedness; in April 1952, for example, the N.A.E. passed a strong resolution condemning U.M.T.

McIntire's denial of the brotherhood of man is from *Twentieth Century Reformation,* p. 60. The A.C.C.C.'s denunciation of Brotherhood Week was reported by the Religious News Service, May 2, 1949. In May 1953, McIntire asked Eisenhower to withhold his endorsement of Brotherhood Week (*Christian Beacon,* May 21, 1953, p. 3). He charged that church literature will "destroy the races" in *The Rise of the Tyrant,* p. 190. His characterizations of the civil-rights program are from the *Christian Beacon,* July 22, 1948, p. 8, and July 5, 1951, p. 8.

PAGE 219. Hamilton represented the A.C.C.C. before a Massachusetts legislative committee, Feb. 20, 1947. McIntire promised *Making Black White* in *Author of Liberty* (Christian Beacon Press, 1946), p. 173. The A.C.C.C. resolution on FEPC was quoted by McIntire in *Russia's Most Effective Fifth Column in America* (1948), p. 29. The 1950 resolution was quoted in *Western Voice,* June 23, 1950, p. 2.

PAGE 220. The Garman release was dated April 15, 1949. Denton's "Bible-burning" was reported in the Akron *Beacon Journal,* Dec. 8, 1952, p. 1.

The statements in commendation of McIntire and the A.C.C.C. are from the following sources: Mrs. Dilling, *Patriotic Research Bureau* (newsletter), Sept. 1943, p. 16; Lovell, *Kingdom Digest,* Aug. 1945, p. 5; *Georgia Tribune,* Aug. 7, 1947, p. 5; Hudson, *America-In-Danger,* March 21, 1945, p. 3; Williams, letter of Sept. 7, 1951; KKK, undated Newsletter of the Imperial Council.

PAGE 221. McIntire's attack upon the World Council is from the "Call" to the 1948 I.C.C.C. Amsterdam meeting; on Mackay, from *Twentieth Century Reformation,* p. 90; on Oxnam, from the *Christian Beacon,* Nov. 8, 1945, p. 1. Ironically enough, Mackay and Oxnam are both accused of anti-Catholicism in some circles.

For examples of how *Our Sunday Visitor* has used A.C.C.C. charges to discredit Protestant leadership, see its issues for March 4, 1951, p. 4; April 8, 1951, p. 2; and Jan. 20, 1952, p. 11.

PAGE 222. *Who's Who in the POAU?* was discussed in Chapter 7. Bordeaux's letter appears in the edition of March 28, 1951, pp. 159-60.

Accounts of the "Frank Fay Rally" and McIntire's role in it appeared in several New York papers: e.g., the *World Telegram,* Jan. 18, 1946, and Jan. 30, 1946.

PAGE 224. The N.A.E.'s resentment was voiced by Stephen W. Paine in *"Separation" — Is Separating Evangelicals;* the quotation is from page 7. One of the many interesting points that Paine makes in his pamphlet is that McIntire and other A.C.C.C. leaders did not fly the "separation" banner until they had been ejected from their denominations. Many A.C.C.C. leaders, he points out, "never made a personal decision to withdraw from their former denominations . . . they stayed in the denomination until they were ejected by action of the church. Yes, they even protested their ejection and appealed to the highest denominational court to reinstate them in their membership privileges in this denomination" (p. 5).

McIntire's remarks are from the following sources: "leaving room for Barthians," *Modern Tower of Babel,* pp. 282-83; against Graham, *The Testimony of Separation,* pp. 88-95; "occupying the middle road," *Christian Beacon,* Dec. 16, 1948, p. 2; against Pentecostal groups, *Twentieth Century Reformation,* p. 202.

PAGE 225. The A.C.C.C.'s 1949 resolution is quoted by McIntire in *Testimony of Separation,* p. 84. The 1950 attack on the I.V.C.F. is noted in Paine's *"Separation" — Is Separating Evangelicals,* p. 41. Shields' remarks are from the *Gospel Witness and Protestant Advocate,* March 6, 1952, p. 3.

Wright's comments are from a letter, Sept. 18, 1952. Ockenga is quoted in *Testimony of Separation,* p. 76.

PAGE 226. Graham's remarks are quoted in *United Evangelical Action,* July 1, 1951. In them, Graham appeared to endorse the Paine pamphlet attacking the McIntire faction. Ayer's statement was quoted by the Federal Council in its pamphlet, *Forces Disrupting the Churches.* Bradbury's remarks are from *The Watchman-Examiner,* Nov. 27, 1952, p. 1099.

Rees's criticism of the American Council was quoted in the New York *Times,* April 15, 1953. The text of Rees's presidential address was published in *United Evangelical Action* of May 15, 1953. Among other keen observations, Rees stated: "American evangelicals should be put on notice that the majority of their conservative brethren in Britain and on the continent of Europe do not view the World Council of Churches with the same alarm or aversion that we display on this side of the Atlantic."

Chapter 10
Seeing "Red"

PAGE 230. Mrs. Dilling's remarks are from the dedication and page 62 of *The Red Network.* Her recent comments are from a newsletter headed "Red Churchmen" (no date).

PAGE 231. Kamp's attack on the YWCA was entitled *Behind the Lace Curtains of the YWCA* (Constitutional Educational League, Inc., 1948). The statement is from page 10.

PAGE 232. Williams' remarks are from the *Williams Intelligence Summary,* Feb. 1952, p. 2.

Flynn's *The Road Ahead* was published in 1949 by the Devin Adair Company of New York. Chapter X was drastically revised in the fourth printing of the special edition distributed by the Committee for Constitutional Government. Perhaps its most incongruous item was Flynn's stout endorsement of McIntire and the A.C.C.C. Apparently Flynn has no aversions to the American Council's fanatical denunciations of his faith. The Federal Council replied to Flynn in a pamphlet, *The Truth About the Federal Council of Churches,* Jan. 6, 1950.

PAGE 233. Peale's remarks are from copies of the original letters.

PAGE 234. Hart's attack on the U.N. is from his Economic Council Letter, No. 206; his criticism of Zionists was quoted in *A Measure of Freedom,* p. 67. For the Buchanan committee reference to Hart, see the Interim Report of the House Select Committee on Lobbying Activities, 81st Congress, Second Session, p. 22.

Robnett outlines the purposes of his organization in a flyer, "What is the Church League of America and the National Laymen's Council?" He referred to "religionists" in *News and Views,* Sept. 1951, p. 1. His remarks concerning "minorityism" are quoted in *The Facts,* May 1951, p. 3.

PAGE 235. Moore's remarks are from *National Republic* of Oct. 1951.

A regular contributor to *National Republic* deserving of brief mention is Evangelist Dan Gilbert, who mixes extreme rightist politics with large doses of fundamentalism. Gilbert edits an irregular *Washington News-Bulletin,* sent out from 511 Eleventh St., N. W., the same address as that of *National Republic.* In the religious realm, Gilbert engages in such worthy activities as the formation of "Ex-Convicts for Christ Clubs." He sponsors a "Prisoners Bible Broadcast" each weekday evening over the high-powered Mexican station, XERF. Through the years, Gilbert has served as a leader in numerous fundamentalist conclaves, such as the World's Christian Fundamentals Association, founded by W. B. Riley (discussed in Chapters 3 and 14). Some have accused Gilbert of sharing Riley-style anti-Semitism, but there appears to be no evidence to support such a charge. In fact, unlike Riley, he was firmly opposed to the Winrod faction.

PAGE 236. Murch's remarks are from *The Growing Super-Church,* pp. 36, 62, 64, 65. The attack on Bennett is on page 42. Bennett's remark is from page 9 of *Communism and Christianity* (Association Press, New York, 1951).

PAGE 237. Gordon's attack on the N.C.C.J. extends from page 45 to 50 in *An Ecclesiastical Octopus* (Fellowship Press, Boston, 1948).

The Robnett articles appeared in March and April, 1952.

PAGE 238. McIntire's remarks are from *Rise of the Tyrant,* pages 253 and 232, respectively. The A.C.C.C.'s criticism of Dulles was reported by the Religious News Service, Nov. 1, 1948. In 1952, the McIntire faction voiced the same sentiment; e.g., *Christian Beacon,* Nov. 6, 1952, p. 8.

PAGE 239. *The Protestant's* remark is from its issue for April-May-June 1950, p. 3. Foster's blast is from page 3 of the *Daily Worker* of April 28, 1953.

The *Christian Beacon* of Jan. 24, 1952, attacked Taft.

McIntire's remark is from *Modern Tower of Babel,* p. 102.

PAGE 240. McIntire's query is from the *Christian Beacon* of Nov. 22, 1951, p. 8. The A.C.C.C.'s resolution was reported in the *Christian Beacon,* Nov. 6, 1952, p. 1.

PAGE 241. Bundy's remarks on page 241 (and the following page) are from an address delivered at a McIntire conference in Latin America in 1951. It has been printed in pamphlet form and in several publications; e.g., *Militant Truth,* Vol. 10, No. 10-9-51-50.

PAGE 242. Bordeaux's remark was quoted in the New York *Times* of March 11, 1953, p. 12. The A.C.C.C. petition was reported in the issue for March 14, 1953, p. 8. The mass meeting was announced in the *Christian Beacon,* March 26, 1953. According to the *Christian Beacon* of May 14, 1952, 25,000 signatures were presented to Rep. Donald L. Jackson of California.

PAGE 243. Oxnam's remark was reported in many newspapers; e.g., the New York *Times,* March 11, 1953, p. 12. Jackson's attack is recorded in the *Congressional Record,* March 17, 1953, p. 2102. The Washington *Post* carried Oxnam's reply on April 5, 1953.

PAGE 244. The statement of the Council of Bishops was reported in the New York *Times* of May 2, 1953, p. 17.

McIntire's remark is from page 3 of *Bishop Oxnam, Prophet of Marx.* This pamphlet was circulated widely and reprinted in some publications; e.g., John R. Rice's *Sword of the Lord,* May 29, 1953.

Kaub's remarks are from his leaflet, *Shall Our Churches Teach Christianity or Communism?*

PAGE 245. *Jesus: A Capitalist* was written by Ray Carroll, Montana author of *The Pixylated Prophet* (contending that Karl Marx was a mental case) and editor of the weekly newsletter *Freedom's Forum.* The quotation is from page 4.

PAGE 246. Kaub's remarks to the editors of *Our Sunday Visitor* were published in *Who's Who in the POAU?* (discussed in Chapter 7), p. 154.

How Red is the Federal (National) Council of Churches? was answered by the National Council in *Plain Facts,* April 24, 1953.

Smith's remarks are from *The Cross and the Flag* of March 1951 (p. 24) and Sept. 1952 (p. 8).

PAGE 249. Kaub's assertion is from page 6 of his brochure. Winrod's remarks are from *The Defender Magazine,* Sept. 1948, p. 6.

PAGE 250. Zoll's record has been brought before the public on many occasions. In 1948, for example, when he founded the National Council for American Education, Pulitzer-prize winner Frederick Woltman of the Scripps-Howard newspapers exposed him in an article headed: "Zoll, Hate-Monger, Promotes New Racket" (New York *World-Telegram,* Aug. 25, 1948). Accounts of Zoll's activities also have appeared in such publications as *McCall's* magazine (e.g., Sept. 1951, Sept. 1952); Arnold Forster's *A Measure of Freedom; The Nation's Schools* (e.g., Jan. 1951, Feb. 1951); *Saturday Review of Literature* (Sept. 8, 1951) — and other sources. For the interesting story of his 1953 marriage to the widow of a millionaire Texas oilman, see the New York *World-Telegram* of April 24, 1953 (p. 3), and *Time,* of May 4, 1953 (p. 100).

Chapter 11

The Hammer and Sickle Behind the Cross

PAGE 252. The advance release of the Interfaith Committee was dated Oct. 1, 1951.

PAGE 253. The *Daily Worker* summary was from its issue of Oct. 8, 1951, p. 3.

PAGE 255. Ironically, Leslie's denunciation of the National Conference of

Christians and Jews was quoted on page 47 of Gordon's *An Ecclesiastical Octopus* (discussed in Chapter 10).

The statements of the Jewish agencies are from a memorandum entitled "The Protestant" distributed by the National Community Relations Advisory Council (Sept. 24, 1946).

PAGE 256. Leslie's anti-Zionist statement is from *The Protestant,* Vol. IX, No. 4, p. 2.

The career of Leslie was traced by Frederick Woltman in the New York *World-Telegram,* Feb. 9, 1944.

PAGE 257. The 1946 schism was reported in many New York newspapers; e.g., *The Times,* Nov. 11, 1946.

The Protestant released the telegram on behalf of Wallace on Jan. 9, 1948.

Leslie's Korea issue, entitled "Common Sense About Korea," was dated July-Aug.-Sept. 1950. His remarks are from pages 7, 16, and 15, respectively.

PAGE 258. Powell's action was reported in the *World-Telegram,* July 17, 1950.

Leslie's acrid attacks against the World Council and its leadership continue in nearly every issue of *The Protestant.* The quotations are from the issues of July-Aug.-Sept. 1950 (p. 10), July-Aug.-Sept. 1951 (p. 11), and July-Aug.-Sept. 1952 (pp. 6, 12).

Henry Smith Leiper was former American secretary of the World Council of Churches; Henry P. Van Dusen, president of Union Theological Seminary in New York City, has been a pioneer in the ecumenical movement; W. A. Visser t'Hooft is General Secretary of the World Council.

PAGE 259. Belfrage's biography of Williams is entitled *A Faith to Free the People* (Dryden Press, 1944). It had been published in England in 1939 as *Let My People Go* and in New York in 1940 as *South of God.* Since the writing of this chapter, Belfrage, a British subject, has been confined to Ellis Island to await deportation hearings. Among the complaints against him, according to Attorney General Herbert Brownell, is that he was formerly research director of the People's Institute of Applied Religion.

Williams' remarks against organized religion are from his handbook, *Religion: Barrier or Bridge to a People's World* (1947), p. 5.

PAGE 260. Williams' secret membership was reported by Frederick Woltman in the New York *World-Telegram,* Aug. 27, 1947.

Williams' remarks reportedly were made at a public assembly in Denver, Colorado, May 17, 1946. This quotation frequently is used by professional vigilantes (discussed in Chapter 10) in an attempt to discredit the National Council of Churches and the Presbyterian Church in the U. S. A.

PAGE 261. Williams' remarks on pages 261-63 are from *Religion: Barrier or Bridge to a People's World.*

PAGE 264. The 1952 E.L.S.A. discussion of peace was reported in *The Witness,* June 26, 1952.

PAGE 265. The Peace Prayer Vigil was lauded in *The Witness* of Oct. 25, 1951, p. 4. Forbes' account of the Crusade for Peace is in the issue of March 29, 1951, p. 3. The article "Our Ostrich Government" is on page 6 of the issue of August 21, 1952.

PAGE 266. Endicott's remarks were made in an address in Canada on May 11, 1952. Uphaus' article was published in *The Witness* of Jan. 29, 1953, pp. 14-16.

Spofford's comments were expressed in a letter of March 9, 1952, the contents of which were repeated in a *Witness* editorial.

PAGE 267. The *New Leader* article of April 16, 1949, entitled "America's Red Dean," was written by Anatole Shub. Woltman's attack is from the New York *World-Telegram* of Aug. 21, 1947.

PAGE 268. Friends of Democracy circulated a 10-page brochure against Shipler and *The Churchman* (no date). Birkhead's remark is from page 9 of the brochure. The *Living Church* was quoted on page 8.

PAGE 269. The materials used in the summary of the Melish case included clippings, leaflets, pamphlets, etc., many of them undated. The pro-Melish forces, organized as the Melish Case Defense Committee, published two booklets, *The Melish Case* and *The Story of a Congregation*. The legal aspects of the case are considered in Leo Pfeffer's *Church, State, and Freedom* (Beacon Press, Boston, 1953), pp. 251-256.

PAGE 273. Philbrick writes of Martha Fletcher's communist ties on pages 246, 254-57, and 293 of *I Led Three Lives* (McGraw-Hill, New York, 1952).

PAGE 275. Arnold's statement, "A high proportion . . .," is quoted from his analysis of the policy slant of the *Christian Register,* written on Nov. 8, 1946.

The statement of policy by the division of publications is taken from "An informal guide in the selection of authors and editorial contributors" written on Feb. 7, 1947. This is from the final draft, other drafts having been written in the several months preceding this statement.

The letter to Stephen Fritchman was sent on April 30, 1947, and printed by the American Unitarian Association under the title: "Letter from the Director of the Division of Publications, American Unitarian Association, to the Editor of *The Christian Register* (in Denver)."

PAGE 277. A "Letter to Unitarians" was first printed on July 1, 1947, and signed by thirty-two persons. Reprinted on August 1, 1947, it contained sixty-nine additional signatures.

PAGE 278. Phelps' letter was published in *Soviet Russia Today,* Nov. 1950. Another paragraph read: "Ninety-five per cent of the U. S. press on the Far East is absolutely false. Believe the opposite, and you will be close to the facts. The South Korean Government first attacked North Korea. It seems that only *Soviet Russia Today* and Harry Ward's Social Action Bulletin of the M. E. Federation are about the only trustworthy papers in the U. S. now." According to Phelps, the letter was written on Aug. 1, 1950, as a private letter. He added: "This private letter was published, without authorization, with such editorial alterations as to make it appear that it had been written directly and intentionally to the editor."

Phelps's statement before the mission board was released, along with the board's comments, on Jan. 22, 1952.

PAGE 282. Davis' *Classmate* article, entitled "Joseph Stalin," was on page 15 of the issue for July 20, 1947.

PAGE 283. Several other non-communists commented favorably on *War, Peace, and You.* On its jacket appeared endorsements from John Haynes Holmes, Abba Hillel Silver, E. Stanley Jones, and others who are not blind to the menacing policies of the Soviet Union.

Chapter 12
God and the "Libertarians"

PAGE 286. "We stand for free competitive enterprise . . ." is the slogan of *Christian Economics,* discussed later in this chapter.

Spiritual Mobilization's credo is quoted often: e.g., *Truth in Action,* Jan. 15, 1953, p. 3.

PAGE 288. Fifield's remarks were reported in *Time,* Feb. 14, 1949, p. 63.

PAGE 289. Fifield's reply to critics is from *Faith and Freedom,* Feb. 1952, p. 12.

PAGE 290. The *Social Action* magazine of May 15, 1951, was written by George Younger, now a Baptist pastor in Pennsylvania. His remarks are quoted from page 5. Spiritual Mobilization circulated a confidential refutation signed by James C. Ingebretsen, vice-president of Spiritual Mobilization.

Niebuhr's comments appeared in *The Reporter* of Feb. 19, 1952, p. 26. Fifield's retort is from *Faith and Freedom,* April 1952, p. 13. Opitz and Niebuhr dueled in the letters-to-the-editor column of *The Reporter* of May 27, 1952, p. 3.

McWilliams' remarks are from *The Nation,* Feb. 7, 1948, pp. 150-52. Ingebretsen's characterization of McWilliams (on the following page) is from the reply to *Social Action.*

PAGE 291. Nodel's remarks are from page 12 of his sermon delivered Dec. 5, 1952, and published in the *Beth Israel Pulpit.*

The two articles exposing *The Iron Curtain Over America* by John O. Beaty were written by V. Orval Watts, a West Coast economist.

The remarks on Spiritual Mobilization philosophy are from *Faith and Freedom,* Sept. 1951, p. 12, and *Theology of Freedom,* a pamphlet by Edmund A. Opitz, p. 16.

PAGE 292. Fifield's program is from *Faith and Freedom,* Sept. 1952, p. 13. His role in the Los Angeles battle against UNESCO materials has been reported in several articles; e.g., Mark A. Hennessey's "Saving Los Angeles from the U. N.," *The Reporter,* Nov. 11, 1952; Dorothy Frank's "I Was Called Subversive," *Collier's,* Mar. 28, 1953.

The criticisms of the social gospel are from the following sources: "pure socialism," *Faith and Freedom,* May 1952, p. 2; "ethical credentials" (Irving E. Howard), *Faith and Freedom,* May 1952, p. 7; *"socialized* covetousness" (Henry C. Link), *Reflections on Faith and Freedom,* p. 105.

Fifield's plea to clergymen is from *Faith and Freedom,* Jan. 1952, p. 10.

PAGE 293. The remark, "Men may differ . . .," is from "The Need of a Golden Calf" by Frank Chodorov, in *Faith and Freedom,* Oct. 1951, p. 6.

Fifield's expressions of alarm are from *Faith and Freedom* of Jan. 1952 (p. 10) and Dec. 1951 (p. 12). He approved of the proposed investigation in the issue of April 1953, p. 19. On page 20 of the same issue the editor takes a contrary view.

Fifield's 1949 survey was reported in the Chicago *Tribune,* Nov. 11, 1949, p. 12. The more recent claims are from *Faith and Freedom,* Feb. 1952 (p. 6) and March 1952 (p. 12).

PAGE 295. Kershner's opposition to pacifism was voiced in *Christian Economics* of Oct. 10, 1950 (p. 2) and Nov. 7, 1950 (p. 2). His comment on Roosevelt is from a letter, Dec. 4, 1952.

PAGE 297. The Vermont preacher (Joseph L. Sullivan) was quoted in *Christian Economics*, May 22, 1951, p. 3. Peale's letter was published in the issue of March 7, 1953, p. 3.

Other remarks on the page are from *Christian Economics* of Feb. 27, 1951 (p. 1) and Jan. 1, 1952 (p. 1).

PAGE 298. Kershner's ideas have been repeated in almost identical words in several speeches and radio broadcasts. The demagogic remarks, for example, are from page 22 of his address, "Ideological Conflicts and the Future"; page 8 of his radio message, "How Much is Freedom Worth?"; etc.

The Christian Freedom Foundation pamphlet was entitled *Christian Liberalism, The New Road to Tyranny*. The quotations are from pages 1 and 3.

PAGE 300. The original donors to the F.E.E. were reported to the House Select Committee on Lobbying Activities, 81st Congress, Second Session, known as the Buchanan committee.

Clinchy's remarks are from a letter, Dec. 5, 1952.

The quotations from F.E.E. spokesmen are from two essays, "Survival of the Species" by Ben Moreell and "Morals and the Welfare State" by F. A. Harper. Both essays are included in the Foundation anthology, *Essays on Liberty*, 1952.

PAGE 301. There has been no attempt in this chapter to present a thorough analysis and critique of so-called "libertarianism." A book scheduled for autumn publication will seek to do this: *Back to the Jungle*, by Herbert Stroup (Beacon Press, 1953). Robert McAfee Brown, former instructor at Union Theological Seminary in New York City, has published two interesting articles on *Christian Economics:* "Is it 'Christian Economics'?" in *Christianity and Crisis*, Nov. 27, 1950; "'Christian Economics' and Theology" in the *Union Seminary Quarterly Review*, June 1951.

PAGE 302. The Laymen's National Committee, Inc., sponsor of National Bible Week and National Sunday School Week, operates from swank headquarters in the Vanderbilt Hotel in New York City. Its chairman is Alfred P. Haake, an economist of the far right. Vice-chairman is George Peck, whose extremist column reportedly is distributed to 4,000 newspapers. Eighty-five per cent of the group's revenue comes from corporations; contributions are not accepted from churches. National chairman for 1952 was Earl Bunting, managing director of the National Association of Manufacturers; in 1953 it is Harry A. Bullis, chairman of the board of General Mills, Inc. Nearly one hundred top businessmen lend their names to the work of the Laymen's National Committee, Inc.

PAGE 303. The remarks of the *Christian Century* are from its issue of Dec. 13, 1950.

PAGE 304. Pew's contributions are listed with the following sources: to Kaub, *Minneapolis Star*, Nov. 30, 1950, p. 8; to McIntire, *ibid.;* to Fifield, *Social Action*, May 15, 1951, p. 19; to Kershner, *ibid.,* p. 21.

PAGE 305. The two 1952 National Council resolutions are recorded in the *Workbook* for the Second General Assembly, pp. 142, 143.

For evidence that Pew intends to continue his attempts to influence National Council policy, see *Christianity and Crisis*, May 12, 1952, p. 63.

PAGE 306. Niebuhr's remarks are from *The Reporter*, Feb. 19, 1952, p. 24.

Chapter 13

The Struggle Within Methodism

PAGE 308. The history of the Methodist Federation from 1907 to 1949 has been traced at Boston University in an unpublished dissertation by John Milton Huber, Jr.

PAGE 309. The General Conference resolutions of 1908, 1924, and 1932 were quoted by Bishop Herbert Welch in the *Christian Advocate,* June 22, 1950.

PAGE 310. Mrs. Dilling's remark is from her book, *The Roosevelt Red Record and Its Background* (1936), p. 280.

The 1935 Conference of Methodist Laymen is reported in the Huber dissertation (p. 220) and the *Social Questions Bulletin,* May 1936 (pp. 2-3). The 1936 General Conference resolutions are recorded in the *Daily Christian Advocate,* May 8, 1936, p. 170.

PAGE 311. The Schultz attack on alleged Protestant pro-communists appeared in the New York *World-Telegram,* Oct. 14, 1947.

All quotations from Woltman are from *The Facts,* a Scripps-Howard pamphlet mentioned in the text (not to be confused with a periodical of the same name published monthly by the Anti-Defamation League).

PAGE 312. Miller's letter was published in *The Churchman,* Feb. 15, 1948, p. 7. The Federation's Commission for Propaganda Analysis should not be confused with the defunct Institute for Propaganda Analysis.

High's remark is from page 138 of the *Reader's Digest* of Feb. 1950.

PAGE 313. Oxnam's remarks are from pages 8 and 9 of his reply to High. Muelder's reply appeared in *Zions Herald,* Feb. 15, 1950, p. 8; Marvin's answer was reprinted in the same issue of *Zions Herald,* p. 9.

PAGE 314. The error regarding the Epworth League — only one of many blunders in the first edition of *100 Things You Should Know . . .* — was corrected in later editions. In a letter to Rep. B. W. Kearney of New York on Nov. 29, 1948, six days after the Federation had been condemned, the Committee reported: "The Committee on Un-American Activities has never investigated nor cited the Methodist Federation for Social Action and there is very little information in file concerning the activities of the group."

Miller attacked the House Committee on Dec. 28, 1948.

PAGE 316. The *Christian Advocate* editorial appeared in its issue of March 6, 1952.

PAGE 318. The 1941 incident involving McMichael was reported in many newspapers at the time.

PAGE 320. The Mecartney brochure, sent to members of the Federation's Executive and National Committees, was answered by Professor Albert E. Barnett, then of the faculty of Garrett Biblical Institute (now at Chandler School of Theology at Emory University). He accused the Mecartney faction of seeking to transform M.F.S.A. into a "Socialist sect." In early 1953, however, Barnett resigned from the Federation, convinced that McMichael's "allegiance lay outside the Methodist framework."

PAGE 321. The bishops' resolution "On Stanley High's Article 'Methodism's Pink Fringe,'" was distributed in leaflet form. The *Christian Advocate* expressed its opinion in its issue of Feb. 9, 1950. The Methodist youth resolution was published in the *Christian Advocate,* Sept. 28, 1950, p. 11.

PAGE 322. Love's prepared remarks were never voiced on the floor of the General Conference; they were reported in the *Social Questions Bulletin* of June 1952, page 4. Those of Bucke were recorded in the issue of May 1952, page 4.

The General Conference resolution on M.F.S.A. read:

"Whereas, The Methodist Federation for Social Action is not now and never has been an official organization or agency of The Methodist Church, and;

"Whereas, The Methodist Church has no control over and is not responsible for the program or pronouncements of the Methodist Federation for Social Action (unofficial), and;

"Whereas, The Methodist Federation for Social Action (unofficial) has no right or authority to speak for or in the name of The Methodist Church, and;

"Whereas, The Methodist Federation for Social Action (unofficial) has continued the use of the word 'Methodist' in connection with its name despite a widespread objection to its doing so, and;

"Whereas, Many members of The Methodist Church have been embarrassed by certain pronouncements of the Methodist Federation for Social Action (unofficial) and by said Federation's continuance of the use of the word 'Methodist,' and;

"Whereas, The Board of Publication of The Methodist Church (an official agency of the church) has requested said federation to vacate the offices which it occupies in the Methodist Building at 150 Fifth Avenue, New York City, with which request said federation has not complied;

"Now, therefore, be it resolved by the 1952 General Conference of the Methodist Church:

"I. That we reaffirm the historic position of The Methodist Church that the General Conference of The Methodist Church is the only body authorized to speak for The Methodist Church.

"II. That The Methodist Church does not approve many of the statements and policies of the Methodist Federation for Social Action (unofficial).

"III. That the General Conference announces and emphasizes that the Methodist Federation for Social Action (unofficial) has no right to take any action which in any way might be construed as speaking for or reflecting the sentiment or position of The Methodist Church.

"IV. That we do hereby request The Methodist Federation for Social Action (unofficial) to remove the word 'Methodist' from its name; and we approve the action of the Board of Publication in requesting said Federation to terminate its occupancy of quarters in the Methodist Building at 150 Fifth Avenue, New York City.

"V. That we do reaffirm the historic position of The Methodist Church of the right of its people to interpret the Christian faith in the field of social and economic relations and to work to bring our social order more nearly into conformity with the teachings of Christ in accordance with the dictates of their own consciences."

PAGE 323. Bishop Love's letter of May 7, 1953, addressed to the Federation's executive committee, also gave as a reason for his immediate resignation the failure of the Federation, as of that date, to abide by the requests of the General Conference that it change its name and vacate its New York office. "As a good Methodist," the bishop wrote, "I believe we should conform to these requests coming from the governing body of our Church."

PAGE 324. The provisions for the Board of Social and Economic Relations are recorded in the Methodist *Discipline,* 1952, Par. 1555-1559. Throckmorton's remarks are from *The Pastor,* Jan. 1953, p. 7; Phifer's are from *Zions Herald,* Sept. 3, 1952, p. 5.

PAGE 326. Satterfield's remarks are from a letter to "Dear Friends" from Satterfield and Dewey Lane (Jackson, Mississippi), May 14, 1952.

PAGE 327. As of Feb. 1953, *Is There a Pink Fringe in the Methodist Church* had been through five printings. The quotation from the memorial is found on page 3.

PAGE 328. A startling account of the possible objectives of the Circuit Riders, Inc., was presented in a letter to the editor of *The Pastor,* Jan. 1953, p. 28.

PAGE 329. Shuler's remarks are from the following issues of *The Methodist Challenge:* Circuit Riders, Nov. 1952, p. 15; loyalty oath, April 1952, p. 4; capitalism, *ibid.;* pacifism, March 1951, p. 8.

PAGE 330. Shuler's early characterization of Smith is from *The Methodist Challenge,* July 1945, p. 13 (reprinted in *The Cross and the Flag,* Oct. 1945, p. 641). De Aryan's remarks are from *The Broom,* July 2, 1945, p. 1. Shuler's 1949 comment concerning Smith is from *The Methodist Challenge,* July 1949, p. 10; the more recent one is from the issue of May 1950, p. 4. Smith's remark is from *The Cross and the Flag,* Feb. 1948, p. 29.

Shuler's other remarks are from the following issues of *The Methodist Challenge:* MacArthur, Aug. 1952, p. 9; U.N., Dec. 1952, p. 14; Spain, Sept. 1951, p. 14; internationalism, July 1949, p. 10.

PAGE 331. The four critical letters quoted are from the *Methodist Challenge* of July 1951, p. 16; Sept. 1951, p. 16; Nov. 1951, p. 16; and March 1952, p. 16.

Shuler's references to Methodist leadership are from the *Methodist Challenge* of July 1952, p. 11; Nov. 1951, p. 4; and Sept. 1951, p. 1.

His reference to McIntire is from the *Methodist Challenge* of Jan. 1953, p. 2; to the Evangelical Methodist Church, March 1952, p. 5.

PAGE 332. Shuler's remark is from the *Methodist Challenge,* Dec. 1952, p. 1.

When people ask him why he does not leave the Methodist Church, Shuler writes them as follows:

"I get a great many inquiries as to why I do not come out of the Methodist Church, and there are many reasons I could mention, none of which might be altogether satisfactory to you.

"First of all, I am a Methodist, I believe in Methodist doctrine. Second, God has blessed my ministry to where this church is now a great citadel, recognized all over the nation, and we carry a testimony to the ends of the whole country, and actually to many foreign lands. Third, our church has become a kind of refuge for many people who cannot go along with the modernism in those other churches and they come here and trust me to hold the fort. Fourth, by remaining inside I avoid the stigma of being a 'come-outer' and am able to write through my magazine, preach from my pulpit and talk over the radio once in a while, as a Methodist preacher, which gives me three times the advantage I would have if I were on the outside.

"There are many other reasons why at my age I think it would be unwise to quit the Methodist Church. The final and best reason is that I have asked God to lead me, and He has led in many other issues that have come my way, but I have felt no leadership from Him to withdraw from the Methodist Church;

in fact, I have felt the leadership to stay in and do what I am doing, fight for the faith."

Rembert Smith's reference to labor unions is from page 5 of his book *Is This the Hour?* (1947).

PAGE 333. The aims of the Society for Reforms of Methodism are included in a leaflet issued by Smith on Jan. 26, 1952.

PAGE 334. Craft's long statement is from *One Methodist Voice*, June 1952, p. 2.

His view of the Negro was expressed in a sermon delivered on Brotherhood Sunday, Feb. 12, 1950. It was published, in part, in *The Cross and the Flag*, May 1950, p. 32.

PAGE 335. Craft's attacks upon varied targets are from many issues of 1952.

PAGE 336. Craft's remarks are from *One Methodist Voice*, May 1952, p. 2.

Chapter 14
Denominational Dilemmas

PAGE 337. Since Chapter 14 was set in type, the name of the Committee Opposing Congregational Political Action has been changed to the League to Uphold Congregational Principles. Some observers believe that the new name suggests that the activities of the group will be broadened to include opposition to the proposed merger with the Evangelical and Reformed Church — and probably to the continued existence of the denomination's General Council itself.

PAGE 338. The quotations from the "Black Book" are from pages 1, 3, 10, and 12. The Council for Social Action, in reply, charged the booklet with sixteen specific errors. The Committee Opposing Congregational Political Action denied the assertion.

PAGE 339. On June 1; 1953, Dr. F. Ernest Johnson, professor emeritus of Teachers College (Columbia University) and recently retired as research director of the Department of Research and Survey of the National Council, assumed the position of editor of *Social Action*. Perhaps the publication will assume a less doctrinaire position on many foreign and domestic issues.

PAGE 341. The background of Herman F. Reissig has become an increasingly important issue between the opposing Congregationalist camps. In the spring of 1951 the issue was raised. The following November, Ray Gibbons prepared and circulated a defense of Reissig, "Let's Look at the Record," with an appended statement by Reissig. The C.O.C.P.A. repeated the charges in a brochure dated Sept. 23, 1952. When they were again answered in the letters-to-the-editor column of *Advance*, official Congregational organ, of Oct. 13, 1952, Payne pressed the issue further in a letter dated March 31, 1952. On April 24, 1953, Reissig himself answered his critics. These materials are available from the parties involved.

PAGE 342. Payne attacked Social Action in a mimeographed brochure headed *"Social Action" Magazine* and distributed in July 1952. His criticism of *Labor Letter* was dated Oct. 3, 1952. His views on Christian Action were contained in a letter to the denomination's Board of Review of Jan. 13, 1953.

The "statement of grievances" is from a circular outlining the purpose and program of the C.O.C.P.A.

PAGE 343. Mikkelson's and Baharian's remarks are from pages 10 and 22 of the mimeographed hearings circulated by C. S. A. Among the many who defended C. S. A. were Liston Pope of the Yale University Divinity School, Emerson G. Hangen, Long Beach (Calif.) pastor, and Ruth I. Seabury, secretary of the American Board of Commissioners of Foreign Missions. Speaking against the Council were Howard Conn of Minneapolis, Jan J. Erteszek of Los Angeles, Eugene E. Wilson of Hartford, and Russell J. Clinchy of the Foundation for Economic Education.

The remarks about the General Council and its composition are from a C.O.C.P.A. report dated Nov. 20, 1952.

PAGE 344. *Destiny for Congregationalism* was published by Modern Publishers, Inc., of Oklahoma City. Burton was formerly pastor of the Second Congregational Church in New London, Conn.

PAGE 345. For the origin of the word "fundamentalist," see the *Watchman-Examiner* of Nov. 27, 1952, p. 1099. The term appeared originally in the issue for July 1, 1920.

PAGE 346. Fosdick was quoted by Stewart G. Cole in *The History of Fundamentalism* (New York, 1931), p. 70. Chapter 5 of Cole's volume deals with the theological cleavage among northern Baptists up to the date of its publication.

PAGE 347. The latest membership claims of the Regular Baptists in the United States were reported in the *Baptist Bible Tribune* of May 29, 1953, p. 5. The claim of the Conservative Baptist Foreign Mission Society to 1,500 contributors was reported in *United Evangelical Action* of June 1, 1952, p. 11.

PAGE 350. The Tulga accusations are from pages 10 and 18 of *The Case Against the World Council of Churches.*

PAGE 351. *Time's* summation of the Norris killing is from its issue of May 19, 1947, p. 70. For Norris' contention, see, for example, *The Fundamentalist,* Feb. 3, 1950, p. 3.

PAGE 352. Norris' references to his seminary are from *The Fundamentalist,* Jan. 14, 1949, p. 1.

(Since Norris' death, the Bible Baptist Seminary has merged with the Akron Baptist Temple Bible College of Akron, O. Dr. Dallas F. Billington, president of the college and pastor of the huge Akron Baptist Temple — which boasts the world's largest Sunday school — has been a long time ally of the World Baptist Fellowship.)

Norris' remarks about Baptist and Methodist leaders are from *The Fundamentalist* of Oct. 22, 1948, p. 2.

PAGE 353. The 1947 convention incident was described in many newspapers and magazines; e.g., *Time,* May 19, 1947.

Norris' attacks are from the following issues of *The Fundamentalist:* on Newton, May 21, 1948, p. 8; on Dawson, Feb. 17, 1950, p. 2; on the Federal Council, Feb. 17, 1950, p. 2, and May 27, 1949, p. 4.

PAGE 354. Norris' remarks concerning the *Protocols* are from his pamphlet, *Did the Jews Write the Protocols?* (no date), p. 3.

Riley's characterization of Norris is quoted in *Trigger Norris,* p. 3. Mrs. Dilling's accusations are from page 5 of her brochure.

PAGE 355. An account of Norris' break with Smith was carried in *Prophecy*

Monthly for April, 1948, pp. 22-23. Smith denounced Norris in *The Cross and the Flag*, July 1948, p. 19.

Norris' statement, as quoted here, was reported in *Our Sunday Visitor* of Sept. 21, 1947, p. 1. In *The Fundamentalist* of May 7, 1948, p. 6, Norris gave a slightly different version of what he had said: "I am glad that you have stood as a Gibraltar here in Europe against the onward sweep of Red Communism, Moscow's conspiracy." Shields's remarks are from the *Gospel Witness and Protestant Advocate* of Sept. 11, 1947, p. 1.

PAGE 357. Noel Smith's characterizations in his booklet are from the following places: Riverside Church, p. iv; Newton, p. 7; seminaries, Chapter 2; R.S.V., p. 50; Southern Baptist Convention, p. 62. His other remarks are from the following issues of the *Baptist Bible Tribune:* Graham, Oct. 17, 1952, p. 1; *Christian Life,* Aug. 10, 1951, p. 4; N.C.C.J., Feb. 29, 1952, p. 4; U.N., Jan. 18, 1952, p. 4; Eleanor Roosevelt, *ibid.;* National Council, Dec. 26, 1952, p. 1, and Nov. 16, 1951, p. 4.

PAGE 358. Peak's plea is from *The Evangelist and Bible Teacher* of Nov. 13, 1952, p. 1; Noel Smith's reply is from a letter, Dec. 26, 1952.

The Watchman-Examiner commented in its issue of July 24, 1952, p. 713; Noel Smith retorted in the *Baptist Bible Tribune* of Sept. 5, 1952, pp. 4-5.

PAGE 359. The resolution of the western section of the World Presbyterian Alliance was included in full in the *Christian Century,* April 8, 1952, p. 411.

Young's remarks are from pp. 3, 6, 8, 7, 9, and 10, of his brochure. His article in *The Cross and the Flag* appeared in the March 1953 issue. Young's brochure has been used by other apostles of discord. Herbert G. Moore, for example, relied upon Young's "research" to "expose" the Presbyterian Church in the U. S. A. in *National Republic,* Nov. 1951.

PAGE 361. The "plight of the Methodists" is discussed in the *Southern Presbyterian Journal* of July 2, 1952, p. 4. The elder quoted is Chalmers W. Alexander of Jackson, Mississippi; his remark is from page 10 of his leaflet, *Unite With the Northern Presbyterian Church? NO!* The "case for segregation" is stated in the *Southern Presbyterian Journal,* Aug. 29, 1951, pp. 4-5.

PAGE 362. The quotation from the *Christian Standard* is from its issue of Nov. 11, 1950, p. 10.

PAGE 363. Elmore's statements are from the *Restoration Herald* of the following dates: Feb. 1952, pp. 2, 10; March 1952, pp. 2, 3; Nov. 1952, p. 2.

PAGE 364. The writer in *Living Church* was Gregory Mabry, whose article, "Glad Tidings of Reconciliation," was reprinted by the Holy Cross Press, 1950.

"Medievalism Rapidly Returning" by Norvin C. Duncan is from *The Churchman* of Nov. 15, 1952, pp. 6-7.

The "deep and thoroughgoing contradiction" is seen by Edwood C. Boggess, chairman of the Doctrine Committee of the American Church Union, in his pamphlet *The Ecumenical Movement and the Episcopal Church.* The A.C.U.'s opposition to the ecumenical movement at the 1952 General Convention was reported in the *Christian Century* of Oct. 1, 1952, p. 1119.

Index

414

American Council of Christian Laymen, 67, 244-250, 304

American Council for a Democratic Greece, 280

American Council for Judaism, 370

American Episcopal Church (Evangelical), 197, 197n

American Ethical Union, 149

American Federation of Teachers, 149, 281

American Flag Committee, 21, 235

American Foundation, 114n

American Freedom and Catholic Power, 151

American Friends Service Committee, 283, 294

American Heritage Protective Committee, 17

American Humanist Assn., 149

American Intelligence Agency, 249

American Jewish Committee, 43n, 50, 77n, 255

American Jewish Congress, 149

American Jewish League Against Communism, 311

American Klansman, 123

American Labor Party, 252

American Legion, 86, 89, 332

American Legion Magazine, 89

American Magazine, 61, 150

American Medical Assn., 48, 49, 51

American Mercury, 86, 90, 90n

American Patriots, Inc., 90, 250

American Peace Crusade, 261, 266

American Peace Mobilization, 319

American Protest, 164

American Protestant Defense League, 163-165

American Protective Assn., 145, 161

American Rangers, 133

American Tract Society, 159

American Tradition in Religion and Education, The, 151

American Union for Nationalist Spain, 223

American Unitarian Assn., 259, 272-277

American Unitarian Youth, 272, 273, 274

American Vigilante Intelligence Federation, 30, 230

American Women Against Communism, 231

American Youth Congress, 318-319

Americanism Bulletin, 53

Americans for Democratic Action, 289

Ancient Order of Hibernians, 222

Anglo-Israelism, Chapter 5 (pp. 92-117)

Anglo-Israelite Guide, 104

Anglo-Saxon Bible Study Group, 103

Anglo-Saxon Christian Assn., 106

Anglo-Saxon Christian Congregation, 103

Anglo-Saxon Federation of America, 94

Anti-Defamation League of B'nai B'rith, 24n, 50, 53n, 65, 69, 126, 138n, 174n, 255

Anti-Defamation League and Its Use in the World Communist Offensive, The, 67

Appraisal of the Protocols of Zion, An, 44

Arcand, Adrien, 67

Architects Behind the World Conspiracy, The, 67

Are These Things So?, 39, 229

Armour and Co., 300

Armstrong, George W., 67, 79-84, 100

Armstrong, R. C., 79

Arnold, Melvin, 273, 274, 275-276

Arrien, John J., 162

Arvey, Jacob, 20, 22, 23

Asbury Theological Seminary, 210

Ashbrook, William E., 239

Asheville Conference (1936), 30-31

Asman, Larry, 64

Assemblies of God, 114, 183

Associated Gospel Churches, 198, 198n

Assn. of Georgia Klans, 122

Assn. for the Preservation of the Southern Presbyterian Church, 361

At Sunset or After 80, 47

Athy, Robert, 30

Atkinson, Henry A., 267

Atlanta *Constitution,* 70

Atom Treason, 67

Atomic Bomb and the End of the World, The, 54

432   Index